THE ORIGIN OF VALUES

SOCIOLOGY AND ECONOMICS
Controversy and Integration

An Aldine de Gruyter Series of Texts and Monographs

SERIES EDITORS

Paula S. England, *University of Arizona, Tucson*
George Farkas, *University of Texas, Dallas*
Kevin Lang, *Boston University*

Values in the Marketplace
James Burk

Beyond the Marketplace:
Rethinking Economy and Society
Roger Friedland and A. F. Robertson (eds.)

Social Institutions:
Their Emergence, Maintenance and Effects
Michael Hechter, Karl-Dieter Opp and Reinhard Wippler (eds.)

The Origin of Values
Michael Hechter, Lynn Nadel and Richard E. Michod

Mothers' Jobs and Children's Lives
Toby L. Parcel and Elizabeth G. Menaghan

Power, Norms, and Inflation: A Skeptical Treatment
Michael R. Smith

THE ORIGIN OF VALUES

Michael Hechter, Lynn Nadel, and
Richard E. Michod

EDITORS

ALDINE DE GRUYTER
New York

About the Editors

Michael Hechter is Professor of Sociology and Fellow at the Udall Center for Studies in Public Policy at The University of Arizona.

Lynn Nadel is currently Acting Dean of the Faculty of Social and Behavioral Sciences and Professor of Psychology at The University of Arizona.

Richard E. Michod is Professor of Ecology and Evolutionary Biology at The University of Arizona.

Copyright © 1993 Walter de Gruyter, Inc., New York

ALDINE DE GRUYTER
A division of Walter de Gruyter, Inc.
200 Saw Mill River Road
Hawthorne, New York 10532

This publication is printed on acid-free paper ∞

Library of Congress Cataloging-in-Publication Data
The Origin of values / Michael Hechter, Lynn Nadel, and Richard E.
  Michod, editors.
        p.   cm. — (Sociology and economics)
    Includes bibliographical references and index.
    ISBN 0-202-30446-9 (alk. paper). — ISBN 0-02-020447-7 (pbk. :
  alk. paper)
      1. Social values—Congresses.   2. Social norms—Congresses.
  I. Hechter, Michael.   II. Nadel, Lynn.   III. Michod, Richard E.
  IV. Series.
  HM73.O75   1993
  303.3'72—dc20   92-27888
                                                     CIP

Manufactured in the United States of America

10 9 8 7 6 5 4 3 2 1

Contributors

GEORGE A. AKERLOF

FREDRIK BARTH

L. LUCA CAVALLI-SFORZA

BARUCH FISCHHOFF

KEITH B. J. FRANKLIN

MICHAEL HECHTER

RICHARD J. HERRNSTEIN

GEORGE MANDLER

RICHARD E. MICHOD

BARRY SCHWARTZ

TIBOR SCITOVSKY

STEVEN P. STICH

LIONEL TIGER

FRANS B. M. DE WAAL

HARRISON C. WHITE

AARON WILDAVSKY

JANET L. YELLEN

Contents

Acknowledgments   *ix*

1   Values Research in the Social and Behavioral Sciences
    Michael Hechter   1

Part I.   Social Scientific Perspectives

2   Are Values Real? The Enigma of Naturalism
    in the Anthropological Imputation of Values
    Fredrik Barth   31

3   On the Social Construction of Distinctions: Risk, Rape,
    Public Goods, and Altruism
    Aaron Wildavsky   47

4   Values Come in Styles, Which Mate to Change
    Harrison C. White   63

5   The Meaning, Nature, and Sources of Value in Economics
    Tibor Scitovsky   93

6   The Fair Wage-Effort Hypothesis in Unemployment
    George A. Akerlof and Janet L. Yellen   107

Part II.   Psychological Perspectives

7   Behavior, Reinforcement, and Utility
    Richard J. Herrnstein   137

8   On the Creation and Destruction of Value
    Barry Schwartz   153

9   Value Elicitation: Is There Anything in There?
    Baruch Fischhoff   187

10   Moral Philosophy and Mental Representation
       Stephen P. Stich   215

11   Approaches to a Psychology of Value
       George Mandler   229

Part III.   Biological Perspectives

12   Biology and the Origin of Values
       Richard E. Michod   261

13   The Neural Basis of Pleasure and Pain
       Keith B. J. Franklin   273

14   Sex Differences in Chimpanzee (and Human) Behavior:
       A Matter of Social Values?
       Frans B. M. de Waal   285

15   How Are Values Transmitted?
       L. Luca Cavalli-Sforza   305

16   Morality Recapitulates Phylogeny
       Lionel Tiger   319

Biographical Sketches of the Contributors   333

Index   337

Acknowledgments

The essays that follow originated in a conference entitled "Toward A Scientific Analysis of Values," held at The University of Arizona, February 1–4, 1989. Despite the evident importance of values in each of the disciplines with which the conference organizers were familiar, we were aware of little ongoing research on the subject. The idea behind the conference was to determine whether recent developments in the social, behavioral and biological sciences might shed new light on the origin, efficacy and measurement of values.

In one guise or another, values play a leading role in nearly every explanatory behavioral theory. In biology, values can be construed as the products of instincts and drives that help channel the organism's motility. In psychology, values are the motives for action, and, as such, they ultimately determine the specific consequences of known reinforcers. In economics, values—generally known as utilities and/or preferences—are one of the two fundamental determinants of all action (constraints external to the agent being the other). In sociology and anthropology values are considered to be basic determinants of social action.

Despite their undeniable theoretical centrality, values are perhaps the greatest black box in all of behavioral science. Science progresses unevenly, of course, and complex and intractable questions often are suppressed in favor of simpler, more tractable ones. Due to problems of conceptualization and measurement, research on value-determination frequently has been consigned to the scientific dustbin. A good deal of knowledge about behavioral outcomes has been acquired at the cost of ignoring the independent role of values in shaping behavior. Thus cognitive scientists have accounted for variations in behavior by studying the consequences of shifts in reinforcers (as in learning theory), and economists have done likewise by studying the consequences of shifts in relative prices (as in comparative statics).

Nevertheless, there are signs that the suppression of value considerations is no longer universally acceptable even in the most traditionally positivistic of disciplines. For example, some leading cognitive scientists have begun to worry about why it is that certain reinforcers reinforce; likewise, some leading economists have begun to worry about the extent of apparently non-self–interested behavior in the real world. Simultaneously, there is new empirical research that bears on issues of value formation. For the most part, however, these forays into research on values have been conducted in mutual isolation by scholars in different disciplines with quite separate research traditions.

Whereas most discussions about values are themselves highly normative exercises in ethics or theology, this conference may have represented the first modern consideration of the problem of values from a frankly positive stance. It brought together the contributions of leading scholars who addressed fundamental questions about values including: What are the determinants of social values, taboos and ideologies? What are the determinants of individual values, such as attitudes toward risk and altruism? What is the nature of motivations and rewards? Finally, several contributors ask if there is an evolutionary basis for the development of values. The conference was organized in three sections emphasizing social scientific, psychological and biological perspectives on values, respectively, and this volume reflects its original format.

The conference planners—the three editors and Lynn A. Cooper of the Columbia University Psychology Department—and the contributors were not the only ones who played a vital role in creating this unusual event. We are grateful to The Alfred P. Sloan Foundation, the Columbia University Center for Social Sciences, and The University of Arizona for their indispensable financial support. Lee Sigelman, then Dean of Arizona's College of Social and Behavioral Sciences, was particularly encouraging. Nancy Henkle took charge of logistics and arrangements with exceptional competence. We are also grateful for the stimulating participation of Douglass C. North, who talked on the economics of ideology.

The following publishers have generously given permission to use their copyrighted works: R. J. Herrnstein, "Behavior, Reinforcement, and Utility." *Psychological Science, 1* 4:217–224. Copyright 1990 by Cambridge University Press; G. A. Akerlof and J. G. Yellen, "The Fair Wage/Effort Hypothesis in Unemployment." *Quarterly Journal of Economics* 105:255–283. Copyright 1990 by MIT Press, Cambridge, Massachusetts; and C. F. Turner and E. Martin, eds. *Surveying Subjective Phenomena.* Copyright 1984 by Russell Sage Foundation.

1

Values Research in the Social and Behavioral Sciences

Michael Hechter

Few concepts are bandied about more liberally in popular, normative, and explanatory scholarly discourse than that of *values*. In the popular realm, parents are eager to have their children associate with peers having the appropriate values, politicians speak of their interest in restoring the traditional values of family, honesty, and hard work to their societies, and academics want to attract scholars with the right kind of values to their departments. In the normative realm, political democracy usually is justified by its ability to provide social policies that, to a greater or lesser extent, are responsive to citizens' values. In the explanatory realm, all action theories assume that behavior is determined not only by constraints emanating from the contexts in which actors are embedded, but also by actors' evaluations of the alternative outcomes they contemplate.[1]

Despite this, calls for renewed attention to values have been gaining momentum in all of the social and behavioral science disciplines.[2] These calls make it seem as if including the full range of human values in social and behavioral explanations is a matter of will. Yet it has seldom been shown how values can be incorporated fruitfully into such explanations.[3]

[1] The idea that the observer's knowledge of the values (or interests) of a subject renders the subject's behavior predictable goes back at least to the seventeenth century. Thus, "If you can apprehend wherein a man's interest to any particular game on foot doth consist you may surely know, if the man be prudent, whereabout to have him, that is, how to judge of his design" (Gunn, 1968: 557).

[2] A brief sampling of these calls includes Sen (1977), Elster (1983), Hirschman (1984), Simon (1986), Wildavsky (1987), Etzioni (1988), Anderson (1990), Calhoun (1991), and Sunstein (1991). Even some economists fully wedded to neoclassical theory (like Becker, 1976: 14) express misgivings about the exogenous assumptions about values in their models.

[3] Apart from a large literature on revealed values, which is critically discussed below.

Nor have any compelling substantive theories of values emerged;[4] indeed, there is a striking absence of discussion about what such theories might consist of. In general, there has been too little appreciation of how difficult it is to incorporate values in social scientific research.

Before assessing the prospects for an enriched role for values in our explanations, it would be wise to recognize one cautionary fact. Whereas 30 years ago values explicitly occupied a central place in all of the social science disciplines (except, perhaps, in economics[5]), use of the concept has declined precipitously in each discipline (for sociology, see Spates, 1983; for political science, see Barry, 1979: 180; for anthropology see Barth, this volume[6]). Despite the strong intuition that evidence about values is needed to fully explain behavior, Stigler and Becker's (1977) claim that no significant behavior has ever been illuminated by assumptions of differences in values (or what they refer to as tastes) probably echoes the current wisdom in social science.[7]

This chapter does not consist of yet another plea for values. Instead, it focuses on how values may be studied so that ultimately they can contribute to our understanding of individual and social behavior. In the first part, I discuss some of the reasons why an explicit concern with values largely has disappeared in social scientific discourse. Progress in scholarly research on values has been slow because of several major impediments: values in all their forms are unobservable; theory in economics, psychology, and sociology provides little guidance for understanding how values shape behavior; simply postulating values is unconvincing

[4] For relevant discussions, see Pollak (1970), von Weiszäcker (1971), Cyert and De Groot (1975), the symposium on Formed Habits, *Journal of Economic Theory, 13* (1976), Elster (1979: 77–86) and Becker (1992). While they are explicitly concerned with endogenizing values, most economic models of state-dependent preferences (such as Karni, 1985) are substantively empty, and purposely so. March's (1988) discussion of variable risk preferences is one of the more substantive attempts to endogenize internal states in recent social science.

[5] Even so, some economists paid them heed. Myrdal (1944) strongly emphasized the importance of values. Spengler (1961: 10), a past President of the American Economic Association, argued that "decision-makers interested in economic development . . . will seek to internalize in a society's members motivational and value orientations that make for economic growth and for political organization favorable to such growth." Similar statements were common among development economists of that era who founded the journal *Economic Development and Cultural Change* as a forum for this kind of research.
[6] Although values would appear to be constitutive of the very enterprise of moral philosophy, they have been neglected even in this discipline (Gaus, 1990: 1).
[7] This is not to imply that values have totally disappeared from view in empirical social science. Inglehart (1990) and others have attempted to document shifts in the content of values in postwar Europe from cross-national survey data, and some demographers (Leasthaege, 1983; Cleland, 1985; Preston, 1987) have argued that value shifts are largely responsible for worldwide patterns of fertility decline. Much of this research is couched in methodologically defensive language, however, and it has only attained marginal attention in its respective disciplines.

when the processes responsible for generating them are unknown; and measurement problems abound. Then I briefly discuss several approaches to the genesis of values. I contend that social researchers will pay heed to values only if these impediments are appreciated and given their due. In the final part, I summarize the contributions to this volume and discuss the directions for future research that they entail.

Four Impediments to the Study of Values[8]

Values Can Take Many Forms, But All of These Are Unobservable

One of the first clues of the troublesome status of values is that they have no consensual definitions. This gives each writer both the obligation and the license to define the term *de novo*. Values are *relatively general and durable internal criteria for evaluation*. As such, they differ from other concepts such as preferences (or attitudes) and norms. Like values, preferences (and attitudes) are internal; unlike them, preferences are labile rather than durable, and particular rather than general. Whereas norms are also evaluative, general, and durable, they are external to actors and—in contrast to values—require sanctioning for their efficacy.

Values differ in a number of ways.[9] They differ with respect to their *scope of control*. Some (such as adherence to an orthodox religion) concern objects and events that are under the actor's control. Others (such as the preference for participating in egalitarian rather than hierarchical groups) necessarily concern objects and events that are beyond any single actor's control.

Values differ in their *scope of application*. Some (for example, the altruism that often is considered responsible for behavior in the nuclear family) are evoked only under specific social situations, whereas others (for example, the reciprocity implicitly expressed in the Golden Rule) may be acted on in nearly all social situations.

Values differ in the degree to which they are *shared socially*. Some are pervasive in groups, whereas others are rare.[10] To see this we have to distinguish between two kinds of socially generated values, the instru-

---

[8] This section of the chapter is drawn from Hechter (1992).

[9] See Mandler (this volume) for the most elaborate attempt to provide a meaning for the term during the conference.

[10] This discussion ignores all pervasive values that result from physiological hard-wiring. Thus, people (as well as all other mammals) have an innate aversion to bitter-tasting substances such as milkweed, many of which are toxic, and an innate attraction to sweet-tasting substances such as bananas, many of which are nutritious (Scott & Yaxley, 1989). Whereas these values are universal in young children, adults can acquire tastes (like that for coffee) that to some degree contravene them.

mental and the immanent (cf. Wright, 1971; Rokeach, 1973).[11] On the one hand, people can act on the basis of *instrumental* values to combine their time and personal endowments to produce fungible resources (such as wealth, status, and power) that then may be exchanged for a wide variety of specific goods. Action on the basis of instrumental values provides means to other ends: it is designed to increase the actor's stock of fungible resources. As their name implies, instrumental values pervade society: they are what enable the economist's incentives to produce their intended effects.[12] The sources of this fundamentally extrinsic basis of values are relatively well understood (Hechter, 1991: 48–49).

On the other hand, people also can act on the basis of *immanent* values to attain goods and ends that are desired purely for their own sake (Hechter, 1987: 42–43).[13] Whereas instrumental values are held commonly by the members of society, immanent values are unlikely to be: they afford us an opportunity to individuate ourselves in social life. Almost everyone in American society prefers more money, status, and 𝗏 wealth to less, but the set of people for whom motorcycles and the music

[11] Not all socially produced pervasive values correspond to the instrumental values described above. Anthropologists long have insisted that values systematically vary across societies. The prototypical American capitalist may place the accumulation of profit above all, but insert that same person in Malinowski's Trobriand Islands and she will endeavor to become the greatest *donor* of goods. One of the most colorful descriptions of a value system that seems weird to us comes from Evans-Pritchard, who commented on the Nuer's overweening interest in cattle: "They are always talking about their beasts. I used sometimes to despair that I never discussed anything with the young men but livestock and girls, and even the subject of girls led inevitably to that of cattle. Start on whatever subject I would and approach it from whatever angle, we would soon be speaking of cows and oxen, heifers and steers, rams and sheep, he-goats and she-goats, calves and lambs and kids. . . . This obsession—for such it seems to an outsider—is due not only to the great economic value of cattle but also to the fact that they are links in numerous social relationships. Nuer tend to define all social processes and relationships in terms of cattle. Their social idiom is a bovine idiom" (Evans-Pritchard, 1940: 18–19). Examples of value differences across social formations abound (see below). To the degree that values are shared by members of a collectivity, they take on the character of an objective reality that may be reflected in prices or in existing institutions and therefore constrain individual action in predictable ways. These kinds of shared values result from the internalization of norms that have to be countenanced in decision-making: they serve to limit expectations, and also may carry sanctions in their wake. At least two things distinguish instrumental values from other kinds of socially produced shared values. First, unlike other shared values (which vary across societies), instrumental ones are universal. Second, they are self-serving, which suggests that they may well have evolutionary origins.

[12] That these instrumental values were also pervasive in early Christian society is revealed by St. Augustine's denunciation of them as constituting the sins of fallen men (Deane, 1963).

[13] These are often referred to as intrinsic values. Rawls' (1971: 62) concept of primary goods—things that every rational person is presumed to want—conflates the distinction between instrumental and immanent values.

of Mozart are jointly immanent values is probably quite small.[14] Behavior that is motivated by immanent values is independent of its effects on an actor's stock of fungible resources, and may even be inconsistent with the attainment of these resources (Schwartz, this volume).

Finally, values differ in the *level of analysis* in social scientific explanations. They enter into social scientific explanations both at the micro and macro levels of analysis. They play an important role as motivating elements in explanations of individual behavior, and often are invoked to explain differences in social outcomes such as institutional arrangements[15] and aggregate rates of productivity, fertility, and crime.[16]

Existing Theoretical Traditions Provide Little Guidance for Understanding How Values Shape Behavior

Classical economists followed Aristotle (*Politics*, Bk. I, Chap. 8) in dividing the source of values into separate components due to exchange and use (Georgescu-Roegen, 1968; Cooter & Rappoport, 1984). One might value a good for the satisfaction garnered by consuming it, as well as for the other goods that might be obtained by exchanging it. Yet this conception could not explain why some goods that were self-evidently very useful (like water) seemed to command lower prices than other much less useful goods (like diamonds).

Early marginalist economists replaced this multivalent conception of value with a unitary one that they termed *utility* (Stigler 1950a,b). They believed that the law of diminishing marginal returns provided them with an objective means of determining what the otherwise ghostly entity of utility consisted of.[17] It then would be possible to make the interpersonal comparisons of utility that were regarded as necessary for utilitarian theories of resource distribution (see Elster & Roemer, 1991). To illustrate, suppose that we live in an oasis deep in the Sahara. Faced with

[14] A critic might respond that this distinction may be overdrawn. For example, might not people seek money not for what it commands in the marketplace, but purely out of the desire to accumulate? A simple thought experiment can dispel the objection. People indeed may accumulate money without spending it, but it is unlikely that anyone would set about accumulating worthless scrip, like confederate dollars or monopoly money. Likewise, people do not tend to seek status as an immanent good, for if they did then they would be indifferent about those granting it to them (that is, the status granted by the homeless would be as valued as that granted by the Nobel Prize committee).

[15] Myrdal (1944) and Lipset (1963) are two well-known examples; for a critical discussion see Barry (1970).

[16] See the references in footnote 7.

[17] Previous to this, of course, classical economists such as Ricardo—and later Marx—had sought an objective basis for value in the amount of labor necessary to produce a given good.

drought, we have only a single indivisible bottle of water to give to one of the two strangers who appear out of the blue one afternoon. Assume that we believe that the bottle should go to the person who receives the greatest value from it. We learn that Bill has wandered for two days in the dunes without having had a drop to drink, and that Bob has consumed a quart of water this very morning. How can we decide whether Bill or Bob should get the bottle of water? The law of diminishing marginal returns enables us to determine that in the usual case Bill is the one who should receive the water. This law seemed to offer an objective basis for the allocation of resources that could generate a robust welfare economics.

Later marginalists, however, insisted that utility could not be determined objectively. Lord Robbins' logic carried the day:

> Suppose elementary barter: A, who has a bottle of whisky, has the opportunity of exchanging it with B, who has a classical record of, say, *Fidelio*. It should be quite easy to ascertain by asking the relative valuations of the objects concerned before exchange. A relates that the classical record is worth more to him than a bottle of whisky; B contrariwise. This at no point involves interpersonal comparisons of absolute satisfaction. But now suppose that A and B fall into conversation about the respective enjoyments and A says to B, "Of course I get more satisfaction than you out of music", and B vigorously asserts the contrary. Needless to say, you and I as outsiders can form our own judgments. But these are essentially subjective, not objectively ascertainable fact. There is no available way in which we can measure and compare the satisfactions which A and B derive from music. (Robbins, 1984: 9).

According to this logic, utility had to be a totally subjective entity and therefore interpersonal comparisons could not be scientifically justifiable.[18] By making utility purely subjective, these theorists paradoxically set the stage for a purely objective economics in which the explanatory status of utility is entirely post hoc.[19]

[18] In Mirowski's (1989: 374) provocative account of the history of economic thought, the later marginalists believed that they had abandoned the earlier substance theory of value for a field theory of value modeled on the principles of physics, but they did so in an incomplete and incoherent fashion.

[19] Economics is not concerned with ends as such. It assumes that human beings have ends in the sense that they have tendencies to conduct which can be defined and understood, and it asks how their progress towards their objectives is conditioned by the scarcity of means—how the disposal of the scarce means is contingent on these ultimate valuations. . . . The ends may be noble or they may be base. The may be 'material' or 'immaterial'—if ends can be so described. But if the attainment of one set of ends involves the sacrifice of others, then it has an economic aspect. Suppose, for instance, a community of sybarites, their pleasures gross and sensual, their intellectual activities preoccupied with the 'purely material'. It is clear enough that

Whereas economists gave up any pretense of developing a substantive theory of values in the late 1930s, psychologists continued to search for one. The question, "What is a reinforcer?" obviously is fundamental for all versions of behaviorism in psychology. Several theories were proposed, including theories of need reduction and drive. Need reduction theory (Hull, 1943) holds that anything that reduces a basic need will serve as a reinforcer; anything that increases a basic need will serve as a punisher. (Basic needs can be defined as goods that are essential to the animal's survival.) It is evident, however, that reducing some animal needs (such as the need for vitamin A) is not generally reinforcing. For many animals, it turns out that very strong reinforcers do not satisfy basic needs (thus, although people are reinforced by positive status, they will not die without it). In the light of difficulties of these sorts, drive theory was proposed. In the course of evolution, needs become internalized in animals in the form of instinctive drives. Thus the fact that a rat would die without food is represented inside the rat by a drive or motivation to obtain food.

> Although originally drives may have corresponded absolutely to needs (and in primitive animals, may do so still), drives are supposed to have gained a certain independence from absolute needs in mammals such as rats, monkeys, and people. An individual monkey would not die without solving puzzles [something observed to be reinforcing] and an individual rat would not die without seeing other rats, but it is probably beneficial for the survival of these species in general for puzzle solving and right sighting to serve as rewards. In nature, a monkey that likes to solve puzzles might incidentally get the banana down from the tree; a rat that likes to see other rats might incidentally find warmth and sources of food. (Rachlin, 1989: 122–123)

Regrettably, the theory is circular because there is no independent measure of what an animal's drives or needs consist of.

Lacking a suitable theory, experimental psychologists have tended to assume that values derive exclusively from objective—hence, measur-

---

economic analysis can provide categories for describing the relationships between these ends and the means which are available for achieving them. But it is not true, as Ruskin and Carlyle and suchlike critics have asserted, that it is *limited* to this sort of thing. Let us suppose this reprehensible community to be visited by a Savonarola. Their former ends become revolting to them. The pleasures of the senses are banished. The sybarites become ascetics. Surely economic analysis is still applicable. There is no need to change the categories of explanation. All that has happened is that the demand schedules have changed. Some things have become relatively less scarce, others more so. The rent of vineyards falls. The rent of quarries for ecclesiastical masonry rises. That is all. The distribution of time between prayer and good works has its economic aspect equally with the distribution of time between orgies and slumber. The 'pig-philosophy' to use Carlyle's contemptuous epithet— turns out to be all-embracing (Robbins, 1984: 24–26).

able—rewards. That supreme individualist Thorstein Veblen carica-
tured the psychologist's version of man as

> a lightning calculator of pleasures and pains, who oscillates like a homoge-
> neous globule of desire of happiness under the influence of stimuli that
> shift him about the area, but leave him intact. . . . Self-imposed in elemen-
> tal space, he spins symmetrically about his own spiritual axis until the
> parallelogram of force bears down upon him, whereupon he follows the
> line of least resistance. (Veblen, [1919] 1961: 73)

A more recent assessment complains that

> The study of concrete rewards has produced a wealth of quantitative detail
> about how reinforcement (the internal mechanism of reward) depends on
> previous deprivation, rate of delivery, the presence or absence of other
> sources of reinforcement, etc. However, in a prosperous society, most be-
> haviour is rewarded by emotional processes that are occasioned by other
> people's social responses, or by tasks or games which are rewarding in their
> own right. It would clearly be desirable if these subtle reward factors could
> be understood in the same framework as visceral ones, but psychology has
> difficulty bridging the gap. (Ainslie, 1986: 135)

Whereas economic theory has virtually nothing to say about the content of individual values, psychological research points to the environment as the principal source of rewarding resources. What seems to be
missing from this account is the awareness, first, that environmentally
determined values may be inconsistent, and second, that some values
may be autonomous and maintained even in opposition to pervasive
environmental rewards. Without this awareness it is difficult to account
for the ambivalence that seems so common in human experience. Nor
can we easily explain the existence of heroes, martyrs, and the kinds of
innovators who are celebrated in popular literature (as in Ayn Rand's
melodramatic classic *The Fountainhead,* modeled on the career of Frank
Lloyd Wright).

Does sociological theory help us come to grips with values? Although
much of Simmel's difficult text on *The Philosophy of Money* (1907) is de-
voted to analysis of valuation, the essential sociological theorist of values
is Max Weber.[20] Perhaps more than any other social scientist in history,
Weber sought to establish a comprehensive theory of social behavior. A
committed comparativist, he understood that action deemed reasonable
in one society might be incomprehensible in another. To account for

[20] Parsons' extensive ruminations about values were effectively challenged by Blake and
Davis (1964).

these systematic differences in behavior, it was necessary to build a social science that was capable of treating not only instrumental action, but also action motivated by values, affect, and tradition. Hence, religious values—for example, those deriving from ascetic Protestantism—might exercise a profound impact on economic action—such as the tendency to accumulate capital.

As part of this project, Weber sought to understand the social determinants of different religious values. He particularly emphasized a causal link between modes of living and propensities to religious values (Weber, [1922] 1968: 468–483). For example, since the lot of peasants is so strongly tied to nature and so little tied to economic rationality, peasants would develop systematic religious ideologies only under the threat of enslavement or proletarianization; since the life pattern of warrior nobles has little affinity with the notion of a beneficent providence or with the systematic ethical demands of a transcendental god, members of this stratum also have little propensity to develop mature religious values. Although it is child's play to challenge the evidence that supports these assertions, Weber's attempt to derive a structural account of value differences between groups and societies remains exceptional in social science.[21] Unfortunately, his followers have found it difficult to move beyond the useful distinction between instrumental and value-oriented action. Nor have they been able to shed much light on the conditions governing trade-offs among these different types of action. As a result, this promising line of analysis has been abandoned in contemporary Weberian scholarship.

Postulating Values in Behavioral Explanations Is Unconvincing When the Processes That Generate Them Are Unknown

Values can be specified simply by postulating them for the relevant actors. In practice, this entails the assumption that all these individuals have homogeneous values, at least within broadly defined boundaries. An important instance is the employment of wealth maximization as a behavioral postulate in economic analyses (Friedman, 1953; Becker, 1976; Stigler & Becker, 1977).[22] Insofar as wealth may be used to purchase goods that satisfy all kinds of values, then it is reasonable to expect everyone to prefer more wealth to less (no matter the content of any specific individual's other values). To the degree that alternatives

---

[21] Perhaps the closest contemporary analogue to Weber's structuralist perspective is found in Kohn's research program relating social class to parenting styles (based on the conceptions in Kohn, 1969).

[22] For animal behavior, the most common behavioral postulate is the maximization of inclusive fitness (Part III, this volume).

may be represented as more or less costly, then all behavior can be analyzed from this point of view.[23]

The problem is that a great deal of individual behavior is not explicable in wealth-maximizing terms.[24] Some behavior seems better explained as the product of status or power maximization. Of course, following Weber, status and power can be added to wealth as postulated values in behavioral models (North, 1981; Lindenberg, 1990), although much precision is lost by doing so. But even then, large difficulties remain. On the one hand, this extension of postulated values rules out unique behavioral predictions, for little is known about the conditions under which motivation stems from wealth instead of from considerations of status or power. On the other hand, this strategy seems difficult to reconcile with findings that individuals sometimes do not appear to be acting to maximize any (or all) of these qualities, but instead act morally, or on the basis of such nonvalue considerations as ritual or habit (Weber, [1922] 1968; Sen, 1977; Etzioni, 1988). Overall, the evidence suggests that actors in modern society are likely to have heterogeneous values. Theory leads to the same conclusion, for if equally endowed actors had identical values then they would have no motive to engage in exchange (Arrow, 1990: 28). Hence, it is reasonable to expect that a more adequate approach to the specification of values may lie elsewhere—in measurement efforts.

Measurement Problems Abound

In principle, values can be measured either by asking people to describe their own values or by imputing their values from observed behavior. Although values are unobservable to others, it makes sense to assume that they are observable to subjects themselves. I cannot presume to know your values because I cannot read your mind, but surely you have the ability to read your *own* mind. This kind of logic gives survey measures of values their intuitive appeal. Yet the values produced by much survey data tend to be labile rather than stable; in addition, they do a poor job of predicting behavior (Schuman & Johnson, 1976; Hill, 1981). These difficulties derive from a variety of sources, among them the fact that people may conceal their values for strategic purposes, that

---

[23] Marxists and ecological determinists also postulate values (that is, interests) but see these as homogeneous within subgroups (such as classes, or groups occupying a similar ecological niche).

[24] In tacit appreciation of these difficulties, even economists—who are most wedded to the wealth-maximization assumption approach—have begun adding unconventional utility arguments to their models (Akerlof and Yellin, this volume; Becker, 1981; Easterlin, 1980; Frank, 1988; Brenner, 1983). Wealth maximization is a good deal more useful in accounting for *aggregate* rather than individual behavior, however, due to the law of large numbers (Hechter, 1987: 31–32).

there is no baseline by which to compare the answers of different respondents,[25] and that there is little cost in misrepresenting one's values (Fischhoff, this volume; for a defense of the use of surveys as measures of values, see Mitchell & Carson, 1989).

Sometimes people may not know what their values really are; hence their answers to probes about values may be unreliable on this account as well (Converse, 1964). The reasons for this subjective unobservability of values are deep. To appreciate them, it is necessary to recall the distinction I drew earlier between instrumental and immanent values. There can be no mystery about the nature of our instrumental values (they are the same as everyone else's in the society!), but how can we discover our immanent values? Introspection is not a reliable guide—it is far better to infer immanent values from past behavior. One means of doing so is periodically to monitor the uses to which we put our fungible resources. Whereas such monitoring may sometimes reveal immanent values for goods allocated by the market (except when we succumb to weakness of will), systematic evidence about our own consumption behavior cannot reveal immanent values for nonmarketed goods and ends (although self-monitoring of the allocation of *time* may help in this respect). Yet it is doubtful that we are capable of doing very well at this kind of internal accounting, for it is a time-intensive activity with significant opportunity costs.[26]

Since behavior can be motivated by instrumental as well as immanent values, we may have no way of telling which of these values was responsible for any given past behavior. Did we invite that person to a party because we really like him, because we are currying his favor for some ulterior purpose, or because of some combination of these different values? No doubt we emphasize our most socially acceptable motives in accounting for our own actions, but whenever instrumental and immanent values lead to the same outcome, the causal priority of these two values is subjectively indeterminate. It follows that we can be certain of our own immanent values only when we see ourselves acting on them *at the expense of instrumental values*. Survey instruments generally do not provide us with the hard choices that are necessary to reveal our immanent values.[27]

[25] Two survey respondents may rate their desire to live in a racially integrated neighborhood as 8 on a Likert scale, for example, but these 8s may not indicate the same intensity of values.

[26] To complicate matters further, it is also conceivable that instrumental values can be displaced into immanent ones over time (Simmel [1907] 1978).

[27] Skepticism about the reliability of questions to elicit an individual's values goes back at least to the Old Testament. Even God did not trust Abraham's professions of loyalty and demanded that he offer his son Isaac to be sacrificed as proof of his faith. God became convinced of Abraham's loyalty only when he began making preparations for his son's demise.

Whenever there is no opportunity to question subjects (as in historical research, for instance) the specification of values must be approached inferentially. Yet doubts about the adequacy of survey measures of values have led to the popularity of inferential measures even when surveys can be carried out.[28] The principal inferential strategy in social science is based on the notion of *revealed preference*. This suggests that values are revealed by choices between known alternatives. If values are stable, then the same preference will reoccur in the future, given the same choice set. The choice of *A* over *B* in this tradition is said to reveal the *preference* of *A* over *B*. Especially when the choice between *A* and *B* involves some risk (and therefore compels the actor to consider the probabilities of attaining each alternative), this preference may have two quite different roots.

Biases in the actor's reasoning constitute the first root of preferences (Nisbett & Ross, 1980; Kahneman, Slovic, & Tversky, 1982). For instance, an actor may choose *A* over *B* because she is not used to considering events that occur only with small probabilities. This implies that if the probabilities involved in attaining the alternatives were much higher, a different choice would have been made. This root of preferences has been studied extensively by decision theorists in the context of one basic experimental paradigm. Subjects are presented with alternative gambles that have the same monetary expectation—thus the alternatives have identical objective values. These experiments provide conditions that are most favorable to preference reversals, for they maximize subjects' indifference to the alternatives. It should come as no surprise that subjects are more likely to reverse themselves in choosing between six of one and a half dozen of another than between alternatives with radically different outcomes. When subjects make inconsistent choices between these alternatives (and this occurs frequently), variations in (objective) value can be ruled out as causes of this preference reversal.

The actor's *differential evaluation of A and of B* is the second root of preferences. Little is known about the social and experiential roots of these values, and they are a principal concern of this volume. This source of preferences may be elicited only by studying choices between alternatives that may be presumed to have different values, but about which biases in reasoning may be ruled out as being principally responsible for determining the choice. Since cognitive biases appear to be fostered in choices between alternatives of similar objective value and between those that involve unusually large amounts of risk, the best way of avoiding them is by studying consequential choices and by minimizing the role of risk in the choice set.

---

[28] For a recent example, note Blinder's (1991) defensiveness about using interview data to investigate the causes of price stickiness.

The most elaborated inferential approach to the measurement of values is von Neumann and Morgenstern's (1944) method of inferring utilities from standard gambles. Although this method would appear to do away with biases resulting from the interview situation, as well as with those due to subjects' ambiguity about their own values, it too entails difficulties. In the first place, people's preferences may be inconsistent with their values: if there is a chance that a given preference may become public knowledge (to a public of any given size), then the decision maker may have an interest in altering it for strategic reasons (for example, to better manage her public impression). In the second place, people's values may have changed (say, due to satiation or to learning) since the last observation was made; thus any simple behavioral projection from past to future choices simply would be erroneous. Whereas there is a large literature on preference reversals (Tversky, Slovic, & Kahneman, 1990), this research has been narrowly focused on cognitive biases alone. Hence its findings contain little of relevance for the study of value-based preferences.

Further, if choice occurs in a setting in which there is any conceivable motive to conceal one's true values, then some unknown part of the resulting choice may be due to strategic considerations rather than to values, and the equation of choice with values will mislead (Sen, 1977; Kuran, 1990).

The Genesis of Values

Even though values unquestionably are difficult to measure, there can be no scientific warrant simply to ignore them. After all, molecules and atoms were unobservables whose existence was hotly debated among scientists of the late nineteenth century (Nye, 1972). The skeptics were persuaded only by the experimental results of a variety of investigators who were committed to the atomic model in the absence of evidence that others found persuasive.

To those willing to accept the intuitive importance of values in explaining both individual and social outcomes, understanding their genesis is critical. The problem is extremely complex, however, for values appear to arise through a bewilderingly large number of pathways.

To some degree values are hard-wired into organisms via the mechanism of natural selection (see Part III, this volume). Hard-wired values can be presumed to be virtually homogeneous within species. If, for example, we are interested in explaining the behavior of marmots, we must have some idea of the kinds of factors that drive, or motivate, marmots to engage in the kinds of behaviors they actually do engage in. Obviously, one of the things that motivates them is the desire for food, so we can apply some theory of food gathering that yields determinate behavioral predictions—an optimal foraging theory—and see how well it accounts for the observed behavior of marmots. In optimal foraging theory, the animal allocates its food-gathering behaviors in such a way as to yield the optimal number of calories per unit of energy expended. With the aid of ideas such as these, we can predict what marmots would do in different kinds of environments, and then carry out experiments to see how well the theory is supported.

To the degree that marmots are motivated to pursue other ends than the mere accumulation of calories (say, to the degree they are driven to consume food partially on the basis of taste, or to engage in behaviors ostensibly unrelated to food gathering, such as gazing at the moon), insofar as these latter ends imply behaviors that diverge from the former ones, we would not expect optimal foraging theory to fully account for the behavior of marmots. To better predict the behavior of marmots, then, we would search for a more complete description of the set of values that motivates marmots' behavior.

One means of finding a highly general theory of marmot behavior would be to posit the existence of one overriding end that dominates (and, perhaps, orders) all the other more particular ends that motivate marmots' behavior and see what implications this conception would have. In evolutionary theory, this overriding end is maximization of Darwinian fitness (or reproductive success).[29] Given the logical plausibility of natural selection, the success of this strategy hinges on the theorists' ability to specify the implications of the general principle of fitness maximization for the pursuit of other, more limited, ends—so that we might be able to predict when marmots are likely to pursue food instead of gazing at the moon. Like all functionalist theories, this one can be used ingeniously to account for all behavior retrospectively; the challenge is to generate empirically falsifiable predictions about behavior.

Collectivities appear to differ systematically along value dimensions. For example, the Nuer vest the highest of values in cattle. Muslims refuse to eat pork, Hindus beef; Americans, no matter how hungry, shy away from eating cats and dogs. Some groups appear to have labor supply curves that are more backward-sloping than others. Some states enact policies that are more redistributive than others. What accounts for differences of these sorts?

---

[29] Alexander (1987: 42) discusses how the principle of inclusive fitness leads to predictions about two kinds of effort that organisms will engage in at different stages of the life course: somatic effort, designed to build the individual's body/self in the prereproductive stage, and reproductive effort, which leads to "altruism."

Rather than viewing these social outcomes as the result of some aggregation of the personal values of the members of the relevant group, social scientists tend to see values as the products of both ecological and institutional conditions. Various mechanisms for the production of values have been proposed, including socialization, situational requirements, institutional functions, and distancing mechanisms (see White, this volume).

Ecological constraints are an obvious starting point for understanding intergroup differences in values. The actual mechanism by which ecology determines values may not be well worked out theoretically, however. In principle, the environment can be the source of both reinforcers and punishers, as well as relative prices. Certain features of the environment may have greater salience for individual life-chances, and therefore may lead to the articulation of clear values. For example, people who are subject to repeated drought may come to value a reliable source of water; those subject to repeated invasion may value security, and so forth.

The values embedded in already-extant institutional structures are also likely to be important.[30] The thrust of many analyses (Barth, Wildavsky, White, & Schwartz, this volume) is to explain personal values by institutional variations. Some concept of values that is embodied by existing social institutions is logically and causally prior to any conception of individual values, therefore.

To some extent, as psychoanalytical theory insists, values also arise from individual experience. Thus we might explain someone's intense commitment to the nuclear family by seeing the family as a source of emotional support that seems especially desirable to people whose relationships to their mothers were attenuated when they were children. This line of analysis can account for heterogeneous values within relevant groups, but it requires such fine-grained data about individual reinforcement histories that it is impractical for most research on social outcomes.

All told, for any individual, some values are selected biologically (we like what's good for us, and dislike what's bad for us; otherwise no survival), some are the by-product of the physical and institutional environments, and the rest are the by-product of personal history. Disentangling the relative weight of these different kinds of factors seems extremely difficult. But it is probably not impossible.

One way of thinking about the problem relies on the notion of a hierarchy of nested values. At the most fundamental level, biological determinants produce values that are common to (or perhaps constitu-

---

[30] One possible mechanism responsible for the effect of social structures on values is adaptive preference formation (Elster, 1983); another is the endowment effect (Samuelson & Zeckhauser, 1988; Kahneman, Knetsch, & Thaler, 1990).

tive of) all human beings. This source of values produces no variation to be explained. Ecological determinants of values indirectly influence the establishment of a set of social institutions that, in turn, highlight certain values at the expense of others. The Nuer provide a good example. Given the nature of the environment that the Nuer occupied, pastoralism was the most viable mode of production. To the degree that the social institutions of all pastoral societies take the same form, the members of such societies will have a set of common values—in addition to those that they share as members of the same species.

Next come institutional determinants. To the degree that ecological (and other environmental) conditions allow for the establishment of different kinds of social institutions, we would expect to find members of these respective societies to have systematically different values. Clearly, there is a great scope for institutional differentiation within the same ecological parameters. And advanced technology certainly loosens the coupling between social institutions and the environment. Hence, in advanced societies, we would expect that more variation in values would be due to social institutions than to ecological variables per se.

The penultimate cause of variation in personal values lies in idiosyncrasies of personal biography, some of which can be explained by individual patterns of group affiliation (Simmel, 1955). Membership in each group may foster particular values. For example, we might expect to see (with a positive probability) certain kinds of common values held by Catholics as against Protestants, by members of the Chamber of Commerce as against union members, and by sociologists as against economists.

Rescuing Values in Prospective Research

Whereas values once occupied a central place in social explanations, research on them has diminished as the four impediments discussed above have come to light. There are good reasons to reassess the concept of values, if only we can understand how they may be studied. Have any new ideas about studying values emerged after three decades of research in the social and biological sciences? After all, this is a period that has witnessed significant new developments in network analysis, rational choice theory, cognitive and physiological psychology, and evolutionary approaches to human and animal behavior.

At least five directions for research on values are suggested by the contributors to Parts I and II of this volume (for Part III, see Michod, this volume): sociohistorical analysis (Barth, Wildavsky, White, and Schwartz, this volume), model-building on the basis of unconventional postulated values (Scitovsky, Akerlof and Yellin, and Herrnstein, this volume), novel measurement efforts (Fischhoff, this volume), new inter-disciplinary research (Stich, this volume), and theoretical synthesis (Mandler, this volume).

Sociohistorical Analysis

Not surprisingly, most of the contributors in the macroscopic social scientific disciplines (with the exception of Schwartz, a psychologist) ad-vocate a sociohistorical approach to value research. Barth notes that although the study of values in anthropology was prominent in the 1950s and 1960s, there is little explicit theory and analysis of values in contemporary anthropology (although a concern with values—norma-tively—seems strong just below the surface). What drove values off cen-ter stage? Meaning has eclipsed explanation in recent anthropology. Problems of cross-cultural epistemology make the imputation of values a very complex task. For Barth, values are not as homogeneous as many social theorists had imagined them to be, but they also are not neces-sarily coherent even when shared. People are routinely beset by deep ambivalence.

Barth suggests that values may be studied first by producing a close empirical description of them or their observable consequences, in the tradition of natural history. This can be done either by describing ob-served regularities of action in a culturally homogeneous population and then by constructing the conceptions of value that would explain these regularities, or by listening to the reasons and judgments people give for their acts. But these strategies sidestep analyses of the mecha-nisms that orient people's choices, actions, and emotions. These mecha-nisms can be unraveled only by discovering the various conceptual un-derpinnings that enhance socially desirable behavior in given contexts. Barth contends that values are always made relevant within the parame-ters set by existing institutions (see also White, this volume). His compar-ison of generosity and greed among the Baktaman and Balinese suggests that the meaning of concepts like sharing refers to individual ways of operating within institutional parameters, and not to the principles on which those institutions are built.

Wildavsky argues that the meanings of critical value distinctions that inform and legitimate public policy are not fixed, but represent movable boundaries that are always subject to cultural contention. He illustrates the argument by considering a number of distinctions that are seldom perceived as parasitic on culture. Thus people with different values tend to place a different interpretation on the same expectation of risk. Those who are opposed to the good tend to regard the risk as involuntary; those who are for it tend to regard the risk as voluntary. The distinction between rape and voluntary consent in sexual relations (which Wildavsky raised well before national debate on this issue reached a crescendo in the summer of 1991) is another case in point. Feminists are trying to increase the power of women to determine voluntary consent by moving the time, criteria, and determination of consent as far forward in time as possible, so as to give females as much control as possible. Likewise, the distinction between public and private goods is another movable boundary that is socially defined. What is to be considered public—and therefore run by government—or private—hence in the province of individuals, families, or groups—is the subject of everyday political dispute. The definition of a public good depends on community fiat: there are not and cannot be any such things as goods that are nonexcludable and in joint supply unless informal understandings or collective decisions make them so. The final illustration concerns the fuzziness of distinctions between self-interested and altruistic behavior. If Wildavsky is correct, then insight into value formation and transformation can come from studies of the correlates and causes of these changing distinctions. Case law would be an obvious place to look for evidence of this kind.

White argues—very much in the spirit of Durkheim—that values come not singly but in symbolic packages that derive from prior institutions. He believes that particular expressions of values are produced by networks that constitute the given institution. All the values consistent with an institution are similar in that they conform to some style. Those subject to the institution make evaluations only in light of these values (this is much the same point that Wildavsky makes in the preceding chapter). White presents an intriguing institutional comparison of village caste in India and academic science, both of which are organized according to the underlying value of purity—worked out in an elaborate structure of hierarchy.

The test of this argument lies in its ability to predict change. Changes in the expression of particular values can be triggered by any number of events, but change in their structure as a package is difficult because style is "coordinated to" institutions. No change in style can take place without corresponding changes in networks and values. The dialectical competition between old styles produces new styles as syntheses (this is what White means by the emblematic phrase "styles mate to change"). The claim is illustrated by showing how Catholic Christianity emerged out of encounters among preexisting Judaic sects, and how rock and roll emerged from the interaction of different networks of producers of popular music. For White, values reflect social action more than they cause it. His case studies are meant to reveal how social contexts combine with accounts of meaning to yield styles that permit effective discourse.

For White, then, values are intrinsically social—a by-product of the interactions that go on in historically defined social networks.

Like the previous contributors, Schwartz is skeptical of the possibility of a purely scientific treatment of values. For him, science characteristically pursues lawful generalizations that are thought to approximate natural inevitabilities, eternal truths. Thus a science of values would be expected to specify the natural laws that govern the determination of human values and their effects on action. But much research in psychology suggests that values are often contextually determined, sociohistorical phenomena, that values can be created and destroyed. In particular, whether activities will be purely instrumental or will possess some intrinsic (immanent) value depends on how those activities are organized. And the way in which activities are organized is subject to historical and cultural change. "Whether and why activities are valuable is a matter not of natural law, but of cultural contingency" (cf. Wildavsky, this volume). Schwartz makes this point by comparing work under feudal conditions with that under capitalist conditions, and by discussing experimental research showing how rewards can have the effect of turning play into work. To illustrate what it means for a domain of activity to be intrinsically valuable, he presents a stylized description of the scientific enterprise.

Historical change in the nature of human values alters the character of social institutions that embody these values and help people pursue them. In modern society, these changes are exemplified by the spread of economic, market considerations into social institutions such as science, education, and the family—institutions that were once thought to embody and to foster nonmarket values. When social institutions are transformed in this way, it becomes easy to mistake contingent, cultural truths for eternal, natural ones. Science tends to tell us that what is the case must be the case, since it is the result of natural law. Applied to human values, such a message would have significant normative consequences, affecting people's conceptions of what is possible, and thus their aspirations and life plans. The task of a "science" of values should instead be to make the historical contingency of values clear, thus opening up discussion of what values people ought to have, and what kinds of social arrangements would best contribute to the development of those values.

Model Building on the Basis of Unconventional Postulated Values

The second set of proposals modifies the economist's tradition of studying values by looking at the empirical implications of models based on postulated values.[31]

---

[31] For a sociological effort in this vein, written subsequent to the conference, see Friedman, Hechter, and Kanazawa (1992).

Scitovsky provides an overview of the treatment of values in modern economics. The values that economists principally are concerned with are the subjective values that people attribute to the sources of their satisfactions and dissatisfactions. Values show what people want and how badly they want it. No objective measures exist to denote the extent of satisfaction. The subjective value that people attach to sources of their satisfactions is always relative and expresses the value of one satisfaction in terms of the equivalent value of another. (Hence money is the best available measure of subjective value.)

Another consequence of our lack of a unit in which to measure satisfaction also prevents us from making interpersonal comparisons. Economists are interested in values as a criterion to evaluate the performance of an economy—how well it allocates resources, coordinates production, and distributes products. To do this one would want a mechanism to aggregate everyone's preferences into a social preference scheme. Arrow (1951) pointed out that this is impossible to do without making interpersonal comparisons. The market does just this for the desires that consumer goods can satisfy. But difficulties arise in the case of collective goods and services.

Economists have a great ability to deal with values in quantitative terms, except for three limits: (1) they can measure the value of only those satisfactions whose sources reach their beneficiaries through consumer markets and of only those pains for which the people who suffer them are compensated through labor markets. (2) Market prices reflect individuals' values accurately only when competition among them is perfect. (3) The values reflected in market prices are not what value means in consumer parlance, but are marginal values. Although the third limit is not severe, the first two are. First, the state's role in the economy has grown enormously, thereby reducing the scope of consumer markets. Second, market failures are both greater and more apparent. Hence measuring the value of collective goods—including such things as equity—is an important challenge to the economic approach to values.

Akerlof and Yellin show how traditional economic analysis may be improved by incorporating novel assumptions about agents' values (see also Herrnstein, this volume). They do so in the context of the fair wage/effort hypothesis, which states that workers have a conception of a fair wage, and insofar as the actual wage is less than this fair wage, they supply a corresponding fraction of normal effort. The reason is that when people are not paid the wage they feel they deserve, they try to get even. (Results from experiments in which workers earn more than their conception of the fair wage are ambiguous.)

Unemployment is anomalous from the neoclassical point of view—for why does the labor market not clear at the going wage? The fair-wage/effort hypothesis suggests that when lay theories about the fair wage leave the fair wage in equilibrium above market-clearing wages, unemployment is the result. This hypothesis is consistent with a variety of literatures in psychology (equity theory) and sociology (relative deprivation and exchange theories), as well as common sense. In addition, this hypothesis explains interindustry wage compression and the existence of a negative correlation between skill and unemployment.

Herrnstein contrasts the treatment of value in economics and psychology, two disciplines that split off from a common Benthamite paternity. As one might expect of close siblings, these disciplines have certain common characteristics. In both traditions, behavior is governed by its consequences, and the relevant consequences can be inferred only from behavior. Neither discipline believes it can get at the essential but subjective hedonic facts, the utility functions or the drives and the associated rewards and punishers, except by noticing how they are revealed in behavior. Despite these similarities, the means by which value is related to behavior differ in the two fields. Herrnstein sees three main points of contention: (1) whereas economics focuses on behavior in exchange, psychology focuses on individual behavior; (2) whereas economics is deductive, psychology is inductive; and (3) whereas economics searches for equilibria driven by utility maximization, psychology is open to the possibility that equilibria can be arrived at on the basis of other behavioral assumptions.

One such assumption is explored in depth herein, namely that individual behavior is based on the principle of matching rather than utility maximization. Whereas maximization requires a sensitivity to marginal returns at each moment, melioration (a process that is based on the matching principle) is based on average returns in utility or reinforcement over some extended period of activity. Herrnstein contends that his theory of melioration is better able to account for individually suboptimal behaviors (such as addiction behavior and various weaknesses of the will) than the traditional rational-choice assumption of utility maximization.

Novel Measurement Efforts

Fischhoff draws attention to a continuum of philosophies among students of other people's values. Adherents to the philosophy of articulated values—among them, experimental psychologists, survey researchers, and economists—believe that if the right kinds of questions are posed they will be sufficient to elicit people's values reliably. At the

other pole are adherents to the philosophy of basic values, such as decision analysts who employ multiattribute utility theory, who hold that
people lack well-differentiated values for all but the most familiar of
evaluation questions—those in which they have had the chance, by trial,
error, and rumination, to settle on stable values. In other cases, people
must derive specific valuations from some basic values through an inferential process. Between these two positions lie intermediate ones. These
hold that although people need not have answers to all questions, neither need they start from scratch each time an evaluative question arises.
Rather, people have stable values of moderate complexity, which provide
an advanced starting point for responding to questions of real-world
complexity.

Each philosophy directs the value researcher to different sets of methodological concerns, and these are amply discussed in Fischhoff's text.
The culmination of the analysis is in Table 3, which—in presenting
conditions favorable to articulated values—suggests a means of reconcil-
ing the different camps by attaining relatively reliable measures of values in response to interrogative probes.

New Interdisciplinary Research

Stich suggests that the typical approach to values taken by moral philosophers may rest on an inadequate cognitive psychology. Moral philosophy suggests that the human mind stores information about values as
definitions that provide individually necessary and jointly sufficient conditions for the applications of the concept being defined, and about
which we already have a great deal of relevant knowledge. It is assumed,
therefore, that the process underlying our ability to classify items into
categories depends on tacitly known necessary and sufficient conditions.
There is some evidence that this traditional account of mental representation is mistaken. Work on categorization in cognitive science has produced several alternative accounts of the processes underlying such
judgments—accounts that do not rely on lists of necessary and sufficient
conditions. One way is that people pick out a set of salient features that
characterizes exemplars, or prototypical members of the category. Another way is that people categorize on the basis of scripts or stories.
Perhaps people store moral knowledge in the form of examples and
stories, but moral doctrines that are cast in the form of necessary and
sufficient conditions are didactically ineffective because they are presented in a form that the mind cannot readily use.

Alternatively, it may be that moral judgments are made on the basis of
rules or principles that specify what sorts of actions are just and unjust,

permissible and not permissible, and so forth. This is similar to the thrust for the search for grammatical intuitions that linguists pursue. Given that there are several kinds of theories about the structures subserving mental representation, it will be necessary to determine which of these theories is correct if we are to pursue the study of values seriously. This requires interdisciplinary collaboration. Stich does not, however, provide any illustrations or exemplars of what this collaborative research might look like.

Theoretical Synthesis

Mandler's ambitions for a theory of values are greater than those of any other contributor. He argues that there are three separate sources of values: biologically determined sources (such as innate approach-and-avoidance tendencies), and two different experiential sources—social and structural ones. Social conditions generate the content and meaning of value structures and permeate all thought and action: living in a particular time and place determines what can be known and, therefore, what can be valued. Cognitive elements are far from context-free—they reflect, incorporate, and constitute the society in which they are formed. Mandler does not dwell much on these social sources of values, however. Instead, he concentrates on structural sources of values generated by the consistencies and discrepancies that are experienced in the course of everyday life. These consistencies and discrepancies, in turn, are recognized on the basis of schemata—abstract mental representations of regularities that enable us to organize our experience.

Values that derive from structural sources, Mandler claims, often have emotional consequences. Occasions for visceral (sympathetic nervous system) arousal follow the occurrence of some perceptual or cognitive discrepancy or the interruption of some ongoing action. Consistency and discrepancy are inherent aspects of our world. Attempts to resolve contradictions in our life lead to new discrepancies and to heightened emotional involvement. One factor that influences judgments arising from structural mechanisms is the frequencies of occurrences and encounters: the more frequently an object or event has been encountered, the more consistent the representational schema. An experience that fits an existing schema is an acceptable event because it is an expected one. This is why we tend to prefer the known to the unknown.

Mandler's principal claim is that schema theory also makes it possible to explain the acceptance and generation of change. Whereas biological and social factors determine the *content* of values, structural factors are primarily responsible for their *dynamics*. Discrepancies and contradictions are the occasions for the development or imposition of new values, for changes in values are most likely to occur when contradictions have to be faced. The outcome of this dialectic between conservatism and openness to change, in turn, is determined by historical and social aspects of the society and by the personal history of the individual within that society.

All told, a number of implicit research programs concerning the genesis and determinants of values can be gleaned from the contributions to this volume. Naturally, these research programs are preliminary; it is difficult to know which, if any of them, will bloom in the future.

Nor is it easy to guess whether interest in the study of values will rebound. Not long ago, values occupied a central place in the various social science literatures (they even had a place in economics!). In the course of three decades of social and behavioral research, the explanatory status of values has declined precipitously. Yet ignoring values has its own risks. Doing without them challenges many cherished institutions and beliefs. Democracy is often justified by its ability to provide policies that are more responsive to citizens' values than the policies provided by other systems of governance. But if people really have no stable values then this justification of democracy is no longer available (Elster, 1983; Sunstein, 1991). When values do not predict behavior this also undermines a principal component of all social theories that are based on intentional action (Tversky et al., 1990). Since neither of these possibilities is especially attractive, there are good reasons to continue searching for measures of values that can predict behavior, the sources of the values, and the conditions under which they sometimes change.

References

Ainslie, G. (1986). Beyond microeconomics. Conflict among interests in a multiple self as a determinant of value. In J. Elster (Ed.), *The multiple self* (pp. 133–176). Cambridge: Cambridge University Press.

Alexander, R. (1987). *The biology of moral systems*. New York: Aldine de Gruyter.

Anderson, E. (1990). *Some problems in the normative theory of rational choice*. Unpublished ms. Department of Philosophy, University of Michigan.

Arrow, K. J. (1951). *Social choice and individual values*. New Haven: Yale University Press.

Arrow, K. J. (1990). Economic theory and the hypothesis of rationality. In J. Eatwell, M. Milgate, & P. Newman (Eds.), *The new Palgrave: Utility and probability* (pp. 25–37). New York: W. W. Norton.

Barry, B. (1970). *Sociologists, economists and democracy*. Chicago: University of Chicago Press.

Becker, G. S. (1976). *The economic approach to human behavior*. Chicago: University of Chicago Press.

Becker, G. S. (1981). *A treatise on the family*. Cambridge: Harvard University Press.

Becker, G. S. (1992). Habits, addictions, and traditions. *Kyklos, 45*(3), 327–346.

Blake, J., & Davis, K. (1964). Norms, values, and sanctions. In Robert E. L. Faris (Ed.), *Handbook of modern sociology* (pp. 456–484). Chicago: Rand McNally.

Blinder, A. S. (1991). Why are prices sticky? Preliminary results from an interview study. *American Economic Review, 81*(2), 89–97.

Brenner, R. (1983). *History: The human gamble*. Chicago: University of Chicago Press.

Calhoun, C. (1991). The problem of identity in collective action. In J. Huber (Ed.), *Macro-micro linkages in sociology* (pp. 51–75). Newbury Park, CA: Sage Publications.

Cleland, J. (1985). Marital fertility decline in developing countries: Theories and evidence. In J. Cleland & J. Hobcraft (Eds.), *Reproductive change in developing countries: Insights from the world fertility survey* (pp. 223–252). London: Oxford University Press.

Converse, P. E. (1964). The nature of belief systems in mass publics. In D. E. Apter (Ed.), *Ideology and discontent* (pp. 206–261). Glencoe, IL: The Free Press.

Cooter, R., & Rappoport, P. (1984). Were the ordinalists wrong about welfare economics? *Journal of Economic Literature, 22*, 507–530.

Cyert, R. M., and De Groot, M. H. (1975). Adaptive utility. In R. H. Day & T. Groves (Eds.), *Adaptive economic models* (pp. 223–246). New York: Academic Press.

Deane, H. A. (1963). *The political and social ideas of St. Augustine*. New York: Columbia University Press.

Easterlin, R. (1980). *Birth and fortune: The impact of numbers on personal welfare*. New York: Basic Books.

Elster, J. (1979). *Ulysses and the sirens: Studies in rationality and irrationality*. Cambridge: Cambridge University Press.

Elster, J. (1983). *Sour grapes: Studies in the subversion of rationality*. Cambridge: Cambridge University Press.

Elster, J., and Roemer, J. (Eds.). (1991). *Interpersonal comparisons of well-being*. Cambridge: Cambridge University Press.

Etzioni, A. (1988). *The moral dimension: Toward a new economics*. New York: Free Press.

Evans-Pritchard, E. E. (1940). *The Nuer*. Oxford: Oxford University Press.

Frank, R. (1988). *Passions within reason: The strategic role of the emotions*. New York: W. W. Norton.

Friedman, D., Hechter, M., & Kanazawa, S. (1992). Valuing children. Paper presented at the Annual Meetings of the American Population Association, Denver, CO.

Friedman, M. (1953). The methodology of positive economics. In M. Friedman (Ed.), *Essays in positive economics* (pp. 3–43). Chicago: University of Chicago Press.

Gaus, G. F. (1990). *Value and justification: The foundations of liberal theory.* Cambridge University Press.

Georgescu-Roegen, N. (1968). Utility. In D. L. Sills (Ed.), *International encyclopedia of the social sciences* (Vol. 15, pp. 236–267). New York: Macmillan.

Gunn, J. A. W. (1968). 'Interest Will Not Lie': A Seventeenth-Century political maxim. *Journal of the History of Ideas, 29,* 551–564.

Hechter, M. (1987). *Principles of group solidarity.* Berkeley: University of California Press.

Hechter, M. (1991). From exchange to structure. In J. Huber (Ed.), *Micro-macro linkages in sociology* (pp. 46–50). Newbury Park, CA: Sage.

Hechter, M. (1992). Should values be written out of the social scientist's lexicon? *Sociological Theory, 10*(2), 215–231.

Hill, R. J. (1981). Attitudes and behavior. In M. Rosenberg & R. H. Turner (Eds.), *Social psychology: Sociological perspectives.* New York: Basic Books.

Hirschman, A. O. (1984). Against parsimony: Three easy ways of complicating some categories of economic discourse. *Bulletin of the American Academy of Arts and Sciences, 37*(8).

Hull, C. L. (1943). *Principles of behavior: An introduction to behavior theory.* New York: Appleton-Century-Crofts.

Ingelhart, R. (1990). *Culture shift in advanced industrial society.* Princeton, NJ: Princeton University Press.

Kahneman, D., Knetsch, J. L., & Thaler, R. H. (1990). Experimental tests of the endowment effect and the Coase theorem. *Journal of Political Economy, 98*(6), 1325–1348.

Kahneman, D., Slovic, P., & Tversky, A. eds. (1982). *Judgement under uncertainty: Heuristics and biases.* Cambridge: Cambridge University Press.

Karni, E. (1985). *Decision making under uncertainty: The case of state-dependent preferences.* Cambridge, MA: Harvard University Press.

Kohn, M. L. (1969). *Class and conformity: A study in values.* Homewood, IL: The Dorsey Press.

Kuran, T. (1990). Private and public preferences. *Economics and Philosophy, 6*(1), 1–26.

Leasthaege, R. (1983). A century of demographic and cultural change in western Europe: An exploration of underlying dimensions. *Population and Development Review, 9*(3), 411–435.

Lindenberg, S. (1990). Homo socio-oeconomicus: The emergence of a general model of man in the social sciences. *Journal of Institutional and Theoretical Economics, 146,* 727–748.

Lipset, S. M. (1963). *The first new nation: The United States in historical and comparative perspective.* New York: Basic Books.

March, J. G. (1988). Variable risk preferences and adaptive aspirations. *Journal of Economic Behavior and Organization, 9*(1), 5–24.

Mirowski, P. (1989). *More heat than light. Economics as social physics: Physics as nature's economics.* Cambridge: Cambridge University Press.

Mitchell, R. C., & Carson, R. T. (1989). *Using surveys to value public goods: The contingent valuation method.* Washington, D.C.: Resources for the Future.

Myrdal, G. (1944). *An American dilemma.* New York: Harper & Bros.

Nisbett, R., & Ross, L. (1980). *Human inference: Strategies and shortcomings of human judgment*. Englewood Cliffs, NJ: Prentice-Hall.

North, D. C. (1981). *Structure and change in economic history*. New York: W. W. Norton.

Nye, M. J. (1972). *Molecular reality*. London: Macdonald.

Pollak, R. A. (1970). Habit formation and dynamic demand functions. *Journal of Political Economy 78*, 745–763.

Preston, S. H. (1987). Changing values and falling birth rates. In K. Davis, M. S. Bernstam & R. Ricardo-Campbell (Eds.), *Below-replacement fertility in industrial societies: Causes, consequences, policies* (pp. 176–195). Cambridge: Cambridge University Press.

Rachlin, H. (1989). *Judgment, decision, and choice: A cognitive/behavioral synthesis*. New York: W. H. Freeman.

Rawls, J. (1971). *A theory of justice*. Cambridge, MA: The Belknap Press of Harvard University Press.

Robbins, L. (1984). *An essay on the nature and significance of economic science* (3rd edition). New York: New York University Press.

Rokeach, M. (1973). *The nature of human values*. New York: Free Press.

Samuelson, W., & Zeckhauser, R. (1988). Status quo bias in decision making. *Journal of Risk and Uncertainty, 1*(1), 7–60.

Schuman, H., & Johnson, M. P. (1976). Attitudes and behavior. *Annual Review of Sociology, 2*, 161–208.

Scott, T. R., & Yaxley, S. (1989). Interaction of taste and ingestion. In R. Cagan (Ed.), *Neural mechanisms in taste*. Boca Raton, FL: CRC Press.

Sen, A. K. (1977). Rational fools: A critique of the behavioral foundations of economic theory. *Philosophy and Public Affairs, 6*, 317–344.

Simmel, G. [1907] (1978). *The philosophy of money*. London: Routledge and Kegan Paul.

Simmel, G. (1955). *The web of group affiliations*. New York: The Free Press.

Simon, H. A. (1986). Rationality in psychology and economics. In R. M. Hogarth & M. W. Reder (Eds.), *Rational choice: The contrast between economics and psychology* (pp. 25–40). Chicago: University of Chicago Press.

Spates, J. L. (1983). The sociology of values. *Annual Review of Sociology, 9*, 27–49.

Spengler, J. J. (1961). Theory, ideology, non-economic values, and politico-economic development. In R. Braibanti & J. J. Spengler (Eds.), *Tradition, values, and socio-economic development* (pp. 3–56). Durham: Duke University Press.

Stigler, G. J. (1950a). The development of utility theory (I). *Journal of Political Economy, 58*, 307–327.

Stigler, G. J. (1950b). The development of utility theory (II). *Journal of Political Economy, 58*, 373–396.

Stigler, G. J., & Becker, G. S. (1977). De gustibus non est disputandum. *The American Economic Review, 67*(2), 76–90.

Sunstein, C. R. (1991). Preferences and politics. *Philosophy and Public Affairs, 20*(1), 3–34.

Tversky, A., Slovic, P., & Kahneman, D. (1990, March). The causes of preference reversal. *The American Economic Review, 80*(1), 204–217.

Veblen, T. [1919] (1961). *The place of science in modern civilisation and other essays.* New York: Russell & Russell.

von Neumann, J., & Morgenstern, O. (1944). *Theory of games and economic behavior.* Princeton: Princeton University Press.

von Weiszäcker, C. C. (1971). Notes on endogenous change of tastes. *Journal of Economic Theory, 3,* 345–72.

Weber, M. [1922] (1968). In G. Roth & C. Wittich (Eds.), *Economy and society.* New York Bedminster Press.

Wildavsky, A. (1987). Choosing preferences by constructing institutions: A cultural theory of preference formation. *American Political Science Review, 81*(1), 3–21.

Wright, D. (1971). *The psychology of moral behaviour.* Harmondsworth, England: Penguin Books.

Part I

Social Scientific Perspectives

2

Are Values Real? The Enigma of Naturalism in the Anthropological Imputation of Values

Fredrik Barth

Contemporary anthropology has little to offer in the way of explicit theory and analysis of values. It takes only the most cursory examination of the titles of recently published books and their chapter headings, or a sampling of the indexes of influential contemporary texts, to discover this striking silence. This is in marked contrast to the 1950s and 1960s, when the study of values was prominent. In important sectors of the literature of that time, the analysis of the value system of a culture was intended to capture the most constitutive, inner core of another way of life; and by the comparative study of values one hoped to reveal the essence of being human.

What happened? It is hardly that questions asked a generation ago have been answered. But sometimes in science, once-central concepts simply fade away as a new perspective emerges; or a paradigm may contain a key conceptual primitive that itself is left unanalyzed; or concepts that are considered unfashionable—but are necessary to grasp the object of study—are discretely introduced into the discipline's descriptive prose without receiving due recognition in the theoretical framework. It is striking that despite the apparent silence on values, the reflexive, critical, and antipositivist thrust of much contemporary anthropology is nourished by normative undercurrents that entail strong value positions and often extensive value counterpoints in the analyses that are pursued. Thus, a widely influential text states under one of its two references to "values" in the index:

> For some, advocacy or assertion of values against a particular social reality
> *is* the primary purpose of cultural critique. However, as ethnographers . . .
> we are acutely sensitive to the ambivalence, irony and contradictions in
> which values, and the opportunities for their realization, find expression
> in the everyday life of diverse social contexts. Thus, the statement and

assertion of values are not the aim of ethnographic cultural critique; rather, the empirical exploration of the historical and cultural conditions for the articulation and implementation of different values is. (Marcus & Fischer, 1986: 167)

Absent from the indexes, perhaps "values" as a concept yet lives a rich but subterranean life in the anthropologists' prose?

But what drove "values" off center stage? Briefly, "meaning" has eclipsed "explanation" in recent anthropology. Thereby some aspects of "value" have been coopted by "meaning," while its place in a paradigm of action has lost its salience. Structuralists following Levi-Strauss search for hidden, deep structure in cultural representations; symbolic anthropologists develop competing paradigms for analyzing symbols; Geertz after 1973 favors "interpretation"; and a younger generation now spearheaded by the postmodernists explore reflexivity, deconstruction, and "multiple voices." A theoretically motivated analysis of values seems to have no place in such concerns.

There are powerful justifications for these reorientations in anthropology, mainly arising from real problems regarding the nature of human behavior and cross-cultural epistemology that make the imputation of values a much more complex task. Few anthropologists today believe that there is a comfortable immediacy in the connection between an observed event and a datum. Imagine you are somewhere in Africa and see a man hand a spear over to another man: What have you observed? Was it an incident of trade? submission? tax? investiture of a vassal? ritual of fealty? bride-price? succession? or a multitude of others? Whatever reality it was part of, that reality is a social and cultural construction, and elaborate culture-specific presuppositions and judgments must intervene before the event is transformed into a datum on interpersonal behavior within that reality. It would appear that any description of values will have to follow after, and be derivative, in relation to these judgments and interpretations.

Such troubling realizations are of course not entirely new (cf. Barth, 1965/1981), but the efforts to display their character and explore their implications have created a new awareness of their magnitude. The struggles to describe parts of reality in another culture's terms (producing an "emic" rather than "etic" account); the acknowledgment that also such accounts will be the ethnographer's constructions or interpretations; the attempts to depict the interactions of ethnographer and natives in this process; the critical labor of deconstructing both anthropology's and Western culture's web of premises, categories, and tacit givens; the realization that interpretation is also the unending challenge for those who live within a culturally constructed world, and the consequent recognition that positioning and multiple voices are inherent features of all cultural phenomena, in contradistinction to the totalizing and integrating assumptions of yesteryear—all these labors have created a drastically changed epistemology for the anthropological project. But though "a scientific analysis of" thereby may fall by the wayside, why do also "values" need to disappear?

It is instructive to go back to the value studies of Kluckhohn and his associates (Kluckhohn, 1951, 1956; Kluckhohn & Strodtbeck, 1961; Vogt & Albert, 1966), or to the very differently articulated perspectives pursued by Firth (1964), to discovery why. Kluckhohn defined values as concepts that regulate "impulse satisfaction in accord with the whole array of hierarchical, enduring goals of the personality, the requirements of both personality and sociocultural system for order, the need for respecting the interests of others and of the group as a whole in social living" (Kluckhohn, 1951: 399). In other words, his very definition incorporates both an emphasis on the complexity of domains and levels, and a troubling double focus on the presumed requirements of both individuals and group—what is often referred to in the literature on values by dichotomizing the desired and the desirable. Firth, less pointedly, incorporates similar specifications in his wording: "To speak of values implies recognition of preference qualities of relationships between means and ends in social contexts. Values involve a grading of things and actions in terms of their relative desirability" (Firth, 1953/1964: 221). The specifications bring out an ambiguity in our intuitive associations with the word: values provide criteria for people's judgment and choice; but they are only a subset of such criteria: those that are socially sanctioned and simultaneously serve the best interests of both the individual and society, integrating the preferences arising from "ought" as well as "want" (Firth, 1953/1964: 221).

As a consequence of such positions, conundrums start proliferating: When do preference criteria for my choices stop being values and merely describe my hedonistic wants? Are we still in the realm of values when prescriptions become so idealized that their effects on action can no longer be traced, and everyone recognizes their expression as mere lip service? What if one's preference criteria are projected on categories of others but not valid for oneself: male standards of femininity, white praise for Uncle Toms, traders' preferences for gullible customers? Or how about such qualities as are ambivalently or mainly vicariously embraced: Robin Hood and other primitive rebels, Don Juan and other macho lovers, and Bonnie and Clyde? These objections are hardly dissolved by introducing remedial terms such as "social deviance" or "value dissonance."

Talcott Parsons imposed greater coherence and consistency in his once so influential conceptual scheme for the analysis of structure and process in social systems. He gave prominent place to "value" as "an element of a shared symbolic system which serves as a criterion or standard for selection among alternatives of orientation which are intrinsically open in a situation" (Parsons, 1952: 12). He thus integrated value as a necessary element in his very concept of social action: "action without cognitive and evaluative components in its orientation is inconceivable within the action frame of reference" (Parsons, 1952: 12). With this (despite a fundamental question begging, which is now more evident than it was then) he retrieved a concept of action that is so deeply embedded in Western everyday understandings, as well as in social scientific thought generally, as to seem compelling and "self-evident." Thus values are established as necessary and fundamental components in the modeling of all human purposive behavior, and value orientations are "the logical device for formulating one central aspect of the articulation of cultural traditions into the action system" (Parsons, 1952: 12).

In my own work, this stimulated my construction of a model of transactions (Barth, 1966)—not to create the moronic maximizer that I am sometimes accused of having fathered but, among other things, to explore processes that generate value convergences. The argument, put very briefly, rested on the idea that through the consummation of reciprocities with others one generates information on the relative evaluations practiced in one's circle and on its margins; and by virtue of the convertability of such objects and acts through transactions into what oneself desires, one will learn to ascribe an equivalent value to them as to that which one seeks for oneself. The conception did not presume the unrealistic coherence, integration, and initial sharing of values that was built into the definitions reviewed above. Yet also it clearly goes too far: I was not able to specify *when* the effects would be generated in empirical social process and when not. I had forced a too-simple and premature closure on the model, as revealed if one tries to apply it to phenomena such as ethnicity or gender.

I would today also point to another, and deeper, flaw in Parsons' formulation: values are not only less shared, but also far less coherent even when shared. We must not blind ourselves to the deep ambivalences embraced by people: wanting and yet not wanting, praising and yet not cherishing, valuing and yet not pursuing, and, most enigmatically, acting on and yet not conceptualizing. Looking more closely, one sees a multivalence of attitudes and conceptions, diversifying the time and place and shades of preference and pursuit in ways only partly captured, partly distorted in Kluckhohn's phrase "the whole array of hierarchical, enduring goals." This is not to deny that actors sometimes pursue systematic, relentless agendas and elaborate, single-minded strategies. But the more one seeks to trace, uncover, and generalize the "hierarchy of" values that underlie such agendas and organize the priorities of people, the more obscure they become: Behind the best-laid plans of mice and men loom nebulous objectives and unresolved alternatives. It is not that values cannot be found—it seems rather as if one finds a surfeit of them: too many, too discrepant, too often disconnected with any field of effective choice, or applied as ways of speaking rather than action, and sometimes, but not always, increasingly vacuous and irrelevant the wider their scope and the more fundamental their pretentions. Empirically, there thus seem to be striking discontinuities between the various levels of discourse on values, and their presumed presence as reasons behind acts.

It seems to me that this is an enigma from which anthropologists have shied away. There has been much work on (culturally operative schemas of) classification and cognition. There has also been much work to unravel the symbolism and evocations of acts within a code of meanings. Lately, there has also been increasingly sophisticated work on the ethnography of emotion. But much less has been done to explore motivations and purposes, and their (degree of) connectedness in terms of the levels and domains of values by which alternative ends are evaluated and priorities of action are sorted.

M.E. research superior to schema

How might one then go about it? If values are "an existing part of nature" in Kroeber's classic formulation (Kroeber, 1949/1952: 136), I would argue that a first step in any study of them must be to produce a close empirical description of them or their observable consequences, in the tradition of natural history. Two different courses seem open:

1. Describe observed regularities of action in a population sharing important cultural premises, and *construct* the conceptions of value that would explain them, i.e., focus on the observable consequences of values.
2. Listen to the reasons and judgments people give for acts: their hopes, moralizing, gossip, praise, envy, pride, and condemnation, i.e., describe the various articulations of values.

Kluckhohn and associates chose mainly the first option. Their key study was made of the five distinct cultural traditions that coexist in the Rimrock area of Texas: Zuni, Navaho, Spanish-American, Mormon, and Texan homestead. A diversity of tests and measures was combined with the anthropologists' cultural interpretations to produce an objective scaling of the cultures on a set of (anthropologist-constructed) dimensions of value orientation.

Firth chose the other course. Warning elsewhere against our tendency to "raise the generalizations to a higher power than the empirical content of the material warrants" (Firth, 1959/1964: 139), he constructed a sensitive description of a particular set of values—relating to authority—in a particular place—Tikopia—by a thoughtful marshalling of contextualized field materials (Firth, 1949/1964) in a way that anticipates the more satisfying aspects of "thick description" (Geertz, 1973).

Both courses have strengths and weaknesses. The description by Kluckhohn and associates can presumably be falsified by other observers, and it offers an instrument for cross-cultural characterizations of value orientations. On the other hand, it tells us little of how Navaho and Mormons conceptualize and articulate their values, how they differ among themselves, and how they justify their positions. It does not even convince us that the value positions formulated by their anthropologists are such as they would themselves embrace. Firth, on the other hand, makes his account compelling by convincing us of his ethnographic perceptivity; but he does not provide concepts that show us how we can emulate him, nor does he explicate a method for cross-cultural comparison of value systems.

But both the immersion into thick description and the exercise in scientistic operationalizing sidestep what I would regard to be the most interesting and fundamental issue: the exploration of what, in different social systems, are indeed the mechanisms/cultural forces at work in orienting people's choices, actions and emotions. Calling these "values," we have anticipated the answer and introduced a particular model of such mechanisms and forces without exposing it to theoretical scrutiny and without questioning its empirical validity or naturalism. I submit that this model incorporates a very simplistic position in moral philosophy: that the connection between a person's concepts and choices is direct and willed (i.e., has a preference character), and can be expressed in relatively simple terms as a normative canon or comparative index. The imagery of "values"also invites us to confound such imputed canons and indexes with standards of exchange (since they are supposed to be shared and socially sanctioned). Since the methodology that is meant to give us access to values is so weak, it becomes only more difficult to overturn this model. As noted above, either we as anthropologists impute a value of our own construction on the basis of the very pattern of behavior that we seek to explain—a vacuous procedure that also ignores the cultural construction of reality. Or else we peruse the various verbal, ritual, and customary expressions of members of a group until we come upon a statement or conception that *seems to us* adequate to motivate the pattern of acts or choices in question. Neither of these methodologies will allow us to transcend our presuppositions and thus make discoveries respecting the *effectiveness* of particular concepts within a culture to valorize emotion, orient choice, and propel action. Rather, they perpetuate a structural–functional presupposition that the main moral and social consequences of any pattern of behavior are those that are normatively intended, and thus ipso facto can serve us, analytically, as the motive and cause of the behavior in question.

Let me provide an ethnographic illustration that can help to cast doubt on these connections. The Baktaman of Western Province, Papua New Guinea (Barth, 1975) had at the time of my fieldwork among them no exposure to the agents of missions or schools, and only first tentative contacts with the then colonial administration. Throughout my fieldwork, I was therefore particularly interested to ascertain, in such a relatively pristine situation, the concepts and perspectives they invoked to interpret themselves and their world, and the social situations and praxis in which such interpretation took place.

Their style of social interaction can generally be characterized as shy and unaggressive—very different, incidentally, from the overt assertion and competitiveness one meets, for example, in the Central Highlands. Participating in the small community they composed, I became increasingly aware of patterns of interaction between them that I found sensitive and attentive to the needs and feelings of others—mainly in ways that seemed consistently to minimize conflict by accommodation, but that also sometimes aimed explicitly at achieving the political manipulation of particular others by humoring them.

Would this justify me in imputing to them values of sociability, consideration, and accommodation? I searched patiently for expressions that might indicate that such values were indeed conceptualized by them. My harvest was very slim indeed. Norms of sharing of (all nonforbidden) foods and of loaning material equipment were widely observed, and accompanying rules were stated. Such rules were also clearly conceptualized in their breach, as when persons hid equipment of theirs that they did not wish to let others use, or when solitary persons or small groups, sometimes including myself, chose to consume particularly desired foods in the privacy of the forest before returning to the camp or village. I was also rewarded for what I intended as generosity and extreme accommodation by once or twice having my beard stroked, and being told they were glad I was staying with them. A concept of "friendship" was also found: a special kind of relationship that could be established through a particular ritual, but the word for which was also used to affirm idiomatically the presence of a positive quality of trust and closeness between two persons. But I was not able to verify a separable conception of generosity, consideration, or sociability in their discourse or their admonition to children. Admittedly, my command of language was never adequate, and negative findings are always questionable. But other conceptions did come through loud and clear. Directly associated with interactions where accommodation was practiced was a clearly con-

ceptualized and expressed fear of sorcery, and a concern to avoid inducing anger. The rationale for acts of sharing, amity, and accommodation,
when given, was consistently that of avoiding the anger of alter; and
when relations deteriorated, the cultural model invoked to anticipate the
actions of neighbors and life-long associates was composed of a grotesque imagery of sorcery-induced sickness and death, the desire for
nocturnal cannibal feasts on corpses, etc.

In other words, I find it empirically plausible that the Baktaman practices of sharing of food is better identified as an *operating strategy* to avoid
sorcery than a *value,* and that the Baktaman practice of tact, amity, and
social accommodation was not generated by concepts that retrieve such
values, but on the contrary was underpinned by concepts that depicted
fellow human beings as destructive and devoid of compassion when
provoked. This seems to provide a logically sufficient model to generate
the behaviors that I observed.

> If you think that irritation or anger in alter may lead to acts that cause
> sickness and death to yourself, it makes good sense to be observant of the
> other's moods and wishes and to be considerate of his interests. Baktaman
> do in fact largely act this way towards each other and also did so towards
> me; it is important to recognize that such tact is an aspect of the *exercise* of
> relationships without being conceptualized as a basic positive morality of
> social relations. The apparent discrepancy between their sensitivity in daily
> events—the genuine pleasure of their company—and the insensitivity and
> violence of some of their acts then disappears. (Barth, 1975: 134 and ff.)

Let me be clear as to what I am asserting. I certainly do not mean to
say that Baktaman do not value good company. What I am saying is that
I think it would be false to impute to them (on the basis of their praxis) a
concept of consideration, altruism, or tact and represent a generalized
value with some such content as the mechanism or cultural force that
generates this pattern of behavior. The desirable result of such acts can,
without special conceptualization, be valued in its particulars. The concepts that I recognize Baktaman as using when they shape their behavior
in this world are those of sorcery, anger, and vindictiveness, and these
are sufficient to explain the patterns of behavior: Where the concept of
sorcery motivates the practice of sociability, the value of sociability can
remain unconceptualized.

If this kind of argument makes sense, we have a slightly different kind
of project on our hands: not to study values, but to discover the various
conceptual underpinnings that, in various cultures at various times, enhance or generate socially desirable behavior. Some of these, in some
cultural traditions, clearly have many or all of the characteristics we
imply with our (most imprecise) concept of values; but we must be pre-

pared to discover that these form only a subclass of what we are exploring. And in discovering what the operative concepts may be and how
they affect behavior, we face a methodological difficulty that is only now
emerging with some degree of clarity in the anthropological literature,
and that has relevance to an even wider field than the study of values.
Pursuing concerns earlier expressed by Firth (1964), Keesing (1982,
1987) articulates it most helpfully in his discussion of normative rules
and cultural codes. "Could it be that the 'cultural code' itself is partly an
artifact of the elicitation process?" he asks (Keesing, 1987: 382), and goes
on to warn us that we "must be weary, in our pursuit of folk models, of
doing what we seemingly have done with folk taxonomies: creating more
global and coherent models than our subjects in fact cognize" (Keesing,
1987: 383).

Indeed, though the particular–generalized dimension is often the
most critical, it is not the only one, as my Baktaman illustration suggests:
a more diverse set of cultural concepts and forces may well impinge on
any particular behavioral domain; and not even the patent presence of
articulated, generalized norms may settle the question of what the mechanisms or cultural forces are that actually orient people's choices, valorize their emotions, and propel their actions.

A counterpointal ethnography may be helpful to focus the problem.
Recent fieldwork by my wife Unni Wikan and myself in North Bali has
given me some familiarity with people who articulate a multiplicity of
value positions in both generalized and vivid ways. Balinese in their
practice of social relations are very sophisticated, but certainly as attentive, considerate, and sociable as were the Baktaman. With familiarity, it
also emerges that a recurring concern of theirs, as of the Baktaman, is
the hazard of evil responses from others—in their case, the fear of
eliciting sorcery by causing offense (Wikan, 1987). But their culture,
including their dominant religion of Bali-Hinduism, differs markedly
from that of the Baktaman in being replete with rich genres of commentary on the tribulations and enigmas of human existence, and teaches
behavioral precepts and morality on a high level of generality and abstraction.

The problem of generosity and greed—presumably a universal human existential theme—can serve as an example. Its most authoritative
expression among Bali-Hindus is perhaps found in the rite-de-passage
of adolescence, where greed is named as one of the six animal passions,
and is symbolically expurgated by the toothfiling ceremony where the
sharp points of the canines are ground down. The same value is expressed in everyday contexts to Balinese youths and intimates in the
standard idiom of urging them to learn to practice the art of giving
without feelings of regret. And the most general philosophical under-

pinnings for these values are found in the *tattwa masi,* the doctrine or teaching of compassion and identification with others (or the "you–me principle" as it is often translated), embracing also all life forms besides mankind.

It would be in line with the program of most contemporary anthropology to proceed to elaborate on the symbolics of this cognitive theme, for example, by exploring the representations of gods and heroes, or the *buta-kala* imagery of the gross aspects of deity: greedy, gluttonous, ugly, and wicked. But the special advantage of an orientation toward values is the way it focuses attention on action. A comparison of Baktaman and Balinese praxis with respect to action brings out an interesting aspect of value concepts such as "generosity" and "greed": their relevance is to the way people modulate their performance of a role, not to the gross circumstances and institutions that structure that role. Anthropologists have sometimes been careless and read the form of an institution directly as evidence for the presence of the values that they judge that institution to entail; whereas I would argue that values are concepts that apply to the judgment of individuals' acts and prestations, not to collective institutions. In this sense, values are always made relevant within a context of parameters set by existing institutions.

Allow me to illustrate, at the risk of laboring the point. Baktaman institutions make usufruct to land freely available to all. Permission to hunt and collect in clan-owned territories is likewise extended to anyone who requests it. The ripening fruits of any particular tree found in the forest may be monopolized—but once it is harvested it must, like all other foods, be shared among those present. Most dwellings are communal and their use limited only by categorical taboos. Tools, equipment, and even items of personal adornment are made available on request.

Bali has generally, and rightly, been depicted by anthropologists as a strongly communally oriented society. But allow me to use the device of depicting it as seen from a Baktaman life-world, and it will appear unbelievably acquisitive and divisive: Gross differences between rich and poor are generated and maintained. Most land is privately owned, and most cultivators obtain access to land only through exploitative contracts of tenancy or wage labor. Activities involving material goods—production and particularly exchange—aim explicitly from each person's point of view at securing the greatest possible material advantage to the person; and the accumulation of material goods is a perennial individual concern. Access to dwellings is limited, and by special invitation only; though there is considerable hospitality in serving snacks and drinks, major meals are almost always monopolized by small, tight family groups, and consumed privately. Just as I felt justified in characterizing Baktaman representations of human vindictiveness as grotesque, the

Baktaman would no doubt characterize as grotesque—if they were able to fathom their import—these Balinese institutions (not to speak of the corresponding Western ones) that deny nonowners all use of land and material objects, alienate most labor, and sustain drastic differences in life chances.

Yet we find it is the Balinese, and not the Baktaman, who conceptualize, embrace, and give eloquent expression to the value of generosity and condemn greed, and who emphasize the percentile of material goods that pass as gifts as a major component of their morality, admonishing that one should learn to give without regrets.[1] The undeniable conclusion must be that concepts of "generosity" and "sharing" are values which only refer to ways of operating *within* the parameters of the established institutions of a society and the social situations defined by them, and not to the principles on which those institutions are built. They enjoin an enduring orientation in the efforts of the *individual* actor, but not in the collective designs for acts of allocation and distribution that are entailed in established institutions.

How do such values assert themselves in the consciousness of the individual actor? Let a small vignette among many illustrate characteristic Balinese concerns. Nyoman, a person with whom I was on quite intimate terms, ruminated one day on his recent experiences:

> I am not a good person. . . . In the boat race the other day, I entered my two boats (manned by hired captains). One of my boats won—I was very proud. The Government gave a prize, 40 kg. rice, to the winning captain. I felt it, in my mind: it was *my* boat, I was not happy. Then, when I went to congratulate the captain, he said: Here is the rice prize, you must take half. I said no, you won the race. He insisted. *Then* I could say 'No' with good feeling, 'you should have the rice; I have rice at home; it is all for you.' But I took it, the diploma.

There can be little doubt that the value of generosity, as a template, plays an active part in Nyoman's shaping of his own act. But clearly also, this takes place within a context defined by other and dominant institutional parameters: competitive racing, first place, property rights, hierarchy, justice. And once these parameters have received public confirmation, there is still a struggle of opposed motives to resolve.

Indeed, this struggle might provide a measure of the relative value placed on the performance of generosity, as compared to other enduring goals. It might be tempting to treat it as a "cost" of obtaining an item

---

[1] A dialectical explanation—that it is the very presence of these excluding social regulations that fosters the conception and ideal of generosity—cannot be dismissed, but seems unenlightening if one cannot give a coherent account of the actions and codifications by which such a dialectic is generated.

of value, and thus make a broader field of choice transitive. But that would be too simple: the major subjective effort goes into making the act *willed*, not that of performing it. One cognitive rationale for this effort is provided by the concept of *karma pala*, which ensures that you will always harvest the moral consequences of your acts: the goodness of your good acts will accumulate and bring results in this life and in later reincarnations, and your bad acts will likewise pursue you with their consequences. But the efficacy of good acts depends, for this purpose, on the sincerity of your intentions: "Insincere good acts and sweet talk do not give good *pala:* the thought and the act must be one!" The model, in other words, sets up a divine accounting of value whereby benefits can accrue only if the subjective work of willing it is done successfully, and the arithmetic of costs and benefits is subjectively transcended.

Furthermore, while the struggle is real, it is motivated only if Nyoman places a particular perspective on these events. At other times, the same Nyoman will pursue elaborate manipulations of social relations to engineer a rip-off: of Balinese as well as tourists, in major land transactions as well as petty deals. This relates to other enduring goals of the person that likewise need attending to: the value of obtaining and accumulating wealth. In taking the measure of the man, this is linked with a model of life stages, whereby the mature man by his wits and his work should have achieved a level of prosperity that provides security and comfort for his family. Nyoman has pursued a checkered and at times frantic career to reach this goal; and sometimes, now in middle life, he reflects on his failure as a person compared to his peers in never having achieved it.

The very boat that won him the diploma was one of his schemes to right this failure, and his contract with the captain was carefully designed to maximize Nyoman's income. In another minor enterprise, he decided to establish a chicken farm. He bought some hens and placed them with a village acquaintance, and provided grains for fodder. He figured that each hen would produce 20 chickens, which would fetch good prices in a few months. As the scheme developed, he would visit occasionally to inspect his fortune; and as the chickens grew so did his delight in feeding them: he would come oftener and oftener, and they would rush up to him to be fed from his hand. The chickens multiplied and grew to delightful proportions, and he enjoyed them so much that he kept postponing the day to start selling them. After a while, difficulties began: counting the chickens he would find some missing, and the villager would serve him tragic stories of how this one was taken by a dog, that one run over by a truck, two had been slaughtered to save the lives of the villager's sick and starving children, and so on. "I got so upset, I could not bear visiting them any more. It is a year now since I have seen my chickens—maybe there are even more of them now, worth a lot of money—if the peasant hasn't eaten them all!"

Can we conclude from such anecdotes that the pursuit of wealth is not such a major value and powerful goal after all? Certainly not, but the story alerts us to two further circumstances: as a scheme unfolds, various values may succeed each other in saliency; likewise, events may call forth a shift in perspective whereby unforeseen models of the objective situation become ascendant. We need to realize that the course of events had produced for Nyoman a situation of danger in terms of a Balinese model of health and life force. Briefly, your life force (*bayu*) depends on your emotional and spiritual condition, as much as on nourishing foods and vitamins; and a strong life force is essential to secure your health and vitality in a world full of illness, misfortune and sorcery (cf. Wikan, 1989 for an analysis of this model and its entailments). Optimism, good thoughts, and harmony all enhance your *bayu* and thus your vitality and resistance, whereas sadness, anger, and confusion weaken it. There could be no doubt that Nyoman's conflicting feelings, distress, and mounting anger at knowing he was being cheated added up to a real health hazard in terms of this model, and his withdrawal from the whole affair was the most expedient way to defend the now acutely threatened value of health. Turning the whole episode into an amusing story, as he did, so it provided an occasion for laughter and gaiety among friends, was a further means of reducing the danger.

In other words, Nyoman's scheme was certainly motivated and shaped by the enduring value that man should seek material wealth; but as it unfolded, other values succeeded it in saliency, influencing a shifting course of events. A project launched in a hopeful spirit in pursuit of one legitimate goal was thus transformed into a quite different one, involving quite other concerns; in this course, we also see alternative models of the world coming to the fore. What might seem, without the proper context, like a very fickle attachment to priorities is no such thing. Life makes unpredictable twists and turns; and the "objective conditions"—objective in terms of cultural models of a supposedly real world—for the pursuit of values are neither predictable to the cultural insider nor transparent to the cultural outsider. Handled less adroitly, Nyoman's relationship to his chicken-tending village partner could, for example, equally well have moved in a third direction, and turned into a nightmare of recrimination, offense, and sorcery disaster. Concerns are multiple, and impinge on even the best-laid plans, requiring urgent attention, whether evasive or constructive. A study of values requires the command of varied and particular cultural insights so one can correctly identify the parameters within which options are conceived by actors, and the changing context of models of the world that are being evoked.

But are not such models ultimately consistent and of a piece, forming a "world view"? Even if the answer were yes—for which I see poor evidence and little plausibility—the question thus posed sidesteps the issue. Orienting oneself in the world by placing a cultural construction on it involves the production of a stream of ad hoc interpretations of it in the passing here and now. Such interpretations will necessarily be tentative, piecemeal, and contradictory to other possible interpretations—so the comforting vision (shared by many anthropologists and many native thinkers) of an ultimate order will in any case remain unrealized.

The main lesson I draw from these two ethnographic illustrations is that to study what we may choose to call values, we must embed our data in the particular context of concepts and practices within which the actors themselves are positioned. We cannot study values simply in terms of their effects, and construct our representations of them on the basis of those effects. No analyst's construct or extract of particular values or generalized value orientations will be able to predict the twists of perspective, the shifting relevance and revocation, that are the essence of human action and its interpretation by actors and their social circles. These events must be seen through the looking-glass of culture, as it is applied by real people as they go about their life; only an elaborate contextualization within the field of templates that actors themselves use, in real-life situations, can retrieve such complex processes and model the reality within which they are living and coping. Since the behavioral effects of values furthermore are secondary, as I have shown, to parameters set by customary institutions and available cultural models of reality, this contextualization is all the more essential.

But if values are so deeply embedded in a complex context that their study becomes so forbiddingly demanding and elaborate, then why study values at all?

I have indeed suggested that the very word is one that tempts us to make unduly simplistic assumptions, and at times has called forth unrealistic expectations. To constitute "values" as a category of phenomena and make it the central object of an empirical and theoretical branch of studies is therefore probably not a productive strategy, certainly not at present. But as part of a project to revitalize the study of social action, the theme of values directs our attention to an area where collective institutions and representations articulate intimately with individual behavior, and thus to an area where the course of social events is significantly shaped. It provides no lodestar, but an orientation that is timely and can help us break out of a constraining contemporary fixation on text, commentary, critique, and symbolics. Furthermore, values in the somewhat restricted sense of articulated concepts that valorize emotion, orient choice, and propel action are cultural products, which in turn affect their producers in very significant ways. Once people articulate, for example, the concepts of "generosity" and "greed," their actions cannot escape being affected by it. There is a vast culture history to explore from this perspective, and a field of comparative analyses to be developed so as to uncover the way and the extent to which different value conceptions generate different effects.

It is possible to sense some of the themes and promises of such a program. Thus, for example, J. B. Haviland has very perceptively shown how a whole genre of value discourse in Zinacantan, that of gossip, "exalts the particular" and fails to articulate general principles (1977: 181). In North Bali, on the other hand—while gossip is variable in form and content and tends mainly to serve a variety of instrumental purposes—much value discourse is cast in terms of generalizing schemata, threefold, fourfold, and eightfold classifications, and the enunciation of grand principles. These general principles are also widely referred to in mundane contexts, and serve the person explicitly and implicitly as templates for thought and judgment—as in Nyoman's reflections on the boat race. This generates a vast body of explicit value theory as part of Balinese tradition of knowledge, and also entails their characteristic self-consciousness about the duties, struggles, and difficulties of transforming such principles into action. A third configuration appears among the Baktaman, who concentrate much of their conceptual work simply on creating and sustaining their cultural construction of the world (Barth, 1987), entertain a fairly limited range of gossip, and neither generalize nor perform the soul-searching of the Balinese. It would not be unreasonable to hope that substantive and systematic comparative analyses of such materials would generate insight into the conditions for the articulation and implementation of different values, as Marcus and Fischer (1986: 167) call for in the passage cited at the beginning of this chapter.

I have stressed the importance of a theoretically motivated analysis of values for the revitalization of the study of social action in the social sciences. It may then seem paradoxical that the ethnographic illustrations I have used point so clearly to the separate and secondary place of value considerations and value discourse as against the parameters set by social institutions and models of the world. Haviland (1977: ix) similarly notes with despair how the gossip he records seems meticulously to avoid drawing attention to the governing constraints—of power, poverty, and exploitation—of the lives it dissects. But we also know that there are genres of value discourse that turn value concepts against institutional parameters and critique them. Values are always involved in the dynamics of people acting *on* their world and their situation—albeit necessarily in terms of their cultural construction of it. Yet that need not prevent them from sometimes, in some ways, wishing to transcend what they see and change their reality. We should give particular attention to the historical situations where values transcend social parameters and introduce additional dynamics into an already complex and inconstant world. This brings us almost full circle back to the brief but ambitious program conceived by Kroeber (1949) in his National Academy address on "Values as a subject of natural science inquiry." The job it calls for is still undone. Perhaps the enhanced sophistication of a critical, reflexive culture theory can be turned to the constructive task of forging the sharper concepts and pursuing the fastidious analyses that could bring that program to fruition.

References

Barth, F. (1966). *Models of social organization.* London: Royal Anthropological Institute (Occasional Papers No. 23).

Barth, F. (1975). *Ritual and knowledge among the Baktaman of New Guinea.* New Haven: Yale University Press.

Barth, F. (1981). *Process and form in social life.* London: Routledge & Kegan Paul.

Barth, F. (1987). *Cosmologies in the making: A generative approach to cultural variation in inner New Guinea.* Cambridge: Cambridge University Press.

Firth, R. (1964). *Essays on social organization and values.* London: The Athlone Press (London School of Economics Monographs on Social Anthropology No. 28).

Geertz, C. (1973). *The interpretation of cultures.* New York: Basic Books.

Haviland, J. B. (1977). *Gossip, reputation, and knowledge in Zinacantan.* Chicago: University of Chicago Press.

Keesing, R. M. (1982). "Cultural rules": Methodological doubts and epistemological paradoxes. *Canberra Anthropology, 5*(1), 37–46.

Keesing, R. M. (1987). Models, "folk" and "cultural." In D. Holland & N. Quinn (Eds.), *Cultural models in language and thought,* (pp. 369–394). Cambridge: Cambridge University Press.

Kluckhohn, C. (1951). Values and value-orientations in the theory of action. In T. Parsons, E. A. Shils, et al. (Eds.), *Toward a general theory of action.* Cambridge, MA: Harvard University Press.

Kluckhohn, C. (1956). Toward a comparison of value-emphases in different cultures. In L. D. White (Ed.), *The state of the social sciences.* Chicago: University of Chicago Press.

Kluckhohn, F. R., & Strodtbeck, F. L. (1961). *Variations in value orientations.* Evanston, IL: Row, Peterson.

Kroeber, A. L. (1952). *The nature of culture.* Chicago: University of Chicago Press.

Marcus, G. E., & Fischer, M. (1986). *Anthropology as cultural critique.* Chicago: University of Chicago Press.

Parsons, T. (1952). *The social system.* London: Tavistock Publications Ltd.

Vogt, E. Z., & Albert, E. M. (Eds.). (1966). *People of Rimrock: A study of values in five cultures.* Cambridge, MA: Harvard University Press.

Wikan, U. (1987). Public grace and private fears: Gaiety, offense and sorcery in North Bali. *Ethos, 15*(4), 337–365.

Wikan, U. (1989). Managing the heart to brighten face and soul: Emotions in Balinese morality and health care. *American Ethnologist, 16*(2), 294–312.

3

On the Social Construction of Distinctions: Risk, Rape, Public Goods, and Altruism

Aaron Wildavsky

We are able to take for granted distinctions among objects and behaviors because by social consensus they are what we think they are. When consensus breaks down, when concepts (and hence the words that refer to them) become politicized, a struggle over meaning and morality takes place. When to classify is to decide, rival moral judgments contend for supremacy.

Most people, I observe, find the social construction of our concepts of the world hard to understand; after all, we are usually not aware of people engaged in building and tearing down such edifices. Since it takes place through repeated interactions at different places and times, among many different people, social construction is even harder to demonstrate. Exactly how this social decision making works its will is not often shown. Yet, without understanding how meanings are constructed, no social theory is possible.

In this chapter I take four well-known distinctions with powerful implications for public policy—the voluntary/involuntary dichotomy to explain the relative (un)acceptability of risks, consent versus coercion in sexual relations, the justification of governmental action based on the dichotomy between public and private goods, and the long-standing efforts to distinguish between selfishness and altruism as a moral basis for evaluating behavior. In each case I seek to show that meanings that seemed fixed are in fact movable boundaries subject to the pulling and hauling of cultural contention.

But how do they move? Who propels them? In what direction? Why? In conclusion, I seek to show how cultural theory helps account for both stability and change in what seems to be immutable. The illustrations are made vivid in the interest of jolting sensibilities to see with a cultural eye.

The Voluntary and Involuntary Are Movable Boundaries[1]

There is a prima facie plausibility in assuming that individuals make a strong distinction between risks they knowingly undertake and risks that are imposed on them. In particular, they accept damage they incur through their own fault or through choice of dangerous sports, drinks, foods. They know that if they want longevity, they should not overeat or drink too much liquor, but that is their affair (unless, of course, there is "prohibition"). What makes them angry is damage they feel they should have been warned against, which they might have avoided had they only known, or damage caused by other people, particularly people profiting from their innocence.

The distinction provides a plausible explanation of the shift in public attitudes to danger. If people are being increasingly deprived of control over their own lives, if people feel helpless, then their sense of outrage at involuntary risks will naturally grow more intense. However, this argument cannot be true, I believe, because the distinction between voluntary and involuntary exposure to danger is not objectively identifiable. Put another way, the people involved decided the risks were unacceptable so they perceived these risks to be involuntary.

If you and I want to go rock climbing, thus voluntarily exposing ourselves to risks, that is presumably our own business and would be all right. If the air contains coal dust or food contains carcinogens, however, that would be all wrong, because the risk to us is involuntary. At first, the distinction appears eminently reasonable; there are indeed risks additional to the standardized risk of daily living that individuals are allowed to assume voluntarily. There are also risks that are unknown or that may be known to some but hidden from others.

There are always unsuspected dangers: some inventions (asbestos, X-rays), introduced to make something safer, turn out to be dangerous and dangers that are present are ignored. Since anything and everything one does might prove risky (perhaps when we know more, an apple a day will prove unhealthy, exercise debilitating, breast-feeding poisonous, or showers enervating), we should ask why people differ in classifying risks as freely taken or coerced.[2] (That the do differ will be demonstrated.)

There are risks we would rather not run but that we undertake to gain other benefits. People do live in Los Angeles, for example, not for the privilege of breathing in smog, but to take advantage of its natural beauty, warm climate, job opportunities, and so on. Life's choices, after

---

[1] This section is largely taken from an early draft of Douglas and Wildavsky (1982).

[2] This sentence appeared in the first draft of this chapter long before the controversy over Alar on apples came into public view.

all, come in bundles of goods and bads that have to be taken whole.[3] Unwanted it may be, but the known risk that comes with the expected reward can hardly be called involuntary. The term would be appropriate only when there is some compulsion or deliberate obfuscation.

The arrow of causality could be reversed. Neighbors and neighborhoods are part of a person's standard of living. The chances of being shot by rival gangs, of being run over by addicts, and much more, are affected by location. Should "undesirables" be kept out of our neighborhoods, then, on the grounds they add to our dangers against our will?

Even as new things add to hazards, they also reduce risks. Are these involuntary benefits to be disregarded? That would make a hash out of Adam Smith's arguments in *The Wealth of Nations* that private exchange yields public benefits, not to say Mandeville's dictum—private vices, public virtues.

There is practically nothing that individuals do in leisure time that does not affect their children or others who enter the home, or even those who provide or share their sports. The climbing instructor has to risk his life rescuing tyros stuck on the mountain; the swimming instructor tries to save a would-be suicide. Voluntary risks are likely to spread danger. Should the amateur climber, the suicidal swimmer, and the smoking drunk be prosecuted or forbidden by law to take risks?

Suppose that one person deliberately injures another. We do not ordinarily speak of this as "risk." Robbers and murderers are called criminals. If a person gets hurt through the negligence of another or merely because a product is faulty, the law of torts enables such people to sue and possibly collect damages. Here I would observe only the enormous differences over time of what is considered negligence and even whether some fault must be proved. In the last few decades, the point is, many actions previously considered voluntary have now been deemed involuntary, that is, actionable in law (Polisar & Wildavsky, 1988, 1989).

The distribution of life chances through any society is hardly equal. Some classes of people face greater risks than others. Poorer people, on average, are sicker, die earlier, and have more accidents than richer people. We cannot say that all classes of people who incur greater risk in the course of their lives incur them voluntarily. A person might prefer to risk an industrial accident, or accept a certain degree of pollution, to being unemployed; the risk incurred is involuntary in the special sense that people would rather things were otherwise. The risks they face may be unwelcome and against their will; they would not accept them if they were rich. Either involuntary risk is an empty logical category, or it has to

---

[3] In Wildavsky (1988) I call this "the axiom of connectedness"—the good and bad health effects of substances and practices are intertwined in the same objects—whose operation exercises a powerful effect on strategies for securing safety.

be a complaint against the particular social system that gives some people a harder life, reflected in risks to which they are exposed.

Voluntary/involuntary is a movable boundary, capable of turning every constraint on choice into injustice, for a moral judgment of who is to be held accountable is enunciated by the boundary between voluntary and involuntary risks. If questions about how the boundary is drawn are raised, risk by risk, they will lead in only one direction: what was taken to be a natural boundary will be discovered to be a socially constructed one. Then political pressures will shift it back, ending with every choice being considered involuntary.

All individuals can in fairness be treated as involuntary visitors on this planet; every conceivable damage they sustain can be attributable to unwished-for destructive agencies. If the pattern of values changes in that direction, ultimately all the sick and unfortunate could be presented as involuntary inhabitants of their own bodies, totally withdrawn from any commitment to social life. Suicides would be owed redress by the implacable institutions that drove them to their undeserved end. All individuals could be shown to have an unlimited right to be compensated for all losses, however incurred, if only the anger against institutions is comprehensive enough.

In *Science*, sociologist Charles Perrow (1986) seeks to distinguish between active and passive risks, active risk being more voluntary and controllable by the individual and passive risk less voluntary and perhaps uncontrollable. This distinction is important because it is often made in justifying why certain risks are more and other risks less acceptable. But the distinction is misleading. One might imagine a static social system whose values, including its rules of accountability, were petrified. The people who conferred meaning on objects must have lived long ago, no one having come along since with any changes to make. Classifications are clearly labeled and immobile. Then, and only then, might one allocate dangers according to those that are active and voluntary and, therefore, acceptable, or passive and involuntary and, therefore, properly subject to governmental regulation or prohibition. Once social change enters the picture, however, the active–passive distinction, becomes a malleable boundary, constantly redrawn by social interaction.

People with different values, I have been arguing, would place a different interpretation on the same expectation of risk. There are people, sometimes called competitive individualists, who believe that risk is opportunity. Conversely, they claim that excessive concern with avoiding risks today is tomorrow's greater danger. Moreover, these interpretations change over time. People on the egalitarian left, for example, consider the dangers stemming from technology (nuclear power or chemical carcinogens) as passive, while they perceive the dangers stemming from casual contact with those suffering from acquired immune deficiency syndrome (AIDS) as active. At the same time, people on the hierarchical right view the dangers of technology as actively chosen, a price worth paying for the benefits of progress, while they view the carriers of AIDS as bringing plague on people who are made their passive victims. Which of these dangers is voluntary? To say a danger is voluntary is tantamount to saying it is acceptable; involuntary dangers, imposed on passive people, by contrast, are unacceptable. Classification and decision are one and the same. Just as we-the-people are the ones who confer meaning on these distinctions, so we are also the ones who change these meanings.[4]

Who Determines When and How a Woman Gives Her Consent?

When I tell people that the distinction between voluntary and involuntary action is not graven in stone but is a social construct, subject to bargaining between affected interests, they are skeptical. The listener has no trouble understanding that objects do not come from nature with their names engraved on them or their value in neon lights. It is people who give names and negotiate values. But when everyone can think of examples of the voluntary and involuntary (say skiers or spelunkers versus the victims of Bhopal or hostages), they feel triumphant.

My next move is to agree with them (as far as I can) by seeking to determine why they feel so certain. The reason, they are quick to tell me, is that the differences are obvious to any intelligent and reasonable person (even going so far as to hint that I might have an ulterior motive or might be congenitally perverse). The distinction seems obvious to them, I counter, knowing from experience my words and reasons will seem like lame excuses, because of near-universal agreement on classification. The boundary separating the voluntary from the involuntary, I claim, is not and cannot be intuitively obvious; boundaries are socially constructed; when this social agreement evaporates or weakens, the "obvious" becomes converted into the politically contested.

Social construction, in my view, is just as real as physical and almost but not quite as easy to spot. A good way to begin is to ask whether there is a fixed distinction between rape and love making by mutual consent. Stipulate in advance that the observed facts are not in dispute. Surely anyone can tell whether and when a woman is forced or voluntarily consents to sexual intercourse. No, I say, not quite. For a time, most people mostly agree. But not all at any time nor most all the time,

[4] These two paragraphs are taken from my response to Perrow (1986), p. 439.

especially when the criteria for ascertaining rape, as they are now, are contested.

These reflections were first spurred by reading accounts of the famous Dr. Ruth Westheimer's visit to Stanford University. At one point a young man described an episode in which he and a young woman made advances to one another, disrobed, got into bed, and were about to consummate the sex act when she demurred.

What did sex therapist Dr. Ruth think of such goings on? Poorly, it appeared. The young woman, Dr. Ruth opined, was wrong in carrying things so far without expecting efforts at consummation.

The rights and wrongs of this particular episode are not my concern here. What does interest me is the response by feminists. They insisted that a woman, no matter what her preceding behavior, had the inviolable right to terminate the sex act until (and, perhaps during, the record is murky) the point of penetration. Such old-time catch phrases as "she wanted it" or "leading on" or "past endurance" were eschewed in favor of pure voluntarism. The woman owned her own body and, as the proprietor, was the sole judge of who or what could enter it and when.

What is happening before our eyes and ears is a negotiation in which feminists are trying to increase the power of women by moving the time and criteria and determination of consent as far forward in time as possible so as to give the female of the species as much control as possible.

In decades past, a term such as "spousal rape" was unknown (at least I never recall hearing it). Marriage presumably meant that a woman had given her consent. Yet we all know that since time immemorial married women have been forced. Only they had no legal redress. Nor could they, except in very unusual circumstances, expect sympathy. Quite the contrary. "You made your bed, now lie in it" was the norm. If marriage was equivalent to consent, and now it isn't, I ask, how did what was once voluntary on all occasions become involuntary when the woman says no? Wasn't it a movement called feminism that was dedicated to the purpose of redrawing boundaries between what is deemed voluntary and involuntary?[5]

Boundaries are power. When one determines that risks from social behavior or technology are voluntary or involuntary, one is deciding

[5] Other major definitional shifts, not appropriate for this illustration, have occurred on fundamental levels. Feminist writers, for instance, have long discussed two interrelated issues: (1) whether rape is a personal crime (against the woman) or a property crime (against those holding a social economic stake in her sexual practices); and (2) whether a woman in a given society has any consent to give: Is willing intercourse with someone not authorized by the males in her family her prerogative or not? And do such "authorized" sex acts take away her right to say no to other men?

important political questions. To say that the hazardous effects are undergone voluntarily is strongly to imply that they are the fault of the injured party, whereas a conclusion of involuntariness implies the desirability of action to redress the grievance, from compensation to regulation. The definition is the decision.

Public versus Private Goods

Laymen (that is, people with a different specialization) are by no means alone in failing to observe a crucial boundary being negotiated. Academics and assorted other thinkers, paid to observe a restricted sphere of events, are especially prone to believe that the distinctions on which their work rests are inherent in nature, the way the world is and has to be. The suggestion that it is artificial, made up, negotiated, a product of huffing and puffing, leads to a reaction not so different from alley cats fighting, except they are not so presumptuous.

In my chosen fields of politics and policy analysis, for instance, the contrast between the private and the public spheres is ubiquitous. A division of fields is based on it, the public belonging to a political science and the private to economics. The belief is that these are not merely traditions of study and thought but that they correspond to real entities that can be pointed to, touched, measured, observed, even manipulated.

As in the earlier analysis of rape, I do not doubt that the public–private distinction is widely used, even, at times, helpful for certain analytic purposes. I do deny that these distinctions are immutable. They, too, are movable boundaries, socially defined, stable for periods of time but not forever.

What is to be considered public, and, therefore, run or regulated by government, or private, hence in the province of individuals, families, or groups, is the subject of everyday political dispute. "How much government" there ought to be is a major area of contention among Western political parties.

Sometimes the debate is carried on by the assertion of rival principles purporting to establish that certain activities naturally "belong to" the private or public sectors. Such arguments will not wash in a culturally plural universe. Adherents of every culture try to make their way of life appear to be natural. Everything, literally, that one can think of has been (or could be) done either publicly or privately. This goes for armies (private mercenaries), taxes (tax farming in which private parties bid for the right to collect revenues), and justice (mediation services). The reverse, seemingly unalterably private matters, such as child-rearing, eating, or sexual practices, have been regulated by the state. Who would have thought a quarter century ago that the state would intervene so frequently and severely in family life in regard to suspected child abuse. Why the term had hardly been heard, let alone intervention sanctioned, yet we know that abuse of children must be millennia old.

Blocked in this direction, making the desired obvious, economists have invented terms that appear to indicate whether the phenomenon in question should be private or public. The starting place is significant because it indicates what is normal and accepted or abnormal and exceptional. Usually, among economists, the private is the thing done, so that exceptions have to be devised to justify governmental intervention.

Among the most amusing such inventions is the concept of "externality," which refers to the effects of an action by one party on another who has not given consent. The classic example is people upstream dumping effluents on people downstream. Because economists judge it inefficient for one party to impose costs on another without their consent, they propose governmental intervention as a remedy either to halt or to reduce or to provide compensation for what is considered this market failure.

Yet externalities are life. Since human life is social life, with each of us, as it is said, a part of the other, everything that is done may well have effects on others, some of which they do not care for. If state intervention is justified by the existence of externalities—a failure to use (or the use of an oppressive smelling) deodorant, setting poor examples for children—then it is justified, period.

"Internalities" could exist only if there were no other people, which there are, or if they did not matter, which they do. I belabor this point to strengthen it: since only other people can judge when they fell affected, it is these others who determine whether an externality exists.[6] As one of my father's favorite maxims had it, when a minyan (that is, the community) tells you you're drunk, fall down!

The claim of externalities makes a good introduction to the assertion that there is a privileged class of goods so essentially public that government is justified in producing them if they are not available at all or, if they already exist, in providing more of them than people are willing to pay for. For the realization that externalities are what we think they are, even what we want them to be, brings us to the irremediable subjectivity of the concept of goods (Douglas & Isherwood, 1978).

[6] The subjectivity of judgments of cost may lead to attempts to objectify the process by taking claims to court. There, under tort law, people must persuade a judge and jury that they have actually suffered harm for which they should be recompensed. Observe that this involves adjudication among private parties and is not, on the face of it, a case for governmental intervention.

A good is not an item in a store with a price tag on it. If that were so, any one of us could put any item in any store at any price. No, a good is something someone values in exchange; someone is willing to give up something else for it. Truly, goods are goods only for those in whose eyes they are good enough. While defining goods according to how each one of us values them in exchange, that is, in terms of our individually perceived opportunity costs, may appear unexceptional, it is not. For if goods depend on our subjective evaluations, so do what is public (or private) about them.

My aim is to bolster Mary Douglas' position, to wit: "Public availability is conferred by the collectivity itself." What enters the list of public goods "depends on community fiat".[7] That and no more than that.

Public goods, as economists define them, appear to be "freebees." They are things people get without paying for them. They are supplied by the state, presumably because people are not wise enough to want to give up something else to get them. But why is government obligated to supply something for which people would not want to pay?

Consider the favorite example of national defense. It is considered a public good by virtue of the fact that even those who do not pay for it, including those, I suppose, who refuse to pay on principle, receive its benefits. The people who paid for protection presumably cannot limit benefits to themselves. Since some of those who benefit do not pay, public goods theorists say, less of this good is produced than it would be if everyone who benefited paid. It follows that government should step in and produce as much of this good for people's welfare as if the shirkers, or, as they are often called, "free riders," had paid their fair share.

A typical assertion in a recent text is that "If . . . our national defense achieves its objective in deterring attack from the Soviet Union, then there is no way that an individual could be excluded from the benefits" (Stiglitz, 1986: 100). This author obviously does not live in Berkeley or other places with "nuclear free zones." Only when there is widespread agreement is the national defense the same for everyone; otherwise, people will, as some do now, seek to exclude themselves from it—others may die as an enemy seeks to destroy a nuclear battleship berthed in

[7] On cultural theory see M. Douglas (1982) pp. 182–254; A. Wildavsky (1987) pp. 3–21; and M. Thompson, R. Ellis and A. Wildavsky (1990). Since writing this essay, a mother paper as it were, I have jointly authored others on these themes—J. Malkin and A. Wildavsky (1991) pp. 355–378; David Fogarty, Claude Jeanrenaud, and Aaron Wildavsky, "Why the concept of externalities does not belong in economics," typescript, June 1992; Magnus Enzell and Aaron Wildavsky, "Hobbes' natural man is a fatalist: Implications of cultural theory for interpreting Hobbes and his critics," typescript, June 1992; Charles Lockhart and Aaron Wildavsky, "The social construction of cooperation: Egalitarian, hierarchical, and individualistic faces of altruism," typescript, August 1992.

their city, but residents of San Francisco will not because their government has refused to accept such an American ship.

The emotional loading of the language used in discussing a subject is often a clue as to its content. Enter the free-rider problem. When a good is available, whether people pay for it or not, they may refuse to contribute their fair share; hence, less of that good would be produced than if everyone revealed their true preference. As Harvey S. Rosen (1988: 53) puts it, "The market mechanism may fail to force people to reveal their preferences for public goods." Or, as Joseph Stiglitz (1986: 102) has it, "The reluctance of individuals to contribute voluntarily to the support of public goods is referred to as the *free-rider problem*." So the moral point will not be missed, Stiglitz (1986: 102) argues that "It is in the interest of all to be coerced to pay taxes to provide for public goods." The action verbs are revealing—force, coerce, reluctance. Whatever happened to free enterprise?

Since when, us ordinary mortals might reply, does anyone have the right to coerce others by claiming they are receiving "benefits" they conspicuously have failed to recognize? Anyone can claim he has conferred benefits on others who should be grateful, and use this alleged ingratitude to have government take their money and spend it on his chosen policies. The doctrine of "false consciousness" is not rescued by being renamed "public goods." Conceptual coercion is not better than any other kind.

Here, I think, we may have a difference of opinion about the meaning of a free society. To individualists freedom means that members of a community pursue what seems to them desirable, not that some members determine what seems good to them and impose it on the rest. The difference is between a conception in which people act on their notions of the good, as in consumer preferences, or in which there is some preexisting standard, like greater equality, that overrides their preferences.

The criterion of public goodness I have been discussing, no doubt with insufficient seriousness, is called "nonexcludability" or you get it whether you pay for it or not. In actual use, nonexcludability depends heavily on an associated concept called free availability or joint supply. The idea is that more for one does not imply less for another or at least the consumption of such goods by certain people does not prevent their consumption by others.

I contend that *there are not and cannot be any such things as goods that are nonexcludable and in joint supply unless informal understandings or collective decisions make them so.*

The concept of public goods is time and situation and culture bound. It is as relative and subjective as anything can get. Later, I will explain how and why different versions of publicness and privateness serve to justify different ways of life (or cultures). Here I wish to show the categorical emptiness, the total nonspecifiability of nonexcludability and joint supply.

First, due to a certain congenital laziness, a challenge to adherents of the utility of the public-versus-private goods distinction: show me that the writers on this subject do in fact classify the same goods in the same way. I doubt it. Second, I claim that everything can be made excludable if the will is there. Isn't medicine socialized in one country and privitized in another, with everything in between found somewhere? Don't tell me whether medicine or food is intrinsically this way or that, a skeptic might suggest, ask whether I want to exclude others from these goods or not. The air and water examples commonly used break down not only when there are shortages but whenever these goods become politicized. When air of the same quality that used to be passable becomes hazardous to your health, stories appear about access to the clear kind, why the poor get the worst, on and on. Nonexcludability and joint supply seem natural only because that is the way it has been for awhile, not necessarily because it has always been that way or nature tells us it has to be so in the future. What, for instance, could be more nonexcludable than climate? Yet, as Gerlach and Rayner (1988) write, "Events have cojoined to place the issue of global climate change on the legislative agenda of the U.S. Congress." Even the weather, about which we used to talk but not act, is no longer nonexcludable. And the same was once true for air and water, illustrations that once were plausible but now are not because their supply and content have become politicized.

Let us take as our last example one that is especially close to the hearts of professors—research. It has been said that there are many benefits of research that cannot (or are not likely to) be appropriated by specific entities. In essence, these entities cannot get paid for the full benefits of research so they are not willing to pay enough for it. Not knowing that they will be benefitted, or how much, these lucky recipients of research benefits will not be willing to pay for as much research as would maximize public welfare. That is quite possible. But that chain of reasoning also supposes that someone knows what is good for the rest of us.

Now if enough of us are persuaded that the proposed expenditures are good for us, or for others we care about, we may well spend the suggested amount. If not, all the criterion of nonappropriability tells us is that some or most people do not want to pay, indeed, cannot be persuaded to pay, but that others who think they ought to pay are prepared to compel them. I prefer the straightforward approach of putting your values up front, as James Tobin (1970) does in his "On limiting the domain of inequality."

When we take this discussion out of its usual context in which society is likened to a single form of social organization, and ask how what some people portray as public goods are viewed in a variety of cultural contexts, we get quite different impressions. Before we do that, however, it may prove useful to try cultural analysis on a commonly raised question and controversy, one in which behavior is classified as benefiting the self or helping others. If anything is self-evident, it is the difference between selfishness and altruism. Or is it?

Self-Interest versus Altruism in Cultural Perspective

As standard a proposition as one could find in all sociology is that behavior considered normative, valued, and prescribed in that culture gets a good grade. Conversely, antinormative behavior is downgraded. As norms change from one culture to another, therefore, we would expect either that selfishness would be honored and altruism disparaged, or if altruism was conventionally honorific, the same behavior that was so designated in one culture would be deemed its opposite in another.

Imagine that we are members of a hierarchy who accept its norms as legitimate. Among these is the sacrifice of the parts for the whole, a norm that led Durkheim to speak of altruistic suicide. Because the person involved has internalized the norm, however, he also believes that sacrificing his own interest is in his self-interest. In a hierarchy, then, it would be failure to sacrifice oneself (the officer lagging behind his men in battle) that would be pejoratively labeled as "selfish."

Turn now to a culture of individualism whose members seek to substitute self-regulation for authority. A norm among individualists (as social a culture as any other) is competition. The honorable and honored thing is to engage in competition so as to win more even if you stand to lose a lot. The winner may be called altruistic because of the risk he voluntarily assumes. But so would the loser, because he did the right thing and can be expected to try again. The selfish individualist might be the one who seeks a subsidy or a tariff or otherwise impedes competition. Given that these terms have achieved a certain tone in society, however, individualists such as Ayn Rand delight in terming what others call altruism, destructive, because it encourages action on behalf of others, simultaneously robbing them of their independence and damaging the economy because no one knows the value of goods better than each individual. Altruistic is selfish and selfish altruistic, Rand maintains, when interpreted in the context of the one right way to live with other human beings. Similarly, she calls seemingly selfish behavior in her favored individualistic culture altruistic because she thinks it leads to a freer and more productive society.

A culture of fatalism, whose members feel ineffectual, erodes the distinction between altruism and selfishness not by reversing but by obliterating it. If you do not affect the world, so it only affects you, any active posture is futile. There is no point in altruism because you cannot help others and, if you could, they would not care. Indeed, they might just as well harm as help you. Nor is there anything to be said for individualism in that you cannot help yourself nor will others help you. Only luck and a dogged avoidance of responsibility, making oneself as inconspicuous as possible, can avoid the blows incessantly raining down on fatalists. Egoism and altruism belong to the active cultures, not the fatalistic.

In the land of the egalitarians, who seek to diminish differences among people, selfishness is setting oneself apart from the group. Egalitarians call for sacrifice, but only on behalf of those who have less, the "unequals." Since the guiding norm is equality of condition, inequality, having more resources than others, exercizing greater power, is the besetting vice. Egoism is either individualism, seeking more than others, or fatalism, refusing to participate, or hierarchy, giving or taking orders. In brief, the concept that is morally bad, selfishness, is adhering to other ways of life, while altruism, the morally good distinction, is supporting one's own culture.

Here we have the meaning of cultural rationality: the rational person supports his or her way of life. To be culturally rational is to relate means to ends in an efficacious manner. To be irrational is to choose means better suited to supporting other cultures. Thus selfishness (your side) is irrational while altruism (my side) is rational. QED.

A Cultural Accounting

I would now like to make a cultural accounting of the preceding four sets of distinctions. When risks come from technology, believers in hierarchy tend to be supportive because they support existing authority. Individualists, who believe that markets are wise, think of risk as opportunity. Fatalists have no preference because they think it does not matter. Egalitarians, by contrast, see corporate capitalism behind the technology, which in cultural terms signifies to them coercive hierarchy and inegalitarian individualism. The cultural premise is that rational people support their way of life. Hence we (the users of cultural theory) predict that people who identify with individualism and hierarchy will tend to perceive technological dangers as small and voluntary while egalitarians see them as large and involuntary. Conversely, when the danger is viewed as social deviance, as from AIDS, egalitarians will perceive the risk from casual contact as small and voluntary, hierarchists as large and involuntary, with individualists in the middle. I think that anyone who follows these issues will see that these classifications improve prediction.

In regard to rape, everyone will agree that force is wrong but they will disagree about what constitutes consent and when it is given. Egalitarians, who want to diminish differences in power, will push the time of consent forward to the last possible moment, giving the deciding voice to the woman (or, as in child-abuse cases, to the child). Supporters of hierarchy, with their patriarchical bent, seeing the husband as head of the family with the wife subordinate to him, will push the time of consent back to the marriage itself, asking for much more stringent proof of much greater coercion. Fatalists have to accept what happens to them. Individualists will make up their rules as they go along.

In no way will individualists accept public goods arguments for further governmental regulation. Viewing private as normal and public as abnormal, they will occupy themselves trying to "privatize" whatever hierarchists wrongly think of as public. Egalitarians, for whom the public arena is of overwhelming importance, because only there do all actively participate and give their consent, tend to view the private as coercive (that is, inegalitarian), a form of hidden hierarchy. Only if they see state power used against "unequals," gays, racial minorities, etc., would egalitarians object.

Reprise

Distinctions between concepts are not found in nature, I have argued, but in us. Meanings are socially constructed and, therefore, socially altered. The categories of cultural theory serve as adequate accounting devices: The rival interpretations of boundaries fit the categories without too much massaging, and predictions of behavior based on which culture individuals adhere to work better than any known alternative.

The most important collective goods a society produces are interpersonal, namely, the shared values justifying social relationships that make up its competing cultures. What do adherents of these cultures compete about? Many, many things, of course, but foremost among them is the ability to make and remake distinctions to support their way of life. They succeed for as long as others regard their distinctions as natural, i.e., in support of the right way to live. In the largest sense, cultural competition is about which concept of rationality (what constitutes reason) and which concept of nature (how the world works) will prevail.

References

Douglas, M., & Wildavsky, A. 1982. *Risk and culture*. Berkeley and Los Angeles, CA: University of California Press.

Douglas, M., & Isherwood, B. (1978). *The world of goods*. London: Penguin.

Douglas, M. (1982). *In the active voice*. London: Routledge & Kegan Paul.

Gerlach, L. P., & Rayner, S. (1988). Managing global climate change: A view from the social and decision sciences. Oak Ridge National Laboratory.

Malkin, J., & Wildavsky, A. (1991) Why the traditional distinction between public and private goods should be abandoned. *Journal of Theoretical Politics, 3*(4) pp. 335–378.

Perrow, C. (1986). Letter to the Editor. *Science, 234,* 783.

Polisar, D., & Wildavsky, A. (1988). From resilience to anticipation: Why the tort law is unsafe. In A. Wildavsky (Ed.), *Searching for safety* (pp. 169–186). New Brunswick, NJ: Transaction Press.

Polisar, D., & Wildavsky, A. (1989). From individual to system blame: A cultural analysis of historical change in the law of torts. *Journal of Policy History, 1,* 129–155.

Rosen, H. S. (1988). *Public finance* (2nd ed.). Homewood, IL: Irwin.

Stiglitz, J. E. (1986). *Economics of the public sector*. New York: W. W. Norton.

Thompson, M., Ellis, R., & Wildavsky, A. (1990). *Cultural Theory: Foundations of socio-cultural viability*. Boulder, Co: Westview Press.

Tobin, J. (1970). On limiting the domain of inequality. *Journal of Law and Economics, 13,* 263–277.

Wildavsky, A. (Ed.). (1988). *Searching for safety*. New Brunswick, NJ: Transaction Press.

Wildavsky, A. (1987). Choosing preferences by constructing institutions: A cultural theory of preference formation. *American Political Science Review, 81* pp. 3–21.

4

Values Come in Styles, Which Mate to Change

Harrison C. White

Values explain and justify intention, agency, and actions. A value may be a guide, but a value may follow rather than precede intention or action, and any value may mislead. Values may be for self and/or for others—be these others peers or agents or onlookers. A value can be explicit, say in a parental scolding on honesty, but in the hurried negotiation of daily living values are implicit, as in prudence accompanying honesty in delivering action.

Either way, a value is made recognizable across different locales and periods by symbols and their use in social action. In the words of Michael Schudson:

> Culture is not a set of ideas imposed but a set of ideas and symbols available for use. Individuals select the meanings they need for particular purposes and occasions from the limited but nonetheless varied cultural menus a given society provides. In this view, culture is a resource for social use more than a structure to limit social action. It serves a variety of purposes because symbols are 'polysemic' and can be variously interpreted; because communication is inherently ambiguous. (Schudson, 1989: 155; Swidler, 1986)

This chapter argues that values do not come as separate coins but in symbolic packages that derive alongside and together with form of social organization. Enormous interaction pressures limit these forms to one of a few, call them institutions. Two of these institutions will be sketched. Each is a correlation of values around social networks.

Particular expressions of values thus come as packages with networks that reflect the underlying institution. For example, the social organization of a science as an institution is reflected in any new theory entertained in that science. All the packages consistent with an institution share similarities: they conform to some style. The population conceives of behaving and misbehaving only in terms of these packages: they evince a style.

...ut test of the argument is predicting change. Changes in expression of particular values can be triggered by environment or by group and individual whim. But change in their structuring as a package, change in style, is difficult because style is coordinated to institution. A style has settled in only through continued reenactments. No change in style can take place without change in organization of networks and values, and conversely.

A new style requires an intermediate period of overlay and melding between one style and another, followed by rejection among styles separate again: that is the specific conjecture. This chapter examines the conjecture for the range in social organization between small-group level and national societies, as well as between instantaneous and epochal. This range is large enough to include social worlds that are relatively self-sufficient, yet small enough for case studies to effectively trace major changes.

Values

A value may range from widely shared on through localized and also on to highly contentious across a population. The primordial form of value is entirely implicit, without language, and yet also completely shared; this form is strict positioning in a pecking order, which determines all aspects of the creatures' lives (Chase, 1980, 1982, 1986, Forthcoming). Some values, however, as in asceticism, may appear to be removed entirely from social interaction. Values can have their own cultural pecking orders, with sacredness enveloping the high ends, but equally striking is their multiplicity of format, from commandments over to mere tones within scripts of interaction.

Earlier theoretical perspectives were typically focused on values in themselves. Talcott Parsons, in his efforts toward a general theory of social action, pushed for transposability and separability of values so that the ultimate ends of different means–ends chains could constitute an abstract system. Thus for Parsons ultimate ends can be cultural facets of coherent social action across a society.[1] By contrast, Erving Goffman

---

[1] "Culture is . . . transmissible from personality to personality by learning and from social system to social system by diffusion. This is because culture is constituted by 'ways of orienting and acting', these ways being 'embodied in' meaningful symbols . . . which are the postulated controlling entities . . . unlike need-dispositions and role-expectations, (symbols) are not internal to the systems whose orientation they control . . . they have external 'objective' embodiments" (Parsons & Shils, 1951: Ch. 3, part II). What had made Parsons' first book (1937) so stunning was its supersession of Pareto's synthesis, a synthesis of an abstract logicoexperimental model of society with a biological/sentimental model.

(1955, 1963, 1967, 1971, 1974) denied this transposability in his push for local phenomenological truth: viz., a "backstage" where reality and valuation of even the simplest social acts must be negotiated afresh, endlessly.[2] He seeks to induce style as well as value out of everyday minutiae of social organization.[3] This reminds us that scientific discourse is subject, like any other discourse, to Ricoeur's (1988) contextual variability.[4]

Parsons seeks to strip values out of styles tied to social organization. Others, such as DiMaggio (1987), March and Olsen (1989), and Merton (1968), push for explanation of style and value only in interaction with tangible organization. These others typically work, like the present chapter, with middle-range orders.

Purity, commitment, and scope are three values on which to focus.[5] After developing theory further, the task will be to show through several examples how each of these values intertwines with a facet of social formation, and how those facets interpenetrate and accompany each other to form an institution. The meanings of a package of values is to be inferred as much from the social architecture as vice versa.

Consider a recent case study of scientific research. Susan Cozzens (1989) dissects a recent controversy over a multiple discovery in neural pharmacology, wherein expressions of the values of honesty and of originality[6] are being negotiated in interaction with constructing a particular discovery through various agencies in a complex social field. One can read a style from this particular social formation for a subdiscipline of science. Multiple networks—of collaboration, of training and sponsorship, of gossip, of friendship, and the like—are sources as well as products of rankings in Cozzens' case. These rankings are both particular, as

---

Pareto had relegated economics to a subordinate role, as unable to shed light on the general ends, the values, that drove and determined the whole means–ends schema of economics. Parsons argued against Pareto's retreat to instinctual biology of the emotions. Parsons argued for a direct sociological interlocking of general ends into a web of values that was exactly *The Structure of Social Action*. Parsons' was a bold vision for linking society to individual by observable cultural fiat.

[2] For a cogent overview of the recent phenomenological position, which situates Goffman with Sachs and Garfinkel, see Rawls (1989). For incisive appreciation and critique of Goffman see Burns (1991).

[3] Even though Goffman seems concerned only with the evanescent, a principle of self-similarity suggests there should be similar stylistic regularities in large and ponderous institutions.

[4] However, I stipulate a self-reproducing social formation in some sort of equilibrium; so values cannot be one-time by-products.

[5] Corresponding in the introductory example to honesty, delivery, and prudence, respectively: By my argument values always appear woven together as a package, in which there is no unique way to specify the canonical warp and woof, anymore than "the" three dimensions of physical space have unique directions.

[6] Corresponding to purity and scope earlier.

scientific pecking orders of investigators in specific subfields surrounding neural pharmacology, and also more general as status-layering, personal and institutional, in the larger scientific field.

Mass-media news conferences were one sort of agency involved. Another was brokering and conciliating by other senior scientists. All meld into activations and adjustments of network and standing among the four different working groups being vied[7] for recognition as co-discoverers. Dual to all this is the semantic negotiation of concepts and perceptions, in struggles over whether there is an "it" to be discovered, and over bounds and shape for this "it"—the "opiate receptor."

The values do not operate as universal guides transposable to this scene. The ordinary language terms of "priority" and "originality" dissolve in confusion amid the bewildering struggles and claims, which manufacture, as convenient, new criteria of connection and information. To transpose—as a term in an algebraic equation or in a sentence—means to change to a new location without altering the value, whereas "priority" transposed to the opiate receptor case is indeed altered.

Value Sets and Networks

Values operate in sets. A value alone is like one hand without the other. Lessons in white lies of tact and adaptability go along with lectures on honesty as a natural package for ordinary living. Or take values in working science: originality (a variant of scope) is a preeminent value, but so also is its complement and obverse in scientists' thinking and talk, the value of truth (a variant of purity). As here, the values in a set need not be seen as hostile but instead may be viewed as natural complements like hammer and chisel.[8]

Values also come within contexts. Take a topical example. Senator Jesse Helms of North Carolina operates in a set of values that you hold too. A set of values comes with a scene, and the national scene that you share with Helms is huge, but it is also abstracted and limited to attitudes and accompanying ties as expressed in public media among entities and actions, which themselves become defined as being public. It is the senator's sequencing and frequencies of use, as well as especially his concrete mappings from values to social actors, that distinguish him from you.

From one population, tribe or town, or factor, to another, even nearby, one may code a somewhat different set of values, and of course distinct networks. But the main shift will be in relative frequencies of use

[7] It is clear that many other individuals and organizations and scientific interest groups also push claims of—and on—particular research groups such as these.
[8] Until some proper calculus has been developed for analysis of discourse—perhaps along some such lines as Abell's (1987)—metaphor and intuition will have to serve.

of a given set (Cornell, 1988). The main shift occurs in how given values are mapped onto sorts of interaction, and in how actors sequence among the set in giving an accounting of action.

Within a given scene there is no unique package, no single set of values ordained. For example, within the discourse of a scientific specialty, priority and precision are another common pair of values, alongside truth and originality, through which to analyze stories of research. Values are not some fixed coins of the cultural realm, and this makes it difficult to discriminate between sets of values (cf., flexible portrayal, in Lorrain, 1973, 1975). At the level of "honesty" and "prudence," which is to say given the degree of abstraction in Parson's pattern variables (e.g., particularist, universalist), a whole package of values that can be operationally distinguished in subjects' appreciations may collapse into one. Distinctions within a set are correlated with concrete social context, so that the package in its concrete correlation is a moving target of analysis.

Take another concrete example, Bob Dylan's adoption in 1965 of electric instruments, followed by many others. Within the preexisting folk-music world, a general value, "genuine" hands-on music from and for the people, was no doubt violated, and indeed there was a ruckus if not a schism. But among the active members of a world, operative values concern much more specific matters than such an abstraction. The change to electric instruments violated some but not others of the set of specific values, so that one could encompass it, cognitively, with rather small adjustments in the set. The shift also at the same time would be impacting social relations, and in particular relations among performers, and between them and new sorts of technicians, all of which would be reflected in shifts in the specific values. Actors, like observers, are as much reading values out of accomplished actions as apprehending them as free-standing guides.

Values reflect and explain away perhaps more than they cause. Change in values derives from fault lines in social patterns shown up by turmoil. An illustration comes from a recent case study of a social movement. Civil Rights values, seen to include purity and effectiveness, were woven into the social fabric of Movement organization. In McAdam's words (1988: 237): "Activism depends on more than idealism. . . . There must also exist formal organizations or informal social networks that structure and sustain collective action. The volunteers were not appreciably more committed to Freedom Summer than the no-shows"— among the college students initially recruited; so that it was position in mobilization networks that tipped who actually came, rather than intensity of individual beliefs in Civil Rights values. Another illustration comes from the early Church (von Campenhausen, 1955).

We see the basis for the correlation of style to overall social arrangement as an institution (White, 1992a). Now look at values from the inside, from individual users' active perspectives. Values help each actor orient in and deal with contingent interactions and environment, which give room to attempts at manipulation, and in particular to agency.[9] Accountings of social actions presuppose a set of values held in common across social networks. Values supply the rhetoric for unending conflicts for control among distinct actors, individual or composite, that generate a set of values in reaching some equilibrium despite duplicity and contention. The resulting value packages and styles serve both to express and to conceal the conflicts and the orientations.

Every identity seeks control by maintaining itself, and to that end establishes, and breaks, ties with other such identities.[10] Each of these ties is a metastable equilibrium of contending control attempts, and as such induces chronic invocations of values, including references to other ties. A set of values comes to be held in common as infrastructure for networks of ties among contending identities and across some levels of organization; liturgies Thompson (1961) came out of such infrastructures.

Network ties go between identities, which are not exogenous but socially constructed. The identities embed out of disciplines of social action, which derive from pecking orders of ecology but recur also in purely social contexts, whether bridge games, children's sports (Fine, 1983), or legislative committees (Padgett, personal communication, and cf. Najemy, 1982). The prototype discipline is interlocked as in recurrent team action for material production, from fishing party to assembly-line group.

Within each such discipline, within an identity, the set of values may be only implicit. Social pressure within a discipline is intense and interlocked enough to establish dominance ordering without articulation in values. Values actively spin out and maintain social ties and their networks, through accountings that interconnect actors and provide bases for institutions and thus styles.

Styles

The values that are the players within a style need not cause what is happening, but the package of values is a medium sufficient for accounting for what happens. Actions may be erratic and zany under the usual

---

[9] Here "agency" connotes reaching through delegation of some immediate chore to obtain longer-lasting control (White, 1985).

[10] By "actor" I designate only the enactor of a script for some social position. I shift to the term "identity" instead when what is at issue is original and unpredictable action by intention—and in particular and especially gaming. An identity may be short or long-lived; it need not be a person. See White (1992a).

pressures of contingency and chance from physical as well as social context, and by the flukes of maneuver for advantage. But the style that drives those actions, by invoking a fixed set of values in accountings thereof, induces perception of regularity: that is its first attribute.

Networks presuppose a set of values. Identities make use of values to maneuver—but of course they can do so effectively only as other actors at least know what they are signaling, and thus only as they share a set of values. Individuals watch one another within disciplines and social networks and imbibe patterns in how to maneuver within and using the package of value.

Thereby individuals acquire a style as they jointly reproduce an institution through their mutually patterned actions. Values impinge on social networks through some profile of transmission distinctive of that institution. A style is measured by a profile of use among a set of values accompanying an arrangement of networks.

Styles with their packages of value and network come in various scopes. For example, a single person can embody a style, which then concerns component identities of the person with their links and values as seen by given others as well as selves. At this level conventional usage differentiates value facets central to the person, values proper or ends, from peripheral value facets, called attitudes. Personality is style exhibiting consistency of ends within the person.

Even about attitudes the main research question has been consistency, evidence for which is at best mixed (Abelson et al., 1958, 1968). Many attitudes, such as those toward political candidates, concern cultural objects on which there is common knowledge concerning others' attitudes. Objects for such attitudes may fall into a known ranking by public esteem or recognition of success. But then consistency or inertia of attitudes in a given person may conflict with central values of the person such as desire for approval and association with success. Why, for example, does a person keep a losing political attitude? It may be because he or she has not yet been convulsed by a mixing of selves needed to change even so apparently labile and isolate a construct as a forlorn political view held by a person, a view actually part of a style.

Levels build up in social formations. "Actor" can become anything from a multinational giant firm (Pratt & Zeckhauser, 1985) to a Goffman creature of the brief encounter. Although style can be seen as a generalization of personality, social formation is easier to observe than personal "insides." Case studies of institutions, not of individual persons, are used below (cf. White, 1992b). A major strength of such case studies is their detailed texture of stories.[11] The analysis here does however presuppose

---

[11] Book-length reports of cases are cited that report the tales and anecdotes that are the raw material of value and style analysis.

self-similarity in which the same principles of style can hold at different levels.[12]

Styles emerge in all contexts, from the most secular to the most sacred.
For example, rock 'n roll music is a style, in that it is a package of values
with profile of performances in an accompanying social world. Rock 'n
roll music came in as lyrical, rhythmical, and organizational vehicle for a
fresh package of values infiltrating a category, the preteens, which was
becoming newly recognized as corporate entity for commercial purpose
(Ennis, 1992). Rock 'n roll emerged as a new style. Equally, every new
Kuhnian paradigm in a science comes in accompanied with a new institution, that is, a repackaging of values together with a realignment of
networks of work and cooperation into a new invisible college.

The second main point of style is how it stitches concrete together with
abstract, cultural with social, value dimension with social network. Style
does not settle tactics or maneuvers but it does shape and constrain
them. Network and dimension weave into larger infrastructure as institution that shapes style via stories and other symbolic accountings. Such
weaving across social and cultural duals occurs only with difficulty and
infrequently, but once accomplished resists change.

Consider a pair of realizations of one institution.

Village Caste and Academic Science

A first institution is illustrated in two very different cultural guises,
caste and science. In the first of these guises, change in institution or
style is generally thought to be precluded, whereas in the other dress the
institution is generally thought to encourage change in style. The specific referent for caste here is the institution observed among central
Indian villages and mapped out in networks of behavior and perception
by Mayer (1960). The second illustration of the same institution, from
an utterly different discourse, is academic science as a social formation in
the United States, of which Cozzens' case earlier is a particular drama.

Accounts of Indian caste in general (Dumont, 1986), emphasize the
value placed on ritual purity and the strict demarcation of bounds for
corporateness. A curious topology underlies and justifies both empha-
ses, within the ongoing networks of kinship across villages. This topology
very much depends on how networks weave together a corporate structure of purity. The topology can be tagged as a metonymy, specifically a
synedoche: "the smaller contains the larger." It is this topology which I
transpose to modern academic science to claim a good fit.

---

[12] The obvious alternative is to introduce auxiliary rules of framing, and scripting that are
special to particular levels and/or contexts.

Meticulous study of a particular system is required to support description of a style and institution. I rely on Mayer's account (1960) of a field of villages in central India. Purity is operationalized with extreme explicitness in villages. There is a ranked series of substances whose passage from one to another grouping permits precise imputation of purity, hence of sociocultural standing.

The groups ranked are local and constitute a partition of all family units within a given village into specific caste groupings. Rankings of each caste can be imputed from observed transactions, especially those on public occasions as in religious feasts and weddings. Party food, cooked in butter, comes at one extreme, then ordinary food, then raw food, and on through smoking pipes, drinking water, and on down through garbage and feces.[13] A generally agreed linear order of village castes is supported thereby.

The village is the site of primary economic activity, farming, and artisanry. Caste matters do not tie directly to most of this ecological activity. Nor do struggles over ownership, over improvement, and change in property, which largely lie outside the scope of the village.

Through marriage kinship cuts across villages. The unit of intimacy is the subset within a village caste who have married into a like subset of an analogous caste in another village, or rather the many such intermarrying sets across a number of villages in the region. Call this the subcaste, a network construction hopping across the region. It is a "sub"caste because within any particular village the persons in the given affinal network are but a subset of the several clusters of blood relatives that make up the whole caste in that village.

Paradoxically, the subcaste is larger than the caste. The reality is that inheritance and marriage, the engines of major change, lie within the subcaste and outside the village. There is both village exogamy and caste endogamy. The corporate reality of a subcaste interlinked through affinal ties across a whole region, this intimate corporateness is broader than the only caste unit that is actually embodied, that of the village. Indeed the subcaste may be comparable to the whole village in size.

Only the subcaste has explicit organization, a council, and like agencies for regulating caste affairs. Wealth flows along subcaste lines, through marriage and inheritance, as do innovations, material, and other. There are only the thinnest threads of purity calibration that can be spun out by the Brahman "priests," themselves scattered as local caste units in villages.

Some mobility can take place without disturbing perceptions of purity value. It is the mobility not of individual persons but of whole subcastes

---

[13] Explicit network modeling of such caste interaction data can be found in Marriott (1959, 1968). No doubt analogues could be uncovered in current Western professional practice.

moving to new villages. They can do so because there are more distinct castes in the region than can ever be found together on the ground of a particular village. The Brahman argues primarily in terms of the four broad *varnas* of their scriptures; so a subcaste new to the village can appear and argue for a location in purity rank within that village in the only way that matters, getting the appropriate exchanges going.

Looking at Mayer's photos of separate caste groups hunkered down in separate locales at feasts, one can almost supply the story sets used to account for and tidy up the value-ranking by purity. Not able to be photographed, but equally central, are the sprawling networks of kinship bonding across other villages that sustain and reproduce the system. A separate set of value facets is embedded in these ties among subcaste segments.

American Academic Science

There is a close parallel to the organization of American academic science. For village read university, and for village caste-group read department in a university. Purity becomes prestige, itself a stand-in for degree of ultimate truth. Subcaste translates into specialty, which is at the heart of science as research, as generator of originality. With this translation, the statements above on Mayer's village caste system can be carried over into the social setup of American academic science.[14]

A pecking order for scientific disciplines is operationalized only among departments within the particular university, physics or mathematics often being top and sociology near the bottom.[15] Degree of scientific purity may be attributed to this order. Ritual pervades this scene, whereas action and excitement and intimacy grow along research networks spreading outside the given university.

Sprawling networks of collaboration and intimacy in actual research reach across the nation on specific subjects. Specialties are concretized in them. For specialty as subcaste read invisible college (Crane, 1972).

Seen from outside within its university, a given department has meaning and indeed coherence. The meaning comes within and expresses a hierarchy of purity and accomplishment, which can vary from one to another university. The hierarchy is enforced by deference behaviors in committee meetings and luncheon interchanges. It is also enforced and

[14] It may be that the dissection below carries through as well to the humanities, with whose organization I am less familiar. Better analogues to the humanities, as well as to professional schools and the like, may be the ethnic enclaves that crosscut villages and castes in a region like Mayer's.

[15] This pecking order varies a little between universities. Sociology, for example, is higher at the University of Arizona than in Ivy League schools.

expressed in larger and more solemn ceremonials, at which symbolic capital can be exchanged like any other.[16] Contents of interchanges can be typed analogously to the discriminations from high to low in the material exchanges among castes within a village, and there is a parallel range of meeting contexts within a village.

Seen from its inside, a university department of science, analogous to a village caste, is a shambles of unrelated specialties. Different collections of specialties will make up that discipline's departments in various universities. And universities differ in their exact menus of departments. All this is parallel to the caste/village/subcaste formation. A specialty spreading across scores of departments is typically much larger than a given university department—just as a given subcaste spreading into scores of villages has more members than are in that caste in a given village (see Figure 1).[17]

Each specialty is the prime world of motivation for its working scientists. And when recruitment of new (faculty) members to the given department comes up, it is recruitment largely along invisible-college networks of specialties active in that department and competing with each other. Just so do marriages and children get formed through networks within a subcaste quite separate from the other subcastes, which together in the eyes of that village make up the weavers (or the blacksmiths or whatever) as a single caste entity. One speciality is linked to its departmental counterparts in different other universities than is another specialty, which is another reason why they tend to operate separately and independently within their own department. Again there is a parallel to Mayer's descriptions for subcastes.

Familiarity of the reader with our academic setting can supply detail and conviction, though excellent case studies such as Cozzens' cited above can help. For overviews to supplement case studies and personal experiences, see, for example, Merton (1973) and Mullins (1973). For longitudinal perspective on values, showing how careers play out in science see Cole and Zuckerman (1979) and Menard (1971).

* * *

This first institution is plausible, and because the caste illustration is a vivid one, it is easy to recognize in other contexts such as modern science.

---

[16] Consider for example the Feast of Grades meetings annual in Arts and Sciences Faculties, at which higher honors for graduating students are negotiated and solemnized. One might speculate that in the university, as in the village, these local ceremonials absorb energies and distract attention from flows of main action and resources through corporative networks.

[17] Even the numbers are quite comparable, for sizes of units and subunits and spread of networks.

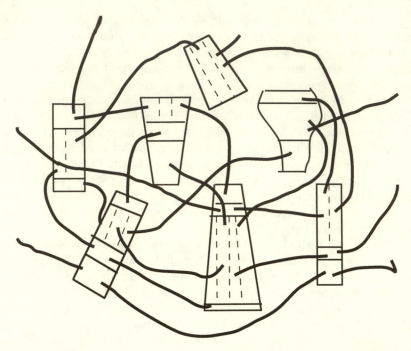

Figure 1. Village caste and university science—Heavy lines for flows of recruits among subcastes/research-specialties; dotted lines mark subcastes, within graded castes/departments in a village/university; only 7 villages and selected flows shown.

A general value—call it purity—is here operationalized in the strongest kind of social ordering, a ranking close to the full linear ordering of the mathematician. But this purity is confined operationally to a small locality, usually a geographic one defined by mundane activities. Purity thus is operationalized only for small populations separately, since linear order can be enforced only through transitivities in chains of behavior that cannot be monitored on a larger scale. Despite its size, this institution is a closest in form to the kernels of social action themselves, to the social disciplines of work teams and the like, which come embedded in social networks.

It is the corporate membership, which intuition tells us should play the role of locality, that in fact sprawls out across localities without, however, interfering with behaviors whose patterns are sufficient to enforce purity. Other value facets, such as intimacy and wealth, accompany these corporate memberships akin to subcaste. What persists and reproduces itself as a robust social formation is the peculiar balancing with social patterns of interpenetrations across values.

Any example of this first institution will tend to be pluralist in value terms, in style, affording parallel sets of story and interpretation specific to locality. Such values have localized facets, which are used for ex post accountings. For a century, purity in caste, like analogous valuations in other climes, had hypnotized observers into treating the social formations of caste on a macro scale as automatic by-products of those values writ large.

With a new generation of anthropologists who were alerted to networks as analytic and phenomenological bases of social topography, values came to be seen as by-products from social pattern rather than as exogenous cause. And it became clear that particular values from the known package were tied together and mapped very differently in the corporate sprawl of networks from the locality layering. It really is a style consisting of complementary dual profiles.

Sociologists of science have been bringing this same new perspective of networks, and their results can be mapped into the same institution as village caste. On some matters one can argue for common predictions. All styles following this institution exhibit social formations that are peculiarly resistant to attempts at external control. This follows from rumination on the illustrations, as well as from the institution's character considered in the abstract—a balanced and stable yet decentralized skeleton.

Caste is argued (Ghurye, 1957; Hocart, 1950), perhaps analogously to other decentralized empires (Reid, 1913), to be the resilient formation that has survived repeated waves of external invaders. The structuring of academic research science can be argued to be a reaction against the emerging dominance of American universities by autocrat Presidents in the early 1900s. It is not particular values taken as abstract symbols that accomplish this transformation, it is a style that embeds value facets operationally into a certain sort of balanced formation.

Change

Coordination of values packages with social network formations into an institution was documented in this first pair of examples. The test, and payoff, is understanding how values and styles change. Five questions will serve as prelude to a conjecture on change.

Questions

Any packaging as style that we discern as observers must also show up in the actors' own terms. These are not accounts of bare values, but are embedded in stories. Social process interleaves with semantic process into sets of stories agreed for discourse, which concern larger actors as well as facets of individual identities.

We should be able to predict whether and when values will tend toward the transposable and universal, and when they remain embedded into a particular institution or style. In the former case only the set and its articulation, not particular values need change in change of style. Question 1 is what are such prediction formulas?

Turn back to the Cozzens case study to provide background. Do the values involved in such a case figure as causes and triggers and incitements to the social actions—or instead do values serve as an accounting scheme for making sense of events only after the fact? That is question 2. One answer has been suggested already, an answer that may be necessary to the transposability of values.

The playing-out of any case erodes sharp boundaries in participants' and observers' perceptions. In Cozzens' case study the playing-out fragments "the" values—honesty and originality in full majesty—into those context-dependent and shifting value facets for which Ricoeur (1988) primes us. Question 3 is how best to represent this fragmenting and shifting of values, whether these be values as harbingers of or as explanations for change? Question 3 requires specification of the initial assertion that values appear in sets; it requires fitting values into localities and dissemination routes. Question 3 reminds us that social organization is a semiordered mess like a glass not a crystal, and its values are tendencies rather than firm regularities.

Question 3, like question 2, affects question 1, on formulas for transposability: Values as triggers may prove less transposable than values as elements in accountings. Values that fragment into numerous subvalues may transpose, but only temporarily or locally. Much more powerful mathematical contexts may be required (e.g., Boyd, 1991), perhaps so many that a metamathematics is required to keep track (Arbib & Manes, 1975; Birkhoff, 1967; MacLane, 1971).

Interaction between valuation and social configuration is indisputable. This leads to question 4: How can social change be valuated—change either as caused by or as attributed from value(s)—when the change itself shapes the value by which it was triggered as well as the values by which it is explained? That is, how does major change coexist with values?

The Mating Game

The chief question of this paper now comes into focus. Question 5: How can values change? Values come locked as distinctive sets into social styles, which map into institutions as structural equivalences built from networks, localities, and orderings.

Conjecture. A new style can emerge only from the superposition, for a time, of two or more existing styles, with attendant institutions, and then only if there follows an untangling and rejection between them. A new style can result in any of several stances vis-à-vis the old styles.

It seems fair to characterize this in shorthand by the aphorism "styles mate to change." We begin with style changes in caste and science. Then another institution will be introduced to further probe the conjecture, continuing on the assumption that examples that are widely divergent in period and ethos will make it easier to pick out important and distinctive features of styles.

Style Change in Caste and Science

The ideology of science holds that change of formulation is easy, a convergence of individual perceptions and cognitions subject only to verification of the truth of findings prompting such reformulation. The social organization of active research in science is in "invisible colleges," each a cluster of networks of workers whose themes cohere around a subfield within any recognized major discipline. In actuality, as studies of invisible colleges show, reformulations, even minor ones, are matters of contention.

The main point is that no conceptual, that is to say cultural reformulation, can take place apart from some change and adjustment in social organization among those concerned, producers and critics and users. And a major reformulation requires a wholesale revamping or even replacement of an invisible college. This is no easy matter. A new paradigm usually turns out, on examination, to be associated with a whole new invisible college.

It is often argued that invisible colleges emerge because of the difficulty of building within a whole discipline a critical mass for and sympathy toward a new line of work. The devil here is the existing, possibly ossified Establishment ensconced within separate departments of the discipline around the country. Certainly no one department is large enough to mount work on the scale of an invisible college. But it is not at all clear that a department is a bad place for generating new ideas;

indeed the crossing of subdisciplines that departments afford would seem almost a precondition for innovation.

The hieratic layering imposed on departments at a given locale may offend and hurt, or exhilarate, but it has almost nothing to do with the bulk of research, which is not implicated across departments. The really extensive and possibly pernicious stratification is that of individuals by reputation cumulated from research networks of invisible colleges (cf. sociology of science cites earlier). What departments do is afford long life to invisible colleges by giving them multiple bases that become very hard to control, much less to change or abolish by any other authority.[18] All can still be well, of course, for innovation and reformulation if leading figures in the invisible college are pure of heart. In short ideology reigns.

Hence change of style, which is also to say change of institution, is difficult. Such change comes only through messes and fights, and emerges out of chaos.) In analytic terms, change can be construed as superposition of distinct styles, here of separate invisible colleges, which for a while overlap and interpenetrate around some new theme or topic. A genuine reformulation, I argue, will prove not to be encapsulable within either of the existing invisible colleges. The new formulation could take over, colonize one of them, the other breaking back off. But more commonly, I suspect from existing studies, the new formulation breaks apart from both antecedents (which thereby disengage) and sets up on its own.[19]

As an example, take the new biophysics after World War II. Or, more recently and close to home, take the emerging new invisible college of social studies of science, which descends from an unquiet and temporary merger of Mertonian and Garfinkel notions and disciples. The list of possibilities is endless.[20] At the end of the paper, possible application of the conjecture to modern mathematics is sketched.

---

[18] Ironically, invisible colleges do provide a way, about the only way, to change local styles of departments, which tend toward an extraordinary degree of ossification when there are no active subdisciplines within to shake them up.

[19] A reader, Paul DiMaggio, comments:
    Interesting . . . What about centralized efforts to use universities rather than departments or networks to implement change by seeding subcaste members in many different departments. I'm thinking of the Ford Foundation's support for behavioral political science in the 50s. It's relatively easy for a centralized agency to convince a university administration that they should take chair money for a new type of person; and because the subdisciplines are spread out, the cost to any department of admitting one new member of a previously unrepresented tribe is low, and easy for the university administration to leverage. In so far as the networks control the central agency (e.g., NSF), this won't work, so it may be a special case.

[20] And of course each would require sustained inquiry with careful definition and measurement.

The conjecture itself, once stated and then exposed to even a sketch exemplification, becomes persuasive on a further ground. It is hard to conceive the contrary, for once the duality of style and institution is pointed out, and once one thinks even casually about one's own experiences in science, it is hard to deny the conjecture that change of style requires change of institution.

But is this just a peculiarity of this particular modern Western enterprise, science? I argue no. Exactly the same line of argument, with obvious changes in parameters of scale and wealth and timing, should apply for field investigators of the Indian village caste scene. In fact, castes do change much more than the stereotype allows for.

Within a village a given caste changes only through influences that come in, via dowry and inheritance and notions, along networks of subcaste. More broadly and regionally a caste makes itself known through the impact of various constituent subcastes, so that it is their changes, ironically, that count. These changes are not common and do not occur easily just because of the way subcastes interlock through village subunits. The record is that major change in subcaste comes through the kind of merger and split we conjectured for science.

But one institution is not enough, it remains but an N of 1 from the point of view of the conjecture proper. The second institution emerges from, and both examples of it will concern, the formation of new styles. Both examples come exactly from overlay of existing styles/institutions.

A Missionary Religion and Rock 'n Roll

Catholic Christianity emerged out of encounters between preexisting Judaic sects, baptismal and Pharisiac (cf. e.g., Dix, 1947; Flusser, 1988; Schoeps, 1969). Doctrine, its existence and its change as a structure of values, is inextricably intertwined in each with its social networks and dimensions of ranks as formed among localities. I argue, as before, that such styles are so locked in that they can change only through turbulent overlay of one on another.

Turbulent overlays were characteristic of the network of cities that constituted Asia Minor and the Syriac region for these sects. In modern terms we would refer to the people involved as lower middle class, often artisans, who became strangers to peasant life and tribal contexts. For centuries there was a diaspora of what we today would call a religion among Hebrews across these cities. Associated on the fringes were God-fearing Gentiles, who did not fully partake of the behavioral proscriptions and prescriptions or the orientation to a single central site in Jerusalem.

Consider this scene when several streams of the infant Christian movement were already established as styles. Their own separate emergences often are too obscure in the historical record to pursue further. For example, the basic facts of heresy and schism between "Gnostics," who were furthest from Judaic concepts, and "Christians" continue to be debated (e.g., Grant, 1966; Robinson, 1988).

Consider the Ebionite Church as one stream. This use of the term Ebionite is anachronistic. Schoeps' basic point (1969) is that the Ebionite Church of Transjordan and Arabia, as a fossil form of Jewish Christianity, held in suspension for several centuries a synthesis of styles different from what we call Christian—and then recruitment of new populations and social networks by Mohammed amidst a new turmoil of social mobility triggered a fully separate new style, the Moslem one. Ebionite is the definite form that came out of the traditionally Jewish strand led in the nascent Christian movement by James, brother of Jesus; its prolonged survival gives us confidence in its reality as a full-blown style, intertwining social and doctrinal value patterns.

⌐Where in the world, literally and figuratively, socially and doctrinally, did Catholic Christianity come from⌐ That is the question. Pauline Christianity is the mission movement already described as an illustration of the second institution. It was overlaid with and in conflict with the Ebionite movement. For some period the two, although discernibly separate, were thoroughly intermixed. Each was genuinely trying to convert and take over and merge with the other, which is the best evidence for intermixing.

The argument is that only such an interim period of intermixing could prompt a radical new style, which we call Catholic Christianity. While the Pauline movement exemplified the second institution, the Ebionite style was very much corporatist, of the first institution above, akin to caste and working science. Some argue that not just this Lewis (Ebionite) Christianity but Judaism itself, in the rabbinic form that we have come to take for granted, was triggered by and in part a reaction to the nascent Christian movements (e.g., Segal, 1986). That is a parallel claim to mine about the generation of Catholicism out of that same stew.

The literature is, of course, immense on the distinctiveness and emergence of Christianity in the lineage today called Catholic (Swete, 1918). Focus on the specific social and organizational formations involved, one strand of the literature, and for just the first generations (see e.g., Dix, 1947). The argument for social and organizational embedding of doctrinal values is a common one. The more familiar variant of this argument is ontogenetic, following what I call a style through a long evolution and family tree. It is represented magnificently by Gottwald (1979).

⌐Focus on a single change, the emergence of a new style. The conjecture is that different styles must not only overlay but *subsequently must repel and blow apart* as part of the cause and signal of the new style.[21] No particular authority need be cited to convince you that the formations, old and new, remaining after the explosion that created the post-Pauline Church, were antithetical one to another! We continue to live among such new turmoils.

The bishop is the key to the emerging Catholic style. The developed Church after the first century is beyond the scope of my middle-level analysis, far too layered and complex. But even in its early period the distinctiveness of the bishops is apparent.

The Pauline mission style permitted feedback between, on the one hand, pattern of network and ranking and, on the other hand, explicit value facets of holiness, of doctrine. There could be a spiral of intensification leading to relapse and split. Such a style has trouble continuing indefinitely to reproduce its social formation. Such a formation invites attempts by organizational entrepreneurs to contrive further explicit social pattern, what we call formal organization.

Then in church as now in modern politics, superposition of diverse local conflicts creates a fertile soil for growing issues. But "issues" are a cultural form not existent until there is a shift from the mission form proper. The overlay of mission form with the Ebionite strand of church, overlay in part in persons and networks as well as doctrine, was requisite to the appearance of what we would recognize as issues. This cognitive situation once created can lead to unraveling in one or more of the overlaid styles.

A rule for splits can be suggested. Heresies, where there is a serious divergence of explicit doctrine, of the structure of values, engender new organizational devices. And indeed the list of early Christian heresies—Gnosticism (Grant, 1966), Arianism (Newman, 1876), Priscillianism, etc.—is also a list of successive new organizational devices installed, from apostolic succession and bishoprics through the first Council of the whole church. Schism, on the other hand, comes from *agreement* on values. When doctrinal disagreement is sufficiently reduced, ethnic and political control and agency attempts may coalesce in such a way as to blow the social formation into separate fragments. This is the clear pattern in the early Church and continues through the Donatist schism (Frend, 1952; Willis, 1950) through the last great schism, between Orthodox and Roman (Meyendorff, 1966).

The bishop at first was merely what we call today the priest, but this was already a revolution in the Pauline formation. In the latter, sacerdotal authority was with the traveling apostle, not in the locally rooted

---

[21] Formally, the argument takes the familiar philosophic form of the dialectic: synthesis emerging from thesis and antithesis.

authority. The bishop–priest's combination of the two authorities supplies the key in helping to contain, as well as generate, doctrinal disagreement and confusion. The bishop could define purity and holiness, and yet he was rooted. Two fixed points of the emerging Church doctrine were one bishop for one city, and anathema on the translation of a bishop from one city to another (Lebretton & Zeiller, 1944).

That completes the sketch of one example supportive of the main conjecture, with respect to an institution different from the previous (caste/science) institution. At least one more example, as different as possible, will help separate the conjecture from particular context. Pick a modern example, one where establishing simple facts is no longer like pulling teeth.

White Pop and Black Pop into Rock 'n Roll

The appearance of rock and roll, hereafter rock 'n roll, as a new style—a new package of values and accompanying social formation across all the participant roles—is a recent and clear example of my conjecture. Indeed the conjecture emerged from a reading of Ennis' (1990) account. In his account, around 1950 there were six preexisting streams of popular music, each with its own base of audience, producers, performers, and disseminators, with overlaps.[22]

Three streams were for black Americans: black popular, gospel, and blues/jazz. They had distinguishable but intertwined and supportive performance, audience, and creator networks. Not just their listeners were segregated from their counterparts in the other cluster of three streams, but also their radio stations, recording companies, agents and critics, playing clubs, and performers.

Call these three the black cluster (analogous to the Pauline missionary institution). The other cluster (analogous to the Ebionite Church) was the white people's. This too had three streams, of mainstream disc jockey,[23] country and western, and folk.

In the early 1950s, quite suddenly, a few songs and music pieces in one cluster began to attract attention in the other. White borrowed black. The values as well as the music, the lyrics of one genre as well as the tunes, for a bit obtained a foothold in the other cluster's social networks of attention and appreciation. At first a song crossed over only after being "arranged" and resung according to conventions and by performers familiar in the other cluster. But even in the first period the

---

[22] For a systematic parsing of production systems of art see Becker (1982).
[23] Until the late forties, Tin Pan Alley had monopolized this stream.

original performance and recording earned a place, even a place on (the bottom of) the "hit" chart of the other stream.

The real causal nexus, Ennis claims, was differential attention to the crossovers by outlets, each relatively marginal and localized within its home stream. Outlets and networks in Memphis, Tennessee, happened to be prominent enough on the black as well as white sides to be catalytic in the overlay. The main key was radio stations small in the national picture but plugged into regional networks of playing clubs and also into networks of smaller record companies.

A crucial catalytic role was played by the disc jockeys, whose interest was development of distinctive new combinations.[24] One might draw an analogy to the role of the bishops above. But, as in the church case, the changing nature of audiences was as important as select leaders.

A particular performer, Elvis Presley, became the seed for the hailstorm, which was the truly new style that was to come out of the temporary overlay of white and black styles. He was the seed not simply because of his musical talent but because of his audience. Presley specialized in a hitherto unattended to fringe, the preteens, present alongside each of the initial six streams, but disdained.

No single theme in the Presley message was different from ones in the mainstreams, but Presley's combination of themes was very different. Moreover, it was explicitly tagged as different and as tied to a particular population, the preteens.[25] The commercial potential had been recognized by clever agents since the preteen mob scenes around the young Frank Sinatra. What was required to realize potential was not a single gimmick, but a retuning and a regrowing of social and performance networks.

There soon followed renewed rejection between the six preexisting streams, styles. There was no enlargement of the canon, but instead a retreat. But out of the overlay had come this new style for a new audience.

An unfailing indicator of the newness of a style is rejection by established critics. For rock 'n roll, as it began to get established and make inroads, there was a veritable frenzy of critical attack. Rarely has there been such a universal shower of opprobrium, presumably because of the

[24] Until Tin Pan Alley got the jockeys' independence suppressed through manipulation of Congressional investigating committees and through abusive use of delays in a Federal court case: the complex story of the rise and fall of disc jockeys is also told by Ennis (forthcoming).

[25] In rock 'n roll a main point of the style is not to deviate from your preteen kin, to hold onto the common style whose detailed balance among values may gyrate blatantly over time, at least as seen through adult critics' eyes.

peculiarly segregated—yet related—status of the preteens in the general population. There was a resonating crescendo of denunciation of the new style as being perverse in content and inane in form. Later, much later, a Leonard Bernstein will rhapsodize about the creative aspects of the new music (in the Beatles).

Conclusion

Values, whether symbolized or implicit, reflect more than they direct concrete social action. They cannot escape the puzzles of polysemic networks that define meanings in general. Philosophers and linguists uncovered these puzzles: "The variability of semantic values, their sensitivity to contexts, the irreducibly polysemic character of lexical terms in ordinary language . . . appears to me to be the basic condition for symbolic discourse and in that way, the most primitive layer in a theory of metaphor, symbol, parable, etc." (Ricoeur, 1977, 321). These polysemic interconnections among meanings in language[26] are simultaneously networks among actors, as Ricoeur says. The case studies above also show more generally how social contexts intertwine with accounts of meaning to yield effective discourse. Style is effective discourse.

Values from Structural Equivalence into Style

Values are as likely to be read out of patterns among affective ties, or from patterns in chains of agency, as from parsing meanings in stories and speeches. This is as true when participants do the reading as when observers do it. That is the first analytic result from this chapter—*values code from social network.* It was illustrated already by the very first example, on Freedom Summer. It was also illustrated by the coding of purity stacking from patterns of ritual interchange among caste, and by the coding of outreach mission from the expanding-tree networks of an early church, and so on.

Networks can bring and indicate change as well as nest actors into shells that block action (Burt, 1990a). Change may be only diffusion of small changes within the envelope of a style with values fixed. But the changes can be larger, raising question 4 above.

Actors situated similarly, in networks and arrays for taking social actions, are actors who are structurally equivalent even when remote. Closeness itself, through direct and indirect connectivity in a network, is but a limiting case. Structural equivalences, within various networks of

---

[26] This is language in actual use, the "parole" of Saussure (1966).

social relations,[27] both enable and imply a degree of similarity across localities. Neighborhood is a by-product and aspect of structural equivalence, one which yields similarity in action, similarity from melding crossings and confoundings by attempts at agency and control.

Structural equivalence is a formulation for network shaping of style that embraces both perception and action. And networks shape sheer connectivity in a social space as well as neighborhoods of equivalence. Styles are profiles in uses of already established values; so styles come as a sort of envelope of intentional uses of stories as shaped by structural equivalence. Observed institutional patterns presumably evolved under simultaneous streams of such pressure from many different actors.

Change in Values as Dimensions

Localities must be constructed socially and symbolically, yet tie to biophysical space of productive, mundane activities. Localities are the junctures between physical, symbolic, and social spaces and embed in the dimensions of each. Valuations play off against network connectivity in emergence of the social/symbolic aspects of localities. Each actor arrays others in value terms, and also each actor connects to others indirectly as well as directly within networks of own ties. Style evolves along with localities as kinds of closeness and distance sort out and play off into a social formation that reproduces itself.

A value has some connotation of ranking, of cumulation, of degree, in short of being in or defining dimension. This has some cognitive basis (De Soto, 1961; De Soto & Albrecht, 1968; Shepard, 1984). Such "dimension" must partake of ordering within social spaces as well as being an ordering in semantic space, and yet it also must have some grounding in mundane space–time of biophysical perception (Gibson, 1950, 1979). A *value as a dimension;* the dimensions of values: that is a second analytic from the studies above.

Change in values is difficult, first, because each value is like a dimension with implications of interlocking, of cumulation in meaning. Change in values is difficult, second, because these interpretations are buttressed and manifested in coordinate social arrangements, And change is difficult, third, because this dual dimensional arrangement

---

[27] The most important advance in sociology in the half-century since Parsons' first book may be operational accountings of networks, which make possible such work as McAdam's cited earlier. For recent general surveys of the state of the art see Freeman, White, and Romney (1989) and Wellman and Berkowitz (1988). For specifics on structural equivalence see Berkowitz (1982); the most advanced mathematical treatment is Boyd (1991). For computations on McAdam's data see Fernandez and McAdam (1988), and for a general formulation of network computations see Burt (1990b).

does not survive constant efforts at fresh control and manipulation from participants unless it is in one of a few robust structures of correlation.

The principal conjecture, borne out so far by these case studies, is that ⌈change in values requires change in style and thus in style's social fitting—and further that only another style, laid down on the same population, can provide resonance and protection for such new arrangement and shift in value packages of style.⌋

Mathematics Is No Exception

Can social pressure be beaten by a science guild?

Can the system of apparently inexorable social pressure against change in style, which is sketched in this chapter, be beaten by any corporate groups given their ideologies? Need the Church be a fake? Can doctors be healers? Do siblings treasure each other? They may require unusual individual movers but exceptions come only in social avenues and then only for a while from cross-pressures in precarious balance. Examination of instances can suggest imitations and variants. One instance is Lipset, Trow, and Coleman (1956) on realization of the value of democracy in trade unions;

Exceptions do not come easy, and they need not be a "good thing," as question 4 earlier suggests. Unless we suppose that in some social institution we have achieved some ultimate perfection, the possibility remains open that a preeminent value is pernicious. Is the operation of social change to be the final arbiter?

⌈This is an essay by a scientist and for scientists.⌋ We hold a value of purity that, in our ethos, should be realized as more than some transcription of social pressures from our institutional arrangements, however astute or benign these latter may be. Will a newer truth be allowed to emerge within, or across, disciplines despite obscurantist blocking and defensive manipulation by scientific elites (Cole & Zuckerman, 1979).

⌈Mathematics is a science, or perhaps not any longer.⌋ Perhaps it is a science no more than the Brahmins are a caste. Mathematics may have changed and become less a science, and perhaps this reflects a change in social organization, away from the classic European days of a free-floating, unspecialized science elite into the modern academic sciences system sketched above. Within this new system, moreover, mathematics surely ranks at the top on purity as much as do Brahmins in the caste realization. Changes of course can still be there, within the subcaste invisible colleges, but at the extremes of the pecking order—mathematics and home economics—are special locations inhibiting participation and interaction with other corporates.

This hypothesis is offered to account for the arresting decay of mathematics attested by Morris Kline in a magisterial 1980 survey. Mathematics was going through great internal dissension in this period. Kline, and the great mathematicians he cites, do not think of the possibility that some social mechanism is at work; they treat decline as a cognitive and cultural issue. (Kline, 1980: 4, 6):

> We must consider first what values won for mathematics its immense prestige, respect, and glory. From the very birth of mathematics as an independent body of knowledge, fathered by the classical Greeks . . . mathematicians pursued truth . . . Godel's theorems produced a debacle . . . the logical principles accepted by the several schools could not prove the consistency of mathematics. . . . The net effect of these new developments was . . . to divide mathematics into an even greater number of differing factions.

Yet it is seen that relations with other sciences may be the key underlying symptom. In the words of Felix Klein, in 1895:

> We cannot help feeling that in the rapid development of modern thought our science is in danger of becoming more and more isolated. The intimate mutual relation between mathematics and theoretical natural science which, to the lasting benefit of both sides, existed ever since the rise of modern analysis, threatens to be disrupted.

But Klein goes on to treat the issue as mathematicians choosing to create arbitrary abstract structures. In the words in 1924 of his successor Richard Courant:

> The last few decades have witnessed a loosening of this connection in that mathematical research has severed itself a great deal from the intuitive starting points. . . . To escape this fate we must direct a great deal of our power to uniting what is separated in that we lay clear under a common viewpoint the inner connections of the manifold facts. Only in this way will the student master an effective control of the material and the researcher be prepared for an organic development. (Kline, 1980: 287, 288)

This sounds like the preoccupation of a top Brahmin caste with its own internal purity! It is a preoccupation that should be charged to a change in social organization as much as to cognitive factors or virtues of individuals.

Acknowledgments

For helpful comments I am indebted to Lynn Cooper, Debra Friedman, Shin-Kap Han, Eric Leifer, Richard Lachmann, Doug McAdam, Walter Powell, Marvin Reiss, Jae-soon Rhee, Ilan Talmud, Ronan Van Rossem, Yuki Yasuda, and Viviana Zelizer. For stern editorial guidance I am indebted to Michael Hechter. Like him, Paul DiMaggio and Priscilla Ferguson suggested both major improvements and many minor corrections.

References

Abbott, A. (1981). Status and status strain in the professions. *American Journal of Sociology, 86:* 819–836.

' Abell, P. (1987). *The syntax of social life.* Oxford: Oxford University Press.

Abelson, R. P., & Rosenberg, M. J. (1958). Symbolic psychologic: A model of attitudinal cognition. *Behavioral Science, 3,* 1–13.

Abelson, R., Aronson, E., McGuire, W., Newcomb, T. M., Rosenberg, M. J., & Tannenbaum, P. H. (Eds.). (1968). *Theories of cognitive consistency: A sourcebook.* Chicago: Rand McNally.

' Arbib, M. A., & Manes, E. G. (1975). *Arrows, structures, and functors: The categorical imperative.* New York: Academic Press.

Becker, H. (1982). *Art worlds.* Berkeley: University of California.

• Berkowitz, S. D. (1982). *An introduction to structural analysis: The network approach to social research.* Toronto: Butterworths.

' Birkhoff, G. (1967). *Lattice theory* (3rd ed.). Providence, RI: American Mathematical Society.

‧ Boyd, J. P. (1991). *Social semigroups.* Fairfax: George Mason University Press.

* Burns, T. (1991). *Erving Goffman.* London: Routledge.

* Burt, R. S. (1990a). *Social contagion and innovation.* New York: Columbia University Press.

Burt, R. S. (1990b). STRUCTURE, Center for the Social Sciences, Columbia University.

‧ Chase, I. (1980). Social process and hierarchy formation in small groups: A comparative perspective. *American Sociological Review, 45,* 905–924.

Chase, I. (1982). Behavioral sequences during dominance hierarchy formation in chickens. *Science, 216,* 439–440.

Chase, I. (1986). Explanations of hierarchy structure. *Animal Behaviour, 34,* 1265–1267.

‧ Chase, I. Forthcoming. *The emergence of order in human and animal behavior.* Cambridge, MA: Harvard University Press.

Cole, J., & Zuckerman, H. (1979). *Fair science: Women in the scientific community.* New York: Free Press.

‵ Cornell, S. (1988). *The return of the native: American Indian political resurgence.* New York: Oxford University Press.

Cozzens, S. E. (1989). *Social control and multiple discovery in science: The opiate receptor case.* Albany, NY: State University of New York Press.

Crane, D. (1972). *Invisible colleges.* Chicago: University of Chicago.

De Soto, C. B. (1961). The predilection for single ordering. *Journal of Abnormal and Social Psychology, 62,* 16–23.

De Soto, C., & Albrecht, F. (1968). Cognition and social orderings. In R.

Abelson, E. Aronson, W. McGuire, T. M. Newcomb, M. J. Rosenberg, & P. H. Tennenbaum (Eds.), *Theories of cognitive consistency: A sourcebook.* Chicago: Rand McNally.

DiMaggio, P. (1987). Classification in art. *American Sociological Review, 52,* 440–455.

Dix, G. (1947). The ministry in the early church. In K. E. Kirk (Ed.), *The apostolic ministry.* New York: Morehouse-Gorham.

Dumont, L. (1986). *A south Indian subcaste.* M. Moffatt (trans.). New York: Oxford University Press.

Ennis, P. (1992). *The seventh stream: A history and geography of Rock 'n Roll to 1970.* Middletown, CN: Wesleyan University Press.

Fernandez, R. M., & McAdam, D. (1988). Multiorganizational fields and recruitment to social movements. In B. Klandermans (Ed.). *Organizing for social change.* Greenwich: JAI Press.

Fine, G. A. (1983). *shared fantasies: Role play games as social worlds.* Chicago: University of Chicago Press.

Flusser, D. (1988). *Judaism and the origins of Christianity.* Jerusalem: Magnes Press.

Freeman, L. C., White, D. R., & Romney, A. K. (Eds.). (1989). *Research methods in social network analysis.* Fairfax, VA: George Mason University Press.

Frend, W. H. C. (1952). *The Donatist church.* Oxford: Oxford University Press.

Ghurye, G. S. (1957). *Caste and race in India.* Bombay: Popular Book Depot.

Gibson, J. J. (1950). *The perception of the visual world.* Boston, MA: Houghton-Mifflin.

Goffman, E. (1955). On face work. *Psychiatry, 18,* 213–231.

Goffman, E. (1963). *Behavior in public places.* Glencoe, IL: Free Press.

Goffman, E. (1967). *Interaction ritual.* New York: Pantheon.

Goffman, E. (1971). *Relations in public.* New York: Harper.

Goffman, E. (1974). *Frame analysis.* New York: Harper & Row.

Goffman, E. (1979). *The ecological approach to visual perception.* Boston: Houghton-Mifflin.

Gottwald, N. K. (1979). *The tribes of Jahweh: A sociology of the religion of liberated Israel, 1250–1050 B.C.E.* Maryknoll, NY: Orbis Books.

Grant, R. M. (1966). *Gnosticism and early Christianity.* New York: Columbia University Press.

Hocart, A. M. (1950). *Caste: A comparative study.* London: Methuen.

Kline, M. (1980). *Mathematics: The loss of certainty.* New York: Oxford University Press.

Lebretton, J., & Zeiller, J. (1944). *A history of the primitive church.* London.

Lipset, S. M., Trow, M. A., & Coleman, J. S. (1956). *Union Democracy.* Garden City: Doubleday.

Lorrain, F. (1973). Some theoretical issues involved in the category-functor approach to social networks. Society of Fellows, University of Michigan.

Lorrain, F. (1975). *Reseaux sociaux et classifications sociales.* Paris: Herman.

MacLane, S. (1971). *Categories for the working mathematician.* New York: Springer-Verlag.

March, J. G., Olsen, J. P. (1976). *Ambiguity and choice in organizations.* Bergen: Universitetsforlaget.

Marriott, M. (1968). Caste ranking and food transactions, a matrix analysis. In M. Singer & B. S. Cohn (Eds.). *Structure and change in Indian society.* Chicago: Aldine.

Marriott, M. (1959). Interactional and attributional theories of caste ranking. *Man in India, 39,* 92–107.

Mayer, A. C. (1960). *Caste and kinship in central India.* Berkeley: University of California Press.

McAdam, D. (1988). *Freedom summer.* New York: Oxford University Press.

Menard, H. W. (1971). *Science: Growth and change.* Cambridge, MA: Harvard University Press.

Merton, R. K. (1968). *Social theory and social structure.* Glencoe, IL: Free Press.

Merton, R. K. (1973). *The sociology of science,* Norman W. Storer, Ed. Chicago: University of Chicago Press.

Meyendorff, J. (1966). *Orthodoxy and catholicity.* New York: Sheed and Ward.

Mullins, N. (1973). *Theories and theory groups in contemporary American sociology.* New York: Harper & Row.

Najemy, J. M. (1982). *Corporations and consensus in Florentine electoral politics, 1280–1420.* Chapel Hill, NC: University of North Carolina Press.

Newman, J. H. (1876). *The Arians of the fourth century.* London: Pickering.

Parsons, T. (1937). *The structure of social action.* New York: McGraw-Hill.

Parsons, T., & Shils, E. A. (Eds.). (1951). *Toward a general theory of action.* New York: Harper & Row.

Parsons, T., Bales, R. F., & Shils, E. A. (1953). *Working papers in theory of action.* Glencoe, IL: Free Press.

Pratt, J., & Zeckhauser, R. (Eds.). (1985). *Principals and agents: The structure of business.* Boston: Harvard Graduate School of Business Administration Press.

Rawls, A. W. (1989). An ethnomethodological perspective on social theory. In D. Helm et al. (Eds.), *Interactional order.* New York: Irvington Press.

Reid, J. S. (1913). *The municipalities of the Roman Empire.* Cambridge: Cambridge University Press.

Ricoeur, P. (1977). *The rule of metaphor,* R. Czerny (trans.). Toronto: University of Toronto Press.

Ricoeur, P. (1988). *Time and narrative: Vol. 3,* K. Blamey & D. Pallauer (trans.). Chicago: University of Chicago.

Robinson, T. A. (1988). *The Bauer thesis examined: The geography of Heresy in the early Christian church.* Atlanta: Edwin Mellen Press.

Saussure, F. de. (1966). *course in general linguistics,* W. Baskin (trans.). New York: McGraw-Hill.

Schoeps, H.-J. (1969). *Jewish Christianity: Factional disputes in the early church,* D. R. A. Hare (trans.). Philadelphia: Fortress Press.

Schudson, M. (1989). How culture works. *Theory and Society, 18,* 153–180.

Segal, A. F. (1986). *Rebecca's children: Judaism and Christianity in the Roman world.* Cambridge, MA: Harvard University Press.

Shepard, R. N. (1984). Ecological constraints on internal representation: Resonant kinematics of perceiving, imagining, thinking, and dreaming. *Psychological Review, 91,* 417–447.

Swete, H. B. (Ed.). (1918). *Essays of the early history of the church and the ministry.* London: Macmillan.

Swidler, A. (1986). Culture in action: Symbols and strategies. *American Journal of Sociology, 51,* 273–286.

Thompson, B. (Ed.). (1961). *Liturgies of the western church.* Cleveland, OH: World.

von Campenhausen, H. (1969). *Ecclesiastical authority and spiritual power in the church of the first three centuries,* 1955, J. A. Baker (trans.). Stanford, CA: Stanford University Press.

Wellman, B., & Berkowitz, S. D. (Eds.). (1988). *Social structures: A network approach.* New York: Cambridge University Press.

Weyl, H. (1949). *Philosophy of mathematics and natural science.* O. Helmer (trans.). Princeton, NJ: Princeton University Press.

White, H. C. (1985). Agency as control. In J. Pratt & R. Zeckhauser (Eds.), *Principals and agents: The structure of business.* Boston: Harvard Graduate School of Business Administration Press.

White, H. C. (1992a). *Identity and control.* Princeton: Princeton University Press.

White, H. C. (1992b). Cases are for identity, for explanation, or for control. In H. Becker & C. Ragin (Eds.). *The logic of social inquiry: What is a case?* New York: Cambridge University Press.

Willis, G. G. (1950). *Saint Augustine and the Donatist controversy.* London: SPCK.

5

The Meaning, Nature, and Source
of Value in Economics

Tibor Scitovsky

The values economists are mainly concerned with are the subjective values people attribute to the sources of their satisfactions and dissatisfactions. Those value judgments show what people want and how badly they want it. We have no objective unit of measurement for denoting the extent of satisfaction; the subjective value people attach to sources of their satisfactions are always relative and express the value of one satisfaction in terms of the equivalent value of another. That is why money, which is general purchasing power over many things, turns out to be the best available measure of subjective value. Our not having a unit in which to measure satisfaction also prevents us from comparing one person's satisfaction and ability to experience it to another person's. The commonsense notion that two people in similar situations would enjoy the same satisfaction in equal measure has been rejected as not proven by present-day economists.

Our interest in the public's subjective value judgments is due to our concern with the economy's ability to allocate resources, coordinate production, and distribute products, so that the public should be provided with the goods and services they want, in the quantities they want them, and in a way that creates the greatest benefit at the least cost as *those benefits and costs are evaluated by the people who experience them.*

To accomplish all that fully, it would be necessary first to aggregate different people's subjective preferences into society's global preferences, which, for some sources of satisfaction, can be a very difficult undertaking. Indeed, Kenneth Arrow was awarded a Nobel Prize for proving that in the general case and for *the entire range* of human needs and desires, it is impossible to carry out such aggregation in a meaningful and reasonable way (Arrow, 1987).

For the greater part of that range, however, the problem of aggregating individual preferences and making the economy cater to them in the way just described can be, and more or less is resolved by competitive markets. The range in question comprises all the needs and desires that consumer goods and services can satisfy. Difficulties arise only in the case of collective and related goods and services. I shall deal with those at length later; but let me first say a few words on how markets resolve the problem for consumer goods.

These are the goods and services that are separable and saleable piecemeal to individuals through consumer markets. Competitive markets establish a single price for each good and service, of which consumers can buy at that price as much or as little as they want and each finds it worth buying whatever quantity renders the value he or she attaches to the last unit bought equal to its market price. As a result, every consumer's marginal valuation of each good he or she buys becomes equal to its marginal valuation by all its other consumers who face the same price, with differences in their needs, tastes, and budgets showing up, not in the values they attribute to them, but in the quantities in which they buy them.

In other words, competitive consumer markets perform three simultaneous functions: (1) they enable everybody to buy a different basket of goods according to what they want and can afford; (2) they bring about a consensus among buyers with respect to the marginal value they attribute to the goods they consume; and (3) they provide the important convenience of making the market-clearing price of each good reflect its identical valuation by all its consumers.

If you then add that those prices are the signals that enable a perfectly competitive economy to utilize and allocate resources and productive methods in best conformity to consumers' preferences, then you have listed all the much-touted advantages of the market economy.

We economists are justly proud of our ability to deal with values in such quantitative terms; but our ability to do that is subject to three limitations. First, we can measure the values people attach to the sources of their pains and pleasures only when those are reflected by market prices, which means that we can measure the value only of those satisfactions whose sources reach their beneficiaries through consumer markets and only of those pains for which the people who suffer them are compensated through labor markets. Second, market prices reflect individuals' subjective valuations accurately only when competition among them is perfect. Third, the values reflected in market prices are not what value means in common parlance but *marginal or incremental values:* the lowest value buyers attribute to the benefit they get from a single unit of what they buy and the highest value sellers place on the cost to them of rendering one unit of their services or of producing one unit of the goods they sell.

The last mentioned is not a serious limitation, because marginal values are the only ones that matter in economics: they contain all the information that has to be transmitted from one economic agent to another to enable markets to perform their coordinating functions. For it is by equalizing the *marginal* valuation of each resource and product by all its sellers and buyers that perfectly competitive markets minimize costs of production, maximize the worth to buyers of the total output, and ensure the best allocation of resources among different industries and producers.

The first two limitations did not, in the beginning, seem too serious either: the first because as recently as 60 years ago, nine-tenths or more of the gross national product consisted of consumer goods and services and the investment needed to produce them; the second because competition seemed more pervasive and more nearly perfect to earlier generations of economists than to today's.

Gradually, however, all that has changed. The state's role in the U.S. economy has more than doubled, which has reduced the scope of consumer markets correspondingly; and the limitations and shortcomings of markets as well as interdependencies between costs and satisfactions that go and do not go through markets have become both greater and more apparent. Since all that detracts from the perfect functioning of the ideal of a perfectly competitive market economy, they are known as market failures, which, no less than the market's accomplishments, are of concern to economists, who, after all, have to develop and advise on policies designed to correct or supplement the functioning of markets. In that connection, we often have to estimate values not reflected or incorrectly reflected by market prices. Some of the time that proves a hopelessly difficult task; but it is not the less important for that. A short discussion of the nature of that task is best introduced by a list of market failures.

To begin with, most markets are imperfectly competitive; though in the all-important consumer markets, at least one side is perfectly competitive, causing prices correctly to reflect buyers' but to overstate sellers' marginal valuations. Second, many important economic goods and services do not reach their beneficiaries through consumer markets, which means that their worth to those whom they benefit or are supposed to benefit are not reflected in market prices. Third, consumers' valuation of their own satisfactions are sometimes unreliable and therefore need overruling or correcting. Fourth, the production and/or consumption of some goods generate favorable or unfavorable side effects, which do not go through the market but which nevertheless must or ought to be estimated and taken into account. I shall say a few words about each of those problems.

Collective Goods

Many goods and services are not separable and cannot be sold piece-meal in quantities appropriate to each consumer's different tastes and budget. National defense, police protection, public parks, roads and city streets, and radio and television programs on the air are some of the more obvious examples of these so-called collective or public goods (Sad-mo, 1987). They are available to everybody in their entirety (i.e., in the same quantity), which causes different people with their differing tastes and incomes to put different values on them. Market exchange between rational individuals cannot, as a rule, ensure the provision of these goods and services in a satisfactory way without agreement among the benefici-aries, owing to a prisoners-dilemma type problem. That is why most collective goods are made available free, usually by the state at taxpayers' expense, but with some provided and financed by private firms that benefit indirectly from providing them to prospective customers.

It is convenient to deal with these latter first. Under imperfect compe-tition, sellers set their prices above the marginal cost to them of the goods and services they sell, which renders it profitable for them to engage in nonprice competition, in the form of advertising the availabili-ty and advantages of their wares and offering prospective buyers various services and conveniences as means of creating goodwill and increasing sales. Examples, in addition to TV and radio programs already men-tioned, are artistically arranged shop windows, elegantly furnished stores, colorful shopping malls, department stores, and the many other attractions that have made shopping and windowshopping many peo-ple's favorite pastime in the advanced market economies. The general public clearly appreciates all those amenities; but there is no way of quantifying the value it puts on them. Suffice it to say that their free provision indemnifies the public to some extent for the profit markup added to the cost of its purchases and compensates for the market's loss of efficiency created by prices that overstate marginal costs. Moreover, the fact that most people prefer to do their shopping in elegant but expensive stores rather than in cheap but unattractive discount houses is clear evidence that they consider those amenities worth their cost.

More important, more valuable, and much more numerous than the privately provided collective services just discussed are those provided by government and paid for out of taxes. The political process gives taxpayers an indirect influence over the nature and quantity of public services provided; but that is very tenuous, which is why economists have always looked for some way of ascertaining the public's value judgments of collective goods similar to those reflected by market prices in consumer markets.

In principle, the worth to the public of a collective good such as national defense could be ascertained if citizens could be prevailed on to state truthfully how much each of them would be willing to contribute to maintaining their country's actual level of national defense. By summing the amounts so named and comparing their sum to the actual level of defense spending, one could tell whether that is insufficient, excessive, or just adequate, and tell it by the same standard that determines the supply of the goods and services sold in consumer markets. (Note the parallelism between the sum of quantities sold at a given price and the sum of contributions offered for a given quantity.) Moreover, the different figures named by different people would be a good guide also for an equitable distribution of the tax burden that national defense imposes.

Needless to say, however, that is not a practical proposition, not only because the public is not well enough informed for its opinion on so complex a subject to have much use, but also because people could not be trusted to reveal the true value they put on defense. They would be tempted to *overstate* it if the survey were known to be designed merely as a guide to help determine the proper level of defense spending; whereas they would be sure to *understate* it if the survey were also to be used for determining each taxpayer's tax assessment. Much thought has gone into trying to find a reliable method for ascertaining what expenditure on collective goods would best conform to what the public wants and believes it can afford but a practical way of doing that is still in the offing.

Equity

A special kind of collective good that deserves special mention is the distribution of income. That is a collective good, because rich and poor alike share the same income distribution; and it is rather special, because one's judgment of it is a moral one; and people's moral judgments are bound to be much more nearly uniform than their judgments of personal gratifications and their sources. After all, to judge the ethical value of an income distribution, one must abstract from one's own position in that distribution, and when people do that, differences in their judgments as to the most desirable distribution may not be all that great. Most of us are fair-minded and compassionate enough to attach value to an equitable distribution, but few would opt for complete equality of incomes, for two reasons. First, because everybody considers economic inducement to seek work and to accept its discomforts preferable to forced labor; and that necessitates some income inequality. Second, because superior status, including superior economic status, is an important source of satisfaction, which most people want to be able to aspire to; and that too is incompatible with income equality.

Our society seems to resolve the conflict between those value judgments by limiting its desire for equality to equality of opportunity and focusing its concern for an equitable distribution of income on the lower end of the income scale. Free education, scholarships, and free or below-cost access to the necessities of life for the needy ensure the former, whereas the last-mentioned, together with relief payments and old-age and unemployment insurance, is also designed to keep people above the poverty line. Only very few of the most advanced countries attack the problem of inequality also at the upper end of the income scale by progressive tax structures.[1]

Merit Goods

Many people believe that the value of some important goods is not, or not fully recognized by a part of the public, owing to ignorance, lack of foresight, or both. Accordingly, they consider it desirable to encourage the purchase and consumption of such goods, called merit goods, by making it compulsory (old-age and unemployment insurance), free (health services in many countries), or subsidized (the performing arts). The provision of a part of poor relief in kind (food, foodstamps, free housing, medicaid) rather than in money is also due to these being considered merit goods (Musgrave, 1987).

Yet another type of merit goods are those whose availability is valued even by people who make no use of them. Hospitals and public transportation are examples, because even those who never use them want to have them available for emergencies, on a standby basis.

External Economies and Diseconomies

Many goods and services affect the well-being not only of their producers and consumers but of third parties as well. These side effects can be favorable or unfavorable; and since they do not go through the mar-

---

[1] The present U.S. tax structure is regressive, because the slight progressivity of the income tax is more than offset by the regressivity of the sales and various excise taxes.

ket, they do not show up in market prices, which is why the market forces that coordinate economic decisions fail to take them into account (Bohm, 1987). It remains for policy makers therefore to correct or supplement market prices whenever external effects arise and are important.

Health services and education are examples of services that generate external economies: the former, because they reduce the spread of contagious diseases, and the latter, because other people benefit from consorting with and having access to the educated. That is another important reason for providing health care and education free.

Most external effects, however, are unfavorable, for reasons to be discussed at the end of this chapter. Think of pollution, degradation of the environment, and the many dangers to health that the modern economy creates. The ideal way of dealing with diseconomies would be to internalize their costs by imposing on their originators a tax or fine that equals the diseconomy's cost to those hurt by them. That would induce them to prevent or offset the diseconomies generated by their activity if the cost of doing so does not exceed the tax, or to limit the activity to the level that maximizes the excess of benefits over costs if preventing or offsetting the diseconomies is impractical or too expensive. That, however, is easier said than done, partly because enforcement can be difficult and expensive and partly also because estimating the social cost of a diseconomy can be a difficult or near impossible undertaking. The subject will be taken up again when we deal with the genesis of diseconomies.

Internal Economies and Diseconomies

Similar to those external effects on third parties are internal side effects that the production and/or the enjoyment of goods and services can have on the transacting parties themselves. Production for the market often has favorable or unfavorable effects on the producer additional to the disutility of the effort involved and the compensation paid for it, just as the consumption of some goods imposes nonmonetary costs on the consumer, which is additional to the market price he or she pays for them. Examples of goods that create the latter are narcotics and other addictive substances and foods harmful to health. Since those nonmonetary costs are usually delayed, not always recognized, and their incidence is often uncertain, many people ignore or discount them, which is why informed opinion favors discouraging their use. Indeed, they could be called demerit goods, since they are the counterpart and exact opposite of merit goods.

To come now to the nonmonetary side effects of work, they can be both negative and positive. The delayed damage to health of many kinds of work has long been ignored or unsuspected; but now that it and its remedies are becoming generally known and much discussed, little remains to be said about it. The best known examples are exposure to radioactivity and the mining, processing, and use of asbestos.

Equally ignored and overlooked are and have long been the positive side effects of work: the challenge of interesting, difficult, responsible, or dangerous work, and the satisfaction and sense of accomplishment that people get out of successfully accomplishing it.

One bad effect of overlooking the intrinsic satisfaction of productive work is the overemphasis on its monetary incentive, which can militate against equity. Keynes and Schumpeter, the two most distinguished economists of the previous generation, both warned against exaggerating the role of profit as the motive force of investment and growth, arguing that investments whose financial returns are drawn out over many years to come are far too risky to be prompted solely by even the best estimates of their expected profits. To use Keynes's words: "If human nature felt no temptation to take a chance, no intrinsic satisfaction (profit apart) in constructing a factory, a railway, a mine or farm, there might not be much investment as a result of cold calculation" (Keynes, 1936: 150).

A good illustration of what's wrong with exaggerating the role of the profit incentive is the Reagan administration's failure to promote innovation, increase productivity, and stimulate the economy by means of tax policies favoring profits. All that increased profits have accomplished was to encourage takeovers instead of investment and growth and to worsen the distribution of income.

Ignoring the intrinsic satisfaction of work has also made us overlook an important negative aspect of technical and economic progress. Most innovations in manufacturing methods of the past century have rendered work more fragmented, more monotonous, less responsible, less creative, and therefore less satisfying to the worker. Karl Marx drew attention to all that a long time ago when he warned against the alienation of workers from their work (Catephores, 1987); but employers and economists alike ignored his warning. Only now, a century later, is worker dissatisfaction generally recognized as a negative side effect of technical progress, which lowers labor productivity, and which is not too difficult to guard against once its existence and importance are recognized.

Scarcity Values

Having surveyed some of the values that market prices fail to reflect but that economists must somehow estimate and take into account, let me take up one of the central concerns of economics, value created by scarcity; and I shall focus on the creation of scarcity by economic growth.

An economy grows when technical progress or a growing labor force increases the capacity to produce and effective demand increases along with it. That condition is usually fulfilled, because the income generated by production always equals the sales value of what is produced, so that growth always creates enough additional purchasing power to pay for the additional output produced. Nevertheless, growth creates problems, because while additional demand usually extends fairly evenly over the whole range of goods and services, additions to supply and productive capacity are usually spotty and uneven. The resulting problems are resolved by price changes, which harmonize the structure of demand and the structure of supply. Some of those price changes are random and more or less cancel and offset one another in the long run; but the prices of those goods and resources that are in fixed supply always and only rise, because they become forever scarcer relative to the increased demand for them.

The simplest and most conspicuous examples of goods in fixed supply are paintings by dead masters and homes in choice locations or of historical value. The demand for them as status symbols is steadily increasing in our increasingly affluent society, which accounts for the rise in their prices relative to other prices in the economy (Hirsch, 1976).

More important are the consequences of the world's ever growing population and its ever growing demand confronting the fixed supply of natural resources. Land is the classic example of a natural resource in fixed supply, and in its case, secularly rising land prices have registered its increasing scarcity in relation to the rising demand for it.

In this country, the inflation-corrected price of land has risen approximately in proportion with the increase in population during the first half of this century; and its rise is likely to accelerate. Bear in mind that in Japan, whose present population density is 12.5 times that of the United States, the average price of land has risen to almost 50 times of what it is here.

The serious consequences that may result as the world's growing population presses against the limits that the fixed quantity of land imposes on the food supply have been pointed out 200 years ago by Malthus; but so far, the great scientific and technical advances in agriculture have postponed the day of worldwide starvation he predicted (Weir, 1987).

Greater, I believe, are the dangers inherent in our ever-increasing demand on the fixed supply of such other natural resources as the purity of our air and fresh water supply and the ozone layer in the stratosphere, because they share the characteristics of collective goods of having no market prices whose rising level would reflect their increasing scarcity and serve as an early warning system to remind us of the need to do something about it.

For the supply of land, together with the depletable mineral resources of the soil, is not only fixed but also separable and saleable piecemeal, in the process of which they acquire market prices that rise as they become scarcer, thereby giving timely and fair warning of the ever-increasing necessity to economize their use. By contrast, the many ingredients of a safe, healthy, pleasant, and beautiful environment are *collective* resources, which means that they do not go through the market, do not acquire a market price, and their husbanding, when necessary, cannot be left to the market but must be undertaken collectively, by the state.

All that created no problem as long as their fixed supply was more than sufficient for our needs, which meant that their marginal value was zero and there was no need to restrict their use. Now, however, when population growth and global economic development make ever greater demands on our environmental resources, these have become scarce, which calls for restricting their use; but their scarcity, instead of imposing a price to measure and warn us of that scarcity, has degraded their quality. That, unfortunately, is the wrong signal in our type of economy, where people look on a change in price as a call for action and for changing their behavior but tend to be helpless and remain inert in the face of a decline in quality.

To illustrate what I mean, compare the husbanding of parking space with that of clean air. Parking space was once a free good; but when increased city traffic made it scarce and put a price on it, that harmonized supply and demand by both encouraging the creation of parking lots and garages and discouraging city driving. Air pollution by contrast, for lack of a market to put a price on the privilege to pollute, degraded the quality of the air, which left the polluters unmoved and caused the general public to suffer in silence.

The authorities did nothing against mere unpleasantness and unsightliness and waited for years before worsening morbidity and mortality statistics made them realize the need for legislation to limit pollution and even then acted half-heartedly. The measures so far enacted against air, water, and soil pollution in the United States are costing about two and one-half to three percent of the GNP and are woefully inadequate and poorly enforced, with the nuclear defense industry and the Defense and Energy Departments the main transgressors of the regulations; and we have done very little as yet about the more global and serious problems of the greenhouse effect and the diminishing ozone layer in the stratosphere.

You will have noticed that the problems of our deteriorating environment have already been mentioned under the name of external diseconomies. Also presented was a theoretically correct solution: monetizing and internalizing external diseconomies by estimating their costs to those hurt by them and imposing those costs in the form of a fine or tax on those whose activity generates the diseconomies. That would be the correct solution, because it would cause the polluters to develop and employ methods capable of eliminating or offsetting the diseconomy or reducing it to the point where the excess of the benefits from the polluting activity over its costs to the public is maximized.

Unfortunately, that is easier said than done, not only because enforcement is difficult and expensive, but mainly because estimating the social cost of a diseconomy can be an extremely difficult undertaking even in the best of circumstances and utterly hopeless in some cases. How is one to estimate the cost to mankind of a rise in the temperature of the earth's surface due to the greenhouse effect, or of the additional ultraviolet radiation due to depletion of the ozone layer when we are still uncertain about their exact effects. We only know that whatever the effects, they may affect millions, even billions of people and generations to come.

Welfare and Growth

I explored in detail that grim subject as a preparation for my next and last topic. Given the central position that economists in their theories accord price as a measure of the value that consumers attribute to individual goods, the idea naturally arose to add together the market value of all the goods and services produced, and use the figure obtained as a measure of the economy's overall performance and the consuming public's welfare. That was the purpose of national product and national income estimates, two seemingly different concepts that nevertheless measure the same thing, considering that every penny spent on what is produced and sold becomes the income of someone who contributed to its production or sale.

Those estimates have become the economist's best known tools and are extremely useful for the first purpose mentioned. Their popular use as an indicator of a nation's welfare is fraught with many pitfalls, which is why economists have never ceased warning against putting them to that use. Let me mention some of them.

First, the satisfaction we get out of consuming goods and services, depends on their quantity and quality, not on their prices. Prices must be used only as weights when adding up physical quantities of dissimilar objects; but changes in prices must be corrected for when comparing the national product of different dates and one wants to measure the change in the *real* national product. A similar, but more complex correction for price differences is also needed when comparing different countries' levels of well-being (Kravis, 1987).

Second, a country's real national product must rise in proportion with its population to keep people's welfare unchanged. To show changes in the average person's economic welfare, one needs estimates of the real national product *per capita of population*.

The last step is to weigh changes in the national product against the costs incurred in producing it. Of the many such costs, some are measurable, others not. The most obvious cost is an increase in labor input, which implies a loss of leisure. A larger output per capita of population may result from increased participation of women and others in the laborforce, from people's working longer hours, having more working days, or from any combination of those three factors, since they all encroach on leisure. To correct for such costs, one would have to express the national product per annual work hours; but that has seldom been done until a recent book documented the great loss of leisure our country's working population has suffered over the past 20 years (Schor, 1991).

Labor, however, is not the only factor of production, capital equipment is another; and the output produced by society's labor input can temporarily be increased by failing to maintain and allowing to deteriorate the country's capital equipment and infrastructure. In time of war, most countries tend to increase their production of war material by letting their capital equipment run down; and the Reagan administration in this country managed to give an exaggerated impression of economic prosperity through the non-maintenance of the country's highway network, bridges, and other infrastructure.

Those were some of the measurable costs to allow for when interpreting the effect on welfare of a rise in the national product; potentially more important are the unmeasurable costs. One of these is the inequity in the distribution of income and in people's access to the necessities of life. For example, our economic performance over the past decade or so has been accompanied by increased inequality in the distribution of income and also by poor people's diminished access to such necessities of life as housing and medical care. We have statistics of the extent of those changes, though no way of numerically expressing the loss of national welfare they represent; but at least we know that appropriate social and economic policies could, if adopted, nullify those costs.

Much less manageable and reversible, and possibly much more serious are the environmental costs of our economic activity; but these have already been discussed in some detail and with ample stress on the difficulty, and in some cases the utter impossibility, of quantifying them. Let me close therefore by just repeating that national product and income estimates are a very incomplete measure of our welfare, which depends on so many other economic and noneconomic factors as well.

References

Arrow, K. J. (1987). Arrow's theorem. In J. Eatwell, M. Milgate, P. Newman (eds.) *The New Palgrave: A Dictionary of Economics* (vol. 1, pp. 124–126). London: Macmillan.

Bohm, P. (1987). External economies. In *The New Palgrave* (vol. 2, pp. 261–63).

Catephores, G. (1987). Alienation. In *The New Palgrave* (vol. 1, pp. 76–78).

Hirsch, F. (1976). *Social limits to growth.* (Harvard University Press, 1976, Cambridge, MA & London).

Keynes, J. M. (1936). *The general theory of employment interest and money.* London: Macmillan.

Kravis, I. B. (1987). International income comparisons. In *The New Palgrave* (vol. 2, pp. 906–909).

Musgrave, R. A. (1987). Merit goods. In *The New Palgrave* (vol. 3, pp. 452–53).

Sadmo, A. (1987). Public goods. In *The New Palgrave* (vol. 3, pp. 1061–1066).

Schor, J. B. (1991). *The overworked American: The unexpected decline of leisure.* Basic Books.

Weir, D. R. (1987). Malthus's theory of population. In *The New Palgrave* (vol. 3, pp. 290–293).

6

The Fair Wage–Effort Hypothesis and Unemployment

George A. Akerlof and Janet L. Yellen

Introduction

This chapter explores the consequences of a hypothesis concerning worker behavior, which we shall call the fair wage–effort hypothesis.[1] According to this hypothesis, workers have a conception of a fair wage; insofar as the actual wage is less than the fair wage, workers supply a corresponding fraction of normal effort. If e denotes effort supplied, w the actual wage, and w^* the fair wage, the fair wage–effort hypothesis says that

$$e = \min (w/w^*, 1) \qquad (1)$$

where effort is denoted in units such that 1 is normal effort. This hypothesis explains the existence of unemployment. Unemployment occurs when the fair wage w^* exceeds the market-clearing wage.[2] With natural specifications of the determination of w^*, this hypothesis may explain why skill and unemployment are negatively correlated. In addition, it potentially explains wage differentials and labor market segmentation.[3]

The motivation for the fair wage–effort hypothesis is a simple observation concerning human behavior: when people do not get what they deserve, they try to

---

[1] Akerlof and Yellen (1988) contains a summary of the results obtained in this chapter.
[2] For evidence of discrepancies between lay theories of fair wages and market-clearing wages, see Kahneman, Knetsch, and Thaler (1986).
[3] Levine (1990) has offered a similar explanation for these phenomena based on worker cohesiveness.

get even. The next section will present five types of evidence for the fair wage–effort hypothesis. *First,* it will draw on psychology, where the fair wage–effort hypothesis corresponds to Adams' (1963) theory of equity. Numerous empirical studies have tested this theory. They are, on balance, strongly supportive. *Second,* in sociology the fair wage–effort hypothesis corresponds to the Blau–Homans (1955, 1961) theory of social exchange. Sociological studies, including studies of work situations, show that equity usually prevails in social exchange. *Third,* the fair wage–effort hypothesis accords with common sense. It appears frequently in literature; it is considered obvious by personnel textbooks; and it explains commonly observed taboos regarding discussion of wages and salaries. *Fourth,* the fair wage–effort hypothesis explains wage compression among individuals with different skills. *Fifth,* simple models of the fair wage–effort hypothesis potentially explain empirically observed unemployment–skill correlations; they also explain why unemployment has not fallen with the rise in education despite lower unemployment of more educated workers.

Having reviewed the evidence for the fair wage–effort hypothesis, we will construct models using this hypothesis. These models differ in the determination of the fair wage w^*. First, w^* is exogenous. Then w^* depends on *relative* wages as well as on market forces. These models provide efficiency wage explanations for unemployment. Yet they are not subject to the criticism that bonding schemes or complicated contracts will reduce or eliminate involuntary unemployment.[4] If such bonds are considered unfair, then they will not be optimal. In relations where fairness is important, grudges due to past events lead to potential future reprisals. In the existing literature this model most closely resembles Summers' (1988) relative wage-based efficiency wage theory. In Summers' model workers compare their own compensation with that of comparable groups in other firms; in our model, in contrast, workers compare their pay with that of co-workers in the same firm.

Motivation for the Fair Wage–Effort Hypothesis

Equity Theory

Adams (1963) hypothesized that in social exchange between two agents the ratio of the perceived value of the "inputs" to the perceived

---

[4] For reviews of this literature and the problems with efficiency wage models, see Akerlof and Yellen (1986), Katz (1986), Stiglitz (1987), and Yellen (1984).

value of the "outcomes" would be equal. In a labor exchange the "input" of the employee is the perceived value of his labor, and the "outcome" is the perceived value of his remuneration. On the firm's side the input is the perceived value of the remuneration, and the outcome is the perceived value of the labor.

In the context of a wage contract, Adams' formula says that the perceived value of the labor input will equal the perceived value of the remuneration. This formula can be translated into economic notation to say that the number of units of effective labor input (denoted e for effort) times the perceived value of a unit of effective labor (denoted w^*) will equal the perceived value of remuneration (denoted w). In other words,

$$e = w/w^*$$

We wish to emphasize that w^*, the perceived value of a unit of labor, will be the *fair* wage, and not the market-clearing wage.

According to psychologists, with both w and w^* fixed, workers who do not receive a fair wage for input of effort $e = 1$ may change *actual* effort e, or they may change their *perceived* effort. Similarly, they may change their perceived level of remuneration (by redefining the nonpecuniary terms of the job). In the theory below, we shall assume that when wages are underpaid workers adjust actual rather than perceived efforts or the perceived value of the nonpecuniary returns to the job.

Psychological experiments have mainly concentrated on discovering whether individuals who are *overpaid* will increase their effort input since psychologists consider this the surprising prediction of Adams' theory. They consider it obvious that agents who feel underrewarded will supply correspondingly *fewer* inputs (Walster, Walster, & Berscheid, 1977: 42). As might be expected, overreward experiments yield ambiguous results. It has been suggested (Walster et al., 1977: p. 124) that this ambiguity occurs because it is less costly for overpaid agents to increase the psychological evaluation of their labor inputs than to increase actual input. These experimental results are consistent with the hypothesis that overpayment does not increase input, and thus that $e = 1$ for $w > w^*$.

While much less work has been done on underpaid subjects, several studies have obtained supportive results.[5] In one revealing study Lawler and O'Gara (1967) compared the performance of workers who were

---

[5] Reviewers consider this implication of equity theory obvious; some experiments have yielded contradictions of the theory, but in all cases there are easy alternative explanations (Goodman & Friedman, 1971).

paid the "going" rate of 25 cents per interview with the performance of interviewers who were seriously underpaid at the rate of 10 cents per interview. The underpaid interviewers conducted far more interviews that were on average of significantly lower quality. Psychologically the lower paid interviewers also had reduced self-esteem—suggesting that workers adjust not only the amount of effort but also their perception of the quality of the labor input when equity is not realized.

In a clever experiment Pritchard, Dunnette, and Jorgenson (1972) hired men to work for a fictitious Manpower firm they realistically set up for their experiment. After the workers had been at work for three days, the firm announced a change in their method of pay. Subjects' earnings were variously adjusted upward or downward. Those subjects with downward adjustments expressed considerable job dissatisfaction on a questionnaire and also performed less well in their work after the change. In a similar experiment Valenzi and Andrews (1971) hired workers at $1.40 per hour, but then announced that, due to the budgetary process involving their grant from the National Institute of Mental Health, some workers would receive more than the stipulated $1.40, and some would receive less. Twenty-seven percent of those who were given the lower wage of $1.20 quit immediately—a result consistent with an upward sloping labor supply curve but also explained by the workers' anger at their unfair treatment.

In what is probably the most revealing experiment, Schmitt and Marwell (1972) gave workers a choice: whether to work cooperatively in pairs or to work alone. When pay was equal, workers chose to work in pairs. However, workers were willing to sacrifice significant earnings to work alone when the pay in pairs was unequal.

Relative Deprivation Theory

The economic consequences of the fair wage–effort hypothesis depend on how the fair wage is determined.[6] According to relative deprivation theory, peoples' conceptions of fairness are based on comparisons with salient others. Psychological theory, however, offers little guide as to which reference groups will be salient. There are three natural possibilities: individuals may compare themselves with others in similar occupations in the same firm, with those in dissimilar occupations in the same firm, or with individuals in other firms. In the relative deprivation model, workers compare themselves with others in the same firm. If workers

---

[6] Most experiments make an implicit assumption regarding the wage considered fair: either some stated wage, a previously received wage, or wages received by others.

compare themselves with similar others who are "close substitutes," we find that equilibrium will be segregated and workers of different abilities will work in different firms. Labor is allocated inefficiently, but there is no unemployment. If workers, however, compare themselves with others who are "dissimilar" or "complements" in production, equilibrium is characterized by unemployment for low-skill workers or by dual labor markets with pay disparities for low-skill workers.

Although the behavioral consequences of relative deprivation have been hard to document (for natural reasons), there is very good evidence that relative deprivation generates feelings of dissatisfaction. (This corresponds exactly to the model proposed.)

Martin (1981) has done an ingenious experiment in a near-field situation that shows that workers are likely to experience feelings of relative deprivation when there are unequal wages. Technicians at a factory were asked to imagine themselves in the position of a technician earning the average pay in a firm similar to their own. They were first asked which pay level—highest or lowest pay of technicians; highest, average, or lowest pay of supervisors—they would most like to know for comparison to their own wage. Most technicians wanted to know the pay of the highest level of technicians—which is consistent with our model that people work less hard if they are paid less than they deserve but not harder if they receive more than they deserve. Those people who receive less are of comparatively little interest (and therefore have little positive influence on work), whereas those people who are paid more are of considerable interest and, if the ratio is deemed inequitable, can have considerable negative impact.

The second part of Martin's experiment is of further importance for our model. After workers had made their comparison choice, they were then given a pay plan and asked to rate it on the basis of being dissatisfying, expected, or just. When the difference in pay of the supervisors and technicians was large, the technicians found the pay levels to be dissatisfying and unjust. This gives an empirical basis for the assumption that low paid workers will feel relatively deprived when workers of other groups receive high wages.

Social Exchange Theory

Sociologists, as well as psychologists, have developed a version of equity theory. Blau's model of exchange (1955) hypothesizes that there will be equivalent rewards net of costs on both sides of an exchange. Blau's model was motivated by his empirical study (1955) of the helping behavior of agents in a government bureaucracy. The agents who did investigative work would consult with other agents concerning difficult problems. Although consultation with other agents, rather than with the supervisor, was against the official rules of the agency, and its existence was denied by the supervisor, on average, agents had five contacts with other agents per hour, most of which were consultations. In this agency agents varied in expertise. Blau noticed that agents of average expertise would consult agents with the greatest expertise only infrequently. In contrast, agents of equal ability consulted with each other frequently. This suggested a puzzle to Blau: why did the average agents not ask for more help from the experts? According to his explanation, the average agents refrained from consulting the experts more because they found it difficult to reciprocate. They were able to pay each expert with gratitude and respect; but there were diminishing returns to the experts from receiving gratitude. The exchanges between the average agents and the experts, Blau concluded, were not carried beyond the point where the two sides of the exchange were of equal value.

Homans (1961) has proposed a similar theory, based on his own observations, Blau's study, and on work on conformity by social psychologists led by Festinger. The Blau–Homans theory is a general theory of social exchange. Homans develops a key proposition regarding social exchange when the subjective equalities are not met on the two sides of an exchange: "The more to a man's disadvantage the rule of distributive justice fails of realization, the more likely he is to display the emotional behavior we call anger" (Homans, 1961: 75). In simple English, if people do not get what they think they deserve, they get angry. It is this simple proposition that underlies our model. Workers whose wage is less than the fair wage w^* will be angry. The consequence of this anger is to reduce their effective labor input below the level they would offer if fully satisfied. This relation is given the simple, natural, functional form $e = w/w^*$ for $w < w^*$.

Empirical Observations of Work Restriction in the Workplace

Sociologists have documented the existence of output restriction in the workplace. In his classic study of 1930 Mathewson (1969) records 223 instances of restriction in 105 establishments in 47 different locations. These observations were recorded from his work experiences as a participant observer, interviews with workers, and from the letters of six colleagues, who were also participant observers. According to Mathewson, "occasionally workers have an idea that they are worth more than management is willing to pay them. When they are not receiving the wage they think fair, they adjust their production to the pay received." This is an exact statement of the fair wage–effort hypothesis. The following, from the bulletin board of a machine shop, expresses the fair wage–effort hypothesis poetically:

I am working with the feeling
That the company is stealing
Fifty pennies from my pocket every day;
But for ever single pennie [sic]
They will lose ten times as many
By the speed that I'm producing, I dare say.
For it makes one so disgusted
That my speed shall be adjusted
So that nevermore my brow will drip with sweat;
When they're in an awful hurry
Someone else can rush and worry
Till an increase in my wages do I get.

No malicious thoughts I harbor
For the butcher or the barber
Who get eighty cents an hour from the start.
Nearly three years I've been working
Like a fool, but now I'm shirking—
When I get what's fair, I'll always do my part.
Someone else can run their races
Till I'm on an equal basis
With the ones who learned the trade by mining coal.
Though I can do the work, it's funny
New men can get the money
And I cannot get the same to save my soul. (Mathewson, 1969: 127)

In the introduction to the reprinted edition of Mathewson, Donald Roy, a sociologist known for his own worker participant observations of restriction in a machine shop, relates a story from his own experience (1952). A machine crew were discontent because of what they considered an unfair ratio between wages and profits. A laminating machine in this factory apparently had extremely odd performance: it would operate perfectly for a long time and then go mysteriously awry. Sheets of heavy paper in the process of lamination would suddenly tear and stick to the machine's rollers, necessitating difficult and sticky work to unwrap the material. The crew operating the machine was putting too much stress on it, causing the paper to tear and stick. Despite the necessity of cleaning the rollers (an unpleasant job relative to tending the working machine) they considered this operation worthwhile to redress their grievances (Roy, 1969: xxiv). The preceding story illustrates that workers reduce their effective labor power if they feel they are getting less than they deserve. It also indicates that they may feel that they deserve a wage higher than that required to induce them to be physically present at their jobs; further, the remuneration of dissimilar agents—in this case the profit earners—enters their calculation of their fair wage.

Studies by Mathewson and Roy are examples of the work of the human relations school of organization. According to this school of thought, workers have considerable control over their own effort and output. This ability of workers to exercise control over their effort, and their willingness to do so in response to grievances, underlies the fair wage—effort hypothesis.

A recent report in *The New York Times* (Salpukas, 1987) concerns the problems generated by two-tier wage systems. Despite the considerable savings in labor costs, many of the companies that adopted such systems are now phasing them out due to the resentment of employees on the job as well as the high turnover generated by the low wages. These wage systems have "produced a resentful class of workers who in some cases are taking their hostility out on customers" (Salpukas, 1987: 1):

> "The attitude on the airplane can be a big problem," said Pat A. Gibbs, the head of the Association of Professional Flight Attendants, which represents the attendants at American [Airlines]. "You can tell that the anger is there." Robert L. Crandall, American's chairman and chief executive, acknowledged in a recent speech that quality of service has suffered because of the pressures that deregulation has brought to cut labor costs.
>
> The lower-paid workers often do just what is required and no more, and sometimes refuse to help the higher-paid workers. . . . 'Having people work side by side for different pay is difficult' said Mr. Olson of Giant Foods. About half of the supermarket chain's workers are in the lower pay tier. (Salpukas, 1987: D22)

Literature, Jealousy, and Retribution

Jealousy and retribution, the relation between equity and performance, are not recent discoveries of psychologists and sociologists: they are part of everyone's experience. Literature offers many excellent examples, such as the story of Joseph (*Bible*, Genesis, 37–50). Joseph's father, Jacob, loved him more than all his children and made him a coat of many colors. When Joseph's brothers saw that their father loved him most of all, they hated him. One day when Joseph was in the countryside they threw him into a pit, from which he was fortuitously rescued and sold into slavery. When Jacob heard of Joseph's presumed death, he wept inconsolably. This sad story of Jacob, Joseph, and his brothers is an example of management failure made worse by inequitable rewards.

Personnel Management Texts

Textbooks on personnel management regard the need for equitable treatment of workers as obvious. By way of illustration Dessler (1984: 223) writes:

> The need for equity is perhaps the most important factor in determining pay rates. . . . Externally, pay must compare favorably with those in other organizations or you'll find it hard to attract and retain qualified employees. *Pay rates must also be equitable internally in that each employee should view his or her pay as equitable given other employees' pay rates in the organization.* [Emphasis in last sentence added.]

Kochan and Barocci, who view equity as most important in "experts,'" opinions of compensation systems, quote approvingly from a War Labor Board project (by William H. Davis): "There is no single factor in the whole field of labor relations that does more to break down morale, create individual dissatisfaction, encourage absenteeism, increase labor turnover and hamper production than obviously unjust inequalities in the wage rates paid to different individuals in the same labor group within the same plant" (Kochan & Barocci, 1985: 249).

Carroll and Tosi (1977: 303) write: "*Pay satisfaction* is influenced by what an individual gets as compared to what he wants and considers fair. The fairness of pay (perceived equity of pay) is determined largely by an individual's comparison of himself and his pay to other reference persons and theirs [sic]."

Wage–Salary Secrecy

Most employees do not openly discuss their wages and salaries except with close friends. Organizations often have a policy of secrecy in regard to wages and salaries. These practices of silence and secrecy are evidence that others' pay is not a matter of indifference to most workers. Personnel textbooks recommend openness about compensation schedules (e.g., Henderson, 1982: 444–446) but also caution at the same time the need for an active program to explain wage and salary payments. The need for such a program is another indication of the common concern about others' pay.

Explaining the equity of a compensation system may not be easy. Most workers believe that remuneration should be according to performance (see Dyer, Schwab, & Theriault, 1976, for a survey of managers that documents this belief). However, most workers view their own performance as superior. In four separate surveys taken by Meyer (1975), between 68 and 86% of workers considered their own performance in the top quartile. In the model of Section IV there is wage compression: wages have less dispersion than their market-clearing levels. Such low dispersion may be partly attributed to workers' positively biased estimation of their own performance: if pay accorded with performance, workers would view the scale as inequitable.

Wage Patterns

The relative deprivation models predict wage patterns that are consistent with empirical findings. These findings constitute additional evidence in favor of our model.

Many studies have documented consistent wage differentials across industries. Slichter (1950) found a correlation between the wages of skilled and unskilled workers by industry. Dickens and Katz (1986), with a far more detailed classification of occupation than skilled and unskilled, find similar correlations across industries; those industries which have high wages for one occupation also have high wages for other occupations. Krueger and Summers (1988) find industry wage differentials in longitudinal regressions controlling for individual characteristics; this suggests that such differentials are not just due to unobserved differences in labor quality. When a given worker moves from one industry to another his or her wage tends to change according to the industry wage differentials. Krueger and Summers show that these industry wage differentials also appear when adjustments have been made for the quality of employment, suggesting that differentials persist above and beyond what can be explained by compensating wage differentials. While no evidence will ever be totally definitive, since each individual has special characteristics and since each job has its own peculiar attributes, these findings clearly point to the existence of different wage scales across industries.

What explains the phenomenon of industry-wide wage differentials? The explanation offered in this chapter is based on fair wages. If firms must pay a high wage to some groups of workers—perhaps because they are in short supply or perhaps to obtain high quality—demand for pay equity will raise the general wage scale for other labor in the firm, who would otherwise see their pay as unfair. Frank (1984) has also documented compression of wages relative to skills. Although he has another interpretation (due to status considerations), his data are consistent with the fair wage–effort hypothesis.

Lazear (1986) and Milgrom and Roberts (1987) have proposed interesting alternative explanations for wage compression. A wage scale with high dispersion gives employees incentives to withhold information from managers in order to increase their influence (Milgrom and Roberts)

Table 1. Unemployment and Skill

Unemployment rates by occupation, April 1987[a]	
Managerial and professional specialty	2.1
Technical, sales, and administrative support	4.3
Service occupations	7.6
Precision production, craft, and repair	6.5
Operators, fabricators, and laborers	9.8
Unemployment rates by education, 1985[b]	
Less than 5 years	11.3
5 to 8 years	13.0
1 to 3 years of high school	15.9
4 years of high school	8.0
1 to 3 years of college	5.1
4 years or more of college	2.6

[a]*Source.* U.S. Department of Labor, *Employment and Earnings,* 34 (May 1987), p. 21, Table A-12.
[b]*Source.* Summers (1986). Table 4, p. 350.

or to undermine the reputations of other workers (Lazear). But fair wage–effort models offer better explanations for wage compression among occupations between which there is low mobility, as found by Slichter and Dickens and Katz. If a secretary has no expectation of becoming a manager, the Lazear–Milgrom–Roberts models would not predict compression of the manager–secretary wage differential.

The behavior of union–nonunion wage differentials is also consistent with the fair wage–effort hypothesis. According to Freeman and Medoff (1984), when plants are unionized, white-collar workers receive boosts in fringe benefits, although their wages do not increase significantly. In 1982 when General Motors negotiated wage concessions with its union employees and thereafter announced bonuses for its executives, the loss of morale amid the ensuing uproar forced a retraction of the proposed bonuses. GM and the UAW subsequently negotiated an "equality of sacrifice" agreement that required white-collar and blue-collar workers to share equally in reductions or increases in pay.[7]

Patterns of Unemployment

As a general rule, unemployment is lower for occupations with higher pay and for workers with greater education and skill. These facts are illustrated in Table 1.[8] Most efficiency wage models offer no natural

[7] See Freeman and Medoff (1984).
[8] Also see Reder (1964).

explanation for these unemployment–skill correlations. Skilled work is probably more difficult to monitor than unskilled work. Worker-discipline models (in the style of Bowles, 1985; Foster & Wan, 1984; Shapiro & Stiglitz, 1984; and Stoft 1982) would thus predict higher unemployment for skilled than for unskilled labor, unless shirking yields significantly greater utility to unskilled than to skilled workers. In contrast, the fair wage–effort model provides a potential explanation of these correlations.

A Rudimentary Model of Unemployment with the Fair Wage–Effort Hypothesis

The Model

This section presents the simplest model of unemployment embodying the fair wage–effort hypothesis. It is assumed that there is a single class of labor with an exogenously determined fair wage w^*. The assumption that the fair wage is exogenous will be relaxed later. The effort e of a given type of labor, according to the fair wage–effort hypothesis, is [Eq. (1), repeated here]

$$e = \min (w/w^*, 1) \tag{1}$$

where w is the wage paid and w^* is the exogenously determined fair wage. If the worker receives more than the fair wage, he contributes full effort of 1. If the worker receives less than the fair wage, he reduces effort proportionately (to maintain the balance between inputs and outcomes).

There are a large number of identical firms, so that the product marker is perfectly competitive. The production function is of the form

$$Q = \alpha e L \tag{2}$$

where Q is output, e is average effort of laborers hired, and L is the labor hired.

Finally, there is a fixed supply of labor, $\bar{L}$, which will work independent of the wage rate.

Equilibrium

In the competitive equilibrium of this model, the unemployment rate is either unity, with no labor hired, if α is less than w^*, or zero, with all labor hired at the wage α, if α exceeds w^*. This occurs because, under the fair wage–effort hypothesis, the marginal cost to the firm of a unit of effective labor is at least as large as w^*, whereas the marginal product of a unit of effective labor is α.

The quantity of effective labor input is the product of e, the average effort of the workforce, and L, the number of workers hired. From the production function, the marginal product of a unit of effective labor is a constant, α. The marginal cost of a unit of effective labor to the firm is w/e—the wage per unit of effort. According to the fair wage–effort hypothesis, (1), this marginal cost is w^* for all wages less than or equal to w^*, and w for wages in excess of w^*. The firm's demand for labor depends on the relationship between the marginal cost and marginal product of effective labor. There are two cases.

Case I: $\alpha < w^*$. If $\alpha < w^*$, the marginal cost of effective labor is at least as large as w^*, regardless of the wage paid by the firm. Since the marginal cost of effective labor exceeds its marginal product, the firm cannot operate profitably. In this case, the demand for labor is zero, and the unemployment rate is unity.

Case II: $\alpha > w^*$. If the aggregate supply of labor exceeds the aggregate demand for labor so that there is unemployment, the firm is free to set its wage at any level. It will choose the wage that minimizes w/e, the marginal cost of effective labor.[9] If the firm chooses to pay any wage between zero and w^*, the marginal cost of effective labor is w^*. Since the marginal cost of effective labor is lower than labor's marginal product, α, every firm should hire an infinite amount of labor, resulting in aggregate excess demand for labor. Under these circumstances, competition for workers will force firms to pay wages in excess of w^*. The demand for labor will also be infinite for any wage between w^* and α, since the marginal product of a unit of effective labor continues to exceed its marginal cost. In contrast, if the wage paid exceeds α, marginal cost exceeds the marginal product of effective labor, and the demand for labor is zero. Since the demand for labor is infinitely elastic at the wage $w = \alpha$, equilibrium is characterized by full employment with all firms paying the "market-clearing" wage, $w = \alpha$.

Discussion

This rudimentary model describes an equilibrium in which employment and the distribution of income are partially determined by the usual economic fundamentals of tastes, technology, and endowments. But in the unemployment case, conceptions of fairness, embodied in the parameter w^*, also affect the equilibrium. In a trivial sense w^* could be

---

[9] According to the fair wage–effort hypothesis, this wage is not unique. Any wage between zero and w^* results in the same effective cost of labor—w^*. Later, we shall assume that in cases of indifference, the firm chooses to pay the fair wage, w^*.

said to reflect tastes; insofar as $w < w^*$, workers prefer to provide proportionately lower effort; but this is not the conventional use of the word tastes. We have assumed that workers reduce effort, not because they are better off doing so in any objective sense, but rather because they are mad. People who are mad (in the American use of the term as well as in the English use of the term) are likely to engage in acts that do not maximize their utility.

Because the model is so very simple and completely linear, the unemployment rate is either zero or one. There are many natural remedies for this. If the production function has diminishing returns, the equilibrium unemployment rate could lie between zero and one. If there are different classes of labor, each with its own value of α and w^*, those laborers with $\alpha > w^*$ will be employed, and those with $\alpha < w^*$ will be unemployed. For each class of labor the unemployment rate would be zero or one, but the aggregate unemployment rate would lie between zero and one. If w^* depends monotonically on the unemployment rate, with $w^*(0)$ being infinity and $w^*(1)$ being zero, there will also be an equilibrium unemployment rate between zero and one. Such a dependence makes sense. At high unemployment rates people may be grateful to be employed so they consider the fair wage low; at low unemployment rates they are unlikely to consider themselves lucky to be employed, and so the fair wage may be high.

Many assumptions in the preceding model call for generalization. For example, w^* should be endogenized. w^* may depend on the wages of other workers who are salient in the worker's life, the profits accruing to the firm's owners,[10] or the worker's past wage history. The production function may be nonlinear; labor of different types may be complements or substitutes; and effort may not enter the production function multiplicatively. The next section explores the consequences of several such complications.

A Relative Deprivation Model of the Fair Wage

This section develops a model with two labor groups, both of which behave according to the fair wage–effort hypothesis. Various outcomes are possible. In one type of equilibrium all firms hire both kinds of labor. In this case, the group with the lower wage experiences some unemployment, while the group with the higher wage rate is fully employed. Thus,

---

[10] The introduction of profits as a determinant of the fair wage explains the finding of Dickens and Katz (1987) and Krueger and Summers (1987) that industry wage premiums are correlated with industry concentration and profitability. It also provides an additional reason, based on fairness, why the premiums paid to different occupations within an industry are positively correlated.

skill, as endogenously defined by earnings, and unemployment are negatively correlated. Equilibria are also possible in which there is a primary and a secondary labor market. Low-skill workers in such an equilibrium experience no unemployment, but there is a wage differential between jobs in the two sectors, and primary sector jobs are rationed. Although not explicitly modeled, wait unemployment could naturally occur. Finally, equilibria also occur in which the two types of labor do not work together. Such equilibria are inefficient.[11]

Assumptions

The key behavioral assumptions concern *endowments, tastes, technology,* and *fairness.*

Endowments. The total supply of labor of types 1 and 2 are $\bar{L}_1$ and $\bar{L}_2$, respectively.

Tastes. Each worker supplies his or her total labor endowment to the market.

Technology and Market Structure. There are a fixed number of identical, perfectly competitive firms. Each firm has a neoclassical production function F, which is adequately approximated by a quadratic form in the effective labor power of the two types of labor:

$$F = A_0 + A_1(e_1L_1) + A_2(e_2L_2) - A_{11}(e_1L_1)^2 + A_{12}(e_1L_1)(e_2L_2) - A_{22}(e_2L_2)^2$$

where L_1 and L_2 are the labor inputs of types 1 and 2 and e_1 and e_2 are their respective levels of efforts.[12]

Fairness. The key assumptions of the model concern fairness. In this regard there are three assumptions. The first is the fair wage–effort hypothesis. The second defines the fair wage in a natural way. And the third says that in case of indifference to profits firms choose to pay fair wages.

(i) *The fair wage–effort hypothesis.* According to the fair wage–effort hypothesis,

$$e_1 = \min(w_1/w_1^*, 1) \tag{4}$$

$$e_2 = \min(w_2/w_2^*, 1) \tag{5}$$

(ii) *Fair wages: determination of w^*.* In the introductory section we motivated the idea of the reference wage. We shall assume here that one

---

[11] Romer (1984) has considered a model with heterogeneous productivities and a common just wage and has reached similar conclusions.

[12] We assume that A_1, A_2, A_{11}, and A_{22} are positive. A_{12} may be positive, in which case the two labor types are termed complements, or A_{12} may be negative, in which case the labor types are termed substitutes.

determinant of the fair wage w^* is the wage received by other members of the same firm. Thus, the fair wage of group 2 depends on the wages received by group 1, and symmetrically, the fair wage of group 1 depends on the wages received by group 2.

We also assume that market conditions influence fair wages. Workers in low demand, all else equal, view their fair wage as lower than workers in high demand. While the study of lay theories of fairness by Kahneman, Knetsch, and Thaler (1986) shows that people's views of fairness do not correspond exactly to market clearing, it clearly reveals that market forces have some impact on the prices and wages that people consider fair. Accordingly, we shall here assume that a second determinant of w^* is the market-clearing wage.

Combining the two arguments, we posit that the fair wage w^* of a group is a weighted average of the wage received by the reference group and the market-clearing wage.[13] Accordingly, we write

$$w_1^* = \beta w_2 + (1 - \beta)w_1{}^c \tag{6}$$

$$w_2^* = \beta w_1 + (1 - \beta)w_2{}^c \tag{7}$$

where $w_1{}^c$ and $w_2{}^c$ are the "market-clearing wages" of groups 1 and 2, respectively.

We define the market-clearing wages, $w_1{}^c$ and $w_2{}^c$, as those wages that would clear the market for labor of a given type in a simple neoclassical economy where workers exert full effort regardless of the wage they are paid. Fixing $e_1 = e_2 = 1$, the quadratic production function (3) yields labor demand functions of the simple form,[14]

$$L_1 = a_1 - b_1 w_1 + c_1 w_2 \tag{8}$$

$$L_2 = a_2 + b_2 w_1 - c_2 w_2 \tag{9}$$

We assume that "own" wage effects are stronger than "cross" wage effects so that $b_1 > c_1$ and $c_2 > b_2$.[15]

The *Marshallian* definition of the market-clearing wage would be

$$w_1{}^c = w_1 - (\bar{L}_1 - L_1)/b_1 \tag{10}$$

$$w_2{}^c = w_2 - (\bar{L}_2 - L_2)/c_2 \tag{11}$$

[13] Alternatively, we could assume that the fair wage depends inversely on the unemployment rate of the group. This assumption yields similar results.

[14] In terms of the parameters of the production function F:

$$a_1 = (A_2A_{12} + 2A_1A_{22})/\blacktriangle; \quad b_1 = (2A_{22})/\blacktriangle; \quad c_1 = -A_{12}/\blacktriangle$$

$$a_2 = (A_1A_{12} + 2A_2A_{11})/\blacktriangle; \quad b_2 = -A_{12}/\blacktriangle; \quad c_2 = (2A_{11})/\blacktriangle$$

where $\blacktriangle = 4A_{11}A_{22} - A_{12}^2 > 0$.

[15] In terms of the production function, this means that $2A_{22} + A_{12} > 0$ and $2A_{11} + A_{12} > 0$ and $2A_{11} + A_{12} > 0$.

The Marshallian market-clearing wage is that wage which, with the other wage held constant, is just enough lower to induce the hiring of the total labor supply of $\bar{L}_1$ or $\bar{L}_2$, respectively.[16] In contrast, we define the *Walrasian* market-clearing wages as those that *jointly* clear both markets.[17]

In summary, the fair wages of types 1 and 2 labor are weighted averages of the wages of the other labor group and its respective Marshallian market-clearing wage [(6) and (7)].

(iii) *Fair Wages Paid When Indifferent.* Finally, we assume that firms have some small preference for paying fair wages. As a result, when their profits are unaffected by payment of fair wages, they prefer to do so.

This model possesses three classes of equilibria. In one type of equilibrium, which is emphasized in the discussion below, all firms hire both types of workers, and some "low-pay" workers are unemployed. We call this the *integrated* equilibrium, since both types of labor work for all firms. In addition, *segregated* equilibria may occur. In *partially segregated* equilibrium some firms hire only low-pay workers, while other firms hire labor of both types. Such an equilibrium has no unemployment, but there are wage differentials for low-pay labor between primary sector (integrated) firms and secondary sector (segregated) firms. In an augmented model such pay differentials could result in "wait" unemployment as workers queue for the better paying jobs. In *fully segregated* equilibrium some firms hire only low-pay workers, while other firms hire only high-pay workers. Both classes of workers are fully employed. Each of these equilibria will be described in turn.

Integrated Equilibria

An integrated equilibrium in this model is characterized by some unemployment for "low-pay" workers and full employment for "high-pay" workers. "Low- (high-) pay" workers are endogenously defined as the labor group that receives lower (higher) pay in equilibrium. Low-pay workers receive their fair wage, which is in excess of market clearing. Their employment is determined by firms' demand at this wage. In contrast, "high-pay" workers receive their market-clearing wage, which is in excess of their fair wage.[18] The structure of pay in equilibrium

---

[16] The reader may wish to note that payment of such a wage while keeping the other wage fixed implies disequilibrium in the other labor market. The Walrasian equilibrium concept of jointly market-clearing wages produces similar results.

[17] These wages satisfy the two demand conditions, equations (8) and (9), with $L_1 = \bar{L}_1$ and $L_2 = \bar{L}_2$.

[18] This assumes that the parameters of the model are such that the Walrasian "market-clearing" wages of the two groups differ. In the singular case in which the Walrasian wages of the two groups are identical, there is no unemployment. In this special case equilibrium coincides exactly with the Walrasian equilibrium without considerations of

exhibits wage compression due to considerations of fairness; the higher is β, the lower is the wage differential. Integrated equilibria are likely to occur when there is significant complementarity in production between high- and low-pay workers. This characterization of the equilibrium is straightforward to justify.

First, *there cannot be an equilibrium in which both groups are fully employed and work at full effort* (except in the razor's edge case in which the Walrasian market-clearing wages of both groups are identical). In such an equilibrium both labor groups would receive wages equal to their respective full employment marginal products.[19] Such an equilibrium cannot prevail, however, because workers with lower pay would consider their wage unfair; as a consequence, these workers would reduce effort below the normal level ($e = 1$). Such a reduction in effort raises the marginal cost of effective labor; in equilibrium, "low-pay" workers experience unemployment because the marginal cost of effective labor of this type exceeds their marginal product.

Second, *equilibrium cannot be characterized by unemployment for the more highly paid group.* Suppose that the more highly paid group experiences unemployment. The firm could unambiguously profit from cutting the wage of these workers. Since workers consider it fair to receive lower pay than the other labor group if they are unemployed, the more highly paid workers must be earning a wage in excess of their fair wage. This group accordingly works at full effort ($e = 1$), and the marginal cost of effective labor services (w/e) for this labor type is equal to the wage w. Now consider the consequences of a cut in the pay of this group. The marginal cost of effective labor (w/e) for this group declines. In addition, this wage cut lowers the pay that the other labor group deems fair, potentially raising the effort that these "co-workers" supply, and lowering the marginal cost of *their* services to the firm as well.

Third, *the "low wage" group is paid its fair wage in equilibrium.* Since low-wage workers experience unemployment, firms can set their wage to minimize the effective cost of their labor services. This is the appropriate objective for profit-maximizing firms because the wage that is paid to low-wage workers has no spillover effect on the marginal cost of effective labor services of high-wage workers. High-wage workers are paid in excess of their fair wage and work at full effort. The marginal cost of "high-wage" labor services is thus equal to the (high) wage irrespective of the wage paid to low-wage workers. The cost of an effective unit of labor

---

[19] With all workers operating at full effort, the firm's demand for labor would be determined by the labor demand functions (8) and (9). The equilibrium wage rates would be determined by the "market-clearing" condition that the demand and supply be equal for labor of each type.

from the "low-wage" group is $w^* = w/e$ if the firm pays any wage between zero and w^* and w if the firm pays in excess of w^*. The "cost-minimizing" wage is nonunique, with the firm's minimum cost of effective labor for the "low-wage" group being w^*. It can achieve minimum cost per effective labor unit by paying any wage between zero and w^*. We have assumed that when profits are unaffected by the firm's wage choice, it will prefer to pay the fair wage. If this assumption is relaxed, there can be "work sharing" equilibria in which a larger number of workers receive less than fair wages and work at less than full efficiency. The equilibrium utilization of "effective" labor services from "low-wage" workers will, however, be identical whether firms pay fair or unfair wages. There could also be equilibria in which different firms pay different wages between zero and w^* to "low-wage" workers.

Fourth, the *"high wage" group is paid its market-clearing wage in equilibrium.* One might imagine that considerations of fairness could lead to equilibria with shortages of skilled labor, with such "high-wage" workers receiving less than the market-clearing wage; however, such equilibria are not possible in our model due to the assumption of perfectly competitive labor markets. In a situation of skilled labor shortage, any individual firm unable to hire its desired level of skilled labor could raise profits by paying an infinitesimally higher wage than its competitors. Such an increase in wages, however, small, would allow this firm to hire as much skilled labor as it wished, thereby increasing profits noninfinitesimally. Profits would increase even if higher wages paid to skilled workers necessitate raising the pay of low-skill workers to maintain fairness.

In order to compute the wages of high and low paid workers and the unemployment rate of low paid workers in equilibrium, it is necessary to identify the "high-pay" group. It follows from the propositions above that the "high-pay" or "skilled" group is the group that would receive higher pay in the corresponding Walrasian equilibrium without fairness effects on efficiency. In the discussion that follows we assume that group 1 is the "high-wage" *skilled* group and group 2 the "low-wage" *unskilled* group. The equilibrium values of w_1 and w_2 and the aggregate employment of the unskilled labor group 2 are determined by three equilibrium conditions:

$$w_2 = w_2^* = w_1 - [(1 - \beta)/\beta c_2](\bar{L}_1 - L_2) \qquad (12a)$$
$$L_2 = a_2 + b_2 w_1 - c_2 w_2 \qquad (12b)$$
$$w_1 = [(a_1 - \bar{L}_1)/b_1] + (c_1 w_2/b_1) \qquad (12c)$$

According to (12a), the wage of unskilled workers is their fair wage as defined by (7) and (11). For the profit-maximizing firm, workers should be hired to the point where the marginal product of effective labor is equal to its marginal cost. Accordingly, (12b) gives the demand for un-

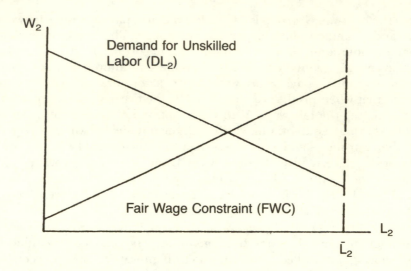

Figure 1.

skilled workers. Since these workers work at full effort, this is given by
the labor demand function (9).[20] Similarly, equation (8) describes the
demand for skilled workers. Equation (12c) shows the equilibrium wage
of skilled workers, w_1, which equates the demand for these workers,
given by (8), with their supply.

The equilibrium is portrayed graphically in Figure 1. The downward
sloping line in Figure 1 shows how the demand for unskilled labor, given
by (12b), varies as w_2 changes, when w_1 adjusts endogenously according
to (12c) to maintain full employment for skilled labor. That is, this "labor
demand" schedule is a partial "reduced form" of (12b) and (12c). The
upward sloping line in Figure 1 is the "fair wage constraint" or "labor
supply" schedule for unskilled labor. This curve is analogous to the "no
shirking constraint" described by Shapiro and Stiglitz (1984). It shows
how the fair (= actual) wage of unskilled workers varies as their employment changes when w_1 again adjusts endogenously according to (12c) to
maintain full employment for skilled labor. The "fair wage constraint" is
a partial reduced form of (12a) and (12c) and is upward sloping because
unskilled workers deem it fair to earn more as their employment rate
rises or their unemployment rate falls. The slope of this constraint depends critically on β, which is the weight that workers attach to peer
comparisons as opposed to market-clearing wages in determining fair
wage norms. In the extreme case in which $\beta = 1$, the fair wage constraint
is horizontal, and the fair (= actual) wage paid to unskilled workers is

[20] We ignore the possibility that (12b) may not be satisfied with equality for any positive
value of L_2, in which case there is a corner solution with $L_2 = 0$.

equal to w_1 and independent of the unskilled unemployment rate. In contrast, if $\beta = 0$, so that workers deem it fair to earn the market-clearing wage, the fair wage constraint is vertical at $\bar{L}_2$.

Comparative Statics: Labor Supply and Productivity Shocks

The system—(12a), (12b), and (12c)—generates predictions concerning the comparative static effects of labor supply and productivity shocks on wages and unemployment. We characterize a productivity shock by a uniform shift in the marginal productivity of type 1 or 2 labor, parameterized as a change in A_1 or A_2 in the production function (3). The complete comparative statics of the model are summarized in Table 2. The most interesting results concern the impact of various shocks on unskilled unemployment. Movements in unskilled unemployment in this model hinge on the shock's impact on the Walrasian equilibrium differential between skilled and unskilled wages. Shocks that raise the Walrasian wage differential are "resisted" by unskilled workers and thus cause higher unemployment, while shocks that reduce the Walrasian differential between skilled and unskilled wages permit unskilled unemployment to fall.

An increase in the supply of skilled labor *unambiguously* lowers the unemployment of unskilled workers because it reduces the Walrasian wage differential between skilled and unskilled wages. Unskilled employment rises even in the case where skilled and unskilled labor are substitutes; in this instance, the increase in skilled labor supply produces a downward shift in the demand for unskilled labor, as depicted in

Table 2. Comparative Static Effects of Labor Supply and Productivity Shocks

Change in	Effect on		
	w_1	w_2	L_2
$\bar{L}_1$	< 0	$\lessgtr 0$ if $\left[1 + \dfrac{b_2(1-\beta)}{c_2\beta} \right] \lessgtr 0$	> 0
$\bar{L}_2$	$\lessgtr 0$ if $A_{12} \lessgtr 0$	< 0	$0 < \dfrac{dL_2}{d\bar{L}_2} < 1$
$\bar{A}_1$	> 0	> 0	< 0
$\bar{A}_1$	$\lessgtr 0$ if $A_{12} \lessgtr 0$	$\lessgtr 0$ if $\dfrac{(1-\beta)}{\beta c_2}$ $\times (b_1 c_2 - b_2 c_1) - c_1 \lessgtr 0$	> 0
$\bar{A}_1$ and $\bar{A}_2$ ($d\bar{A}_1 = d\bar{A}_2$)	> 0	> 0	0

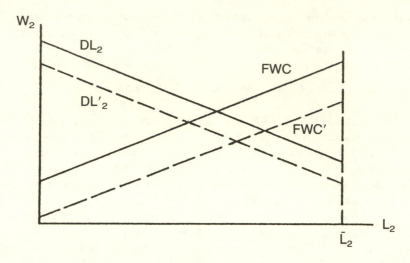

Figure 2.

Figure 2. Nevertheless, the employment of unskilled workers rises because the "fair wage constraint" shifts down by even more. The wage
deemed fair by unskilled workers falls by an amount that is equal to the
wage cut suffered by skilled workers.

As might be expected, an increase in the supply of unskilled labor
leads to an increase in unskilled unemployment. Graphically, this shock
shifts the fair wage constraint to the right by the amount of the increase
in unskilled labor. An increase in the size of a labor force group is
commonly believed to result in increases in the unemployment rate of
that group. Our model is thus consistent with the observation that the
unemployment of teen-agers and highly educated people has increased
as these groups have increased their share of the labor force.

A simple way of parameterizing productivity shocks is by a uniform
shift in the respective marginal products of the two types of labor. In
terms of the production function (3), this corresponds to changes in A_1
and A_2, respectively.[21] Such an increase in the productivity of skilled
labor raises the Walrasian wage differential: the Walrasian equilibrium
wage of skilled labor rises, and the Walrasian equilibrium wage of unskilled workers remains unchanged. The consequence is an increase in
unemployment of unskilled workers who "resist" any widening of the
wage differential. Graphically, this shock leaves the demand for unskilled workers unchanged but shifts the fair wage constraint up; un-

---

[21] Other possible parameterizations of productivity shocks, such as labor-augmenting neutral changes that alter the effective labor power of a given labor type in the production
function (3), lead to less clearcut results.

skilled workers consider it fair to receive higher wages when skilled workers receive pay hikes. According to this model, productivity increases of skilled workers produce an uneven pattern of gains. Both skilled and unskilled workers achieve wage gains; but unskilled workers experience an increase in unemployment.

An increase in the productivity of unskilled labor (an increase in A_2) lowers the Walrasian differential between skilled and unskilled wages, and causes an unambiguous reduction in unskilled unemployment.

The model can also be used to analyze the impact of a simultaneous increase in the productivity of skilled and unskilled labor, as might occur if education levels rise across the board. While increases in A_2 lead to a reduction in unskilled unemployment, increases in A_1 have the opposite effect. Our model provides one possible explanation of why unemployment rates in the United States have not fallen in the face of a general increase in education. Summers (1986: 348) has calculated that with constant education-specific unemployment rates, increases in education between 1965 and 1985 should have caused a 2.1% reduction in unemployment. In our model, as people upgrade their own skill through increased education, they decrease their own probability of unemployment but increase the probability of unemployment of those with less skill. An across-the-board increase in education consequently may not decrease aggregate unemployment. Indeed, in our model an equal increase in the productivity of skilled and unskilled labor leaves unemployment absolutely unchanged.

The discussion above assumes that the equilibrium of the system is symmetric and integrated, with all firms behaving identically and hiring both types of labor. Asymmetric equilibria are also possible, however, in which firms pursue different hiring strategies but earn identical profits. The system consisting of Eqs. (12a), (12b), and (12c) describes an equilibrium only if two further conditions are satisfied. First, no firm can profitably switch from hiring both types of labor to hiring only low paid labor. Second, firms that hire high-pay workers must also find it optimal to hire some low-pay workers. If the first condition is violated, equilibrium, if it exists, will be asymmetric and segregated: some firms will hire *only* low-pay workers. Two types of segregated equilibria—partially and fully segregated—are possible. We shall discuss these in turn.

Partially Segregated Equilibria

Partially segregated equilibrium may occur because, even if the three key equilibrium conditions in Eq. (12) are satisfied, a firm adopting a "deviant" strategy may earn higher profits. Deviant firms would take advantage of the availability of low-pay, unemployed labor who are willing to work at their reservation wage. In our model, with a vertical labor supply schedule, this wage is zero. Deviant firms hiring only low-pay workers need not be concerned with fairness. The condition under which such deviation is profitable is conceptually simple: starting from a potential equilibrium satisfying (12), a firm hiring only low-pay labor at a zero wage must make greater profit than the firm that hires both types of labor at the fair wage equilibrium. The condition for profitable deviation can easily be described in terms of producer surplus: if the surplus achieved by a firm hiring both types of labor at the integrated equilibrium exceeds the surplus of a firm hiring only low-pay workers at their reservation wage, then no deviation is profitable. A deviant strategy will not be profitable if high- and low-pay labor are sufficiently complementary in production. A deviant strategy will *always* be profitable if the two types of labor are perfect substitutes in production.

If deviation is profitable, then exit by deviants would occur. As deviant firms are established, unemployment of low-pay workers is eliminated, and the wage of low-pay workers in segregated firms is bid up to the point where segregated and integrated firms earn identical profits. A partially segregated equilibrium, provided that it exists, has the following properties: high-pay workers are fully employed at integrated firms; low-pay workers are fully employed but divided between integrated and segregated firms; integrated and segregated firms earn identical profits; "low-pay" workers earn more at integrated than at segregated firms. The equilibrium corresponds to standard descriptions of the dual labor market; jobs for "low-skill" workers occur in both a primary and secondary sector. Good jobs for low-skill workers in the primary sector are rationed. If pay disparities cause "wait" unemployment as workers queue for jobs in the primary sector[22] (a simple modification of our model), then the partially segregated equilibrium would also exhibit unemployment.

Fully Segregated Equilibria

The profitable entry of deviant firms, which destroys the potential equilibrium satisfying (12), may lead to an interesting "corner" solution. The fair wage of low-skill workers depends inversely on their unemployment. As deviant firms hire low-pay workers, their unemployment falls, and the fair wage rises.[23] In consequence, integrated firms will reduce their employment of low-pay workers. This process may lead to equilib-

[22] See, for example, Hall (1975).
[23] In a more complicated model the fair wage would also depend on the wage differential between the two sectors.

rium at a corner in which firms with high-pay labor are unwilling to hire *any* low-pay workers at their fair wage. If the two types of labor are perfect substitutes in production, only fully segregated equilibria can occur. Firms hiring high-pay-workers are unwilling to hire any low-pay workers, since the marginal product of the first unit of low-pay labor at such firms is less than the fair wage of low-pay workers. Firms hiring low-pay workers are similarly unwilling to hire any high-pay workers. In the absence of integration in the workplace, low-pay workers work at full effort since considerations of fairness do not apply. The introduction of any high-pay workers into a segregated low-pay workplace potentially causes a significant reduction in effort by a low-pay workforce as considerations of fairness become relevant to their effort on the job.

The fully segregated equilibrium has full employment of both types of labor with no wage differentials, full effort, and market-clearing wages for each group of labor. Still, fairness significantly affects the allocation of resources and efficiency in production, except in the limiting case in which both types of labor are perfect substitutes. In a fully segregated equilibrium considerations of fairness prevent firms from combining labor in the production process, even though it is almost always efficient to do so.

Conclusion

This chapter has presented a theory whereby effort depends on the relation between fair and actual wages. This framework easily generates involuntary unemployment and rationalizes wage compression. The theory conforms to common sense, and also to sociological and psychological theory and observation.

Like all real efficiency wage models, the equilibrium of our model exhibits neutrality: if all exogenous nominal variables change proportionately, then all endogenous nominal variables also change in proportion; and real variables such as the unemployment rate remain unchanged. As a consequence, this model might be regarded as irrelevant to an explanation of cyclical fluctuations in unemployment. Plausibly, however, the level of nominal wages perceived to be fair does not rapidly change in proportion to shifts in nominal aggregate demand. In this instance, our model predicts that aggregate demand shocks will produce cyclical variations in unemployment, thus yielding demand-generated business cycles.

Acknowledgments

We would like to thank Samuel Bowles, Daniel Kahneman, David Levine, John Pencavel, David Romer, and Lawrence Summers for helpful comments and discussions. We also gratefully acknowledge financial support from the Sloan Foundation (for the first author), from the Guggenheim Foundation (for the second author), from the Institute for Industrial Relations, and from the National Science Foundation under grants SES 86-005023 and SES 88-07807 administered by the Institute for Business and Economic Research at the University of California, Berkeley.

References

Adams, J. S. (1963). Toward an understanding of inequity, *Journal of Abnormal and Social Psychology, 67*, 422–436.

Akerlof, G. A., & Yellen, J. L. (1986). Introduction. In G. A. Akerlof & J. L. Yellen (Eds.). *Efficiency-wage models of the labor market.* Cambridge, England: Cambridge University Press.

Akerlof, G. A., & Yellen, J. L. (1988). Fairness and unemployment. *American Economic Review, Papers and Proceedings, 78*, 44–49.

The Holy Bible: King James Version. (1974). New York: New American Library.

Blau, P. M. (1955). *The dynamics of bureaucracy: A study of interpersonal relations in two government agencies.* Chicago: Chicago University Press.

Bowles, S. (1985). The production process in a competitive economy: Walrasian, neo-Hobbesian and Marxian models. *American Economic Review, 75*, 16–36.

Carroll, S. J., & Tosi, H. L. (1977). *Organizational behavior.* Chicago: St. Clair Press.

Dessler, G. (1984). *Personnel management* (3rd ed.) Reston, VA: Reston Publishing Co.

Dickens, W. T., & Katz, L. F. (1987). Interindustry wage differences and industry characteristics. In K. Lang & J. S. Leonard (Eds.), *Unemployment and the structure of labor markets* (pp. 48–89). New York: Basil Blackwell.

Dickens, W. T., & Katz, L. F. (1986). Industry wage patterns and theories of wage determination. Mimeo, University of California.

Dyer, L., Schwab, D. P., & Theriault, R. D. (1976). Managerial perceptions regarding salary increase criteria. *Personnel Psychology, 29*, 233–242.

Foster, J. E., & Wan, H. Y., Jr. (1984). Involuntary unemployment as a principal-agent equilibrium. *American Economic Review, 79*, 476–484.

Frank, R. H. (1984). Are workers paid their marginal products? *American Economic Review, 77*, 549–571.

Freeman, R. B., & Medoff, J. L. (1984). *What do unions do?* New York: Basic Books.

Goodman, P. S., & Friedman, A. (1971). An examination of Adams' theory of inequity. *Administrative Science Quarterly, 16*, 271–288.

Hall, R. E. (1975). The rigidity of wages and the persistence of unemployment. *Brookings Papers on Economic Activity*, 301–335.

Henderson, R. I. (1982). *Compensation management: Rewarding performance* (3rd ed.). (Reston, VA: Reston Publishing Co.

Homans, G. C. (1961). *Social behavior: Its elementary forms.* New York: Harcourt Brace Jovanovich.

Kahneman, D., Knetsch, J., & Thaler, R. (1986). Fairness as a constraint on profit seeking: Entitlements in the market. *American Economic Review, 76,* 728– 741.

Katz, L. F. (1986). Efficiency wage theories: A partial evaluation. In S. Fischer (Ed.), *NBER macroeconomics annual 1986.* Cambridge, MA: MIT Press.

Kochan, T. A., & Barocci, T. A. (1985). *Human resource management and industrial relations.* Boston: Little Brown.

Krueger, A. B., & Summers, L. H. (1987). Reflections of the interindustry wage structure. In K. Lang & J. S. Leonard (Eds.), *Unemployment and the structure of labor markets* (pp. 17–47). New York: Basil Blackwell.

Krueger, A. B., & Barocci, T. A. (1988). Efficiency wages and the inter-industry wage structure. *Econometrica, 56,* 259–293.

Lawler, E. E., & O'Gara, P. W. The effects of inequity produced by underpayment on work output, work quality and attitudes toward the work. *Journal of Applied Psychology, 51,* 403–410.

Lazear, E. P. (1986). Pay inequality and industrial politics. Hoover Institution, Palo Alto, CA, mimeo.

Levine, D. I. (1991). Cohesiveness and the inefficiency of the market solution. *Journal of Economic Behavior and Organization, 15,* 237–255.

Martin, J. In L. L. Cummings, & B. M. Staw (Eds.), Relative deprivation: A theory of distributive injustice for an era of shrinking resources. *Research in organizational behavior: An annual series of analytical essays and critical reviews* (Vol. 3) Greenwich, CT: JAI Press.

Mathewson, S. B. (1969). *Restriction of output among unorganized workers* (2nd ed.) Carbondale, IL: Southern Illinois University Press.

Meyer, H. (1975). The pay for performance dilemma. *Organizational Dynamics.*

Milgrom, P. & Roberts J. (1987). Bargaining and influence costs and the organization of economic activity. Working Paper 8731, Department of Economics, University of California, Berkeley.

Pritchard, R. D., Dunnette, M. D., & Jorgenson, D. O. (1972). Effects of perceptions of equity and inequity on worker performance and satisfaction. *Journal of Applied Psychology Monograph 56,* 75–94.

Reder, M. W. (1964). Wage structure and structural unemployment. *Review of Economic Studies, 31,* 309–322.

Romer, D., (1988). The theory of social custom: A modification and some extensions, *Quarterly Journal of Economics, 90,* 717–727.

Roy, D. (1952). Quota restriction and goldbricking in a machine shop. *American Journal of Sociology, 57,* 427–442.

Roy, D. F. (1969). Introduction to this edition. In S. B. Mathewson (Ed.), *Restriction of output among unorganized workers* (2nd ed.). Carbondale, IL: University of Southern Illinois Press.

Salpukas, A. (1987). The 2-tier wage system is found to be 2-edged sword by industry. *The New York Times, 137,* (July 21) 1 and D22.

Schmitt, D., & Marwell, G. (1972). Withdrawal and reward allocation as re-
    sponses to inequity. *Journal of Experimental Social Psychology, 8,* 207–221.
Shapiro, C., & Stiglitz, J. E. (1984). Equilibrium unemployment as a worker
    discipline device. *American Economic Review, 74,* 433–444.
Slichter, S. (1950). Notes on the structure of wages. *Review of Economics and
    Statistics, 32,* 80–91.
Stiglitz, J. E. (1987). The causes and consequences of the dependence of quality
    on price. *Journal of Economic Literature, 25,* 1–48.
Stoft, S. (1982). Cheat threat theory: An explanation of involuntary unemploy-
    ment. Mimeo, Boston University.
Summers, L. H. (1986). Why is the unemployment rate so very high near full
    employment? *Brookings Papers on Economic Activity* 339–383.
Summers, L. H. (1988). Relative wages, efficiency wages, and Keynesian unem-
    ployment. *American Economic Review, Papers and Proceedings, 78,* 383–388.
Valenzi, E. R., & Andrews, I. R. Effects of hourly overpay and underpay inequity
    when tested with a new induction procedure. *Journal of Applied Psychology,
    60,* 22–27.
Walster, E., Walster, G. W., & Berscheid, E. (1977). *Equity: Theory and research.*
    Boston: Allyn and Bacon.
Yellen, J. L. Efficiency wage models of unemployment. *American Economic Review,
    74,* 200–205.

Part II

Psychological Perspectives

7

Behavior, Reinforcement, and Utility

Richard J. Herrnstein

Nature has placed mankind under the governance of two masters, *pain* and *pleasure*.

(Jeremy Bentham, 1789)

Jeremy Bentham, father of British utilitarianism, no more discovered "pain and pleasure" than Isaac Newton discovered that apples fall from trees. The simple facts of reward and punishment, like those of gravity, are part of ordinary experience. But, with the sentence quoted above, Bentham (1789) opened Chapter 1 of his *Introduction to the Principles of Morals and Legislation,* in which he gave such impetus to what he called the Principle of Utility that, two centuries later, it continues to be the flywheel of behavioral and social science, as well as of political, moral, and legal philosopy. Despite its age and its importance, questions remain unanswered about utility (or its synonyms in other disciplines, such as reward and punishment or reinforcement)—how to define it, to formalize it, to square it with ethics, to delimit its scope, to account for its evolutionary origins, to uncover its physiology, and to use it or not to use it for the good of oneself or the world.

Bentham and the other early utilitarians are, then, common intellectual ancestors to modern psychologists and economists, as well as to other students of human behavior. But, despite the common ancestry, economics and psychology soon diverged to such an extent that mutual incomprehensibility has become the major barrier to any attempt to unify the two disciplines at any level.

This essay will not try to review, let alone undo, two centuries of divergent intellectual evolution, much of which is just sensible division of labor among specialists. It focuses instead on the divergence at the level of theories of individual behavior. Here, the two traditions have arrived at conclusions that are often at odds. Both the economic and the psychological theories are incomplete, but at least one of them is fundamentally wrong, and is bound therefore to foster false conclusions. The conclusions affect not just how we think about ourselves, but also how we would design the environments that shape our behavior and that are, in turn, shaped by how we behave.

Although the principle of utility applies to individual behavior, economic thinkers naturally concentrate on exchange. Adam Smith's (1776) familiar example of a butcher selling meat to a customer exemplifies the molecule, if not the atom, of economic theory. Seller and buyer, both self-interested, establish the price at which each improves his lot by trading the money for the meat. This is the invisible hand at work, and what it was presumed to be doing is guiding the parties in exchange toward the best possible distribution of goods, services, and money. In time, economists elaborated this simple notion in so many distinctive ways that their approach to behavior is only barely recognizable to most psychologists.

Yet, it seems beyond question that the two disciplines must rest on a common foundation, namely a theory of individual human behavior. The following observations are offered in the hope of pinpointing where economics and psychology most relevantly diverge in their underlying theories of individual behavior.

By focusing on behavior in exchange, economics defined a subject matter that approaches individual behavior only indirectly, based as it is on multiple agents. The laws of individual behavior could be obscured when the data comprise exchanges rather than individual acts. For example, when the exchange takes place in competitive settings (a setting that includes, say, other butchers and other customers), competition per se may be decisive.

Economics has been formalistic or deductive when it characterizes individual behavior, rather than naturalistic or inductive. Economists have assumed that individuals are fundamentally rational, by which they mean that individuals tend to maximize utility. Theoretical economists invest time and effort in deducing the implications of utility maximization in myriad circumstances.

To outsiders, it is hard to tell whether economists believe in rationality as fact or definition, which is to say, by virtue of empirical evidence or as a useful tautology. Those may seem to be the only two alternatives, but an article in a leading journal of economics says, "Although the neoclassical hypothesis [i.e., utility maximization] is *not* a tautology, no criticism of that hypothesis will ever be successful" (Boland, 1981). Similarly, the prominent economist, Gary Becker, wrote, "The combined assumptions of maximizing behavior, market equilibrium, and stable preferences, used relentlessly and unflinchingly, form the heart of the economic method" (Becker, 1976: 4). Those sentences capture well the hold of the maximization assumption over economic theory.

Economists recognize that the rationality assumption is often contradicted by actual behavior, but rarely does this inspire a search for some other fundamental assumption about behavior (for discussions of this mismatch between theory and data from the psychological and economic viewpoints, respectively, see Tversky & Kahneman, 1986; Zeckhauser, 1986). Rather, to the extent that the irrationalities cannot be blamed on sheer random error, they typically lead to a search for subsidiary principles, concerning systematic distortions of perception of probability and time, failures in memory, insufficient information, erroneous rules of thumb for calculating outcomes, and the like.

In short, much seems to be at stake for economic theorists in their assumption of utility maximization. Possibly, what is at stake is a further, rarely stated assumption—that any assumption about behavior other than that of maximization would exact too great a price in lost rigor, as if the clarity and precision of formal economic analysis under the assumption of rationality is worth a certain amount of error in the prediction of behavior.

The deductive economic approach has exploited the implications of a concept of an economic equilibrium. The idea that a system is drawn toward certain well articulated outcomes defines mathematical structures of proven worth in the physical sciences, where they have given shape to such concepts as entropy and least effort. But the idea of an equilibrium state for the behavior of an individual actor says little about how an actual person comes to behave in a given way. Economic theory is not committed to any particular process or mechanism guiding the flow of behavior, which gives rise to the last of the characteristics I wish to note.

Somehow we maximize, the theory says, and how we do so is not the concern of economic theorists. The conventions of economic theorizing require only that the theorist show that someone's investments or behavior do or do not satisfy the assumption of optimality. Behavior is seen to be unaccounted for until it can be shown to be consistent with utility maximization or it is explained why not.

We can contrast this list with the approach of behavioral psychology, from which the competing theory arises. Behavioral psychology has searched for the processes that control behavior, rather than for the equilibria that those processes might produce. Lacking a presupposition about the ends of behavior, psychology has been far more inductive than deductive.

The occasion for this essay is a body of evidence from the psychological laboratory consistent with the notion that an individual's allocation of behavior tends to approach an equilibrium, but not necessarily the equilibrium required by utility maximization. Many of the systematic departures from rationality that are part of everyday experience can be interpreted as exemplifying a principle of equilibrium that differs from utility maximization. The tools of formal analysis are as readily applicable to this new principle of equilibrium as to the rationality assumption of standard economics.

Melioration, Matching, and Suboptimality

The present approach takes the view that behavior is generically suboptimal, though still orderly, and that optimality is the exception rather than the rule (Herrnstein & Prelec, 1991; Prelec, 1982; Vaughan & Herrnstein, 1987). The governing theory for this approach is based on numerous laboratory experiments exploring the law of effect in animals and humans. The theory is built around the idea that choice is guided by the law of effect to produce a particular sort of limited optimization, one that happens to be susceptible to serious lapses from rational choice.

Data from the behavior laboratory crystallize around what has been called the *matching law* (Herrnstein, 1961, 1970), which has been observed in several hundred experiments on various species, including human (Bradshaw & Szabadi, 1988; Davison & McCarthy, 1988; de Villiers, 1977; de Villiers & Herrnstein, 1976; Williams, 1988). The matching law states that, at equilibrium, an individual's behavior is distributed over alternatives in the choice set so as to equalize the reinforcement returns per unit of behavior invested, measured in time, effort, or any other dimension of behavior constrained to a finite total. Any systematic deviation from equality in reinforcement per unit of behavior invested is destabilizing, driving behavior toward an equilibrium in which the deviation is absent.

The dynamic process that yields matching at equilibrium has been called *melioration* (Herrnstein, 1982; Herrnstein & Prelec, 1989; Herrnstein & Vaughan, 1980; Prelec, 1982). The notion of melioration is simply a restatement of the principle of reinforcement itself: other things equal, more reinforced responses occur more often than less reinforced responses. A rise or a fall in the reinforcement of a response causes the rate of occurrence of the response to change in the same direction. Should there be an inequality in unit returns from two alternatives, behavior "meliorates," redistributing itself toward the more lucrative, hence stronger, alternative. The melioration process continues until the stronger response displaces all others, or, because the reinforcement returns from an alternative may depend on its level of occurrence, equilibrium is attained with several alternatives left in the response set, each yielding the same returns per unit at a given allocation among them, which is the matching law. The most salient observable difference between the matching law and the equilibria implied by standard economic analysis is that, at a matching equilibrium, a person may not be allocating behavior optimally, given his own utility functions, as will be shown below.

As noted earlier, standard economic analysis and reinforcement theory may both properly claim descent from the utilitarian conceptions of the eighteenth and early nineteenth centuries. Both of them depict behavior as being adaptive. They differ in that the adaptation implied by the matching law is limited by the person's tendency to credit, as it were, the returns he receives to a particular response alternative, rather than to keep a global account of returns across his entire repertoire, which the modern theory of rational choice requires him to be able to do. This limitation in mental bookkeeping entails a limitation in our general capacity to discover optimal allocations of our behavior, although particular circumstances determine whether the limitation is grave, trivial, or, in certain cases, nonexistent.

It should soon be evident that the fundamental difference between matching and utility maximization is that matching is based on average returns (in utility or reinforcement) over some extended period of activity, while maximization requires a sensitivity to marginal returns at each moment.[1] Where the marginal and average returns to response alternatives are equal or bear certain other specifiable relations to each other, we would expect to find no large difference in the predictions of theories relying on one or the other of them (see Herrnstein & Prelec, 1991, for the general case). The customary economic assumption about the marginal utility of a commodity (or other sources of utility) is that it decreases as the rate of consumption increases. Figure 1 illustrates allocation across two such commodities in the kind of chart that matching theory usually focuses on.

It is assumed for this example that the subject is constrained so that consumption of the two commodities, 1 and 2, is exhaustive and mutu-

---

[1] For the distinction between rates of reinforcement on the average and at the margin, consider a subject distributing its behavior across a set of alternatives. The average rate of reinforcement for each alternative is the ratio between the total amount of reinforcement received from the alternative and the time invested in the alternative, at that allocation of behavior. The rate of reinforcement at the margin for each alternative, at a given allocation of behavior, is estimated by the change in reinforcement received from that alternative associated with a marginal change in the time allocated to that alternative, which is to say, the derivative of the function relating the reinforcements received from each alternative to the time spent engaging in it.

ally exclusive, and that the average utility (or value or reinforcement) obtained from each commodity during an extended period of observation is inversely and linearly related to how much of it is consumed in the period. The lines designated as *V*1 and *V*2 in Figure 1 show the reinforcement received from one or the other of two commodities per unit of allocation of behavior invested in it, given a long-term allocation in commodity 1 represented along the x-axis (the consumption of commodity 2 being the complement). With a linear decrease in the average yield as a function of allocation to an alternative, the marginal returns also decrease linearly, albeit twice as rapidly (these relations are expli-

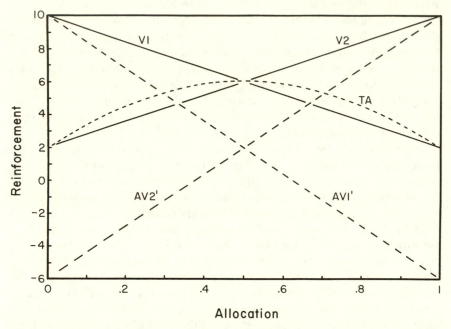

Figure 1. Showing the interaction between several reinforcement variables and the allocation to one or the other of two mutually exclusive, exhaustive alternatives, in a hypothetical procedure. The abscissa gives the allocation to the 1-alternative; the 2-alternative is its complement. *V*1 and *V*2 plot the rates of reinforcement per unit of allocation to the 1-alternative and the 2-alternative, respectively. Their intersection is the matching point. *AV*1′ and *AV*2′ plot the marginal changes in the number of reinforcements associated with a marginal change in allocation to the 1- and 2-alternatives, respectively. Their intersection is the optimal allocation, also shown by the maximum value of *TA*, which plots the total number of reinforcements obtained from both alternatives. Equations are given in the appendix.

cated in the Appendix). The marginals at each long-term level of allocation are traced by the lines labeled $AV1'$ and $AV2'$.

Diminishing returns may arise externally or internally. The reinforcement per unit invested may deplete with the average time spent consuming it or with the rate of consumption, over a period of observation. In repetitive choices between, for example, two berry bushes over some period of time, the average quality and number of berries per visit may bear an inverse relation to the average rate at which we visit a bush. But reinforcement returns may diminish, or otherwise change, because of internal processes—pizza too many evenings or too many trips to a museum may take the edge off the pleasure. Repeated exposures may also enhance reinforcement: we may come to love Mozart more if we listen to it more, over some range of consumption rates. Any of these cases may be represented as in Figure 1, with appropriately drawn functions.

The curve labeled TA in Figure 1 depicts the aggregate reinforcement returns over the two commodities. Standard economic analysis, as well as common sense, says we should find the maximum on this curve, at the point where the joint returns are best and the marginal returns are equal. In this environment, melioration implies the same outcome, for the maximum of the aggregate curve coincides with the crossing $V1$ and $V2$ curves, which is the equilibrium point conforming to the matching law.

The picture in Figure 1 needs only a slight change in order to highlight the fundamental difference between matching and maximization. In Figure 2, the two commodities still yield linearly diminishing average returns with increased consumption, but because of their mutual asymmetry, the maximum of the aggregate returns (the maximum of the TA curve or the intersection of the $AV1'$ and $AV2'$ lines) has shifted toward alternative 2, relative to the matching point at the intersection of the $V1$ and $V2$ lines. Common sense is equivocal here (shall we equalize the averages or the marginals?), but the evidence from the laboratory suggests that in environments like this, no less than that depicted in Figure 1, subjects equalize the averages and thereby match, but here they do so at some cost in overall gains.

Note, further, that in both figures the aggregate returns, the TA curves, are relatively flat in the intermediate range of allocations. Flatness means that overall reinforcement is insensitive to the overall allocation of behavior, while the difference in average returns for each commodity, the $V1$ and $V2$ lines taken separately, interacts sharply with the allocation. The behavior of subjects in controlled experiments is usually narrowly concentrated around the matching point (Williams, 1988), even when the overall returns are not much affected by allocation. In

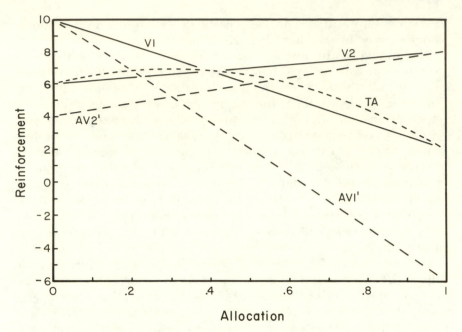

Figure 2. Except for differences in the equations plotted, the same as Figure 1. See text and appendix for details.

deed, even when the aggregate returns have zero slope in the region of observed allocations, subjects still approximate matching (Vaughan & Miller, 1984).

The laboratory evidence, then, supports three related propositions. First of all, subjects allocate their behavior optimally when doing so also satisfies melioration and the matching law. Secondly, when matching and maximization make divergent predictions, behavior is often closer to matching than to maximization. Finally, in situations in which maximization does not narrowly constrain allocation, subjects still conform relatively sharply to the matching law (see Vaughan & Herrnstein, 1987).[2]

Figures 3 and 4 repeat the examples depicted in Figures 1 and 2, respectively, using coordinates more familiar to economists and to those psychologists who have lately adopted economic approaches to behav-

[2] This, of course, is the author's reading of the evidence. Others may, and do, differ (see Commons, Herrnstein, & Rachlin, 1982, for some competing theories among behavioral psychologists). The author's reading appears, at least for the moment and in regard to the matching law itself (if not to the melioration principle), to approximate the predominant one (e.g., Davison & McCarthy, 1988; Williams, 1988), but it is by no means unanimously accepted. It is also a reading based primarily on the results of experiments using animal subjects. The laboratory data from human subjects are generally supportive, but would not on their own substantiate matching as the principal challenge to utility maximization.

ioral data. Since the two alternatives in each of those examples provide access to the same reinforcement, the reinforcements from the alternatives are assumed to be perfectly substitutable, and the indifference curve is therefore linearly decreasing and complementary (see Appendix). Figure 3 shows how the linearly decreasing utility indifference (i.e., equal reinforcement) curve implied by Figure 1 forms a tangent with the "budget constraint" in this procedure, which is to say, the constraint imposed by an experimental session in which the subject has a given amount of time or behavior to allocate to one or another of two alternatives. The subject earns reinforcement from both alternatives, with the number depending on how behavior is allocated and on the $V1$ and $V2$ functions plotted in the previous figures. The filled circle plots the allocation that conforms to matching (i.e., M) and to the utility (or reinforcement) maximum (i.e., O).

Figure 4, however, exemplifies the challenge to maximization theory implicit in matching. The reward structure in Figure 2 also implies linearly decreasing indifference curves, but now the tangent to the bud-

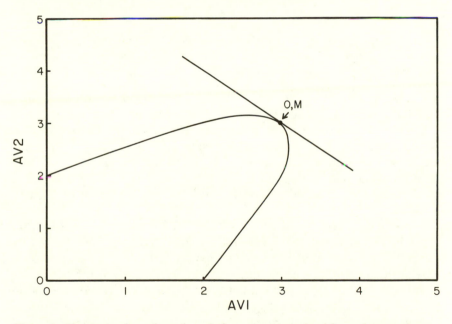

Figure 3. The curve shows how the reinforcements received from the two alternatives trade off with each other, given the procedural constraints implied by the functions plotted in Figure 1. The linearly decreasing line is the locus of equal total reinforcements (i.e., the assumed indifference curve) tangent to the constraint curve, namely, a total of 6 reinforcements. Filled circle is at the optimal (O), as well as the matching (M), distribution of reinforcements, given the constraints.

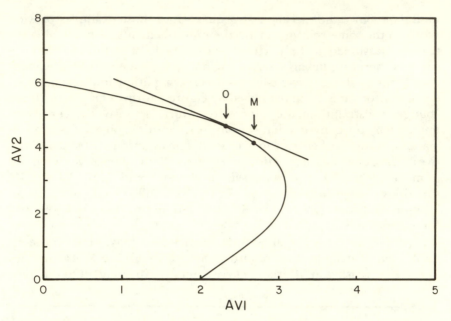

Figure 4. Same as Figure 3, for the functions plotted in Figure 2. The assumed indifference curve is at a total of 6.9 reinforcements. Filled circles at *O* and *M* show the optimal and matching distributions, respectively.

get constraint (that is, the optimal allocation, *O*) is no longer at the matching point (*M*). The evidence suggests that, in situations like this, subjects allocate suboptimally, approximately matching. The separation between matching and maximization can be large, small, or nil, depending upon the contingencies of reinforcement for the alternatives. The location of the matching point is not determined, nor even identifiable, by the variables in standard indifference charts like those in Figures 3 and 4.

   If utility maximization is generically violated by behavior, it is natural to ask how so momentous a fact of nature could have been overlooked by the proponents of rational choice theory as it is applied in economics. The answer is not that economists have generally carved off for themselves the rational bit of human behavior, leaving the irrational residue for the other social sciences to grapple with. As Hirshleifer has written, explaining the "expanding domain" of economics, *"There is only one social science . . .* Thus economics really does constitute the universal grammar of social science" (Hirshleifer, 1985: 53, italics in original).

   One must agree with Hirshleifer that the logic of modern economics makes it inherently imperialistic: "It is ultimately impossible to carve off a distinct territory for economics, bordering upon but separated from other social disciplines. Economics interpenetrates them all, and is reciprocally penetrated by them" (Hirshleifer, 1985: 53). It is, in fact, the underlying assumption of rationality, the very assumption I suggest is false, that ties the social sciences together, in the view of modern economic theory.

Utility Is Indivisible But Essential

The Principle of Utility can still be a matter of debate 200 years after Bentham's enunciation of it because utility is invisible. We may observe behavior and its objective consequences, but, however carefully we observe or deeply we probe, utility itself will remain out of reach of direct observation. The invisibility of utility is a particular instance of the inscrutability of subjective states in general. Like force in physics, utility names a relationship between observables, but is not itself observable.

We have strong intuitions about utility. We expect people to place positive subjective value on food, companionship, the admiration of others, and negative subjective value on losses of status, wealth, health, and so on. Most of the time, most of us may behave accordingly, hence our intuitions. But a person may differ in these respects from other people, at least sometimes. From time to time, we surprise each other or ourselves by our choices. When we defy intuition, it is impossible, on that one occasion, to tell whether the source of the surprise is an uncommon, aberrant, even potentially self-destructive, utility function, or a generic principle of choice that occasionally guides behavior in some way other than rationally, given the person's own utility function. It is only by looking at behavior in many situations, varying along many dimensions, that we are able to build a consistent case for one or the other of those explanations.

For the traditional economist, committed to utility maximization as the fundamental choice rule, explaining behavior has had only one degree of freedom, the utility functions themselves. Only postulations about the nature of the motivational substratum are at hand for saving the theory (see, for example, the treatment of addiction by Becker & Murphy, 1988). Many economists have lately been willing, even eager, to expand the conception of utility beyond the limits of mere wealth, to the "deeper successes that are not made of gold and silk," in the words of George Bush's inaugural address (quoted in the *New York Times* by Passell, 1989, in a quite pertinent article on Robert Frank's book, *Passions within Reason,* 1988), or in such works as Scitovsky's (1976) book on *The Joyless Economy* and many others. The arguments about a surprising bit of behavior are often concerned with competing inferences about the underlying utilities (see, for example, Caporael, Dawes, Orbell, & van de Kragt, and associated commentary, 1989, in regard to "selfishness"). But few economists have been willing to explore the possibility that the explanation lies elsewhere than in the utility functions.

For behavioral psychologists, in contrast, there have always been two degrees of freedom, for the behavioral rule itself was in question, not just the motivational substratum. Only by systematically varying the circumstances in which choices are made—by doing controlled experiments, in other words—can we find a rule for interpreting behavior that will explain behavior in terms of its consequences, whether or not the behavior violates our intuitions.

Conclusions

The empirical tradition of behavioral psychology gives us a picture of choice that is partially, though not wholly, inconsistent with the rational choice theory of modern economics. The similarities are worth noting. In both theories, behavior is governed by its consequences and the relevant consequences can only be inferred from behavior. Neither discipline believes it can get at the essential but subjective hedonic facts, the utility functions or the drives and the associated rewards and punishers, except by how they are revealed in behavior.

The bootstrap operation differs, however, in the two disciplines. Economics assumes generic rationality. Behavioral psychology assumes nothing generically about behavioral equilibria, but, in the course of experiments on human and animal behavior, it discovered the law of effect, which was then refined into the matching law.

We have suggested that matching is the equilibrium point produced by melioration, a process in which response classes compete for the organism's behavioral investment, coming into equilibria where the benefits per unit investment are stably equalized (see Herrnstein & Prelec, 1991, for stability conditions). The matching law is as capable of being the basis for inferences about utility as the principle of utility maximization, but the inferences may differ. The matching point may be suboptimal, but it need not be. The class of maximizing equilibria can be shown to be a subset of the class of matching equilibria, given the process of melioration (Herrnstein & Prelec, 1991).

In traditional economics, the utility functions are inferred but not explained. Economics provides what Hirshleifer called a "grammar" for deriving and expressing the utility functions, but no economic theory says where they come from. The evolutionary origins and physiological mediation of the rewards and punishers for species or individuals are, in contrast, traditional matters of concern for behavioral psychologists. And, in addition to those biological roots, behavioral psychologists study the modification of the rewarding and punishing powers of stimuli by Pavlovian conditioning. For motivation, as for other elements in their theories of individual behavior, psychology has less grammar and more laboratory data than economics.

A fundamental difference between the disciplines is the status of response classes. In a utility-maximizing theory, no fundamental significance attaches to how the organism subdivides its own behavior, except insofar as one or another "accounting scheme" is more or less inherently costly or pleasurable. The theoretical maximizer operates by the principle of "universal accounting" (Luce, 1990), treating costs and benefits across all alternatives as fungible. According to the principle of melioration, however, the accounting scheme is decisive in determining the equilibrium point, as described above (and discussed at further length by Herrnstein & Prelec, 1991).[3] No comprehensive theory of how organisms arrive at particular accounting schemes is at hand, a gap in theory that will in time need to be filled.

The interaction between choices and returns, we also noted, may arise in the environment or in motivational states. It is plausible that the environmental sources are public and visible: we can all see that too many visits to the fishing grounds deplete the stock, hence reduce the average reward per visit at a later time.

For intraindividual interactions grounded in motivational states, it may be less possible to accumulate comparable public wisdom or, at any rate, to supply it in a timely fashion. We may know as a general rule that eating or drinking too much or exercising too little can be dangerous, but suboptimal rates of indulgence may show no visible traces until considerable utility has been forgone. The suboptimalities arising in motivational externalities (the economist's "changes in tastes") are therefore likely to remain more uncontrolled, hence of greater potential danger, than those in environmental externalities, at the individual level.

Because of the invisibility of utility, economists have argued that the ostensible irrationalities involved in obesity, addiction, etc., are really not irrationalities at all, but only the result of peculiarities of one sort or another in utility functions. Economic man may harm himself objectively, but he cannot fail to satisfy the demands of utility maximization, according to modern economic theory. While not excluding the possi-

---

[3] The concept of "framing," well known to economists but uncovered by psychological experiments on behavior (e.g., Tversky & Kahneman, 1981, 1986), is another manifestation of the significance of the way behavior is being partitioned.

bility of peculiar and self-destructive utility functions, the theoretical alternative proposed here holds that the principle of action itself, above and beyond the sources of utility, can lead to maladaptive behavior. The present alternative says that people may need help in their pursuit of subjective satisfaction, let alone objective well-being.

In short, after 200 years, we descendants of Bentham can agree about the primacy of pains and pleasures; we can agree even that, as Hirshleifer more recently said, there is only one social science. But now, to pursue that social science, and to use it to design social institutions, we need to reconcile the divergent answers provided by empirical approaches, such as that of behavioral psychology, with the formal structures of economic theory.

Appendix

Equations for the variables plotted in Figures 1–4 are given below. In these equations, allocation to the 1-alternative is represented by X, and to the 2-alternative, by $1 - X$.

$$V1 = b - a(X)$$
$$V2 = b' - a'(1 - X)$$
$$AV1 = X(V1)$$
$$AV2 = (1 - X)(V2)$$
$$AV1' = d(AV1)/dX$$
$$AV2' = d(AV2)/d(1 - X)$$
$$TA = AV1 + AV2$$

For Figures 1 and 3, the parameters are $a = a' = 8$; $b = b' = 10$. For Figures 2 and 4, the parameters are $a = 8$; $a' = 2$; $b = 10$; $b' = 8$.

$V1$ and $V2$ give the average rates of reinforcement per unit of allocation to each of the two alternatives. $AV1$ and $AV2$ give the numbers of reinforcements from each alternative at each allocation. $AV1'$ and $AV2'$ give the marginal change in reinforcements for each alternative given a change in allocation to it. TA gives the total number of reinforcements from both alternatives, at each allocation.

The indifference curve in Figure 3 plots a segment of the line:

$$6 = AV1 + AV2$$

The indifference curve in Figure 4 plots a segment of the line:

$$6.9 = AV1 + AV2$$

Acknowledgments

Thanks are owed to too many people to list by name, for providing the impetus for this work, for finding gaps in my argument, and for suggestions for improvement. There are doubtless gaps remaining, but fewer than there would have been without the help received. Thanks are, finally, owed especially to the Russell Sage Foundation, for providing support during the academic year 1988–1989, and an environment rich in discussion on the general subject of behavioral economics.

References

Becker, G. S. (1976). *The economic approach to human behavior.* Chicago: University of Chicago Press.

Becker, G. S., & Murphy, K. M. (1988). A theory of rational addiction. *Journal of Political Economy, 96,* 675–701.

Bentham, J. (1789). *Introduction to the principles of morals and legislation.* In *The works of Jeremy Bentham.* (1962). New York: Russell & Russell.

Boland, L. A. (1981). On the futility of criticizing the neoclassical maximization hypothesis. *The American Economic Review, 71,* 1031–1036.

Bradshaw, C. M., & Szabadi, E. (1988). Quantitative analysis of human operant behavior. In G. Davey & C. Cullen (Eds.), *Human operant conditioning and behavior modification* (pp. 225–259). New York: Wiley.

Caporael, L. R., Dawes, R. M., Orbell, J. M., & van de Kragt, A. J. C. (1989). Selfishness examined: Cooperation in the absence of egoistic incentives. *Behavioral and Brain Sciences, 12,* 683–739.

Commons, M. L., Herrnstein, R. J., & Rachlin, H. (Eds.). (1982). *Quantitative analyses of behavior, Vol. II: Matching and maximizing accounts.* Cambridge, MA: Ballinger.

Davison, M., & McCarthy, D. (1988). *The matching law: A research review.* Hillsdale, NJ: Erlbaum.

de Villiers, P. A. (1977). Choice in concurrent schedules and a quantitative formulation of the law of effect. In W. K. Honig & J. E. R. Staddon (Eds.), *Handbook of operant behavior* (pp. 233–287). Englewood Cliffs, NJ: Prentice-Hall.

de Villiers, P. A., & Herrnstein, R. J. (1976). Toward a law of response strength. *Psychological Bulletin, 83,* 1131–1153.

Frank, R. H. (1989). *Passions within reason: the strategic role of the emotions.* New York: Norton.

Herrnstein, R. J. (1961). Relative and absolute strength of response as a function of frequency of reinforcement. *Journal of the Experimental Analysis of Behavior, 4,* 267–272.

Herrnstein, R. J. (1970). On the law of effect. *Journal of the Experimental Analysis of Behavior, 13,* 243–266.

Herrnstein, R. J. (1982). Melioration as behavioral dynamism. In M. L. Commons, R. J. Herrnstein, & H. Rachlin (Eds.), *Quantitative analyses of behavior, Vol. II: Matching and maximizing accounts* (pp. 433–458). Cambridge, MA: Ballinger.

Herrnstein, R. J., & Prelec, D. (1991). Melioration: A theory of distributed choice. *Journal of Economic Perspectives, 5,* 137–156.

Herrnstein, R. J., & Vaughan, W., Jr. (1980). Melioration and behavioral allocation. In J. E. R. Staddon (Ed.), *Limits to action: The allocation of individual behavior* (pp. 143–176). New York: Academic Press.

Hirschleifer, J. (1985). The expanding domain of economics. *The American Economic Review, 75,* 53–68.

Luce, R. D. (1990). Rational versus plausible accounting equivalences in preference judgment. *Psychological Science, 1,* 225–234.

Passell, P. (1989, January 25). Why it pays to be generous. *New York Times,* p. D2.

Prelec, D. (1982). Matching, maximizing, and the hyperbolic reinforcement feedback function. *Psychological Review, 89,* 189–230.

Scitovsky, T. (1976). *The joyless economy: An inquiry into human satisfaction and consumer dissatisfaction.* Oxford: Oxford University Press.

Smith, A. (1776). *Inquiry into the nature and causes of the wealth of nations.* London: W. Strahan & T. Cadell.

Tversky, A., & Kahneman, D. (1981). Framing of decisions and the psychology of choice. *Science, 211,* 453–458.

Tversky, A., & Kahneman, D. (1986). Rational choice and the framing of decisions. *The Journal of Business, 59,* S251–S278.

Vaughan, W., Jr., & Herrnstein, R. J. (1987). Stability, melioration, and natural selection. In L. Green & J. H. Kagel (Eds.), *Advances in Behavioral Economics* (Vol. 1, pp. 185–215). Norwood, NJ: Ablex.

Vaughan, W., Jr., & Miller, H. L., Jr. (1984). Optimization versus response-strength accounts of behavior. *Journal of the Experimental Analysis of Behavior, 42,* 337–348.

Williams, B. A. (1988). Reinforcement, choice, and response strength. In R. C. Atkinson, R. J. Herrnstein, G. Lindzey, & R. D. Luce (Eds.), *Stevens' handbook of experimental psychology* (Vol. 2, pp. 167–244). New York: Wiley.

Zeckhauser, R. (1986). Comments: Behavioral versus rational economics: What you see is what you conquer. *The Journal of Business, 59,* S435–S449.

8

On the Creation and Destruction of Value

Barry Schwartz

> Finally, there came a time when everything that men had considered inalienable became an object of exchange, of traffic, and could be alienated. This is the time when the very things which till then had been communicated, but never exchanged; given, but never sold; acquired, but never bought—virtue, love, conviction, knowledge, conscience—when everything, in short, passed into commerce. It is the time of general corruption, of universal venality.
>
> Karl Marx, *The Poverty of Philosophy*

Can there be a science of values? If so, what might it look like? How should it begin? In this chapter, I will suggest that as the term *science* is ordinarily understood, the most likely result of attempts to construct a science of values will be to reify phenomena that are historically specific and context dependent into timeless generalizations. These generalizations may then take on normative force, becoming a kind of ideology that helps shape social life and social institutions in a way that makes the generalizations self-fulfilling. It may be possible to construct a science of values that is both illuminating and useful, but only if we understand *science* to include the critical examination of history and of culture.

To tell this story, I will first say something about what science, as traditionally understood, is. Then, I will sketch what a traditional science of values might look like. Next, I will attempt to exemplify the shortcomings inherent in a traditional approach by discussing phenomena that illustrate how the values of individuals can be changed—created and destroyed—by certain kinds of experience. These phenomena also illustrate how changes in individual values can contribute to the transformation of social institutions and of the values embodied by these institutions.

Science

The practice of science depends on a set of metaphysical and epistemological commitments that are so commonplace that they rarely rise to the level of explicit consideration or discussion, at least among scientists. However, it is useful to review them, especially in a context in which the extension of a science to a categorically new domain (values) is being considered. Lacey (1988) has recently rendered these commitments in a form that is especially useful for the present discussion.

First, science presupposes that there is an objective causal order that is ontologically independent of human inquiry, perception, and action, an order whose character does not vary with the theoretical commitments, interests, or values of the people investigating it.

Second, science presupposes that underlying this objective causal order are laws that are independent, both ontologically and causally, of human inquiry, perception, and action. These laws capture the state of the world as it is, and their generative (predictive) power defines and circumscribes possible future states of the world.

The principal aim of science is to create theories that are adequate representations of these laws. These theories can be developed with methods and practices that are known to provide adequate representations of the way the world is. And they can be evaluated by appeal to widely accepted criteria for assessing the adequacy of possible theories. The criteria for evaluation depend on data that meet the following conditions:

1. The truth value of any datum can be recognized by anyone with suitable training, simply through making the appropriate observations.
2. All parties to theoretical disputes accept the relevance of a given set of data to the disputes, though they may differ on how those data may best be characterized.
3. Only data in this class are relevant to the resolution of theoretical disputes.
4. Data that represent replicable experimental results have special status in evaluating theoretical representations of a domain.

The data set on which a theory is based can never be exhaustive. Data are always being created, both in experiment, and in the scientist's selection of what to focus on and what to ignore. Nevertheless, the rebuttable presumption is that the data under consideration at any given time are *representative* of the data set as a whole. When theories conflict, theory choice is based on an assessment of which theory has greater explanatory and predictive power with regard to data that meet the above conditions. And importantly, theory choice is based on nothing else.

Values

Now that we have before us a picture of "canonical" science, what about values? What are the entities that we are to imagine studying and understanding scientifically? I take values to be principles, or criteria, for selecting what is good (or better, or best) among objects, actions, ways of life, and social and political institutions and structures. Values operate at the level of individuals, of institutions, and of entire societies.

A social institution embodies individual values when, in the normal course of its operation, the institution offers people roles that encourage behavior that displays the values, and fosters conditions for the further expression of the values. Thus, for example, elite liberal arts colleges embody the value of intellectual cultivation to a high degree. They embody the value of cooperation and group solidarity to a lesser degree, and the value of service to the poor hardly at all. An entire social order embodies a value to the extent that it provides conditions that nurture social institutions that embody the value. The values that an individual can express are very much constrained by the character of the social institutions and the social order in which that individual lives. Indeed, social stability probably depends on a meshing of personal values and institutional opportunities for their expression.

Science and Values

What, then, might a science of values look like? One possibility is that a science of values would discover, by empirical inquiry, the large and varied set of objects, experiences, and actions that different people value. Such a science would not be especially illuminating. It would not tell us *why* (that is, under what conditions) certain objects, experiences, and actions are valued over others. We could enrich the science by adding to the set of values a set of boundary conditions that specifies when some objects, experiences, or actions will be valued rather than others. Still richer would be a more abstract characterization of what people value, so that deep similarities that underlie surface differences might be detected. For example, the claim that people value whatever makes them feel good, or whatever maximizes utility, or whatever promotes inclusive reproductive fitness, if true, might permit us to unify quite diverse individual value schemes. The surface diversity could be the result of institutional requirements and constraints that have a heavy hand in determining what will make individuals feel good, or give them utility, or promote their reproductive fitness. Disciplines such as behavior theory, economics, and sociobiology, which purport to discover the hidden universal laws of human motivation by which all societies operate, are presumeably guided by this kind of theoretical aspiration.

Problems for a Science of Values

These brief remarks on science and on values are intended to lay the groundwork for a discussion of the problems that arise when the two are combined. My focal concern is the dynamic interplay between human values and social institutions. And the problem I am concerned with is this: the "value scientist," using whatever empirical methods are at his or her disposal, identifies the values that characterize both individuals and institutions at a given time and place. From this empirical work, the scientist makes inferences about underlying causal laws. These are taken to be "laws of nature," generalizations about the way the world must work. But in actual fact, they may not be laws of nature. Instead, they may be facts of history that arise out of the interplay of human beings *making* their institutions and in turn being made by them. Claims that are *contingently* true of people located at a particular time and place become reified into laws of nature.

And to this problem we can add a further one. None of the epistemological criteria of science that I outlined above would ensure that we could detect this reification if it occurred. That is, a careful scientist, following all the rules, could easily confuse observations about what *is* the case for evidence about what *must be* the case (see Schwartz & Lacey, 1982, 1988; Lacey & Schwartz, 1986, 1987). In short, the metaphysical commitments of science make it difficult for the scientist to detect that the phenomena being investigated violate those commitments. Detection of the contingent, historical character of generalizations about values requires a perspective that is both metaphysically and epistemologically more inclusive than science.

I will illustrate these problems by examining a particular example of how values can be created and destroyed. By looking at how these value changes occur, and at how they are reflected in the character of our social institutions, I will try to illustrate what the limitations are to a science of values.

The Destruction of Value and the Creation
of New Means–Ends Relations

The part of experimental psychology known as behavior theory or reinforcement theory has focused historically on how instrumental or operant behavior is controlled by its consequences. The study of how behavior is controlled by consequences has had built into it the presumption that means and ends—operant responses and reinforcers—are both conceptually and empirically distinct. The relation between the particular response one requires an organism to make and the reinforcing consequence of that response is *arbitrary*. It does not exist prior to the experimental intervention (e.g., Schwartz, 1989). The various means to reinforcement are essentially interchangeable with one another, and they have no value apart from their relation to the consequences they produce. These kinds of arbitrary response–outcome relations are studied because they are thought to be paradigmatic of means–ends relations that characterize human behavior. The automobile assembly line worker can perform anywhere on the line for his or her weekly wage. Which particular task is required is a matter of indifference, as long as the rate and quantity of reinforcement are held constant.

It is undeniable that some human activities reflect the kind of means–ends relation that characterizes studies of operant conditioning. However, the relation between means and ends need not have this arbitrary form. For some activities, means and ends are interconnected. To see the point, consider the concrete example of a man who works as an automobile mechanic from nine to five each day, and then goes home to pursue his hobby—restoration of old cars to running order. On his job, fixing cars is an operant. The weekly paycheck is the reinforcer. He would not be fixing cars were it not for the paycheck, and he would just as soon do some other kind of work for an equivalent or greater paycheck. Thus his job, the operant, is a means, and his paycheck, the reinforcer, is an end, and there is no special relation between the means and the end that could not be duplicated by substituting some other job for his current one.

The situation is quite different when he gets home. Now, fixing cars is both means and end, operant and reinforcer. While it is true that he does not tinker with cars just for the sake of tinkering—achieving the goal of a smooth-functioning automobile is an important influence on his activity—it is also true that he would not be satisfied with any old means of achieving that goal. He would not, for example, be satisfied with hiring someone else to restore the old cars for him. The reinforcing consequences of the activity are a part of the activity itself, and other kinds of activity are not interchangeable with it in the service of the same

r. Indeed, we might even say that "owning old cars that run well is not even properly a reinforcer, for it will not increase the likelihood of any operant except for "fixing old cars." Similarly, the operant "fixing old cars" is not properly an operant, since it will not be reinforced by any reinforcer except "having old cars that run well."

The distinction between this man's job and his hobby should be familiar. Some people have jobs that are like this man's; they are simply means to an end—pure operants performed solely for the wage that would be given up immediately if a bigger wage came along. Other people are fortunate enough to have jobs that are more like this man's hobby. While the wage is certainly significant, and without it people would not do the job (just as for the hobbyist, having a finished, working automobile is crucial, and without it, he would abandon his hobby), it is not everything. There are aspects of the job itself that make it more than just a means and make people unwilling to substitute other jobs that pay just as well or better. So even though people work at these jobs for the wage, the jobs themselves are both operant and reinforcer.

The relevance of this means–ends distinction to the creation and destruction of values is this: whether activities will be purely instrumental or will possess some intrinsic value or connection to the ends they produce depends on how those activities are organized. And the way in which activities are organized is subject to historical and cultural change. Thus, whether and why activities are valuable is a matter not of natural law, but of cultural contingency. Nowhere is this more clearly in evidence than in the history of the workplace.

Centuries ago, what came to be modern industrial society was feudal. Large portions of land were controlled by lords. The majority of the population worked the lord's land, as serfs. These serfs had no legal alternative to the work they did. In return for his protection, serfs were required to work the lord's land, and to turn over a fixed proportion of their yield to him. They had no choice of the terms they would work under, or of the conditions of their work. They could not hire themselves out to the highest bidder. Nor could the lord sell off his land. The details of the relation between serf and lord were part of a long-standing set of political and social practices that was neither based strictly on economic considerations nor changed on the basis of these considerations. This network of political and social practices is what economic historian Karl Polanyi had in mind when he said, "man's economy, as a rule, is submerged in his social relationships" (1944: 46).

If the factors operative in the choice of work were different in feudal than in modern times, so also was the nature of the work itself. Serfs, and other premodern workers, engaged in a wide variety of different activities in the course of a day. Their work required flexibility and decision making. The rhythm and pace of their work changed with the seasons. In addition, the work they did for the lord was integrated into the rest of their daily activities. They did not leave home for the shop, work from 9 to 5, then return home to engage in personal pursuits. This pattern of work is in sharp contrast to the modern factory worker, who does the same thing all day, every day, with no flexibility or decision making required.

Over a period of several hundred years after feudalism ended, the descendants of serfs eventually became wage laborers. This change coincided with other changes in work that resulted in the emergence of the factory system. By the end of the eighteenth century in England, many of masses of people were not only working for wages, but were free to hire themselves out to the highest bidder. Moreover, with increasing mechanization and division of labor, work became less and less varied and flexible. When the factory system was fully in place, behavior in the workplace seemed a perfect exemplification of the laws of operant behavior in operation.

Industrialization, as we now know it, did not come all at once (Hobsbawm, 1964). For a time, even when masses of people were working for a wage, the wage they received and the way they did the work were largely determined by social custom, not by the competitive market. That is, workers did not hire themselves out to the highest bidder, and bosses did not try to extract maximal output for minimal cost. Thus, complete control of work by wage rates (reinforcement rates) was not characteristic of early industrialization. This is not to suggest that work was uninfluenced by the reinforcement contingencies. Clearly, if workers received no pay at all, they would not have worked. However, pay rates did not exert the same kind and degree of control over workers as reinforcement rates exert over animals.

As industrialization proceeded, however, wages came completely to dominate the work people chose and the way they performed it. Workers learned to sell their labor to the highest bidder. And the reason that work came to be completely dominated by the wage is that custom, its principal competitor for control, had been systematically and intentionally eliminated. A central component of the final stages of development of the workplace, in its modern form, was a movement explicitly designed to eliminate custom as an influence on behavior. The movement was one of the earliest examples of what is now called "human engineering." It went by the name of "scientific management" and its founder and leader was Frederick Winslow Taylor.

Taylor (1911/1967) argued that custom interfered with efficiency and productivity. What industry needed was a set of techniques for controlling the behavior of the worker that was as effective as the techniques used for controlling the operation of machines. Accomplishing this control involved two distinct lines of human engineering. First, one would need to discover the rates and schedules of pay that resulted in maximal output (e.g., Gilbreth, 1914). Second, one would need to break up customary ways of doing work, and substitute for them minutely specialized and routinized tasks that could be accomplished mechanically and automatically. The idea was to strip work down to its simplest possible elements, to eliminate the need for judgment and intelligence, and to wrench work free of its customary past. With this done, there would be no possible source of influence on work except for the schedule of pay. And the schedule of pay was something the boss could control.

Thus, work as pure means, as purely operant behavior, is a relatively recent human invention. It is an invention that took all value out of work itself, and located it instead in the wage, the consequence. And it is an invention that was abhorrent to most of the workers subjected to it. As Marglin (1976) has pointed out, bosses had enormous difficulty in harnessing the efforts of their workers. Workers chafed at the confining discipline of the factory. They malingered, they failed to appear, they quit altogether. Harnessing the worker was difficult, and for the successful boss, it was a singular achievement. But eventually, the problem of inducing workers to put up with the conditions of the factory disappeared. Eventually, what for one generation was the wrenching out of a complex network of customs and social relations was for another "only natural." So it was that scientific managers could see themselves as merely increasing the efficiency of work rather than transforming its very character. And so it may be that the reinforcement theorist, looking around at the "natural" order of things, can see his principles as reflecting an eternal necessity of human nature rather than an historical contingency (see Schwartz, Schuldenfrei, & Lacey, 1978, for a more detailed discussion of this process).

Creation of New Means–Ends Relations: Laboratory Evidence

I am suggesting that the historical transformation of the nature of work provides evidence that value can be destroyed. Supporting evidence can be found in several lines of experimental research. One such line can be summarized as showing how rewards can have the effect of "turning play into work." People are given the opportunity to engage in a variety of activities that might be regarded as pleasurable: solving various puzzles, for example. These are activities people would happily engage in in the absence of any reinforcement. The twist in these demonstrations is that even though no reinforcement is necessary to keep people at the activities, they get it anyway, typically in the form of money.

And the reinforcement has two effects. First, predictably, it gains control of the activity, increasing its frequency. Second, and more significant for our purposes, when reinforcement is later withdrawn, people engage in the activity even less than they did before reinforcement was introduced. The withdrawal of reinforcement does not simply reduce responding to its prereinforcement, baseline levels; it eliminates responding almost completely (see Deci, 1975; Greene, Sternberg, & Lepper, 1976; Lepper & Greene, 1978; Lepper, Greene, & Nisbett, 1973).

In one particular demonstration (Lepper et al., 1973), the experimental subjects were nursery school children. They were given the opportunity to draw with felt-tipped drawing pens, an activity that seems to have almost unlimited appeal to young children. After a period of observation, in which experimenters measured the amount of time the children spent playing with the pens, the children were taken into a separate room where they were asked to draw pictures with the pens. Some of the children were told they would receive "Good Player" awards (reinforcement) if they did the drawing; others were not. A week later, back in the regular nursery school setting, the drawing pens were again made available, with no promise of reward. The children who had received awards previously were *less* likely than the others to draw with the pens at all. If they did draw, they spent less time at it than other children, and drew pictures that were judged to be less complex, interesting, and creative. Without the prospect of further awards, their interest in drawing was only perfunctory.

What is important to note about this demonstration is that it is not an example of the failure of the principle of reinforcement. On the contrary, the awards seemed to gain control over the behavior. If they had continued to be available for drawing in the classroom, there is little doubt that high rates of drawing would have been maintained. The point of the demonstration is that prior to the introduction of the reinforcement contingency, something else was influencing the drawing, and that other influence was suppressed or superceded by the reinforcement contingency. Clearly, this laboratory demonstration is an example of how value can be destroyed.

Another series of experiments indicating that reinforcement can usurp control of an activity from other sources has been going on in my laboratory over the past several years (Schwartz, 1982, 1988). In a prototypical procedure, subjects are seated in front of a matrix of light bulbs, five across by five down. Beside them are two push-buttons and a counter to keep track of their score. Periodically, the top left bulb in the matrix lights up, signalling the start of a trial. "This is a game," subjects are told. "By pushing the two buttons, you can change the position of the illuminated light in the matrix of lights. If you do it right, you get a point. What I want you to do is to figure out the rules of the game; figure out what you have to do to earn a point."

A subject might first push the left button, and observe that the light moves down one position. She might then push the right button, and observe that the light moves across one position. Left, right, left, right. After four alternations, all the lights go out, and the subject gets a point. The next trial begins, and she pushes the buttons in exactly the same order, and again gains a point. She does the same thing, with the same result, on the third trial. Thinking she has the game figured out, she calls over the experimenter. "You have to start on the left and alternate between left and right. Four alternations get you a point." "Wrong" says the experimenter, "try again."

The subject realizes she has made a silly mistake. The experimenter wants to know what one has to do to get a point—what is *necessary*. All that she has discovered is one particular way to do it—what is *sufficient*. The way to find out what is necessary is to vary what one does on each trial, in systematic fashion. For example, to test whether it is necessary to alternate, starting on the left, one starts a trial on the right. The name of this game is "experimental science." There is a phenomenon, the getting of points, and the task is to discover its causes. One goes about this task by formulating guesses or hypotheses, and by doing experiments to test the hypotheses. The process one goes through in attempting to discover the rules of the game is precisely the one that scientists go through as they attempt to discover the rules of whatever "natural game" they are studying. And the process has two essential ingredients: formulation of hypotheses and tests of the hypotheses by systematic variation in experiment.

Moreover, there is nothing about these processes that is unique to science. People engage in them frequently, if somewhat less systematically, in everyday life. Someone interested in learning how to bake bread might find a recipe, and follow it carefully, step-by-step, with the bread turning out delicious. Now if all one cares about is knowing *a* way to make good bread, this recipe will be followed every time the need for bread arises. Similarly, if all our game-player cares about is finding *a* way to get points, once he or she finds that left–right alternation succeeds, he or she will never deviate from it. But suppose one wants to know more than *a* way to make good bread. Suppose one wants to discover the most efficient way to make good bread. Now, what the baker must know is the essentials of good bread baking, what is necessary to make good bread—

the rules, as it were, of bread baking. And as in the case of the button-pushing game, this requires experimentation, the formulating and testing of hypotheses.

In our experiments, college students were asked to try to discover the rules of the game. When they succeeded in discovering a rule, it was changed, and the students did it again. They were given no instructions about how one might most effectively tackle the problem. Sometimes, the students were told that they would get a few cents for each point they earned in the process of discovering the rule. Sometimes they were told they would get a dollar for each rule they discovered. Sometimes, they were able to get a few cents for every point and a dollar bonus for every rule. Finally, sometimes no monetary rewards were available at all.

Think about how these various contingencies of reward might affect students' behavior. Suppose they could earn money for every point. This would put them in conflict. If what they care about is discovering the rule, they will vary their responses from trial to trial. But if what they care about is earning as much money as possible, once they find a successful sequence of responses, they will stick with it. After all, every time they experiment by varying their sequences of responses, they risk failing to earn a point. When one experiments with bread baking technique, one risks producing lousy bread. If, in contrast, they earn money only by discovering the rule, then there is no conflict. Both the contingency of reward and the intrinsic demand of the task itself encourage them to vary their response sequences systematically and intelligently.

When students played the game, these varying conditions of reward made no difference at all. In all cases, students varied their responses from trial to trial with great efficiency. Almost every one of them discovered each of the rules, and they did so quite rapidly. The reinforcement contingencies failed to have any impact. But there is more to the story. Another group of students was exposed to the same set of problems with the same contingencies of reward as the first set. What distinguished the two groups was that this second group had had prior experience playing the game. The prior experience was this: they were brought into the laboratory, shown the game, and told that every point they scored would earn them two cents. They were then given one thousand opportunities (trials) to play the game. Note that there was nothing in the instructions they received urging them to discover the rule. They could have tried to if they wished, of course, but they could also just find a sequence of responses that worked, and stick with it, earning as much money as possible. And that is what they did. Each student settled on a particular sequence of responses that occurred on about 90% of all trials. The little game and the contingency of reinforcement had turned the subjects into assembly-line

workers, engaged in the same task, done the same way, over and over
again, completely controlled by the reinforcement contingency.

What happened then when these newly formed factory workers were
instructed to discover the rules? Compared to the first, inexperienced
group, they were much less effective. They discovered fewer of them,
and took longer in discovering the rules when they were successful. And
unlike the first group, what they did was powerfully influenced by the
prevailing contingency of monetary reward. They were especially ineffective at discovering rules if each point they got earned them money.
Some of the results of this experiment are presented in Figures 1 and 2.
Figure 1 presents the percentage of problems solved by naive and pretrained subjects in each of the four different reward conditions, and
Figure 2 presents the number of trials per solution across the same
subjects and conditions.

That we obtained this result is surprising, for several reasons. First, we
were dealing with a group of bright college students, people who get
their kicks from acting like scientists. Nevertheless, pretraining seemed
to overcome this orientation, or at least to place the game outside the
problem-solving domain. And it did so though the sums of money up for
grabs were rather trivial. Second, we might have expected their previous

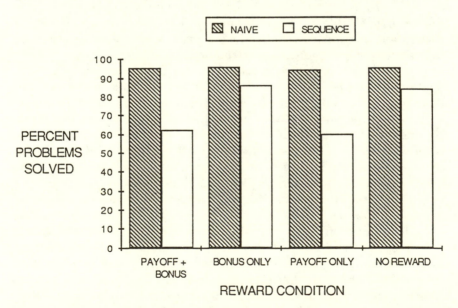

Figure 1. Percent of sequence problems solved by pretrained and naive subjects
in each of four different incentive conditions identified on the X-axis. Data are
from Schwartz (1982).

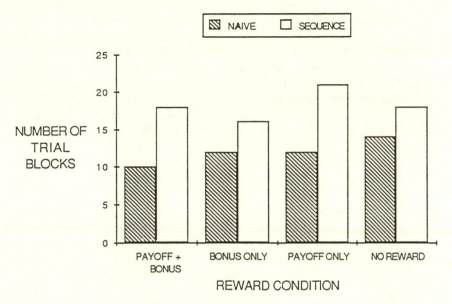

Figure 2. Mean number of trial blocks required per problem by naive and pre-trained subjects in each of four different incentive conditions identified on the X-axis. Data are from Schwartz (1982).

experience to make them better rather than worse at discovering the rules. No doubt they had tested and rejected some hypotheses while developing their stereotyped response sequences. For example, they probably learned that how fast they pushed the buttons, or which hand they used, made no difference. The inexperienced subjects did not know these things when the rule discovery task began. Finally, one of the rules that the pretrained students had to discover was the very same rule that had been in effect during their 1000 trials of pretraining. But even here, they were less effective than students who came to this problem competely naive.

We have followed up these initial findings (Schwartz, 1988) to determine the extent to which the negative effects of rewarded pretraining will generalize to problem-solving situations that are different from the pretraining situation. We have evaluated how pretraining affects subjects' ability to assess accurately the degree of correlation between their actions and environmental events, and how pretraining affects subjects' ability to apprehend and evaluate the truth value of statements of different logical form. I will describe each of these studies briefly.

There is a large literature concerned with assessing how accurately people estimate the degree of contingency or correlation between two environmental events, or between their action and some outcome. In general, the results of such studies indicate that humans are inaccurate in various systematic ways in assessing contingencies (e.g., Allan & Jenkins, 1980; Alloy & Abramson, 1979; Arkes & Harkness, 1983; Crocker, 1981; Einhorn & Hogarth, 1978; Jenkins & Ward, 1965), an outcome that is somewhat surprising in light of the apparent accuracy of pigeons and rats when faced with similar tasks (e.g., Alloy & Tabachnik, 1984; Rescorla, 1972; see Schwartz, 1989 for a textbook review of this literature).

There have been a few attempts to reconcile the two literatures, the most sweeping of which was offered by Alloy and Tabachnik (1984), who suggested that accuracy in contingency assessment is largely determined by whether assessment is based on expectations derived from past experience or upon analysis of current situational data. Humans are perhaps especially susceptible to having theories based on past experience shape expectations that in turn influence the perception of current events. These theory-based perceptions are the source of various biases that have been well documented in the psychological laboratory, in applied clinical or industrial settings, and even in the history of science (e.g., Alloy & Tabachnik, 1984; Einhorn & Hogarth, 1978; Nisbett & Ross, 1980; Platt, 1964; Tweney, Doherty, & Mynatt, 1981).

One particular source of error in contingency judgment has often been called a "confirmation bias." It refers both to people's tendency to seek evidence that can only confirm but not falsify hypotheses, and to overvalue confirming evidence and undervalue disconfirming evidence when it does appear (e.g., Einhorn & Hogarth, 1978; Schwartz, 1982; Wason & Johnson-Laird, 1972; but see Baron, 1985; and Klayman & Ha, 1987, for a critical discussion of confirmation bias). A suggestive account of where this particular bias might come from was offered by Einhorn and Hogarth (1978). They suggested that in natural settings, people rarely have the opportunity to falsify hypotheses. A variety of practical constraints operate to make only partial tests of hypotheses possible, and these partial tests are often of the sort that make confirmation easy and disconfirmation difficult. These practical constraints can lead to habits of inference that prevent people from either collecting the appropriate data, or processing appropriate data in an appropriate fashion, even in circumstances in which practical constraints are absent. It appears from our research that a history of reinforcement for successful responses may create just such habits of inference. When a subject evolves a particular sequence of responses to produce payoffs, his or her orientation is toward producing desirable outcomes rather than true generalizations, and this tendency persists even in the face of explicit instructions to do otherwise.

We therefore examined whether a history of reinforcement for correct sequences of responses in fact reduces accuracy in a contingency detection task conducted in a different context. The study was a replication of contingency detection experiments reported by Alloy and Abramson (1979). They found that judgments of contingency were inaccurate in several ways. When the environmental events in question were frequent, people judged that they controlled their occurrence, even when in fact they did not. Also, when the environmental events in question were hedonic in nature (wins or losses of money), contingency estimates were affected by the hedonic nature of the events. People gave higher estimates of their ability to control good outcomes than of their ability to control bad ones though the actual degree of control that they had was the same.

More specifically, Alloy and Abramson (1979) gave subjects a series of trials in which they could either push a button or not push it in any 3-second period. At the end of the 3 seconds, either a light would come on or it would not. This was the environmental event the control of which subjects had to estimate. The actual degree of control that subjects had was manipulated by manipulating two conditional probabilities: the probability of the light given a response; and the probability of the light given no response. When these probabilities were equal, subjects had no control. When they were unequal, subjects had control to a degree that could be quantified as the difference between the two conditional probabilities. After a series of such trials, subjects were asked to estimate the degree of control they had, on a 100-point scale.

In our experiment, there were three major groups of subjects. Two of them had been previously exposed to the button-pushing, light matrix task described above (see Figures 1 and 2). Group Sequence experienced a 300-trial session of the task in which correct sequences (four pushes, in any order, on each of the two buttons) earned $.02, 1 or 2 days prior to the contingency estimation task. Group Rule experienced three sequence problems in which correct sequences had to include four responses on each button and satisfy additional constraints (for example, beginning with two left-button pushes), and they were instructed to discover the rule that determined whether or not they earned points. These subjects were paid $5 for participating in the session, which occurred a day or two prior to the contingency estimation task. Finally, the third group, Group Naive, had no pretraining.

Subjects were seated at a console that contained a push button and a red light. They were then read instructions that described the task (see Schwartz, 1988, for verbatim instructions). They were then given a series of five blocks of 40 trials. In each trial, they could either push the button or refrain from pushing it, and either the red light would go after the trial or it would not. At the end of the forty trials, they had to estimate, on a 100-point scale, the degree to which their behavior controlled the illumination of the red light. An estimate of 0 indicated that they thought they had no control, and an estimate of 100 indicated that they thought they had complete control. The conditional probabilities of a red light given a response or not in the five blocks of trials were .75–.75, .75–.50, .75–.25, .50–.50, and .25–.25. Subjects received these blocks in random order.

The results of our experiment are presented in Figures 3–5. Conditional probabilities (of the light coming on after a button press or no button press) are on the X-axis and estimates of control are on the Y-axis. Figure 3 presents control estimates across three series where degree of control actually varied. The data are presented separately for the different pretraining groups. It is clear from the figure that subjects in Group Rule were quite sensitive to the degree of actual contingency, while subjects in Group Sequence were insensitive. The naive subjects were in the middle; their estimate of control in the .75–.25 series was significantly higher than in the other two.

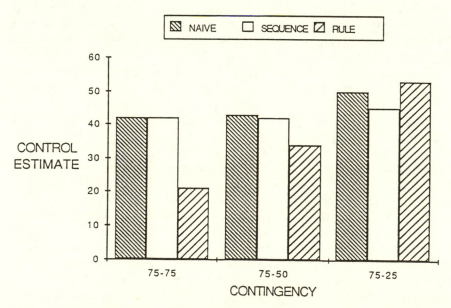

Figure 3. Estimates of control in the conditions in which the actual control that subjects had varied. Data are presented separately for each pretraining group. Data are from Schwartz (1988).

Figure 4 presents similar data from the problem series in which subjects had no control. The data for naive subjects were very much like those reported by Alloy and Abramson; the degree of control was consistently overestimated (since actual control was zero), and the magnitude of the overestimation varied directly with the frequency of the outcome. For Group Sequence, the effect of frequency was diminished as estimates of control were high at all frequencies. For Group Rule, the effect of frequency of outcome was also diminished as all estimates of control were quite modest.

Finally, Figure 5 presents data that compare estimates of control when outcomes are positive with estimates of control when outcomes are negative. Some subjects (Win) started with no money, and won a quarter whenever the light came on. Others (Lose) started with $10, and lost a quarter whenever the light came on. The *Y*-axis in Figure 5 represents the *difference* between Win and Lose estimates of control under the three different degrees of actual contingency. Since contingency estimation should be independent of whether outcomes are positive or negative, accurate performance should yield difference scores close to zero. The scores of Group Rule are close to zero. Naive subjects give substantially higher estimates of control when they are winning than when they are

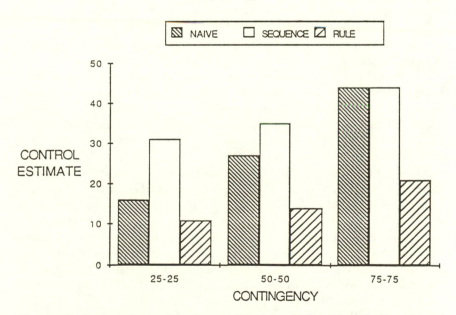

Figure 4. Estimates of control in the conditions in which subjects had no control but the overall frequency of the outcome varied. Data are presented separately for each pretraining group. Data are from Schwartz (1988).

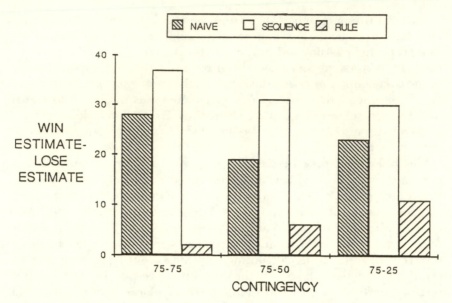

Figure 5. Difference scores between estimates of control when subjects could only win money and estimates of control when subjects could only lose money. Data are presented separately for different pretraining groups across different contingency conditions. Data are from Schwartz (1988).

losing. For Sequence subjects, the disparity between winning and losing is even higher.

The bias that reveals itself in inaccurate estimates of contingency relations has also been investigated in other contexts. Perhaps the best known of these is the so-called "selection task" (Wason, 1964; Wason & Johnson-Laird, 1972). Subjects are shown four cards, two of which have letters (A or B), and two of which have numbers (1 or 2), and are made to understand that each card has a letter on one side and a number on the other. They are then read a proposition and asked to select the card or cards they would have to inspect to assess the validity of the proposition. The proposition is typically of the conditional form, if p, then q. For example, the proposition might be: "If there is an A on one side, there is a 1 on the other."

Propositions of this form are false only when the antecedent (p) is true and the consequent (q) is false. So faced with four cards displaying A, B, 1, and 2, and the proposition "If there is an A on one side, there is a 1 on the other," the schooled logician would know that the A card (p) and the 2 card (not-q) would have to be examined. The other two cards, while relevant to evaluating some kinds of propositions, are not relevant to this one.

Schooled logicians may know this, but typical college students do not. Very few subjects choose all and only the relevant cards. The most common choices are of card A alone, or of card A and card 1. The evidence on card A is relevant to efforts at either confirmation or falsification of the proposition (a 1 on the hidden side confirms and a 2 falsifies). However, the evidence on card 1 can only confirm (an A on the hidden side confirms and a B is irrelevant). The fact that subjects choose card 1, which can only confirm, and ignore card 2, which can only falsify, is what leads to the conclusion that subjects come to tasks like this with a confirmation bias.

Does pretraining of various kinds enhance or diminish people's tendencies to appreciate the value of some kinds of evidence and ignore the value of other kinds? Does it enhance or impair their ability to apprehend the logical form of various propositions? We asked these questions experimentally by assessing the effects of pretraining on people's behavior when they were required to test propositions that were presented in varying linguistic but equivalent logical forms.

There were three groups of subjects in the experiment. Group Sequence subjects experienced a 300-trial session in which correct sequences earned $.02. Group Rule subjects were paid $5 for the session, experienced three sequence problems, and were instructed to discover the rule that determined whether or not they earned points. Group Naive had no pretraining. Within 2 days of their pretraining, all subjects then experienced an identical test phase of the experiment. In the test phase, they were seated in front of the sequence apparatus, and given a series of problems. For each problem, they were given a diagram of the light matrix with one of the 25 squares shaded. Beneath the diagram was a statement, like, for example, "if you go through the shaded square, you get a point," or "to get a point, it is necessary to go through the shaded square." Their task was to test the statement by doing "experiments" with the light matrix. That is, they had to determine whether the statement was true or false by giving themselves trials with the matrix.

Subjects were then given a series of eight problems, each including a matrix diagram with one shaded square and a statement. These materials occupied about half of an 8.5 by 11 inch piece of white paper. The remainder of the sheet was available for subjects to use for taking notes, framing hypotheses, or whatever they thought useful. Four of the eight problems contained statements that were logically equivalent forms of the claim "if p, then q," with p standing for the shaded square and q standing for the getting of a point. Each of these statements was a claim about *sufficiency*. The other four problems contained statements that were claims about *necessity*, logically equivalent to "if *q*, then *p*." Specifically, the eight statements were these:

Sufficiency

1. If the light goes through the shaded square I get a point.
2. To get a point, it is sufficient for the light to go through the shaded square.
3. Either the light does not go through the shaded square, or I get a point.
4. The light went through the shaded square only if I got a point.

Necessity

5. If the light does not go through the shaded square, I don't get a point.
6. To get a point, it is necessary for the light to go through the shaded square.
7. Either I didn't get a point, or the light went through the shaded square.
8. I get a point only if the light goes through the shaded square.

Subjects received these eight problems in random order, and for each subject, a random half of both the necessity and the sufficiency statements were true. Because we expected that pretraining might enhance an already existing tendency in subjects to treat questions about necessity as if they were questions about sufficiency, the results of the experiment were analyzed separately for the two types of statements. Figure 6 presents data on accuracy; the percentage of correct conclusions for each group on each subset of the problems. On the problems asking about sufficiency, there were differences between the groups, but they were not statistically significant. On the necessity problems, differences were significant; rule pretrained subjects were significantly more accurate than naive ones, who in turn were significantly more accurate than sequence pretrained subjects.

A second measure of performance was the number of trials subjects took in evaluating each problem, and these data are presented in Figure 7. First, evaluations of necessity took more trials than evaluations of sufficiency. Second, within problem types, there was a significant effect of pretraining. In the case of both types of problems, Group Sequence took significantly more trials than either of the other groups, which did not in turn differ from each other.

When hypotheses make claims about sufficiency, they can be falsified only by trials in which the shaded square is in fact illuminated. The statement that, for example, "if the middle square in the 5×5 matrix is

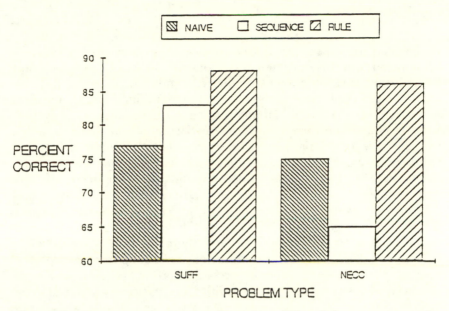

Figure 6. Percentage correct guesses about the validity of the statements to be tested. Data for statements about sufficiency are on the left, and data for statements about necessity are on the right. Data are presented separately for each pretraining group. Data are from Schwartz (1988).

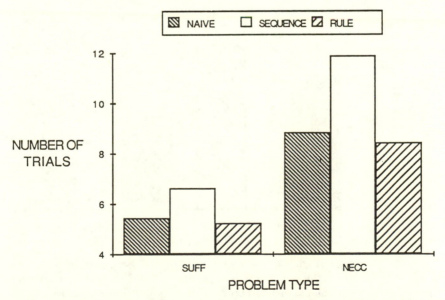

Figure 7. Mean number of trials per statement taken by subjects prior to making their guesses about statement validity. Data for statements about sufficiency are on the left and data for statements about necessity are on the right. Data are presented separately for each pretraining group. Data are from Schwartz (1988).

illuminated you get a point" is tested only by trials in which that square is illuminated. Conversely, statements about necessity can be falsified only by trials that *do not* illuminate the square in question. To assess the claim that "you get a point only if the middle square is illuminated," one must generate trials that avoid illuminating the middle square.

We evaluated, for each subject, the proportion of trials generated that actually were appropriate tests of the proposition in question. In other words what proportion of trials that evaluated statements about sufficiency were actually tests of sufficiency, and what proportion of trials that evaluated statements of necessity were actually tests of necessity? The data are presented in Figure 8. On sufficiency problems, both pretrained groups generated a significantly higher proportion of trials that actually tested for sufficiency than did the naive subjects. This might lead to the conclusion that both kinds of pretraining improved performance. However, the data from necessity problems suggest quite a different conclusion. Here, the Rule group was significantly better than the Naive group while the Sequence group was significantly worse. The

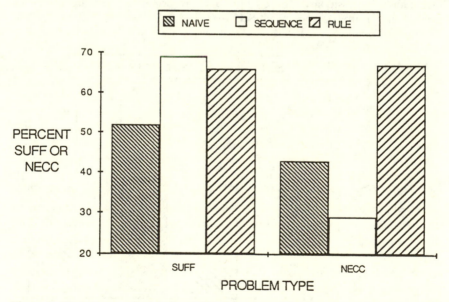

Figure 8. Percentage of trials in which the tests subjects generated were appropriate to the claims in the statements being tested. Thus data on the left present the percent of tests of statements about sufficiency that were actually tests of sufficiency, while data on the right present the percentage of tests of statements about necessity that actually were tests of necessity. Data are presented separately for each pretraining group. Data are from Schwartz (1988).

appropriate conclusion from these data seems to be that rule pretraining indeed helps subjects in their analysis of the logical form of various propositions so that they understand what claim is being made and test it correctly. In contrast, sequence pretraining induces subjects to treat all logical claims as claims about sufficiency, and to test them as such. Or alternatively, perhaps it induces them to attempt to produce positive results and ignore logic all together. This will improve the accuracy and appropriateness of subjects' behavior only as long as the claims in question actually *are* about sufficiency. It seems, therefore, that the kind of bias identified and studied by Wason and Johnson-Laird (1972) and by Einhorn and Hogarth (1978) is ameliorated by experience with systematic hypothesis testing and rule discovery and exacerbated by experience generating particular behavior patterns to produce particular outcomes.

In these experiments we have experimental simulations of the historical process I argued for above. Exposure to contingencies of reinforcement creates an efficient, stereotyped pattern of behavior that can be executed with effortless and mechanical precision, just like work on the assembly line. The contingency makes it possible for people to do the right thing, over and over again. Lapses of attention have no cost, because attention is not required. Lack of intelligence has no cost, because intelligence is not required. The people become an extension of the machinery, a realization of Taylor's Scientific Management vision.

That this automatization is achieved at the expense of another potential influence on the nature of the activity becomes apparent when these students are later asked to discover rules, detect contingencies, or test logical claims. Students without pretraining know what rule discovery means. They have been participating in a tradition of rule discovery or problem solving for years, and it is a relatively simple matter to plug this new challenge into one's traditional wisdom from previous ones. The pretrained students are a part of this same tradition. But they have been induced, by their pretraining, to place this particular task outside it. The debilitating effect of this pretraining is modest. But one can imagine that if they were required to engage in this pretraining task for 8 or more hours a day, day after day, week after week, year after year, the effect might be considerably more dramatic. And if everyone around them was engaged in a similarly repetitive activity, the effect might be more dramatic still. For instead of simply failing to locate this task in the problem-solving tradition, that tradition might erode and disappear all together. Adam Smith (1776/1937: 734–735) of all people, captured this possibility most forcefully. He had this concern about the side effects of factory work:

> The man whose life is spent in performing a few simple operations . . .
> has no occasion to exert his understanding, or to exercise his invention in
> finding out expedients for difficulties which never occur. He naturally
> loses, therefore, the habit of such exertion and generally becomes as stu-
> pid and ignorant as it is possible for a human creature to become.

Exactly so.

Practices and Their Contamination

The research just described explores an example of how activities that
are valuable in themselves can be transformed into activities that are
simply means to ends that could be attained in other ways. To appreciate
better the general character and significance the transformation of value
reflected in this research, we need a clearer idea of what it means for a
domain of activity to be valuable in itself. What is it that participants
strive for when they engage in activities that are not purely instrumental?

This question has been illuminated by Alasdair MacIntyre, in his book
After Virtue (1981). MacIntyre attempts in that book to reconstruct a
moral philosophy, and central to that attempt is the concept of a *practice*.
Practices are certain forms of complex and coherent, socially based,
cooperative human activities. Among their characteristics are these:

1. They establish their own standards of excellence, and indeed, are
    partly defined by those standards.
2. They are teleological, that is, goal directed. Each practice estab-
    lishes a set of "goods" or ends that is internal or specific to it, and
    inextricably connected to engaging in the practice itself. In other
    words, to be engaging in the practice is to be pursuing these inter-
    nal goods.
3. They are organic. In the course of engaging in a practice, people
    change it, systematically extending both their own powers to
    achieve its goods, and their conception of what its goods are.

Thus practices are established and developing social traditions that
are kept on course by a conception of their purpose that is shared by the
practitioners. And most importantly, the goals or purposes of practices
are specific or peculiar to them. There is no common denominator of
what is good, like utility maximization, by which all practices can be
assessed.

We can illustrate the concept of a practice and its significance by considering an example of a practice in some detail. The collection of activ-

ities referred to as "science" is a practice. Sciences are certainly complex, social activities. They establish their own standards of excellence. They have a set of "goods," the pursuit of which partly defines them. And they develop. The goal of science is to discover generalizations that describe and explain the phenomena of nature.

Different scientific disciplines develop traditions that provide guidance as to which generalizations are worth going after, which methods are best suited for going after them, and which standards should be used for determining whether one has succeeded. Now not all people who do what looks like scientific work are engaged in the practice of science. People who do experiments to achieve impressive publication records are not engaged in the practice. The goods they seek—fame, wealth, status, promotion—are not internal to science. Science is just one means to those goods among many. It is certainly true that people who are pursuing such external goods may do good science; that is, they may contribute to the development of the practice. But they are not themselves practitioners. And if everyone engaged in science were to start pursuing these external goals, the practice of science would cease to exist. The core of the practice of science—the thread that keeps it going as a coherent and developing activity—lies in the actions of those whose goals are internal to the practice.

And these internal goals are not commensurable with other kinds of goals. The scientist does not choose from among a variety of market baskets, each containing some amount of truth and some amount of status and money, the one market basket that maximizes his preferences. One does not bargain away portions of truth for portions of something else, at least not if one is working within the practice of science. But in the experiments I just described, some of the experimental subjects did precisely this. They bargained away truth, or more accurately, the best techniques for discovering truth, in return for money. For subjects who were pretrained to perform a particular task for monetary reward, the problem solving task was not "pure" science. It was an amalgam of truth seeking and money seeking, of doing what will yield a general principle and doing what works. These students struck a compromise between two competing masters when they faced the problem-solving task. Their compromise was not necessarily deliberate, but it was there nevertheless. They forsook traditional methods of doing good science that their untrained colleagues followed, so that they could earn more money.

One does not need our laboratory demonstrations to see this compromise between scientific and economic objectives. Economic considerations have been affecting the behavior of real scientists, doing real science, for years, and continue increasingly to do so. It is not good science to do the same experiment again and again—to repeat what works. Yet with research success, promotion and the granting of tenure largely determined by rate of publication, many scientists do so. Each experiment is a minor variant on the preceding one, because such mechanical and unimaginative variation is the quickest road to print. It is not good science to decide what to study on the basis of what people are willing to pay for. Yet government agencies are able to manipulate fields of inquiry by shifting funding from one domain to another. It is not good science to keep ones results a secret, keeping others in the dark, or even intentionally misleading them. Yet in areas that are hot, scientists often do this, as a way of protecting claims to priority, even at the cost of scientific progress. Above all, it is not good science to lie—to misrepresent results willfully, or to invent results of experiments that were never conducted. Yet, in the last few years, several examples of blatant falsification have been uncovered at major research institutions. This last perversion of science, presumably in the interest of self-aggrandizement, is especially crippling. Science must proceed on the presumption that its practitioners always tell the truth, even if they are not always successful at finding it. Were this presumption seriously undermined, science would grind to a halt. All experiments would have to be repeated by all interested parties, to make sure of the veracity of published reports.

Spurred by the growing number of research partnerships between universities and industry, concerned scientists worry that it is just a matter of time before corporate concerns start taking control of the university laboratory, dictating which problems are to be studied, who is to be hired to study them, what information is allowed to be publicly disseminated when, and the like. At the very least, even if they do not dictate the direction of research, or encourage distortion, corporate sponsors can be expected to exert substantial control on communication. It does them little good to foot the bill for research if everyone can gain access to its products, through the scientific journals, at the same time they do. If the practice of delaying or witholding publication becomes widespread enough, it will create substantial doubt among scientists about just how accurate and up to date the reports they see in their journals really are (see Schwartz, 1986, for further discussion of this and other examples).

Economic Imperialism and the Destruction of Value

The distinction between internal and external goods, and the concept of a practice more generally, is illuminated by the notion of "economic imperialism" (see Hirsch, 1976; Schwartz, 1986). Economic imperialism is the spread of economic calculations of "interest" to domains that were once regarded as noneconomic. It is the infusion of a practice with the pursuit of external goods. This pursuit pushes a practice in directions it would not otherwise take, and in so doing, undercuts the traditions that comprise it. Economic imperialism evaluates practices by a common, economic denominator, abandoning the ones that fall short and encouraging the ones that do not, without regard to the internal goods that each practice possesses uniquely. And whenever internal and external goods conflict, economic imperialism moves in the direction of maximizing the latter, sometimes at the cost of eliminating the former.

This is arguably what happened in the factory, as I indicated above. Tailoring, for example, is a practice. There are goods internal to it that help to shape it even though people do it to earn their livelihood. The pursuit of livelihood does not completely determine the character of weaving just because of these other, internal goods. But when tailoring is organized by the assembly line, the goods internal to it disappear. Assembly line work is not a practice. Good assembly line workers show up for work, and work just as hard and as fast as they are told. What they are doing on the line does not matter. There is no developing tradition of which they are a part. The goods of assembly line work are entirely external. This was part of the point of creating the assembly line to begin with. And economic imperialism threatens to turn other practices into the essential equivalent of assembly line work, by moving them always in the direction of maximization of marginal productivity, utility, or profitability, at the expense of their traditional, internal goods.

For MacIntyre, the concept of a practice has a central place in a theory of what it is to be a good person. Good people possess just those characteristics, or virtues, that permit them to engage successfully in practices. The list of these virtues is fairly traditional—justice, honesty, courage, wisdom, respect, constancy, determination, and so on. And the continued existence and development of practices depend on the continued existence of people who possess these virtues. Thus, our judgment of moral worth is bound up with our judgment of the set of practices to which that worth contributes. What then happens to moral worth if the practices disappear, if economic imperialism transforms them into simply means to external goods? If that happens, there is only one practice—the practice of utility maximization. And the good person will be the good utility maximizer. Virtuous, moral people will be indistinguishable from rational, economic agents. By penetrating and transforming the set of practices that comprise human, social life, economic imperialism will have created the conditions under which its conception of human nature is true.

Hirsch (1976) identifies many aspects of modern life that once were largely independent of economic considerations but are now becoming increasingly pervaded by them. One example he discusses is education.

With increasing competition among members of society for good jobs, employers keep erecting new hurdles that must be jumped before job entry is possible. First high school degrees were required, then college degrees, then special training programs, then masters degrees, then doctoral degrees, then doctoral degrees at only a handful of select, certified institutions. The training one receives in these various programs may or may not be relevant to the requirements of the job; relevant training is really not the essential point. What is critical is to make the path to the job arduous enough so that only a few dedicated souls will embark on it.

These hurdles have a profound effect on the way people view education. With education so closely tied to job entry, and job training, it becomes an "investment" in one's future. The money spent on school is expected to be returned, *in kind*, and with interest, later on. One can put a dollar value on a college degree by surveying the wages paid on the jobs to which it gives access. It is easy to imagine people engaged in the following kind of calculations: a degree from Harvard will cost $80,000. If one took that money and invested it, and entered the job market 4 years earlier than one otherwise would, would the interest on investment coupled with the extra years of earning power compensate for the high-paying jobs forgone? Or perhaps the calculations might go like this: Harvard will cost $80,000, while the state university will cost $30,000. Will the job opportunities provided by the Harvard degree pay back the extra $50,000 invested?

It is easy to see how thinking about education in these terms—as an economic investment—can affect what people want out of education, and thus how they evaluate what they get. If enough people assessed their education in these terms, what actually went on in the college classroom would surely change. Colleges and universities would have to be sensitive to market demand; they would have to provide what students wanted, or the students would go elsewhere. The goal of education would shift from creating well-informed, sensitive, and enlightened citizens to creating skilled workers. This is an example of economic imperialism. To the claim that one cannot put a dollar value on having an educated citizenry comes the reply, of course one can. One simply looks at how much extra salary the education makes possible. Extra salary becomes the yardstick for evaluating the effectiveness of an educational institution. Before long, the institution changes what it does, so that the creation of extra salary potential becomes the goal itself, instead of just a measuring stick.

Another example of economic imperialism is that our everyday social relations—as friends, neighbors, spouses, and parents—are taking on an economic component. In part, this comes from the fact that consumption takes time. If one has money only for the essentials of life, finding the time in which to consume them is not an issue. But if there is money for stereos, video recorders, dinners in nice restaurants, the theater, and vacations, one must find the time to decide which stereo, restaurant, play, or resort to partake of. In addition, one must find the time actually to partake of it. Dinner at home is an hour; dinner out is an evening. No matter how rich a person is, time is a resource that cannot be increased; there are only 24 hours in a day.

The pressure for time to consume has real costs. It produces what Hirsch calls "the economics of bad neighbors." Time spent being sociable is time taken away from consumption. Chatting over the backyard fence or helping a neighbor cut down a tree are actions taken at a cost of using the video recorder, or going into town for a nice dinner. Whether we like it or not, the decision to be sociable becomes an economic decision, another example of the spread of economic considerations to traditionally noneconomic domains. Many people have experienced how much harder it has become to find the time to spend a quiet evening sipping beer and chatting with a few friends. It is becoming increasingly rare for such occasions to develop spontaneously; they must be planned days, or even weeks, in advance. And of course it seems ludicrous to "plan" an evening of casual conversation. So instead it becomes a dinner party. This, in turn only adds to the time pressure, since now food must be purchased, and an impressive meal must be prepared.

In the economic world, people get what they pay for. Certainly, they get nothing more, and vigilance is required to see that they do not get less. People are not in business for their health, after all. So what happens when social "goods" become economic? Presumably, people start getting only what they pay for in social relations as well as economic ones. In the economic world, people are prepared to operate on this assumption. Products come with explicit guarantees, services are provided in accordance with detailed and specific contracts. People enter into exchanges with their eyes open, expecting, and guarding against, the worst. They are not so prepared in the social world. People assume that friends, lovers, families, doctors, and teachers will act with good will, doing, insofar as is possible, what is best for them. As a result, they ask no guarantees, and write no contracts. People trust that part of what it means to be a spouse, lover, parent, doctor, or teacher ensures that people close to them will behave honorably, truthfully, courageously, and dutifully in social interactions.

As social relations become commercialized, however, this assumption grows more and more suspect. Increasingly, people feel the need to have things written down in contracts. Increasingly, they feel the need to be able to hold others legally accountable—whether doctors, lawyers, teachers, or even friends or lovers—to have a club to wield to ensure that they are getting what they pay for out of their social relations.

One might argue that this shift from a dependency on what is implicit in various social relations to what is explicit and contractual is merely a recognition of cold, hard reality. But what the person who makes this argument fails to realize is that the process of commercialization of social relations affects the product. By treating the services of doctors and teachers as commodities being offered to the wary consumer, we change the way doctors doctor and teachers teach. Doctors practice defensively, doing not what they regard as the best medicine, but what they regard as the best hedge against malpractice suits. Medical costs soar, but medical care does not improve. Teachers teach defensively, making sure their students will perform well on whatever tests will be used to evaluate their progress, at the expense of genuine education. Test scores go up, but students are no wiser than before.

There is, in short, a self-fulfilling character to the commercialization of social relations. The more we treat such relations as economic goods, to be purchased with care, the more they become economic goods about which we must be careful. The more that an assumption of self-interest on the part of others governs social relations, the truer that assumption becomes. As Hirsch (1976: 88) has said, "the more that is in the contracts, the less can be expected without them; the more you write it down, the less is taken—or expected—on trust."

Probably, not even the most committed economist is sanguine about this vision of the world. If it is true that moral traditions depend on practices, and practices can be corrupted by the pursuit of external goods, and the pursuit of external goods is encouraged by economic imperialism, then all we have to do is be vigilant, and keep economic considerations from penetrating into all our practices. By keeping practices relatively pure, we can preserve a proper place for morality in a highly industrialized, productive, and affluent culture.

But choosing to keep practices pure, and economic and noneconomic goods distinct, is not a decision that can be easily made individually. If few others make that choice, and instead enter practices with external orientations, the practices themselves will change so that the pursuit of previously internal goods will no longer be possible. Return for a moment to the experiments in which intelligent college students treated a scientific, problem-solving situation as if it were an assembly line job. All that the experiments really did was trick them. They knew what problem solving was, and what it required, and they knew what mechanical, repetitive activity was, and what it required, and the experiments merely induced them to treat an instance of the former as if it were the latter. It was a trick that could easily be corrected. But suppose there was no practice of science left as we know it. Suppose science had been completely penetrated by economic imperialism. What help would it be to the students then to be told that they were supposed to be doing science? What would "doing science" mean? The economist may expect that economic imperialism can be exercised in moderation, but the problem is that there may be nothing left to provide that moderation.

Conclusion

Systematic inquiry into the character of human values should help us answer questions like these:

1.   Where do values come from?
2.   How do values change?
3.   How do values influence the actions and life plans of individuals?
4.   How are values embodied in social institutions?
5.   How does the shape of social institutions influence or constrain the formation of values in individuals?

I have tried to suggest in this chapter that science, as ordinarily understood, is probably not the best way to develop answers to questions such as these. This is because the real answers to questions such as these lie in the particulars. People are situated in particular times and places, are influenced by particular social norms and institutions, and contribute to the development of new social norms and institutions. Attempts to extract what is timeless and universal about the formation of human values from the particulars that are important at any given time or place are likely to lead to distortion. This distortion can be especially serious if historical contingencies are mistakenly identified as natural laws.

Gould (1987) has recently written about the difference between the universal and the historical in the study of geology. Gould refers to the universal as "time's cycle," to highlight its repetition or recurrence. He refers to the historical as "time's arrow," to highlight its uniqueness and directionality. Gould (1987: 15–16) says of the distinction that

> Time's arrow and time's cycle is, if you will, a "great" dichotomy because each of its poles captures, by its essence, a theme so central to intellectual (and practical) life that Western people who hope to understand history must wrestle intimately with both—for time's arrow is the intelligibility of distinct and irreversible events, while time's cycle is the intelligibility of timeless order and lawlike structure. We must have both.

We must have both. But what this chapter has tried to suggest and to illustrate is that in the domain of human values, it is time's arrow that should properly do most of the explanatory work.

Acknowledgments

The research and analysis reported in this chapter was supported by a Eugene M. Lang Faculty Fellowship and by grants from the National Science Foundation. Alan Heubert and Heidi McBride provided invaluable assistance in the design, execution, and analysis of the experiments.

References

Allan, L. G., & Jenkins, H. M. (1980). The judgment of contingency and the nature of the response alternatives. *Canadian Journal of Psychology, 34,* 1–11.

Alloy, L. B., & Abramson, L. Y. (1979). Judgment of contingency in depressed and nondepressed students: Sadder but wiser? *Journal of Experimental Psychology: General, 108,* 441–485.

Alloy, L. B., & Tabachnik, N. (1984). Assessment of covariation by humans and animals: The joint influence of prior experience and current information. *Psychological Review, 91,* 112–149.

Arkes, H. R., & Harkness, A. R. (1983). Estimates of contingency between two dichotomous variables. *Journal of Experimental Psychology: General, 112,* 117–135.

Baron, J. (1985). *Rationality and intelligence.* New York: Cambridge University Press.

Crocker, J. (1981). Judgment of covariation by social perceivers. *Psychological Bulletin, 90,* 272–292.

Deci, E. L. (1975). *Intrinsic motivation.* New York: Plenum.

Einhorn, H. J., & Hogarth, R. M. (1978). Confidence in judgment: Persistence of the illusion of validity. *Psychological Review, 85,* 395–416.

Ferster, C. B., & Skinner, B. F. (1957). *Schedules of reinforcement.* New York: Appleton-Century-Crofts.

Gilbreth, L. (1914). *The psychology of management.* New York: Sturgis and Walton.

Gould, S. J. (1987). *Time's arrow, time's cycle.* Cambridge: Harvard University Press.

Greene, D., Sternberg, B., & Lepper, M. R. (1976). Overjustification in a token economy. *Journal of Personality and Social Psychology, 34,* 1219–1234.

Hirsch, F. (1976). *Social limits to growth.* Cambridge: Harvard University Press.

Hobsbawm, E. J. (1964). *Labouring men.* London: Weidenfeld and Nicholson.

Jenkins, H. M., & Ward, W. C. (1965). Judgment of contingency between responses and outcomes. *Psychological Monographs, 79* (1, Whole No. 594).

Klayman, J., & Ha, Y. (1987). Confirmation, disconfirmation and information. *Psychological Review, 94,* 211–228.

Lacey, H. (1988). Realism and the value freedom of science. Unpublished manuscript.

Lacey, H., & Schwartz, B. (1986). Behaviorism, intentionality and sociohistorical structure. *Behaviorism, 14,* 193–210.

Lacey, H., & Schwartz, B. (1987). The explanatory power of radical behaviorism. In S. Modgil & C. Modgil (Eds.), *B. F. Skinner: Consensus and controversy* (pp. 165–176). New York: Falmer Press.

Lepper, M. R., & Greene, D. (Eds.) (1978). *The hidden costs of reward.* Hillsdale, NJ: Erlbaum.

Lepper, M. R., Greene, D., & Nisbett, R. E. (1973). Undermining childrens' intrinsic interest with extrinsic rewards: A test of the "overjustification" hypothesis. *Journal of Personality and Social Psychology, 28,* 129–137.

MacIntyre, A. (1981). *After virtue.* South Bend: University of Notre Dame Press.

Marglin, S. (1976). What do bosses do? In A. Gorz (Ed.), *The division of labour* (pp. 13–54). London: Harvester Press.

Marx, K. (1955). *The poverty of philosophy.* London: Lawrence and Wishart.

Nisbett, R., & Ross, L. (1980). *Human inference: Strategies and shortcomings of social judgment.* Englewood Cliffs, NJ: Prentice-Hall.

Platt, J. R. (1964). Strong inference. *Science, 146,* 347–353.

Polanyi, K. (1944). *The great transformation.* New York: Rinehart.

Rescorla, R. A. (1972). Informational variables in Pavlovian conditioning. In G. H. Bower (Ed.), *The psychology of learning and motivation* (Vol. 6, pp. 216–282). New York: Academic Press.

Schwartz, B. (1982). Reinforcement induced behavioral stereotypy: How not to teach people to discover rules. *Journal of Experimental Psychology: General, 111,* 23–59.

Schwartz, B. (1986). *The battle for human nature.* New York: W. W. Norton.

Schwartz, B. (1988). The experimental synthesis of behavior: Reinforcement, behavioral stereotypy, and problem solving. In G. H. Bower (Ed.), *The psychology of learning and motivation* (Vol. 22, pp. 93–135). New York: Academic Press.

Schwartz, B. (1989). *The psychology of learning and behavior.* New York: W. W. Norton.

Schwartz, B., & Lacey, H. (1982). *Behaviorism, science and human nature.* New York: W. W. Norton.

Schwartz, B., & Lacey, H. (1988). What applied studies of human operant conditioning tell us about humans and about operant conditioning. In G. Davey & C. Cullen (Eds.), *Human operant conditioning and behavior modification* (pp. 27–42). New York: Wiley.

Schwartz, B., Schuldenfrei, R., & Lacey, H. (1978). Operant psychology as factory psychology. *Behaviorism, 6,* 229–254.

Smith, A. (1753/1976). *The theory of moral sentiments.* Oxford: Clarendon Press.

Smith, A. (1776/1937). *The wealth of nations.* New York: Random House.

Taylor, F. W. (1911/1967). *Principles of scientific management.* New York: W. W. Norton.

Tweney, R. D., Doherty, M. E., & Mynatt, C. R., Eds. (1981). *On scientific thinking.* New York: Columbia University Press.

Wason, P. C. (1964). The effect of self-contradiction on fallacious reasoning. *Quarterly Journal of Experimental Psychology, 16,* 30–34.

Wason, P. C., & Johnson-Laird, P. N. (1972). *The psychology of reasoning.* Cambridge: Harvard University Press.

9

Value Elicitation: Is There Anything in There?

Baruch Fischhoff

Eliciting people's values is a central pursuit in many areas of the social sciences, including survey research, attitude research, economics, and behavior decision theory. These disciplines differ considerably in the core assumptions they make about the nature of the values that are available for elicitation. These assumptions lead to very different methodological concerns and interpretations, as well as to different risks of reading too much or too little into people's responses. The analysis here characterizes these assumptions and the research paradigms based on them. It also offers an account of how they arise, rooted in the psychological and sociological contexts within which different researchers function.

We begin with the following examples:

> Taken all together, how would you say things are these days—would you say that you are very happy, pretty happy, or not too happy?
>
> National Opinion Research Center (NORC), 1978

> Think about the last time during the past month that you were tired easily. Suppose that it had been possible to pay a sum of money to have eliminated being tired easily and immediately that one time. What sum of money would you have been willing to pay?
>
> Dickie, Gerking, McClelland, and Schulze (1987: 19)

> In this task, you will be asked to choose between a certain loss and a gamble that exposes you to some chance of loss. Specifically, you must choose either: Situation A. One chance in 4 to lose $200 (and 3 chances in 4 to lose nothing). OR Situation B. A certain loss of $50. Of course, you'd probably prefer not to be in either of these situations, but, if forced to either play the gamble (A) or accept the certain loss (B), which would you prefer to do?
> Fischhoff, Slovic, and Lichtenstein (1980: 127)

600 people are ill from a serious disease. Physicians face the following choice among treatments: Treatment A will save 200 lives. Treatment B has 1 chance in 3 to save all 600 lives and 2 chances in 3 to save 0 lives. Which treatment would you choose, A or B?

Tversky and Kahneman (1981: 454)

Problematic Preferences

A Continuum of Philosophies

A critical tenet for many students of other people's values is that "If we've got questions, then they've got answers." Perhaps the most ardent subscribers to this belief are experimental psychologists, survey researchers, and economists. Psychologists expect their "subjects" to behave reasonably with any clearly described task, even if it has been torturously contrived in order to probe esoteric theoretical points. Survey researchers expect their "participants" to provide meaningful answers to items on any topic intriguing them (or their clients), assuming that the questions have been put into good English. Economists expect "actors" to pursue their own best interests, thereby making choices that reveal their values, in whatever decisions the marketplace poses (and economists choose to study).

This article examines this *philosophy of articulated values* both in its own right and by positioning it on a continuum of philosophies toward value formation and measurement. At the other end of this continuum lies what might be called the *philosophy of basic values*. It holds that people lack well-differentiated values for all but the most familiar of evaluation questions, about which they have had the chance, by trial, error, and rumination, to settle on stable values. In other cases, they must derive specific valuations from some basic values through an inferential process.

Perhaps the clearest example of this latter perspective might be found in the work of decision analysts (Raiffa, 1968; von Winterfeldt & Edwards, 1986; Watson & Buede, 1988). These consultants lead their clients to decompose complex evaluation problems into basic dimensions of concern, called *attributes*. Each attribute represents a reason why one might like or dislike the possible outcomes of a decision. For example, the options facing someone in the market for a car are different vehicles (including, perhaps, none at all), whose attributes might include cost, style, and reliability.

The relative attractiveness (or unattractiveness) of different amounts of each attribute is then captured in a *utility function*, defined over the range of possible consequences (e.g., Just how much worse is breaking down once a month than breaking down twice a year?). After evaluating the attributes in isolation, the decision maker must consider their relative importance (e.g., Just how much money is it worth to reduce the frequency of repairs from annual to biennial?). These tradeoffs are expressed in a multiattribute utility function. Having done all of this, the consequences associated with specific actions are then evaluated by mapping them into the space spanned by that function.

Between the philosophies of articulated values and basic values, lie intermediate positions. These hold that although people need not have answers to all questions, neither need they start from scratch each time an evaluative question arises. Rather, people have stable values of moderate complexity, which provide an advanced starting point for responding to questions of real-world complexity. Where a particular version of this perspective falls on the continuum defined by the two extreme philosophies depends on how well developed these partial perspectives are held to be.

Each of these philosophies directs the student of values to different sets of focal methodological concerns. For example, if people can answer any question, then an obvious concern is that they answer the right one. As a result, investigators adhering to the articulated values philosophy will worry about posing the question most germane to their theoretical interests and ensuring that it is understood as intended. On the other hand, if complex evaluations are to be derived from simple evaluative principles, then it is essential that the relevant principles be assembled and that the inferential process be conducted successfully. That process could fail if it required too much of an intellectual effort and, also, if the question were poorly formulated or inadequately understood. If people have thought some about the topic of an evaluation question, then they have less far to go in order to produce a full answer. Yet, even if people hold such partial perspectives, there is still the risk that they will miss some nuances of the question and, as a result, overestimate how completely they have understood it and their values regarding the issues that it raises.

A Choice of Paradigms

The effort to deal with these different worries in a systematic fashion has led to distinct research paradigms (Kuhn, 1962). Each such paradigm offers a set of methods for dealing with its focal worries, along with empirical tests of success in doing so. Each has evolved some theory to substantiate its approach. As paradigms, each is better suited to answering problems within its frame of reference than to challenging that frame. Thus, for example, the articulated values paradigm is better at devising additional ways to improve the understanding of questions than at determining whether understanding is possible.

This is, of course, something of a caricature. Many investigators are capable of wearing more than one hat. For example, survey researchers have extensively studied the properties of the *don't know* response (Smith, 1984). Still, when one is trying to get a survey (or experiment or economic analysis) out the door, it is hard to address these issues at length for every question. It may be easier to take *no answer* for an answer in principle than in practice. At the other extreme, it may be unprofitable for a consulting decision analyst to deal with situations in which the answer to a complex evaluation question is there for the asking, without the rigamarole of multiattribute utility elicitation.

To the extent that studies are conducted primarily within a single paradigm, it becomes critical to choose the right one. Table 1 summarizes the costs of various mismatches between the assumed and actual states of people's values. Above the diagonal are cases in which more is expected of people than they are prepared to give. The risk here is misplaced precision, reading too much into poorly articulated responses and missing the opportunity to help people clarify their thinking. Below the diagonal are cases in which too little is expected of people. The risk here is misplaced imprecision, needlessly complicating the task and casting doubt on already clear thinking.

The choice of a paradigm ought to be driven by the perceived costs and likelihoods of these different mismatches. Thus, one might not hire a survey researcher to study how acutely ill individuals evaluate alternative medical procedures, nor might one hire a philosopher to lead consumers through the intricacies of evaluating alternative dentifrices. Evaluation professionals should, in turn, devote themselves to the problems most suited to their methods.

Yet, it is in the nature of paradigms that they provide clearer indications of relative than of absolute success. That is, they show which applications of the set of accepted methods work better, rather than whether the set as a whole is up to the job. After describing these paradigms in somewhat greater detail, I will consider some of the specific processes by which work within them can create an exaggerated feeling for the breadth of their applicability.

As a device for doing so, I will highlight how each paradigm might interpret several sets of potentially puzzling results, namely those produced by the studies posing the four evaluation questions opening this article. In each case, two apparently equivalent ways of formulating the question produced rather different evaluations. Assuming that the stud-

Table 1. Risk of Misdiagnosis[a]

Assumption made	Proper assumption		
	Articulated values	Partial perspectives	Basic values
Articulated values	—	Get incomplete values Inadvertently impose perspective	Get meaningless values Impose single perspective
Partial perspectives	Promote new perspectives Distract from sharpening	—	Impose multiple perspectives Exaggerate resolvability
Basic values	Shake confidence Distract from sharpening	Discourage Distract from reconciliation	—

[a]Above diagonal: misplaced precision, undue confidence in results, missed opportunity to help. Below diagonal: needless complication, neglect of basic methodology; induced confusion.

ies were competently conducted, an articulated values perspective would hold that if the answers are different, then so must the questions have been. Any inconsistency is in the eye of the beholder, rather than in the answers of the respondents.

A basic values philosophy leads to quite a different interpretation: If their responses are buffetted by superficial changes in question formulation, then people must not know what they want. As a result, none of the evaluations should be taken seriously. At best, they reflect a gut level response to some very general issue. According to the intermediate, partial perspectives philosophy, each answer says something about respondents. However, neither should be taken as fully representing their values.

A Sample of Problems

Happiness. Surveys sometimes include questions asking respondents to evaluate the overall state of their affairs. Answers to these questions might be used, for example, as barometers of public morale or as predictors of responses on other items (i.e., for statistical analyses removing individual mood as a covariate). In reviewing archival data, Turner and Krauss (1978) discovered the apparent inconsistency revealed in Figure 1. Two respected survey organizations, asking virtually identical happiness questions, produced substantially different proportions of respondents evaluating their situation as making them *very happy*. If the temptation of naive extrapolation is indulged, then quite different societies seem to be emerging from the two surveys (happinesswise, at least).[1]

After a series of analyses carefully examining alternative hypotheses, Turner and Krauss (1978) concluded that the most likely source of the response pattern in Figure 1 was differences in the items preceding the happiness question. In the NORC survey, these items concerned family life; in the Survey Research Center (SRC) survey (Campbell, Converse, & Rodgers, 1976), they were items unrelated to that aspect of personal status.[2]

If respondents have fully articulated values, then different answers imply different questions. Inadvertently, the two surveys have created somewhat different happiness questions. Perhaps Happiness$_1$ (from the NORC survey) emphasizes the role of family life, whereas Happiness$_2$ (from the SRC survey) gives respondents more freedom in weighting the different facets of their lives.

---

[1] The two questions did differ slightly in their introductory phrase. One began "taken all together," the other "taking all things together." Only the bravest of theoretician would try to trace the pattern in Figure 1 to this difference.

[2] Subsequent research (Turner, 1984; Turner & Martin, 1984) has shown a somewhat more complicated set of affairs—which may have changed further by the time this chapter is printed and read. Incorporating the most recent twists in this research would change the details but not the thrust of the discussion in the text.

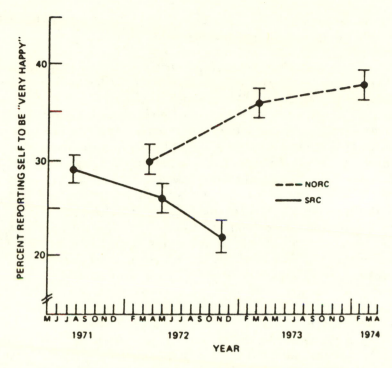

Figure 1. Trends in self-reported happiness, 1971–1973.

Note. Estimates are derived from sample surveys of noninstitutionalized population of the continental United States, aged 18 and over. Error bars demark ±1 standard error around sample estimate. NORC, National Opinion Research Center; SRC, Survey Research Center. Questions were "Taken all together, how would you say things are these days—would you say that you are very happy, pretty happy, or not too happy?" (NORC); and "Taking all things together, how would you say things are these days—would you say you're very happy, pretty happy, or not too happy these days?" (SRC). From "Why Do Surveys Disagree? Some Preliminary Hypotheses and Some Disagreeable Examples" (p. 166) by C. F. Turner, 1984, in C. F. Turner and E. Martin, *Surveying subjective phenomena*, New York: Russell Sage Foundation. Copyright 1984 by the Russell Sage Foundation. Reprinted by permission.

From the opposing perspective, the same data tell quite a different story. If a few marginally related questions can have so great an impact, then how meaningful can the happiness question (and the responses to it) be? Conceivably, it is possible to take all things together and assess the happiness associated with them. However, as long as assessments depend on the mood induced by immediately preceding questions, that goal has yet to be achieved.

According to the partial perspectives philosophy, the two responses might be stable. However, neither should be interpreted as a thoughtful expression of respondents' happiness. Achieving that would require helping respondents generate and evaluate alternative perspectives on the problem, not just the one perspective that happens to have been presented to them.

Headache.   According to Executive Order 12291 (Bentkover, Covello, & Mumpower, 1985), cost–benefit analyses must be conducted for all significant federal actions. Where those actions affect the environment, that often requires putting price tags on goods not customarily traded in any marketplace. For regulations governing ozone levels, one such good is a change in the rate of subclinical health effects, such as headaches and shortness of breath. In order to monetize these consequences, resource economists have conducted surveys asking questions like the second example in the set of quotations at the beginning of this article (Cummings, Brookshire, & Schulze, 1986; Smith & Desvousges, 1988).

In Dickie et al.'s (1987) survey, people who reported having experienced being tired easily estimated that they would be willing to pay $17, on average, to eliminate their last day of feeling tired easily. Later in the same survey, the interviewer computed the overall monthly cost of eliminating each respondent's three most serious ozone-related health effects. This was done by multiplying how much people reported being willing to pay to eliminate the last occurrence of each effect by the number of reported episodes per month, then summing those products across symptoms. Respondents were then asked, "On a monthly basis is [_] what you would be willing to pay to eliminate these three symptoms?" (p. 20, Appendix 1). If respondents recanted, they were then asked what monthly dollar amount they would pay for the package. The markedly reduced dollar amount that most subjects provided was then prorated over the individual health effects. By this computation, respondents were now willing to pay about $2 to eliminate a day of being tired easily.

From a regulatory perspective, these strikingly different estimates indicate markedly different economic benefits from reducing ozone levels. [Indeed, the Office of Management and Budget (A. Carlin, personal communication, 1987) has seriously criticized the Dickie et al., 1987, study as a basis for revising regulations under the Clean Air Act.] From an articulated values perspective, they imply that the two questions must actually be different in some fundamental ways. For example, people might be willing to pay much more for a one-time special treatment of their last headache than for each routine treatment. From a basic values perspective, these results indicate that people know that symptomatic relief is worth something, but have little idea how much (even after an hour of talking about health effects). As a result, respondents are knocked about by ephemeral aspects of the survey, such as the highly unusual challenge to their values embodied by the request to reconsider. The investigators in this study seem to have adopted a partial perspectives philosophy. They treat respondents' values seriously, but not seriously enough to believe that respondents have gotten it right the first time. Rather, respondents need the help provided by showing them the overall implications of their initial estimates (Furby & Fischhoff, 1989).

Gamble. In samples of people shown the third example (Fischhoff et al., 1980), most people have preferred the gamble to the sure loss. However, they reverse this preference when the sure loss is described as an insurance premium, protecting them against the potentially greater loss associated with the gamble (Fischhoff et al., 1980; Hershey & Schoemaker, 1980). This difference is sufficiently powerful that it can often be evoked within subject, in successively presented problems.

From an articulated values perspective, the appearance of equivalence in these two versions of the problem must be illusory. Observers who see inconsistency in these responses must simply have failed to realize the differences. Perhaps, as a matter of principle, people refuse both to accept sure losses and to decline insurance against downside risks. In that case, these seemingly superficial differences in description evoke meaningful differences in how people judge themselves and one another. People want both to preserve a fighting chance and to show due caution. How they would respond to a real-world analog of this problem would depend on how it was presented.[3]

From a basic values perspective, these results show that people know that they dislike losing money, but that is about it. They cannot make the sort of precise tradeoffs depicted in such analytical problems. As a result, they cling to superficial cues as ways to get through the task.

In this case, some subsidiary evidence seemingly supports the intermediate perspective. When both versions are presented to the same person, there is an asymmetrical transfer effect (Poulton, 1968, 1989). Specifically, there are fewer reversals of preference when the insurance version comes first than when it comes second. This suggests that viewing the sure loss as an insurance premium is a relevant perspective, but not one that is immediately available. By contrast, respondents do realize, at some level, that premiums are sure losses. Studies of insurance behavior show, in fact, some reluctance to accept that perspective. For example, people prefer policies with low deductibles, even though they are financially unattractive. Apparently, people like the higher probability of getting some reimbursement, so that their premium does not have to be viewed as a sure loss (Kunreuther et al., 1978).

Disease. About two-thirds of the subjects responding to the fourth problem (Tversky & Kahneman, 1981) have been found to prefer Treatment A, with its sure saving of 200 lives. On the other hand, about the

---

[3] Thus, these results would lead one to expect lower renewal rates on insurance policies were subscribers to receive periodic bills for sure losses, rather than for premiums.

same portion prefer the second treatment when the two alternatives are described in terms of the number of lives that will be lost. In this version, Treatment A now provides a sure loss of 400 lives, whereas Treatment B gives a chance of no lives lost at all.

Applying the alternative philosophies to interpreting these results is straightforward. One difference in this case is that there is not only some independent evidence but also some theory to direct such interpretations. The discrepancies associated with the three previous problems were discovered, more or less fortuitously, by comparing responses to questions that happened to have been posed in slightly different ways. In this case, the discrepancies were generated deliberately. Kahneman and Tversky (1979) produced the alternative wordings as demonstrations of their *prospect theory*, which predicts systematic differences in choices as a function of how options are described, or *framed*. The shift from gains (i.e., lives saved) to losses is one such framing difference.

Prospect theory embodies a partial perspectives philosophy. It views these differing preferences as representing stable derivations of intermediate complexity from a set of basic human values identified by the theory. The sources of these differences seem ephemeral, however, in the sense that people would be uncomfortable living with them. Adopting an articulated values philosophy here would require arguing that people regard the different frames as meaningfully different questions— and would continue to do so even after thoughtful reflection.

In the absence of a theoretical account (such as prospect theory) or converging evidence (such as the asymmetrical transfer effect with the sure-loss—premium questions), one's accounting of seemingly inconsistent preferences becomes a matter of opinion. Those opinions might reflect both the particulars of individual problems and the general orientation of a paradigm. The next section describes these paradigms. The following section considers how they could sustain such different views on the general state of human values.

The Paradigms

However the notion of *paradigm* is conceptualized (Lakatos & Musgrave, 1970), it is likely to involve (1) a focal set of methodological worries, (2) a corresponding set of accepted treatments, (3) a theoretical basis for justifying these treatments and directing their application, and (4) criteria for determining whether problems have been satisfactorily addressed. Table 2 characterizes the three paradigms in these terms. This section elaborates on some representative entries in that table.

Table 2. Three Paradigms for Eliciting Values

Worry	Treatment	Theoretical base	Test of success
Assumption: People know what they want about all possible questions (to some degree of precision)			
Inappropriate default assumptions (for unstated part of question)	Examine interpretation, specify more, manipulate expectations	Nonverbal communication, experimenter–interviewer effects, psycholinguistics	Full specification, empathy with subjects
Inappropriate interpretation of stated question	Use good English, consensual terms	Survey technique, linguistics	Sensible answers, consensual interpretation of terms
Difficulty in expressing values	Choose correct response mode	Psychometrics, measurement theory	Consistency (reliability of representation)
Strategic response	Proper incentives, neutral context	Microeconomics, demand characteristics	Sensible answers, nonresponse to "irrelevant" changes
Assumption: People have stable but incoherent perspectives, causing divergent responses to formally equivalent forms			
Deep consistency in methods across studies (failing to reveal problem)	"Looking for trouble": multiple methods in different studies; "asking for trouble": open-ended questions	Framing theory, new psychophysics, multiple disciplines, anthropology	Nonresponse to irrelevant changes
Eliciting values incompletely (within study)	Multiple methods within study, open ended	Same as above, counseling skills	Inability to elicit more
Inability to reconcile perspectives	Talking through implications	Normative analysis, counseling skills	Unpressured consistent response to new perspectives
Assumption: People lack articulated values on specific topic (but have pertinent basic values)			
Pressure to respond	Measure intensity, allow no response, alternative modes of expression	Survey research, social psychology	Satisfaction, stability among remainder
Instability over time	Accelerate experience	Attitude formation, behavioral decision theory	Stable convergence
Inability to relate	Client-centered process	Normative (re)analysis	Full characterization
Undetected insensitivity	Ask formally different questions	Normative analysis	Proper sensitivity

Philosophy of Articulated Values

Investigators working within this paradigm have enormous respect for people's ability to articulate and express values on the most diverse topics. Indeed, so great is this respect that investigators' worrying often focuses on ensuring that evaluative questions are formulated and understood exactly as intended. Any slip could evoke a precise, thoughtful answer to the wrong question (Fischhoff & Furby, 1988; Mitchell & Carson, 1989; Sudman & Bradburn, 1982).

A hard-won lesson in this struggle involves recognizing the powerful influence that social pressures can exert on respondents (DeMaio, 1984). As a result, investigators take great pains to insulate the question–answerer relationship from any extraneous influences, lest those become part of the question. To prevent such complications, interviewers and experimenters stick to tight scripts, which they try to administer impassively in settings protected from prying eyes and ears. Lacking the opportunity to impose such control, economists must argue that marketplace transactions fortuitously have these desirable properties, in order to justify interpreting purchase decisions as reflecting just the value of the good and not the influences, say, of advertising or peer pressure.

At first blush, this protectiveness might seem somewhat paradoxical. After all, if people have such well-articulated preferences, why do they need to be shielded so completely from stray influences? The answer is that the investigator cannot tell just which stray influence will trigger one of those preferences. Indeed, the more deeply rooted are individuals' values, the more sensitive they should be to the nuances of how an evaluation problem is posed.

For example, it is considered bad form if the demeanor of an interviewer (or the wording of a question) suggests what the investigator expects (or wants) to hear. Respondents might move in that direction (or the opposite) because they aim to please (or to frustrate). Or, they might be unmoved by such a hint because they are indifferent to the information or social pressure that it conveys. Because a hint becomes part of the evaluation question, its influence is confounded with that of the issues that interested the investigator in the first place.

Unfortunately, the logical consistency of this position can border on tautology, inferring that a change is significant from respondents' sensitivity to it and inferring that respondents have articulated values from their responses to changes in questions now known to be significant. Conversely, responding the same way to two versions of a task means that the differences between them are not irrelevant and that people know their own minds well enough not to be swayed by meaningless variations.

The potential circularity of such claims can be disrupted either by data or by argument. At the one extreme, investigators can demonstrate empirically that people have well-founded beliefs on the specific questions that they receive. At the other extreme, they can offer theoretical reasons why such beliefs ought to be in place (bolstered, perhaps, by empirical demonstrations in other investigations). Developing these data and arguments in their general form has helped to stimulate basic research into nonverbal communication, interviewer effects, and even the psycholinguistics of question interpretations (e.g., Jabine, Straf, Tanur, & Tourangeau, 1984; Rosenthal & Rosnow, 1969; Turner & Martin, 1984).

Within this paradigm, the test of success is getting the question specified exactly the way that one wants and verifying that it has been so understood. A vital service that professional survey houses offer is being able to render the questions of diverse clients into good English using consensual terms. This very diversity, however, ensures that there cannot be specific theory and data for every question that they ask. As a result, the test of success is often an intuitive appeal to how sensible answers seem to be. The risks of circularity here, too, are obvious.[4]

Assuming that respondents have understood the question, they still need to be able to express their (ready) answer in terms acceptable to the investigator. The great edifice of psychometric theory has evolved to manage potential problems here by providing elicitation methods compatible with respondents' thought processes and investigators' needs (Coombs, 1964; Nunnally, 1968). The associated tests of success are, in part, external—the ability to predict responses to other tasks—and, in part, internal—the consistency of responses to related stimuli. The risk in the former case is that the theoretical tie between measures is flawed. The risk in the latter case is that respondents have found some internally consistent way to respond to questions asked within a common format and varying in obvious ways (Poulton, 1989).

Perhaps surprisingly, the main concern of early contingent valuation investigators was not that respondents would have difficulty expressing their values in dollar terms. On the contrary, they feared that subjects would be able to use the response mode all too well. Knowing just what they want (and how to get it), subjects might engage in strategic behavior, misrepresenting their values in order to shift to others the burden of paying for goods that they value (Samuelson, 1954). In response, investigators developed sophisticated tasks and statistical analyses. Applica-

[4] One is reminded of the finding that undetected computational errors tend to favor investigators' hypotheses. A nonmotivational explanation of this trend is that one is more likely to double-check all aspects of procedure, including calculations, when results are surprising (Rosenthal & Rosnow, 1969).

tions of these methods seem to have allayed the fears of many practitioners (Brookshire, Ives, & Schulze, 1976).[5]

Philosophy of Basic Values

From the perspective of the philosophy of basic values, people's time is very limited, whereas the set of possible evaluative questions is very, very large. As a result, people cannot be expected to have articulated opinions on more than a small set of issues of immediate concern. Indeed, some theorists have argued that one way to control people is by forcing them to consider an impossibly diverse range of issues (e.g., through the nightly news). People who think that they can have some opinion on every issue find that they do not have thoughtful opinions on any issue (Ellul, 1963). The only way to have informed opinions on complex issues is by deriving them carefully from deeply held values on more general and fundamental issues (Rokeach, 1973).

Taking the headache question as an example, a meaningful answer is much more plausible from someone who has invested time and money in seeking symptomatic relief, which can serve as a firm point of reference for evaluating that special treatment. [Economists sometimes call these *averting behaviors* (Dickie et al., 1987).] Otherwise, the question seems patently unanswerable—and the wild discrepancies found in the research provide clear evidence of respondents' grasping at straws.

From the perspective of this paradigm, the existence of such documented discrepancies means that not all responses can be taken seriously. As a result, investigators adhering to it worry about any aspects of their methodology that might pressure respondents to produce unthoughtful evaluations. In this regard, an inherent difficulty with most surveys and experiments is that there is little cost for misrepresenting one's values, including pretending that one has them. By contrast, offering no response may seem like an admission of incompetence. Why would a question have been posed if the (prestigious?) individuals who created it did not believe that one ought to have an answer? With surveys, silence may carry the additional burden of disenfranchising oneself by not contributing a vote to public opinion. With psychological experiments, it may be awkward to get out, or to get payment, until one has responded in a way that is acceptable to the experimenter.

One indication of the level of perfunctory responses in surveys may be seen in the repeated finding (Schuman & Presser, 1981) that explicitly

---

[5] The processes by which these fears were allayed might be usefully compared with the processes by which psychology convinced itself that it knew how to manage the effects of experimenter expectations (Rosenthal, 1967).

offering a *don't know* option greatly increases the likelihood of subjects offering no opinion (e.g., from 5 to 25%). Yet, even that option is a rather crude measure. Respondents must determine how intense a degree of ignorance or indifference *don't know* implies (e.g., Does it mean absolutely, positively having no idea?). Investigators must, then, guess at how respondents have interpreted the option.

Hoping to say something more about the intensity of reported beliefs, survey researchers have conducted a lively debate over alternative statistical analyses of seemingly inconsistent attitudes (e.g., Achen, 1975; Converse, 1964). Its resolution is complicated by the difficulty of simultaneously evaluating questions and answers (Schuman & Presser, 1981; Smith, 1984). For example, one potential measure of value articulation is the stability of responses over time. When people say different things at different times, they might just be responding randomly. However, they might also have changed their underlying beliefs or settled on different interpretations of poorly worded questions. Changes in underlying opinions may themselves reflect exogenous changes in the issues addressed by the question (e.g., "My headaches are worse now than the last time I was asked") or endogenous changes in one's thinking (e.g., "I finally came to realize that it's crazy to be squirreling money away in the bank rather than using it to make myself less miserable").

A striking aspect of many contingent valuation studies is the high rate of refusals to provide acceptable responses among individuals who have already agreed to participate in the study (Cummings et al., 1986; Mitchell & Carson, 1989; Tolley et al., 1986). These protest responses take several forms: simply refusing to answer the evaluation question, offering to pay $0 for a good that one has admitted to be worth something, and offering to pay what seems to be an unreasonably high amount (e.g., more than 10% of disposable income for relieving a headache). For investigators under contract to monetize environmental goods, these responses are quite troublesome.[6] For investigators who have the leisure to entertain alternative perspectives, these responses provide some insight into how respondents having only basic values cope with pressure to produce more. It is perhaps a testimony to the coerciveness of interview situations how rarely participants say *don't know*, much less try to bolt (as they have in these contingent valuation studies).

The term *protest response* implies hostility toward the investigator. Some of that emotion may constitute displaced frustration with one's own lack of articulated values. The investigator's "crime" is forcing one to confront not knowing exactly what an important good is worth. Per-

[6] In actual studies, investigators sometimes just throw out protest responses. At times, they adjust them to more reasonable values (e.g., reducing high values to 10% of disposable income).

haps a more legitimate complaint is that investigators force that confrontation without providing any help in its resolution.

As mentioned, investigators within the articulated values paradigm provide no help as a matter of principle. Elicited values are intended to be entirely those of the respondent, without any hint from the questioner. This stance might also be appropriate to investigators in the basic values paradigm in cases in which they want to know what is in there to begin with when an issue is first raised. However, basic values investigators might also be interested in prompting the inferential process of deriving specific values from general ones. That might be done nondirectively by leaving respondents to their own devices after posing an evaluative question and promising to come back later for an answer. In the interim, respondents can do whatever they usually do, such as ruminate, ask friends, listen to music, review Scripture, or experiment. Such surveys might be thought of as accelerating natural experiences, guided by descriptive research into how people do converge on values in their everyday life.

Alternatively, investigators can adopt a multiply directive approach. They can suggest alternative positions, helping respondents to think through how those positions might or might not be consistent with their basic values. Doing so requires a normative analysis of alternative positions that might merit adoption. That might require adding professions like economics or philosophy to the research team. Surveys that present multiple perspectives are, in effect, respondent centered, more akin to decision analysis than to traditional question-centered social research, with its impassive interviewers bouncing stimuli off objectified respondents. Studies that propose alternative perspectives incur a greater risk of sins of commission, in the sense of inadvertently pushing subjects in one of the suggested directions, and a reduced risk of sins of omission, in the sense of letting respondents mislead themselves by incompletely understanding the implications of the questions that they answer.

As shown in the discussion of the questions opening this article, a clear hint that people have only basic values to offer is when they show undue sensitivity to changes in irrelevant features of a question. It can also be suggested by undue *in*sensitivity to relevant features. Figure 2 shows the proportion of women who reported that they expect no additional births, either in all future years (left side) or in the next 5 years (right side).[7] In each panel, there was considerable agreement between responses elicited by two respected survey houses. So, here is a case in which all of the irrelevant differences in procedures (e.g., interviewers,

---

[7] This is a question of prediction, rather than of evaluation, except in the sense that intentions to have children reflect the perceived value of having them.

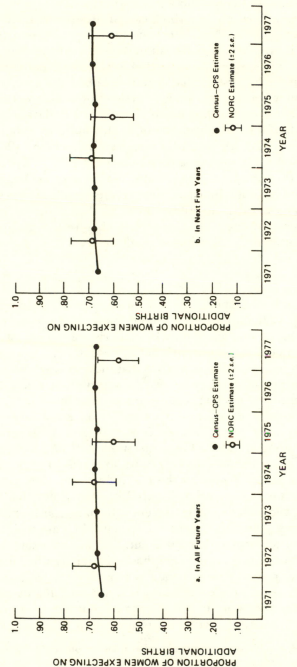

Figure 2. Estimates of fertility expectations of American women: proportion of women expecting no further children in (a) all future years, and (b) the next 5 years. Samples included only married women aged 18–39; sample sizes in each year were approximately 4,000 (Census-CPS) and 220 (NORC). CPS, Current Population Survey; NORC, National Opinion Research Center. From "Why Do Surveys Disagree? Some Preliminary Hypotheses and Some Disagreeable Examples" (p. 192) by C. F. Turner, 1984, in C. F. Turner and E. Martin, *Surveying subjective phenomena*, New York: Russell Sage Foundation. Copyright 1984 by the Russell Sage Foundation. Reprinted by permission.

sampling, preceding questions) had no aggregate effect on responses. Across panels, however, there is a disturbing lack of difference. If there are women who intend to give birth after the next 5 years, then the curves should be lower in the left panel than in the right one. Although the investigators took care to specify time period, respondents either did not notice or could not make use of that critical detail.

An analogous result in contingent valuation research was Tolley et al.'s (1986) finding that people were willing to pay as much for 10 days worth as for 180 days worth of a fixed improvement in atmospheric visibility. Even more dramatic is Kahneman and Knetsch's (Kahneman, 1986) finding that respondents to a phone survey were willing to pay equal amounts to preserve the fisheries in one Ontario lake, in several Ontario lakes, and in all of the lakes in Ontario. These results could, of course, reflect articulated values based on utility functions that flattened out abruptly after 10 days and one lake. More likely, they reflect a vague willingness to pay a little money for a little good.

Philosophy of Partial Perspectives

By adopting an intermediate position, individuals working within the partial perspectives paradigm must worry about the problems concerning both extremes. On the one hand, they face the risk of inadequately formulated and understood questions, preventing respondents from accessing those partially articulated perspectives that they do have. On the other hand, investigators must worry about reading too much into expressions of value produced under pressure to say something.

These worries may, however, take on a somewhat different face. In particular, the existence of partial perspectives may give a deceptive robustness to expressions of value. Thus, investigators using a single method may routinely elicit similar responses without realizing the extent to which their success depends on the method's ability to evoke a common perspective. That fact may be obscured further when a family of related methods produces similar consistency. It takes considerable self-reflection for investigators to discern the structural communalities in methods that seem to them rather different. Speculative examples might include a tendency for surveys to emphasize hedonic rather than social values by asking respondents for their personal opinions, or for experimental gambles to encourage risk taking because participants cannot leave with less than they went in with,[8] or to discourage emotional involvement because the scientific setting seems to call for a particularly

[8] The need to protect human subjects poses this constraint. Even without it, there would be problems getting people to risk their own money in a gamble contrived by some, possibly mistrusted, scientist.

calculating approach. Discovering the perspectives that it inadvertently imposes on itself is part of the continuing renewal process for any scientific discipline. In the social sciences, these perspectives may also be imposed on the people being studied, whose unruly behavior may, in turn, serve as a clue to disciplinary blinders (e.g., Furby, 1986; Gergen, 1973; Gilligan, 1982; Wagenaar, 1989).

Research methods may create consistent response sets, as well as evoke existing ones (Tune, 1964). When asked a series of obviously related questions on a common topic, respondents may devise a response strategy to cope with the experiment. The resulting responses may be consistent with one another, but not with responses in other settings. Indeed, those investigations most concerned about testing for consistency may also be the most vulnerable to generating what they are seeking. Think, for example, of an experiment eliciting evaluations for stimuli representing all cells of a factorial design in which each factor is a different outcome attribute. Why not come up with some simple rule for getting through the task?

For example, Poulton (1968, 1989) has conducted detailed secondary analyses of the quantitative estimates elicited in psychophysics experiments in an effort to capture the subjective intensity of physical stimuli (e.g., sweetness, loudness). He argued that the remarkable internal consistency of estimates across stimulus dimensions (Stevens, 1975) reflects the stability of investigators' conventions in setting up the details of their experiments. Although subjects have no fixed orientation to such unfamiliar forms of evaluation, they do respond similarly to structuring cues such as the kind of numbers to be used (e.g., integers vs. decimals) and the place of the standard stimulus in the range of possibilities.[9] The (nontrivial) antidotes are what might be called *looking for trouble* and *asking for trouble*—eliciting values in significantly different ways and using sufficiently open-ended methods to allow latent incoherence to emerge.

Economists hope to reduce these problems by discerning people's values from the preferences revealed in market behavior. Such actions ought to be relatively free of pressures to respond. After all, you don't have to buy. Or do you? Even if choices are voluntary, they can only be made between options that are on offer and with whatever information respondents happen to have. For example, you may hate ranch style homes but have little choice other than to choose one that makes the best of a bad situation in some locales. In that case, the preferences thereby

[9] Many contingent valuation studies have elicited values by asking subjects questions such as "Would you pay $1, $2, $3, . . . ?" until they say no. One might compare the implicit structuring of this series of questions with that achieved by "Would you pay $10, $20, $30, . . . ?" or by moving down from $100 in $1 increments.

revealed are highly conditional. Furthermore, even if the choice sets are relatively open and well understood, they may be presented in ways that evoke only a limited subset of people's values. By some accounts, evoking partial perspectives is the main mission of advertising (by other accounts, it is just to provide information). Some critics have argued that some perspectives (e.g., the value of possessing material goods) are emphasized so effectively that they change from being imposed perspectives to becoming endorsed ones.[10]

If one wants to predict how people will behave in situations presenting a particular perspective, then one should elicit their values in ways evoking that perspective.[11] If one wants to get at all their potentially relevant perspectives, then more diverse probing is needed. This is the work of many counselors and consultants. Although some try to construct their clients' subjective problem representation from basic values (along the lines of decision analysis), others try to match clients with general diagnostic categories. Each category then carries prognoses and recommendations. As mentioned, the counselor stance is unusual in social research. Like any direct interaction, it carries the risk of suggesting and imposing the counselor's favored perspective. Presumably, there is a limit to how quickly people can absorb new outlooks. At some point, they may lose cognitive control of the issue, wondering perhaps, "Whose problem is it, anyway?"

How Could They Think This Way?

Described in its own right, any paradigm sounds like something of a caricature. Could proponents really believe that one size fits all when it comes to methodology? Surely, decision analysts realize that some values are already so well articulated that their decomposition procedures will only induce confusion. Surely, survey researchers realize that some value issues are so important and so unfamiliar in their details that respondents will be unable to resist giving uninformed answers to poorly understood questions. Surely they do. Yet, equally surely, there is strong temptation to stretch the envelope of applications for one's favored tools.

Some reasons for exaggerating the applicability of one's own discipline are common to all disciplines. Anyone can exaggerate the extent to which they are ready for a challenge. Each discipline has an intact cri-

[10] This is just the tip of the iceberg regarding the methodological difficulties of inferring values from observed market behavior (Campen, 1986; Fischhoff & Cox, 1985; Peterson, Driver, & Gregory, 1988). In many cases, technical difficulties make inferring values from behavior an engaging fiction.
[11] Fischhoff (1983) considered some of the difficulties of predicting which frames are evoked by naturally occurring situations.

tique of its competitors. People who ask questions know what they mean and also know how they would answer. What might be called anthropology's great truth is that we underestimate how and by how much others see the world differently than we do. Paradigms train one to soldier on and solve problems, rather than to reflect on the whole enterprise.

The inconsistent responses opening this article present an interesting challenge for that soldiering. As shown in the discussion of those results, each paradigm has a way to accommodate them. Yet, investigators in the basic values paradigm seem much more comfortable with such accommodation. They seem more ready to accept them as real (i.e., produced from sound, replicable studies) and much more ready to see them as common. Basic values investigators sometimes seem to revel in such discrepancies (e.g., Hogarth, 1982; Nisbett & Ross, 1980), whereas articulated values investigators seem to view them as bona fide, but still sporadic, problems (e.g., Schuman & Presser, 1981).[12] Insight into these discrepant views about discrepancies can be gained by examining the institutional and methodological practices of these paradigms.

Interest in Discrepancies

Basic values investigators would like to believe that there are many robust discrepancies "out there in the world" because they serve a vital propose for this kind of science. Discovering a peculiar pattern of unexpected results has been the starting point for many theories (Kahneman & Tversky, 1982). McGuire (1969) has gone so far as to describe the history of experimental psychology as the history of turning artifacts into main effects. For example, increased awareness of experimenter effects (Rosenthal, 1967) stimulated studies of nonverbal communication (e.g., Ekman, 1985). In fact, some critics have argued that psychology is so much driven by anomalies that it tends to exaggerate their importance and generality (Berkeley & Humphreys, 1982). Anomalies make such a good story that it is hard to keep them in focus, relative to the sometimes unquirky processes that produce them (Fischhoff, 1988).

Interest in Order

On the other hand, articulated values investigators are more interested in *what* people think than in *how* they think. For these purposes, all

---

[12] This observation was sharply drawn by Professor Robert Abelson at a meeting of the National Research Council Panel on Survey Measure of Subjective Phenomena (Turner & Martin, 1981). This section of the chapter is, in large part, an attempt to work up the pattern that he highlighted.

these quirks are a major headache. They mean that every question may require a substantial development effort before it can be asked responsibly, with elaborate pretesting of alternative presentations. The possibility of anomalies also raises the risk that respondents cannot answer the questions that interest the investigators—at least without the sort of interactive or directive elicitation that is an anathema within this paradigm.

Of course, investigators in this paradigm are concerned about these issues. Some of the most careful studies of artifacts have come from survey researchers (e.g., Schuman & Presser, 1981). Classic examples of the effort needed to tie down the subjective interpretation of even seemingly simple questions may be found in the U.S. Department of Commerce studies of how to ask about employment status (Bailar & Rothwell, 1984). However, every research program with resource constraints is limited in its ability to pursue methodological nuances. When those nuances could represent fatal problems, then it is natural to want to believe that they are rare.

For survey research houses, these constraints are magnified by the commercial pressures to keep the shop open and running at a reasonable price. To some extent, clients go to quality and will pay for it. However, there is a limit to the methodological skepticism that even sophisticated clients will tolerate. They need assurance that investigators have the general skill needed to create workable items out of their questions. Clients might know, at some level, that "different questions might have produced different answers" (according to the strange wording that quality newspapers sometimes append to survey results). However, they still need some fiction of tractability.

Ability to Experiment

A further constraint on articulated values scientists is their theoretical commitment to representative sampling. The expense of such samples means that very few tests of alternative wording can be conducted. Conversely, it means that many discrepancies (like the happiness questions) are only discovered in secondary analyses of studies conducted for other purposes. As a result, there are typically confounding differences in method that blur the comparison between questions.

By contrast, basic values scientists are typically willing to work with convenience samples of subjects. As a result, they can run many tightly controlled experiments, increasing their chances of finding discrepancies. Multiple testing also increases the chances of finding differences by chance. If they are conscientious, these scientists should be able to deal with this risk through replications (which are, in turn, relatively easy to conduct). This indifference to sampling might reflect a self-serving and cavalier attitude. On the other hand, it may be the case that *how* people think might be relatively invariant with respect to demographic features that are known to make a big difference in *what* they think.

Precision of Search

The theories that basic values scientists derive to account for discrepancies are not always correct. When they are, however, they allow investigators to produce inconsistent responses almost at will. Much of experimental psychology is directed at determining the precise operation of known effects. For example, at the core of prospect theory is a set of framing operations designed to produce inconsistencies. The prevalence of phenomena under laboratory conditions has, of course, no necessary relationship to their prevalence elsewhere. Some extrapolation of prevalence rates from the lab to the world would, however, be only natural (Tversky & Kahneman, 1973). Furthermore, continuing absorption with a phenomenon should sharpen one's eagerness and ability to spot examples. Investigators who want and expect to see a phenomenon are likely to find it more often than investigators who do not. It would be only natural if the confirmation offered by such anecdotal evidence were overestimated (Chapman & Chapman, 1969).

The theoretical tools for seeking nuisance effects in an articulated values study would likely be more poorly defined. For example, the question might be posed as generally as "How common are order effects?" Given the enormous diversity of questions whose order might be reversed, the answer is, doubtless, "very low" in the domain of all possible questions. However, with questions of related content, order effects might be much more common (Poulton & Freeman, 1966). Moreover, questions are more likely to appear in surveys with somewhat related ones, rather than with completely related ones—even in amalgam surveys pooling items from different customers. Without a theory of relatedness, researchers are in a bind. Failure to find an order effect can just be taken as proof that the items were not related.[13]

---

[13] A related example—for which I have unfortunately misplaced the reference and must rely on memory—is the finding that people respond more consistently to items on a common topic when those are grouped in a survey than when the questions are scattered. An (expensive) attempt to replicate this finding took as its common topic attitudes toward shop stewards, and found nothing. That could mean that the first result was a fluke or that *shop stewards* is not a meaningful concept, of the sort that could induce consistent attitudes when brought to people's attention.

Criterion of Interest

Surveys are often conducted in order to resolve practical questions, such as which candidate to support in an election or which product to introduce on the market. As a result, the magnitude of an effect provides the critical test of whether it is worthy of notice. Unless it can be shown to make a difference, who cares? Laboratory results come from out of this world. If they cannot be mapped clearly onto practical problems, then they are likely to seem like curiosities. The psychologists' criterion of statistical significance carries little weight here. Survey researchers, with their large samples, know that even small absolute differences can reach statistical significance.

On the other hand, not all survey questions have that direct a relationship to action. One can assess the effects of being off by 5% in a preelection poll or a product evaluation, as a result of phrasing differences. However, in many other cases, surveys solicit general attitudes and beliefs. These are widely known to be weak predictors of behavior (Ajzen & Fishbein, 1980). As a result, it may be relatively easy to shrug off occasional anomalies as tolerable. Discrepancies should become more important and, perhaps, seem more common as the questions driving research become sharper. The discrepancies associated with contingent valuation studies have come under great scrutiny recently because of their enormous economic consequences. Changes in wording can, in principle, mean the difference between success and failure for entire companies or industries.

Thinking About Lability

How common are artifacts? is an ill-formed question, insofar as there is no clear universe over which the relative frequency of instances can be defined. Nonetheless, investigators' intuitive feeling for overall frequency must determine their commitment to their paradigms and their ability to soldier on in the absence of definitive data. Understanding the nature and source of one's own disciplinary prejudices is essential for paradigms to be used wisely and to evolve. Understanding other disciplines' (more and less legitimate) prejudices is necessary for collaboration. Implicit assumptions about the nature of human values seem to create a substantial divide among the social sciences. If they were to work together, the focal question might shift from how well articulated are values to where are they well articulated. Table 3 offers one possible set of conditions favorable to articulated values. Turner (1981) offered another. It

Table 3. Conditions Favorable to Articulated Values

Personally familiar (time to think)
Personally consequential (motivation to think)
Publicly discussed (opportunity to hear, share views)
Uncontroversial (stable tastes, no need to justify)

Few consequences (simplicity)
Similar consequences (commensurability)
Experienced consequences (meaningfulness)
Certain consequences (comprehensibility)

Single or compatible roles (absence of conflict)
Diverse appearances (multiple perspectives)
Direct relation to action (concreteness)
Unbundled topic (considered in isolation)

Familiar formulation

---

might be informative to review the evidentiary record of discrepancies and nondiscrepancies in the light of such schemes.

Acknowledgments

Preparation of this article was supported by National Science Foundation Grant SES-8175564 and by the Carnegie Corporation of New York, Council on Adolescent Development. The views expressed are those of the author. My special thanks go to Robert Abelson, who suggested the juxtaposition that is explored here, and to Charles Turner, who has stimulated concern for nonsampling error for many years. My thinking on these issues has benefited from discussions with many people, including Lita Furby, Robyn Dawes, Paul Slovic, Sarah Lichtenstein, Amos Tversky, Daniel Kahneman, Alan Randall, and Robin Gregory. I have also received valuable comments from participants in the National Research Council Panel on Survey Measure of Subjective Phenomena; the conference, "Towards a Scientific Analysis of Values"; and the U.S. Forest Service Conference on Amenity Resource Valuation.

References

Achen, C. H. (1975). Mass political attitudes and the survey response. *American Political Science Review, 69,* 1218–1231.
Ajzen, I., & Fishbein, M. (1980). *Understanding attitudes and predicting social behavior.* Englewood Cliffs, NJ: Prentice-Hall.

Bailar, B. A., & Rothwell, N. D. (1984). Measuring employment and unemployment. In C. F. Turner & E. Martin (Eds.), *Survey measure of subjective phenomena* (pp. 129–142). New York: Russell Sage Foundation.

Bentkover, J., Covello, V., & Mumpower, J. (Eds.). (1985). *Benefits assessment: The state of the art.* Amsterdam: Reidel.

Berkeley, D., & Humphreys, P. (1982). Structuring decision problems and the "bias" heuristic. *Acta Psychologica, 50,* 201–250.

Brookshire, D. S., Ives, C. C., & Schulze, W. D. (1976). The valuation of aesthetic preferences. *Journal of Environmental Economics and Management, 3,* 325–346.

Campbell, A., Converse, P., & Rodgers, W. (1976). *The quality of American life: Perceptions, evaluations, and satisfaction.* New York: Russell Sage Foundation.

Campen, J. T. (1986). *Benefit, cost, and beyond.* Cambridge, MA: Ballinger.

Chapman, L. J., & Chapman, J. P. (1969). Genesis of popular but erroneous psychodiagnostic observations. *Journal of Abnormal Psychology, 74,* 271–280.

Converse, P. E. (1964). The nature of belief systems in mass politics. In D. E. Apter (Ed.), *Ideology and discontent.* Glencoe, NY: Free Press.

Coombs, C. H. (1964). *A theory of data.* New York: Wiley.

Cummings, R. D., Brookshire, D. S., & Schulze, W. D. (Eds.). (1986). *Valuing environmental goods: An assessment of the Contingent Valuation Method.* Totowa, NJ: Rowman & Allenheld.

DeMaio, T. J. (1984). Social desirability and survey measurement: A review. In C. F. Turner & E. Martin (Eds.), *Survey measure of subjective phenomena* (pp. 257–282). New York: Russell Sage Foundation.

Dickie, M., Gerking, S., McClelland, G., & Schulze, W. (1987). *Improving accuracy and reducing costs of environmental benefit assessments: Vol. 1. Valuing morbidity: An overview and state of the art assessment* (USEPA Cooperative Agreement No. CR812954-01-2). Washington, DC: U.S. Environmental Protection Agency.

Ekman, P. (1985). *Telling lies.* New York: Norton.

Ellul, J. (1963). *Propaganda.* New York: Knopf.

Fischhoff, B. (1983). Predicting frames. *Journal of Experimental Psychology: Learning, Memory, and Cognition, 9,* 103–116.

Fischhoff, B. (1988). Judgment and decision making. In R. J. Sternberg & E. E. Smith (Eds.), *The psychology of human thought* (pp. 153–187). New York: Wiley.

Fischhoff, B., & Cox, L. A., Jr. (1985). Conceptual foundation for benefit assessment. In J. D. Bentkover, V. T. Covello, & J. Mumpower (Eds.), *Benefits assessment: The state of the art* (pp. 51–84). Amsterdam: Reidel.

Fischhoff, B., & Furby, L. (1988). Measuring values: A conceptual framework for interpreting transactions with special reference to contingent valuation of visibility. *Journal of Risk and Uncertainty, 1,* 147–184.

Fischhoff, B., Slovic, P., & Lichtenstein, S. (1980). Knowing what you want: Measuring labile values. In T. Wallsten (Ed.), *Cognitive processes in choice and decision behavior* (pp. 117–141). Hillsdale, NJ: Erlbaum.

Furby, L. (1986). Psychology and justice. In R. L. Cohen (Ed.), *Justice: Views from the social sciences* (pp. 153–203). New York: Plenum.

Furby, L., & Fischhoff, B. (1989). *Specifying subjective evaluations: A critique of Dickie et al.'s interpretation of their contingent valuation results for reduced minor health symptoms* (U.S. Environmental Protection Agency Cooperative Agreement No. CR814655-01-0). Eugene, OR: Eugene Research Institute.

Gergen, K. J. (1973). Social psychology as history. *Journal of Personality and Social Psychology, 26,* 309–320.

Gilligan, C. (1982). *In a different voice: Psychological theory and women's development.* Cambridge, MA: Harvard University Press.

Hershey, J. R., & Schoemaker, P. J. H. (1980). Risk taking and problem context in the domain of losses: An expected utility analysis. *Journal of Risk and Insurance, 47,* 111–132.

Hogarth, R. M. (Ed.). (1982). *New directions for methodology of the social sciences: Question framing and response consistency.* San Francisco: Jossey-Bass.

Jabine, T. B., Straf, M. L., Tanur, J. M., & Tourangeau, R. (Eds.). (1984). *Cognitive aspects of survey methodology: Building a bridge between disciplines.* Washington, DC: National Academy Press.

Kahneman, D. (1986). Comment. In R. D. Cummings, D. S. Brookshire, & W. D. Schulze (Eds.), *Valuing environmental goods: An assessment of the Contingent Valuation Method.* Totowa, NJ: Rowman & Allenheld.

Kahneman, D., & Tversky, A. (1979). Prospect theory. *Econometrica, 47,* 263–292.

Kahneman, D., & Tversky, A. (1982). On the study of statistical intuitions. *Cognition, 11,* 123–141.

Kuhn, T. S. (1962). *The structure of scientific revolution.* Chicago: University of Chicago Press.

Kunreuther, H., Ginsberg, R., Miller, L., Sagi, P., Slovic, P., Borkin, B., & Katz, N. (1978). *Disaster insurance protection: Public policy lessons.* New York: Wiley.

Lakatos, I., & Musgrave, A. (Eds.). (1970). *Criticism and the growth of scientific knowledge.* Cambridge, England: Cambridge University Press.

McGuire, W. J. (1969). Suspiciousness of experimenter's intent. In R. Rosenthal & R. L. Rosnow (Eds.), *Artifact in behavioral research.* San Diego, CA: Academic Press.

Mitchell, R. C., & Carson, R. T. (1989). *Using surveys to value public goods: The Contingent Valuation Method.* Washington, DC: Resources for the Future.

National Opinion Research Center. (1978). *General Social Surveys, 1972–1978: Cumulative codebook.* Chicago: Author.

Nisbett, R. E., & Ross, L. (1980). *Human inference: Strategies and shortcomings of social judgment.* Englewood Cliffs, NJ: Prentice-Hall.

Nunnally, J. C. (1968). *Psychometric theory* (2nd ed.). New York: McGraw-Hill.

Peterson, G. L., Driver, B. L., & Gregory, R. (Eds.). (1988). *Amenity resource valuation: Integrating economics with other disciplines.* State College, PA: Venture.

Poulton, E. C. (1968). The new psychophysics: Six models for magnitude estimation. *Psychological Bulletin, 69,* 1–19.

Poulton, E. C. (1989). *Bias in quantifying judgments.* London: Erlbaum.

Poulton, E. C., & Freeman, P. R. (1966). Unwanted asymmetrical transfer effects with balanced experimental designs. *Psychological Bulletin, 66,* 1–8.

Raiffa, H. (1968). *Decision analysis.* Reading, MA: Addison-Wesley.

Rokeach, M. (1973). *The nature of human values.* New York: Free Press.

Rosenthal, R. (1967). Covert communication in the psychological experiment. *Psychological Bulletin, 67,* 356–367.

Rosenthal, R., & Rosnow, R. L. (Eds.). (1969). *Artifact in behavior research.* San Diego, CA: Academic Press.

Samuelson, P. (1954). The pure theory of public expenditure. *Review of Economics and Statistics, 36,* 387–389.

Schuman, H., & Presser, S. (1981). *Questions and answers.* San Diego, CA: Academic Press.

Smith, T. (1984). Nonattitudes: A review and evaluation. In C. F. Turner & E. Martin (Eds.), *Survey measure of subjective phenomena* (pp. 215–256). New York: Russell Sage Foundation.

Smith, V. K., & Desvousges, W. H. (1988). *Measuring water quality benefits.* Boston: Kluwer-Nijhoff.

Stevens, S. S. (1975). *Psychophysics: Introduction to its perceptual, neural, and social prospects.* New York: Wiley.

Sudman, S., & Bradburn, N. M. (1982). *Asking questions: A practical guide to questionnaire design.* San Francisco: Jossey-Bass.

Tolley, G. et al. (1986). *Establishing and valuing the effects of improved visibility in the eastern United States* (USEPA Grant No. 807768-01-0). Washington, DC: U.S. Environmental Protection Agency.

Tune, G. S. (1964). Response preferences: A review of some relevant literature. *Psychological Bulletin, 61,* 286–302.

Turner, C. F. (1981). Surveys of subjective phenomena: A working paper. In D. Johnson (Ed.), *Measurement of subjective phenomena.* Washington, DC: U.S. Government Printing Office.

Turner, C. F. (1984). Why do surveys disagree? Some preliminary hypotheses and some disagreeable examples. In C. F. Turner & E. Martin (Eds.), *Surveying subjective phenomena* (pp. 159–214). New York: Russell Sage Foundation.

Turner, C. F., & Krauss, E. (1978). Fallible indicators of the subjective state of the nation. *American Psychologist, 33,* 456–470.

Turner, C. F., & Martin, E. (Eds.). (1981). *Surveys of subjective phenomena.* Washington, DC: National Academy Press.

Turner, C. F., & Martin, E. (Eds.). (1984). *Surveying subjective phenomena.* New York: Russell Sage Foundation.

Tversky, A., & Kahneman, D. (1973). Availability: A heuristic for judging frequency and probability. *Cognitive Psychology, 5,* 207–232.

Tversky, A., & Kahneman, D. (1981). The framing of decisions and the psychology of choice. *Science, 211,* 453–458.

von Winterfeldt, D., & Edwards, W. (1986). *Decision analysis and behavioral research.* New York: Cambridge University Press.

Wagenaar, W. A. (1989). *Paradoxes of gambling behavior.* London: Erlbaum.

Watson, S., & Buede, D. (1988). *Decision synthesis.* New York: Cambridge University Press.

10

Moral Philosophy and Mental Representation

Stephen P. Stich

Let me begin with a bit of autobiography. I am, by profession, a teacher of philosophy. Year in and year out, for the last 15 or 20 years, I have taught a large undergraduate course on contemporary moral issues—issues such as abortion, euthanasia, reverse discrimination, genetic engineering, and animal rights. Over the years, I have written a handful of papers on some of these topics. However, most of my research and writing has been in a very different domain. It has been concerned with problems in the philosophy of language, the philosophy of mind, and the philosophy of psychology. During the last decade, much of my work has been on the philosophical foundations of cognitive science, and I have spent a great deal of time thinking and writing about the nature of mental representation.

For a long time I assumed that the two branches of my professional life were quite distinct. However, a few years ago I began to suspect that there might actually be important connections between them. The invitation to participate in the Tucson conference on the Scientific Analysis of Values has provided the motivation to set out my suspicions a bit more systematically. In reading what follows, do keep in mind that it is very much a first stab at these matters. I suspect that much of what I have to say is seriously oversimplified, and no doubt some of it is muddled or mistaken.

Here is an overview of what is to come. In Sections I and II, I will sketch two of the projects frequently pursued by moral philosophers, and the methods typically invoked in those projects. I will argue that these projects presuppose (or at least suggest) a particular sort of account of the mental representation of human value systems, since the methods make sense only if we assume a certain kind of story about how the human mind stores information about values. The burden of my argument in Section III will be that while the jury is still out, there is some evidence suggesting that this account of mental representation is mistaken. If it is mistaken, it follows that two of the central methods of moral philosophy may have to be substantially modified, or perhaps abandoned, and that the goals philosophers have sought to achieve with these methods may themselves be misguided. I fear that many of my philosophical colleagues will find this a quite radical suggestion. But if anything is clear in this area, it is that the methods we will be considering have *not* been conspicuously successful, though it certainly has not been for want of trying. So perhaps it is time for some radical, empirically informed rethinking of goals and methods in these parts of moral philosophy.

In Section IV, I will take a brief look at a rather different project in moral philosophy. This project, I will argue, is compatible with a wide range of theories about the structures subserving mental representation. But to pursue the project seriously, it will be necessary to determine which of these theories is correct. And that is a job requiring input from anthropologists, linguists, artificial intelligence (AI) researchers, and cognitive psychologists as well as philosophers. If this is right, a surprising redrawing of traditional disciplinary boundaries is in order. For a central project in ethics will turn out to be located squarely within the domain of cognitive science.

I. Plato's Quest: The Analysis of Moral Concepts

> Well said, Cephalus, I replied; but as concerning justice, what is it?—to speak the truth and to pay your debts—no more than this? And even to this are there not exceptions?

With this passage in the *Republic*,[1] Plato launches a long inquiry whose goal is to find the definition of justice. Let me pick up the quote where I left off, since the next few sentences provide a paradigm for the process of inquiry Plato will pursue.

> Suppose that a friend when in his right mind has deposited arms with me and he asks for them when he is not in his right mind, ought I to give them back to him? No one would say that I ought or that I should be right in doing so, any more than they would say that I ought always to speak the truth to one who is in his condition.
>   You are quite right, he replied.
>   But then, I said, speaking the truth and paying your debts is not a correct definition of justice.
>   Quite correct, Socrates.[2]

[1] Plato (1892), *The Republic* I, 331, p. 595.
[2] Plato (1892), *The Republic* I, 331, p. 595.

Much the same pattern recurs frequently in Plato's dialogues. Here's another example.

> *Socrates.* I abjure you to tell me the nature of piety and impiety, which you say that you know so well, and of murder, and of other offenses against the gods. What are they? Is not piety in every action always the same?
>
> *Euthyphro.* To be sure, Socrates.
>
> *Socrates.* And what is piety, and what is impiety? . . . . Tell me what is the nature of this idea, and then I shall have a standard to which I may look, and by which I may measure actions, whether yours or those of any one else, and then I shall be able to say that such and such an action is pious, such another impious.
>
> *Euthyphro.* I will tell you, if you like. . . . Piety . . . is that which is dear to the gods, and impiety is that which is not dear to them.
>
> *Socrates.* Very good, Euthyphro; you have now given me the sort of answer which I wanted. But whether what you say is true or not I cannot as yet tell. . . .
>
> The quarrels of the gods, noble Euthyphro, when they occur, are of a like nature [to the quarrels of men]. . . . They have differences of opinion . . . about good and evil, just and unjust, honorable and dishonorable. . . .
>
> *Euthyphro.* You are quite right.
>
> *Socrates.* Then, my friend, I remark with surprise that you have not answered the question which I asked. For I certainly did not ask you to tell me what action is both pious and impious: but now it would seem that what is loved by the gods is also hated by them.[3]

Throughout the history of philosophy, there has been no shortage of authors who have followed in Plato's footsteps, seeking definitions of such central moral notions as justice, goodness, obligation, responsibility, equality, fairness, and a host of others. Typically, those pursuing these projects share with Plato a cluster of assumptions about how the game is to be played. The first is that a correct definition must provide *individually necessary and jointly sufficient conditions* for the application of the concept being defined. It must specify what every instance falling under the concept, and only these, have in common. If there are exceptions to the definition—either cases that fit the definition but to which the concept does not apply, or cases that do not fit the definition to which the concept does apply—then the definition is mistaken.

A second widely shared Platonic assumption is that we already have a great deal of knowledge relevant to the definition we seek. The central strategy in testing a proposed definition is to compare what the definition says to what *we* would say about a variety of actual and hypothetical

[3] Plato (1892), *Euthyphro*, 5–7, pp. 386–389.

cases. On the definition offered by Cephalus, justice requires paying your debts. But we would not say that a man is unjust if he refuses to return the weapons of a friend who is no longer in his right mind. So Cephalus's definition must be mistaken. To make this sort of test work we must suppose that we already know whether or not refusing to return the arms would be unjust—we must have this sort of knowledge prior to articulating the sought after definition. Indeed, the Platonic inquiry seems to make the most sense if we assume that we already know necessary and sufficient conditions for the application of the concept, and that this knowledge is being put to work in guiding our judgments about the various cases, both real and hypothetical, that are offered as potential counterexamples to proposed definitions. Though of course at the beginning of the inquiry our knowledge of necessary and sufficient conditions is largely tacit; it is not available in a form that enables us to specify those conditions. If it were, the Platonic quest for definitions would be much easier than it is.

A third assumption underlying the Platonic project is that it will do some good to articulate and make explicit the necessary and sufficient conditions that, presumably, we already tacitly know. Socrates motivates his request for a definition by saying that when he has it "then I shall have a standard to which I may look, and by which I may measure actions, . . . and then I shall be able to say that such and such an action is pious, such another impious." There is something of a paradox lurking here, however. For, as we have just seen, the method that Plato and the many who follow him invoke seems to require that we already know how to "measure actions . . . and say that such and such an action" is just or pious or what have you. Judgments about the applicability of the term we are seeking to define are the *input* into the process of testing proposed definitions. Having noted this paradox, I do not propose to pursue it any further, since doing so would take us too far afield.

II. Morally Relevant Difference Arguments

My second example of a project in moral philosophy that seems to make some strong assumptions about the mental representation of values is one that I find myself pursuing over and over again in my courses in contemporary moral issues. To motivate the project for my students, I begin with the observation that if two cases are to be judged differently from a moral point of view—if, for example, one action is judged morally right while another is morally wrong—then it must be the case that there is some nonmoral feature with respect to which they differ. Two cases that are *exactly* the same in every descriptive or nonmoral respect must be morally the same as well. Philosophers like to make this point by saying that the moral properties of a situation *supervene* on the nonmoral properties. Once the latter have been determined, the former are fixed as well.

Now, by itself, this principle of the supervenience of the moral on the nonmoral cannot do much work for us, since in the real world there are no two cases that are exactly alike. There will always be *some* differences between any two situations. However, if we are going to draw a moral distinction between a pair of cases, the descriptive differences between them must be differences that we take to be *morally relevant*—they must be aspects of the situation that we are seriously prepared to accept as justifying the drawing of a moral distinction. And if they justify the drawing of a moral distinction in the case at hand, then presumably they justify the drawing of a parallel moral distinction in other cases that differ in the same way.

All of this will be a bit clearer if we consider an example. The illustration I will use is one of my favorites in the classroom—the issue of animal rights. I begin the discussion by noting that most people have reasonably stable and reasonably clear views about what is right and wrong in this domain. The goal I propose to the students is the apparently modest one of making their own views explicit.

Most students are not vegetarians. They are prepared to say that there is nothing morally wrong with the practice of raising and slaughtering a variety of agricultural animals for no better reason than that some people like to eat the meat of those animals. There is, in particular, nothing at all morally wrong with raising pigs destined for slaughter and ultimately for pork chops and ham sandwiches. Nonvegetarian students typically do not condone the *cruel* treatment of farm animals. And, of course, some of the most powerful arguments of animal rights advocates turn on what are alleged to be the intrinsically cruel nature of modern farming methods. But for the purposes of the current illustration, let us leave the issue of cruelty to one side. Let us assume that the animals we are considering are treated well and slaughtered as painlessly as possible. Under these circumstances most of my students are prepared to agree, indeed insist, that there is nothing wrong with raising cows, pigs, and other common farm animals for food.

Now consider a parallel case. Suppose a group of very wealthy gourmets decide that it would be pleasant to dine occasionally on human flesh. To achieve their goal they hire a number of couples who are prepared to bear infants to be harvested for the table. Typically, my students' first reaction to this proposal is horror and disgust, accompanied with considerable moral indignation. They are quite certain that such a practice would be morally intolerable. Very well, then, I ask, what is the morally relevant difference between farming children and farming animals? Why do you draw a moral distinction between babies and pigs? To start the ball rolling, I note that there are all sorts of features that distinguish adult humans from pigs that they cannot appeal to here. It is not the case that a human baby is more intelligent than an adult pig, or more self-conscious, or more rational, or more aware of its environment. With respect to all of these features, adult pigs are *superior* to babies.

Well, the answer usually comes back, perhaps it is true that an adult pig is more intelligent and self-aware than a human infant. But the difference is one of *potential*. Human babies have the potential to become significantly more intelligent, rational, self-aware, etc. than any pig can ever be. Human babies grow up to be moral agents. Pigs do not. And it is the potential for developing in these ways that marks the moral boundary between pigs and babies.

Ah, I reply, not so fast. Let me change the case a bit. Suppose that our gourmets, sensitive to concerns about potential, have arranged to treat the sperm with which the women are impregnated. The treatment makes some small changes in the genetic make-up of the sperm, with the result that the children produced are all very severely retarded. None of *these* children has the potential for developing into rational, reflective adults. On any reasonable measure, none of them will ever be as rational as a normal adult pig. Or, if you prefer, we can imagine yet another variation on the theme. Suppose our gourmets have entered into an arrangement with the administration of several large hospitals. Whenever there is an extremely senile patient in one of the hospitals who has no close relatives or friends, the patient is turned over to the gourmets, and ends up in the stew at their next banquet. Here again, there is no potential for rationality, or for becoming a moral agent. The people who end up on the dinner table have less potential, along these lines, than a normal adult pig.

At this point the students are generally getting a bit uncomfortable, and it is common for someone to propose that the crucial difference between the pig and the senile person or the severely retarded child is simply that the latter two are *humans*—they are members of *our* species. It is the difference between humans and nonhumans that marks a major moral boundary. A first response to this suggestion, one that often comes from another student, is the observation that this is *speciesism*—a doctrine that bears a distressing similarity to racism. But if a student is unmoved by the analogy, the following tale will typically be very unsettling. Suppose it were to be found that some small group of people living among us—people of Icelandic descent, for example—turn out not to be able to have children when married to partners outside their group. On further investigation it turns out that the Icelanders are incapable of interbreeding with the rest of us because they are actually genetically different from us. They have a different number of chromosomes, and a significantly different genetic structure. They are, in short, members of a different species. The difference went unnoticed for so long because Icelanders generally marry other Icelanders. Despite the differences, however, Icelanders typically make exemplary citizens, and they are often the best of friends with non-Icelanders. Some of them do superb science, others write first rate poetry, and a fair number of them are skilled at sports. Nonetheless, they are members of another species. And because of the difference in species, our gourmets conclude they are morally justified in having the occasional Icelander for dinner—as the main course.

Not at all surprisingly, the students find this morally repugnant, and they concede that mere difference in species is not enough to mark the moral boundary they seek. Indeed, what often happens at this point in the discussion is that students start to question their initial moral judgments. If it is so *hard* to specify the morally relevant difference between pigs and babies, perhaps that is because there are no differences that they are prepared to take seriously. Perhaps when the issue at hand is killing for food, pigs and babies should not be treated differently. Perhaps what we do to pigs is horribly *wrong*. It is not at all uncommon for students to suffer a small moral crisis when confronted with these considerations. And in at least a few cases students who came back to visit a number of years later have told me that they had been strict vegetarians ever since taking my course.

The search for morally relevant differences between harvesting pigs and harvesting people is in some ways quite different from the Platonic search for definitions. In Plato's project, we are seeking to characterize conditions for the application of a particular moral notion such as justice or responsibility or piety. In debating the morality of using animals for food, we are seeking to characterize an important moral boundary—the boundary between those creatures that it is morally acceptable to kill simply to satisfy our own tastes, and those that it would be morally repugnant to kill for this reason. However, there are also some important similarities between the two endeavors. In both investigations, we are trying to specify the extension of categories by seeking necessary and sufficient conditions. We want an account that will cleanly divide cases into two distinct classes—the just and the unjust, or the things it is permissible to kill for food and the things it is not permissible to kill for food. Also, it seems that in both cases we must assume that we already know a great deal about the categories we are seeking to characterize. The methods proceed by testing proposed conditions against our "intuitive" judgments about actual and hypothetical cases. And, as we noted earlier, it is plausible to suppose that if this process is to succeed we must already have something like a set of tacitly known necessary and sufficient conditions to guide our judgments about particular cases. Thus, both the Platonic quest for definitions and the search for morally relevant differences appear to presuppose a view about the process underlying our ability to classify items into categories: *Categorization exploits tacitly known necessary and sufficient conditions.* In the section that follows, I will sketch some of the reasons to suspect that this account of categorization may be mistaken.

III. Categorization and Concepts

In the psychological literature, the cognitive structures underlying categorical judgments are generally referred to as *concepts.*[4] And in psychology, as in philosophy, there is a long-standing tradition that insists that concepts must specify necessary and sufficient conditions. However, since the early 1970s there has been a growing body of experimental literature challenging this "classical view" of concepts. Perhaps the most well known work in this area has been done by Elenore Rosch and her associates.

In one series of experiments it was shown that people can reliably order instances falling under a concept when asked how "typical" or "representative" the instances are. Thus, for example, an apple will be rated as a more typical fruit than a lemon; a lemon will be rated as more typical than a coconut; and a coconut will be rated as more typical than an olive (Mervis, Catlin, & Rosch, 1976; Rosch, 1978; Malt & Smith, 1984). What is important about these ratings is that they predict performance on a wide variety of tasks including categorization.

If subjects are asked whether a particular item is or is not a fruit, and are told to respond as quickly as possible, their responses are faster for more typical instances and slower for less typical instances (Smith, Shoben, & Rips, 1974). Also, when subjects are asked to generate examples of subcategories of a given concept they mention typical ones before atypical ones. Thus, for example, subjects asked to name kinds of fruit will mention apples, peaches, and pears before blueberries, and blueberries will be mentioned before avocados or pumpkins (Rosch, 1978).

Now if a concept is the cognitive structure that subjects are using when they make categorical judgments, then these results begin to make the classical view of concepts look a bit problematic. For if concepts specify

[4] Philosophers too sometimes use the term "concept" in this way, though they also use the term in some very different ways. For a useful discussion of the contrast, see Rey (1983, 1985), Smith, Medin, and Rips (1984), and Smith (1989).

necessary and sufficient conditions, they apply equally to every instance of the concept, and it is not obvious why some instances should be more typical, easier to categorize and easier to recall.

Another line of research that has been taken to undermine the classical view of concepts suggests that typicality effects can be explained by appeal to properties that are common in members of the category, though they are not necessary conditions for membership in the category. In a number of studies, subjects were provided with a list of instances or subcategories falling under a given concept, and they were asked to specify properties of the items on the list. Thus, for example, if the category in question is *birds,* subjects will be given a list that includes *robin, canary, vulture, chicken,* and *penguin.* The properties that subjects offer for *canary* might include *has feathers, flies, small size, sings,* etc. Only the first two of these would be offered for *vulture,* and only the first for *penguin.* Given these data, we can compute what Rosch and her associates call the *family resemblance score* for various kinds of birds. This is done by assigning to each property (*has feathers, flies,* etc.) a number proportional to the number of bird kinds for which the property was mentioned. (Thus the number assigned to *has feathers* would be higher than the number assigned to *sings.*) Having weighted the properties, the family resemblance score for a particular kind of bird is simply the sum of the weights of the properties mentioned for that bird. The high family resemblance score for *robin* indicates that robins have many properties that occur frequently in other kinds of birds, while the low family resemblance score for *chicken* and *penguin* indicates that these birds do not have many of the properties that occur frequently in other sorts of birds. Not surprisingly, the family resemblance score turns out to be an excellent predictor of typicality, and thus an excellent predictor of categorization speed, recall, etc.

In light of these results, a number of investigators have proposed accounts of concepts that are at odds with the classical (necessary and sufficient conditions) view. One widely discussed idea is that a concept consists of a set of salient features or properties that characterizes only the best or "prototypical" members of category. This prototype representation will, of course, contain a variety of properties that are lacking in some members of the category. The prototypical bird flies, but emus do not. On the prototype view of concepts, objects are classified as members of a category if they are sufficiently similar to the prototype—that is, if they have a sufficient number of properties specified in the prototype representation. The more similar an item is to the target prototype, the faster one can determine that it exceeds the similarity threshold. Thus a more typical member of a category will be recognized and classified more rapidly than a less typical one.

Another proposal for dealing with the experimental results posits the mental representation of one or more specific exemplars. An exemplar is a specific instance of an item falling under a concept—the spaniel that was my boyhood companion (for *dog*) or the couch in our living room (for *couch*). On this view, categorization proceeds by activating the mental representations of one or more exemplars for the concept at hand, and then assessing the similarity between the exemplars and the item to be categorized. When developed in detail, exemplar models and prototype models yield different predictions, and there are some sophisticated empirical studies aimed at determining which model is superior in various conceptual domains (see, for example, Estes, 1986).

Recent research strongly suggests that neither the prototype approach nor the exemplar approach can tell the whole story about conceptual representation, even for simple object concepts such as *fruit* and *bird* (Medin & Smith, 1984; Smith, 1990). The consensus seems to be that conceptual representation is a complex affair combining prototypes or exemplars with less observationally salient, more theoretical features. Also, it may well turn out that conceptual representation works differently in different domains. If this is right, then the mental representation of "goal derived" categories, such as *things not to eat on a diet* and social concepts such as *extrovert* or *communist* may have a format that is quite different from the mental representation of *apple, fruit,* or *dog* (Barsalou, 1987).

While the empirical story about the mental structures underlying categorization is far from complete, it should be clear that much of the work I have been reviewing poses a major challenge to the two methods in moral philosophy sketched in Sections I and II. For both of those methods assume that categorization exploits tacitly known necessary and sufficient conditions, and much of the empirical work on categorization suggests that classical necessary and sufficient conditions play little or no role in the process. To the best of my knowledge, there have been no empirical studies aimed at exploring the mental representation of moral concepts like *justice* or *responsibility.* Nor has anyone looked carefully at the cognitive structures underlying our ability to use categories such as *things it is morally acceptable to kill for food.* However, if the story for those concepts is at all like the story elsewhere, it will explain why it is that moral philosophers working with the methods I sketched have been so unsuccessful for so long. For if the mental representation of moral concepts is similar to the mental representation of other concepts that have been studied, then the tacitly known necessary and sufficient conditions that moral philosophers are seeking *do not exist.*

Exemplar models of conceptual representation, and more sophisticated variations on the theme that invoke "scripts" or stories, also suggest an explanation for the fact that those engaged in moral pedagogy generally prefer examples to explicit principles or definitions. Myths, parables, fables, snippets of biography (real or fanciful)—these seem to be the principal tools of a successful moral teacher. Perhaps this is because moral knowledge is *stored* in the form of examples and stories. It may well be that moral doctrines cast in the form of necessary and sufficient conditions are didactically ineffective because they are presented in a form that the mind cannot readily use.

IV. Some Alternative Models for the Mental Representation of Moral Systems

The two projects in moral philosophy that we have looked at so far seem to presuppose that the mental structures underlying moral judgments are rather like definitions—they specify individually necessary and jointly sufficient conditions for the application of moral concepts. The psychological models that challenge this presupposition offer alternative accounts of conceptual representation, accounts that do not involve necessary and sufficient conditions. But these alternatives are still very much *like* definitions. Indeed, as Quine pointed out long ago, a typical dictionary definition of a word such as *tiger* or *lemon* will not offer necessary and sufficient conditions. Often it will present a list of features of a typical tiger or a typical lemon—very much in the spirit of the prototype account of mental representation (Quine, 1953).

However, in the philosophical literature there is a venerable tradition that suggests a rather different account of how moral judgments are made. Instead of relying on something akin to definitions, this tradition assumes that our moral judgments are derived from an interconnected set of *rules* or *principles* specifying what sort of actions are just or unjust, permissible or not permissible, and so on. There are some clever ways in which certain systems of rules can be recast as a set of necessary and sufficient conditions. Thus the distinction between these two approaches is not a hard and fast one. Still, in many cases the style and complexity of rule-based theories give them a very different appearance and a very different feel.

In his seminal book, *A Theory of Justice,* John Rawls (1971: 46) urges that a first goal of moral philosophy should be the discovery of the set of rules or principles underlying our reflective moral judgment. These principles along with our beliefs about the circumstances of specific cases should entail the intuitive judgments we would be inclined to make about the cases, at least in those instances where our judgments are clear, and there are no extraneous factors likely to be influencing them. There is, of course, no reason to suppose that the principles guiding our moral judgments are fully (or even partially) available to conscious introspection. To uncover them we must collect a wide range of intuitions about specific cases (real or hypothetical) and attempt to construct a system of principles that will entail them.

As Rawls notes, this method for uncovering the system of principles presumed to underlie our intuitive moral judgments is analogous to the method used in modern linguistics. Following Chomsky, linguists typically assume that speakers of a natural language have internalized a system of generative grammatical rules, and that these rules play a central role in language production and comprehension. The rules are also assumed to play a central role in the production of linguistic intuitions—the more or less spontaneous judgments speakers offer about the grammaticality and other linguistic properties of sentences presented to them. In attempting to discover what a speaker has internalized, linguists construct systems of generative rules, and check them against the speaker's intuitions. However, the internalized rules are not the only psychological system that plays a part in producing reported intuitions. Memory, motivation, attention, and other factors all interact in the production of the judgments speakers offer. Thus the rules the linguist produces should not be expected to capture the exact details of the speakers' judgments. As in the case of moral principles, we expect the rules to capture only the clearest intuitions, and even these may be ignored when there is some reason to suspect that other factors are distorting the subject's judgment.

Now, as Rawls (1971: 47) observes, it is very likely that the grammatical rules for a natural language such as English will "require theoretical constructions that far outrun the ad hoc precepts of our explicit grammatical knowledge." So if the analogy between grammar and ethics is a good one, "there is no reason to assume that our sense of justice can be adequately characterized by familiar common sense precepts" (Rawls, 1971: 47). It may also be the case that the principles underlying our moral intuitions, like those underlying our grammatical intuitions, are both numerous and enormously complex. Indeed, in the case of language, Chomsky has long maintained that the rules are so complex that they could not possibly be learned from the relatively limited data available to the child. Rather, he contends, the range of grammars that it is possible for a child to learn is a small and highly structured subset of the set of logically possible grammars. Thus much of the fundamental structure of the grammars that children ultimately internalize must be innate. One of the more intriguing possibilities suggested by the analogy between grammatical theory and moral theory is that, as we learn more about the mental representations underlying moral judgment, we may find that they sustain a similar sort of "argument from the poverty of the stimulus." Thus it may be that "humanly possible" moral systems are a very small subset of the logically possible systems, and that much of the structure of moral systems is innate, not acquired.

Though grammatical knowledge was one of the first domains to be systematically investigated by cognitive scientists, there has been a great deal of work on the mental structures underlying other sorts of knowledge, belief, and skill during the last two decades. Mathematical knowledge, knowledge of various sciences, and common sense knowledge in various domains have all been explored. The cognitive systems underlying various skills, from chess and computer programming to musical composition and medical diagnosis, have also been investigated. Theories attempting to account for people's abilities in these areas have invoked a wide range of knowledge representing systems, some of them rather like the generative systems that loom large in linguistics, and others quite different. What makes this work relevant to our current concerns is that many of the knowledge or belief systems that have been explored are at least roughly analogous to moral systems. In many cases people can offer a complex, subtle, and apparently systematic array of judgments about particular cases, with little or no conscious access to the mechanisms or principles underlying these judgments. Thus, while Rawls was certainly right in noting parallels between ethics and grammar, there are other analogies that are at least as plausible. Perhaps the mental structures underlying moral judgment are similar to those underlying expert medical diagnosis, or commonsense physical intuition. Perhaps the best analogy is with the knowledge structures that guide our expectations in reading stories about restaurants and other common social situations.

Which account of the mental representation of moral systems is best is certainly not a matter to be settled a priori. The question is an empirical one. But it is, I think, the sort of empirical question that is best approached in a resolutely interdisciplinary way. Philosophers have lavished a great deal of attention on the exploration of moral intuitions, and have amassed a very substantial body of cases illustrating the richness, subtlety and complexity of our moral judgments. Linguists and deontic logicians have studied the semantic and logical structure of moral language. Anthropologists have much to say about the moral systems in cultures very different from our own. AI researchers, particularly those concerned with knowledge representation, have explored the strengths and weaknesses of many strategies for storing and using complex bodies of information. And, of course, cognitive psychologists have a sophisticated bag of tricks for testing hypotheses about the form and content of mentally represented information.

It is my strong suspicion that progress in understanding how people represent and use moral systems will not be made until scientists and scholars from these various disciplines begin to address the problem collaboratively. Indeed, one of my goals in writing this chapter is to convince at least some of my readers that it is time to launch such a collaborative effort.

A final note: If I am right about the way to make headway in understanding how moral systems are mentally represented, and if Rawls is right in suggesting that such an understanding is a first essential step in moral philosophy, then the beginnings of moral philosophy fall squarely within the domain of cognitive science.

References

Barsalou, L. (1987). The instability of graded structure: Implications for the nature of concepts. In U. Neisser (Ed.), *Concepts and conceptual development: Ecological and intellectual factors in categorization* (pp. 101–140). Cambridge: Cambridge University Press.

Estes, W. (1986). Array models for category learning. *Cognitive Psychology, 18,* 500–549.

Malt, B., & Smith, E. (1984). Correlated properties in natural categories. *Journal of Verbal Learning and Verbal Behavior, 23,* 250–269.

Medin, D., & Smith, E. (1984). Concepts and concept formation. *Annual Review of Psychology, 35,* 113–138.

Mervis, C., Catlin, J., & Rosch, E. (1976). Category structure and the development of categorization. In R. Spiro, B. Bruce, & W. Brewer (Eds.), *Theoretical issues in reading comprehension* (pp. 279–307). Hillsdale, NJ: Lawrence Erlbaum.

Plato (1892). *The dialogues of Plato,* translated by B. Jowett. Vol. I. New York: Random House.

Quine, W. (1953). Two dogmas of empiricism. In *From a logical point of view* (pp. 20–46). Cambridge, MA: Harvard University Press.

Rawls, J. (1971). *A theory of justice,* Cambridge, MA: Harvard University Press.

Rey, G. (1983). Concepts and stereotypes. *Cognition, 15,* 237–262.

Rey, G. (1985). Concepts and conceptions: A reply to Smith, Medin & Rips. *Cognition, 19,* 297–303.

Rosch, E. (1978). Principles of categorization. In E. Rosch & B. Lloyd (Eds.), *Cognition and categorization* (pp. 27–48). Hillsdale, NJ: Lawrence Erlbaum.

Smith, E. (1989). Three distinctions about concepts and categorization. *Language and Mind, 4,* 1, 2, 57–61.

Smith, E. (1990). Categorization. In D. Osherson & E. Smith (Eds.), *Thinking: An invitation to cognitive science* (Vol. 3). Cambridge, MA: MIT Press.

Smith, E., Medin, D., & Rips, L. (1984). A psychological approach to concepts: Comments on Rey's 'concepts and stereotypes.' *Cognition, 17,* 265–274.

Smith, E., Shoben, E., & Rips, L. (1974). Structure and process in semantic memory: A featural model for semantic decisions. *Psychological Review, 81,* 214–241.

11

Approaches to a Psychology of Value

George Mandler

Psychologists have been reluctant to consider either the origins of the perception of value or the place of value in the origins of their perceptions of psychological phenomena. The present chapter attempts to identify the parameters within which a psychology of value could be developed. I shall deal only peripherally with certain innate sources of value such as biologically determined approach and avoidance tendencies, and identify two major *experiential* sources of values: social and structural. *Social* conditions generate the content and meaning of value structures and permeate all thought and action; values are not learned by a neutral organism, but the very conditions of living at a particular time and place—in a specific historical, social, and biological milieu—determine what can and will be known and valued. Cognitive contents are not only not context free—they reflect, incorporate, and constitute the society in which they are formed. *Structural* sources of values refer to the changes and products generated by the consistencies and discrepancies we experience in individual and social action; values arising out of these conditions have special relations to affective conditions. Consistency as well as discrepancy and disorder are inherent aspects of our world. The attempted resolutions of contradictions in our life lead in turn to new discrepancies. Order arises in part out of repeated experiences with our personal world, giving rise to a conservative organism who prefers the known to the novel, the old to the new. Change implies contradictions and emotional involvement. The two sources of value—social and structural—are not separable; they are interdependent and interactive. "Rational" systems of values are generated by systems of schemas that reflect both the social context and requirements of cognitive consistency. A psychology of value can attempt to identify proximal origins of values, but it is constrained in the effort by the values of the society in which it operates.

Introduction

The purpose of this conference was to initiate or to revive a concern with the problem of value that has been ignored and avoided by the scholarly community. Psychology is particularly guilty of pretending that there is no problem of value, neither as a problem of the psychological representation of value, nor as reflected in psychology as such. This avoidance has been incomprehensible to some and comfortable to others, and one psychologist noted the lack of attention to value by predicting that "[i]t is quite possible that future generations will look back upon this period in utter perplexity." In fact, this expectation of future perplexity is a quote from a paper on value by Wolfgang Köhler, written 45 years ago! I wanted to share Köhler's sense of unbelief that psychologists in the first half of the century refused to consider problems of value. They excluded it because, as Köhler quotes his colleagues, "scientific psychology . . . deals with strictly neutral facts, just as does physics." Philosophers of science and of society have since agreed that there are no "neutral" facts, but psychologists have still avoided the problem. The dissection of psychology and psychologists that would be necessary in order to understand the social and scientific matrix that created this phobia would have to be the topic of a lengthy chapter of its own.

Some 10 years ago I presented a speculative essay on the problem of value at a Carnegie Mellon conference (Mandler, 1982).[1] The purpose was in part to expose some budding ideas to public inspection, but also to invite and generate some discussion of the problem itself. The invitation was, apparently, declined. Psychology in general is still valueless (though, of course, *not* value free). I shall now try again. What I intend to do is to present further developments of the notions expressed then. I shall operate under some assumptions that need to be spelled out because I expect that they may not be shared by all the contributors to the present enterprise.

I do not intend to address the issue of innate basic value orientations—whether human beings are a priori good or bad, aggressive or cooperative. Thus, I shall not speculate about Panglossian perfection or Augustinian evil. I believe that we now have enough sophisticated evidence both from anthropology and from primate studies (e.g., Geertz, 1973; Schweder, 1982; Strum, 1987) to realize that human and simian diversity place relatively weak constraints on the range of possible human values. Nor do I intend to analyze in detail the expression of the more obvious "built in" behaviors that are usually interpreted as indica-

---

[1] See also Ch. 9, G. Mandler (1984), and, for a discussion of the function of values in education, G. Mandler (1989a,b).

tions of value. Human beings, from birth on, like sweet tastes and retreat from looming objects. They startle at loud noises, cling to supporting objects, and avoid loss of support. These, and several other, avoidances and withdrawals form the basis for many human values, but in themselves they account for a very small proportion of the values that govern our social lives. Liking candy, shrinking from heights, and avoiding thunder inform little of our everyday lives.

Most of my exposition will be weighted toward what might be called "simple" values. I am interested in the origins of people's calling an event pleasant or noxious, an experience joyous or frightening, and how we come to have preferences for certain foods, music, paintings etc. In that sense I tend toward an explication of tastes rather than values in the sense of moral, rational values (and their justification). Simple values, as I use the term, are values that are generally not debatable—one either likes or does not like clothes, pictures, people, foods. Complex values— on the other hand—are debatable and sometimes require justification. Why is it good to be humane or cooperative, to believe in democratic values, to assert one's opposition to capital punishment? Sometimes these values too are held uncritically and automatically, but they too generally fall into the category of moral values. The latter have been the philosophers' province, those philosophers who usually wish to construct or discover systems of moral judgments that are *rationally* defensible, i.e., values for which reasons and justifications are available and accessible. No intent to explicate such complex values should be read into the following sections. I shall return to a brief attempt at defining the psychological problem of rational, complex value judgments in a later section.

I shall also try to avoid defining values in terms of other psychological phenomena. I want to get at fundamental psychological processes that are intrinsic to the development and construction of values. In contrast, some philosophers, as in the utilitarian tradition, have tended to approach values in terms of wishes, strivings, or interests. Ralph Barton Perry (1926), for example, tried to define values in terms of valuable objects being of interest or in terms of interest taken in them.

Most of my discussion will be concerned with the structural basis for the persistence and change of values, which I shall show to be a function of the structure of the schemas that inform our view of the world. I shall contrast these with "social" values that determine the contents of the structures and schemas. I choose the term "social" to indicate that most of our values arise directly out of the structure and content of the social order. I juxtapose social and structural only to distinguish between primarily structural mechanisms and mainly contextual social ones. I do not imply that structural, schematic mechanisms are independent of the social matrix. Obviously, the social context determines what schemas can be constructed. However, neither for the structural argument, nor the social one, shall I address the mechanisms whereby social values are acquired. I avoid this topic primarily out of ignorance. I do not believe that there is just a single learning mechanism, or even that the basic "laws of learning" are generally known. We understand some of the conditions under which new actions and beliefs are acquired, but we know too little about the varieties of learning mechanisms to make even an approximate statement about the acquisition of values, beliefs, or attitudes. I will, however, address the conditions in which these acquisition processes operate, i.e., the social structures that make one or the other value more or less likely to be acquired.

Before I start and lest I forget: Social scientists have been prone to propose and look for single dimensions of causation—single causes and unique deterministic chains. I too find myself at times a victim of this particular social disease. I must therefore remind the reader and myself that values are not unidimensional. Psychologists in particular have advocated monolithic mechanisms for such complex phenomena as learning, perception, and intelligence. In part this has been a function of the psychologists' successful use of the experimental method that has often been most useful in isolating the effect of single variables and processes. However, the human organism not only responds complexly to the world, but it is also a redundant fail-safe system—there are a variety of processes and mechanisms that address a particular problem of adaptation and environmental demand. There are, for example, many learning mechanisms and there are a variety of ways of generating values and the experience of value. In the world of daily experience and social intercourse, values are multidimensional and overdetermined. Not only are there different sources of value, but the expression in action and thought of some value orientation is usually derived from more than one source.

I shall start with a short discussion of the definition of value, followed by a presentation of a view of emotional experience that I have developed over the past 25 years. I start there because I have become convinced that the problem of value is at the heart of human emotional experience. I do not assert the converse, that emotion is at the heart of the problem of value. Values, even simple preferences, do not arise out of emotion; rather they contribute to emotional experiences. One might consider emotions to be a common language metaphor for the intense expression of values.

After developing the theme of the role of values in the experience of emotion, I shall concentrate on what I believe to be a central condition that gives rise to value attributions and experiences—the emergence of stable schemas that create a conservative view of the world on the one hand, and contradictions among these schemas that produce novelty and value change on the other hand. That exposition will be concerned with the *structural* basis of value, because it is the schematic structure as such that gives rise to a sense of familiarity/acceptance and also determines the sign or direction of consequent values when schemas are interrupted or inconsistent with current evidence. I shall then continue with some thoughts about the social contexts that define and generate values, together with some comments about a psychological basis of rational complex values. For analytic purposes, I shall initially discuss the three sources of values—innate, structural, and social—as independent phenomena. I shall include in my conclusion the assertion of their interdependence.

What Is a Value?

Despite quarrels about definitions that have been one of the hallmarks of the social science enterprise, one can find general agreement that what is needed for a psychological approach to value is some representation that shapes our likes, dislikes, preferences, prejudices, and social attitudes, that informs (but does not constitute) our moral judgments and—in general—that makes it possible for us to say what is good and what is bad. Generally speaking, we exercise simple values unconsciously. We know what we like. Choices and preferences come unbidden and usually without deliberation. We know what people we like, what foods and works of art we prefer, and we know that automatically, without reflection. And we "exercise" many of our social values of competition and cooperation, humanism and racism, altruism and self aggrandizement, patriotism and chauvinism in a similar fashion. I recognize the fact that many of our complex, moral values are "rational," i.e., they are debatable and often require or bring forth justifications. On the other hand, we often fail to inquire into the state of our values in everyday life, and when challenged often rely on social norms or rationalizations. On the one hand, our response may be: "I just do;" on the other we may have reasoned justifications that may be no more than appeals to socially acceptable formulas, given without further examination. Some of this latter behavior is best described as "false consciousness;" people believe that they know what values they are exercising, and insist on (moral, ethical) bases for choices that are often no more than rationales generated by institutions and groups through their dominance of the social means of communication. In general, society and the norms produced by it not only generate rationalizations, but also constrain the possible values and system of values to which anyone can appeal as justifications for actions or ideas.

If one needs a definition of value, one might adopt one proposed by Milton Rokeach, a psychologist who has contributed more than most to the psychological study of value. He defines instrumental and terminal values as enduring prescriptive and proscriptive beliefs in the preferability of modes of actions and of end-states. A value is a standard that guides actions in much of the individual's everyday life, and values are hierarchically organized along a continuum of importance (Rokeach, 1973: 25). Rokeach also asserted that such beliefs "transcend" attitudes toward objects and situations. But that is surely not always the case. A person may have a strong prescriptive belief that stealing or lying is wrong, but adjust the appropriate actions as a function of the situation or person that is encountered. Similarly, the same action executed by different persons or institutions may be differentially evaluated. Rokeach claimed social and cultural universality and generality for a number of terminal and instrumental values. One needs to approach such a claim with caution. For example, ambition and obedience are included in Rokeach's list, as is the prosperous life, but the absence of cooperation and selflessness as instrumental values, or economic equality as a terminal value suggests that the system is—not unexpectedly— biased toward the existing American "way of life." As to how these values are specifically acquired, Rokeach is no more helpful than others. He notes that values are "the result of all the cultural, institutional, and personal forces that act upon a person throughout his lifetime" (1973: 23). How these "forces" produce personal values is left open.

There is one psychologist who has made a heroic effort to place value squarely within our science—Wolfgang Köhler. His William James lectures in 1934–1935 placed value within the notion of requiredness— values are demanded by the structure of both the phenomenal and the physical world (Köhler, 1938). Value is an instance of the recognition of requiredness which is determined by the Gestalten—the inherent patterns of our physical, neural, and phenomenal worlds. Facts do not just happen or exist, but they extend in specific contexts toward other facts with a quality of acceptance and requiredness.[2] The world consists of segregated contexts that have physical and valuative properties that are displayed as contexts and systems, that is, properties such as values are characteristics of structured contexts. Furthermore, any part of a context has properties (such as values) that are determined by the position

[2] Köhler's presentation anticipates a later development that arose out of Gestalt psychology—the ecological psychology of James Gibson, whose "affordances" are very similar to the requiredness invoked by Köhler.

of that fragment as part of the larger context or system. These contextual systems change and develop historically, but such a change is not subjective, e.g., imposed by the individual's phenomenology. Rather, historically changed systems (as, for example, the acceptance of minor chords in music) are as objectively real as the preference for sweet over bitter substances.

There are certain appealing qualities to a view of the world as determined by objective structures, but Köhler wants to avoid subjectivity to the point of caricature. Consider the following quote from a later (1944) paper:

> [Irresistible womanly charm] is a value attribute on which women have a monopoly. It would be absurd to maintain that when the intensely male interests . . . impinge upon the neutral appearance of women, female charm develops in these objects as an illusory projection of the males' conations. (Köhler, 1944)

I believe many psychologists today would opt for "absurdity." This does not deny that there are "objective" characteristics of female (and male) sex objects, *qua* sex objects, nor that there are historical and social standards of beauty, but pulchritude (and its various social and cultural variations) is surely "in the eye of the beholder."

Emotion and Value

As I have noted, my concern with spelling out a psychology of value derives directly from my attempt over the years to delineate a psychological theory of emotional experience (most recently in Mandler, 1984, 1990). What follows is a necessarily brief outline, with a major emphasis on affective values and their origins.

The theory addresses the subjective experience of emotion. It is not a theory of emotional behavior, which may or may not be accompanied or followed by positive or negative emotional experience. This contrast avoids a confusion that has been with us at least since Charles Darwin—a confusion that equates the observation of affectively categorized behavior with emotional experience. The display of "emotional" behavior by other animals, for example, may be no more than just behavior—a particular action pattern released by internal or external events. The theory is constructivist and views the construction of emotion as consisting of the concatenation of a cognitive evaluative schema with visceral arousal that is perceived as emotional intensity. This conscious construction is a unitary experience, even though it may derive from separate and even independent schematic representations (Mandler, 1985; Marcel, 1983). Such a view of emotion only approximates the commonsense meaning of the term. To ask "what is an emotion?" is not—in principle— answerable. The term is a natural language expression that has all the advantages (communicative and inclusive) and disadvantages (imprecise and vague) of the common language. However, it is exactly for communicative purposes that one needs to approximate the common meaning as a first step.

I have focused on two dimensions out of the many available from analyses of common language "emotions": the notion that emotions express some aspect of value, and the assertion that emotions are "hot"— they imply a gut reaction, a visceral response. The cognition of values— what is good or bad—provides the quality of the emotional experience, and the visceral reaction generates its quantitative aspect. An analysis of the concatenation of value and visceral arousal addresses natural language usage as well as theoretically interesting problems. Given the many different possible evaluative states, one of the consequences of such a position is that it leads to the postulation of a potentially innumerable number of different emotional states. There are of course regularities in human thought and action that produce general categories of these constructions, categories that have family resemblances and overlap in the features that are selected for analysis (whether it is the simple dichotomy of good and bad, or the appreciation of beauty, or the perception of evil). These families of occasions and meanings construct the categories of emotions found in the natural language (and psychology). The emotion categories are fuzzily defined by external and internal situations.

The common themes found within the categories of emotions vary from case to case, and they have different bases for their occurrence. Sometimes an emotional category is based on the similarity of external conditions (as in the case of some fears and environmental threats). Sometimes an emotional category may be based on a collection of similar behaviors (in the subjective feelings of fear related to avoidance and flight). Sometimes a common category arises from a class of incipient actions (as in hostility and destructive action). Sometimes hormonal and physiological reactions provide a common basis (as in the case of lust), and sometimes purely cognitive evaluations constitute an emotional category (as in judgments of helplessness that eventuate in anxiety). Others, such as guilt and grief depend on individual evaluations of having committed undesirable acts or trying to recover the presence/comfort of a lost person or object. All of these emotional states involve evaluative cognitions, and their common properties give rise to the appearance of discrete categories of emotions.[3]

The problem of *cognitive evaluation* is common to all emotion theories. Even advocates of a small vocabulary of fundamental or basic emotions need to have an analytic mechanism whereby the individual evaluates the current scene. For the basic emotion theorist such evaluations could then be postulated to elicit prepackaged emotions. For all theories of emotion the problem of value involves the different external and internal sources that lead us to see some person or event as good or bad, as evil or benign, as harmful or beneficient.[4] I shall return to a more detailed discussion of the sources of these values after considering the quantitative aspect of emotion, particularly because it introduces the concept of discrepancy, which will continue to be central to this tale.

If evaluative cognitions provide the quality of an emotional experience, then visceral activity provides its intensity and peculiar "emotional" feel. As a first approximation I assume that degree of autonomic (sympathetic) arousal can be mapped into the felt intensity of an emotion. Affective judgments can obviously occur without visceral involvement. To say that something is pretty or fine or awful or even disgusting may be said quite dispassionately and unemotionally. What we need to understand are the occasions when visceral activity (however slight) cooccurs with these judgments or affects.

In one version of the common understanding of emotion, the occurrence of some visceral or gut reaction is generally assumed. Emotions are said to occur when we feel "aroused," "agitated," when our "guts are in an uproar," etc. The reference is almost invariably to some autonomic nervous system activity, such as increased heart rate, sweating, or gastrointestinal upheavals. The autonomic nervous system has been systematically implicated in quasiemotional activity ever since Walter Cannon (e.g., 1929) delineated the function of the sympathetic and parasympathetic systems in fight/flight reactions, giving them a function over and beyond energy-expending and energy-conserving in keeping the internal environment stable. However, if one looks at the literature on

---

[3] For an extensive analysis of these various evaluative states from a somewhat different point of view, see Ortony, Clore, and Collins (1988).

[4] Other psychologists have also looked to the problem of value as basic to emotional experience. For example, Toda (1982) suggests that "emotions reveal values and . . . we do evaluate, very often, the utility of a state by the emotions it may arouse" (p. 205). While undoubtedly we anticipate outcomes in terms of their positive or negative (emotional) consequences, I would argue that "emotions reveal values" not just by their consequences, but also as a function of their very structure.

the ANS, one is faced with a lack of any principled account of the sources of ANS activation.

I have argued that a majority of occasions for visceral (sympathetic nervous system) arousal follow the occurrence of some perceptual or cognitive discrepancy, or the interruption or blocking of some ongoing action.[5] Discrepancies and interruptions depend to a large extent on the organization of the mental representations of thought and action. Within the purview of schema theory, these discrepancies occur when the expectations generated by some schema are violated. This is the case whether the violating event is worse or better than the expected one— and accounts for visceral arousal in both unhappy and joyful occasions. Most emotions follow such discrepancies, just because the discrepancy produces visceral arousal. And it is the combination of that arousal with an ongoing evaluative cognition that is the subjective experience of an emotion. Interruption, discrepancies, blocks, frustrations, novelties etc. are occasions for ANS activity. Whether or not an emotional construction accompanies such arousal depends on the evaluative activity of the individual. It is the concatenation of an evaluative process and ANS arousal that produces emotion.[6]

The notion of discrepancy as the basis for much of the intensity of human emotions may at first sound out of place when one is dealing with the positive emotions. However, some reflection discloses that the complexity of human thought practically always produces ambivalences and alternative outcomes for positive as well as negative events. Fear of the loss of the loved one, anticipation of possible negative outcomes even for the most joyful occasions, and alternative constructions of negative outcomes illustrate the ambivalences that provide the discrepancies for most emotional occasions (see also Mandler, 1990).

The effects of situational or life stress are excellent examples of unexpected events producing visceral arousal, negative or positive evaluations, and emotional experiences. Berscheid (1983) has imaginatively described the conditions of interpersonal interactions that lead to interruptions and discrepancies and therefore to emotional reactions. When a relationship is meshed, when one individual's actions depend on the actions of the other, then the two people involved may become occasions for each other's interruptions. The actions of the other are essential for one's own action. Thus, emotional reactions are more likely in such meshed relationships than they are when the two lives are—in effect— parallel, when the actions of the two are not independent.

[5] Discrepancies are only a sufficient, not a necessary condition of sympathetic arousal. Other sources of sympathetic nervous system arousal can and do also play a role in emotional experience.

[6] For evidence for this assertion see Mandler (1964) and MacDowell and Mandler (1989).

Finally, the construction of emotions requires conscious capacity. The experience of emotion preempts the limited capacity of consciousness. Limited capacity refers to the fact that conscious contents are highly restricted and limited at any one point in time. Whenever some particular construction preempts conscious capacity, then other processes that require such capacity will be impaired. The best example is found in stress and panic reactions when emotional reactions prevent adequate problem-solving activities. Emotional experiences may inhibit the full utilization of our cognitive apparatus, thoughts may become stereotyped and canalized, and tend to revert to simpler modes of problem solving. However, the effects of emotion are not necessarily intrusive and deleterious. In part, it will depend on other mental contents and mechanisms that are activated by the emotional experience and that may become available for dealing with stressful situations. For example, stress tends to focus attention on the perceived central aspects of a situation, and such focusing may be useful. The relationship of "emotions" to discrepancies and autonomic nervous system recruitment also points to their adaptive function; emotions occur at important times in the life of the organism and may serve to prepare it for more effective thought and action when focused attention is needed.

Before I turn to a more detailed discussion of the sources of value, I need to give a brief introduction to the concept of schemas.

The Nature of Schemas

The notion of the schema has been with us at least since Immanuel Kant. A schema is a coherent unit of structured representation that organizes experience. Schemas are not carbon copies of experience, but abstract representations of experiential regularities. Schemas range from the very concrete, involving the most primitive categorization of perceptual experience, to the very abstract, representing general levels of meaning such as "love" or "justice." Abstract schemas subsume more concrete schemas; the resulting structure is hierarchical. Schemas are built up in the course of experience and interaction with the social and physical environment. They organize and interpret our world, and they organize experience in that current encounters are defined and interpreted in terms of the schemas laid down by past similar and cognate experiences. Currently active schemas define what we are likely to see, hear, and remember, and also determine what we are unlikely to hear or see. Thus, we note the "time" when looking at a clock in a public square, but are unlikely to see (process) the precise form of the numerals. New information activates and constructs relevant schemas that in turn organize our experience of the world.

The activation of schemas proceeds automatically from the most concrete to the most abstract relevant schemas. At the same time, and also automatically, activated high-level schemas pass activation to lower schemas (top-down processing) which constrain further perception. Expectations are those elements of schemas activated by top-down processing that are not directly supported by input evidence. Expectations influence what will be attended to by influencing the ease with which new evidence may be interpreted. Expectations are not met when evidence is not found for all or part of an activated schema; the result is a lack of congruity in schematic processing. This discrepancy is one of the causes of autonomic (sympathetic) nervous system arousal, in part to prepare the organism to cope with a changing environment.

Schemas are not rigidly bounded representations but are best seen as dispositional. Currently available information constructs (out of distributed features of previously developed schemas) a particular representation that responds both to the immediate information and to the regularities (schemas) generated by past events. Since schemas develop through experience, it is important to consider how they change. The single most important description of such a development has been provided by Jean Piaget, who analyzed the process of schema development in terms of *assimilation,* the integration of new elements or input into existing schemas, and *accommodation,* the change in schemas caused by input that cannot be assimilated.

Sources of Values

In my discussions of emotion I have distinguished three general classes of values—those arising out of actions and behaviors, socially acquired values, and structurally determined values. In the development of these notions, I have changed this classification slightly. The "action" and "social" categories determine the contents of value structures, while the structural factors are primarily responsible for the persistence as well as the change of values.

In the case of actions, individuals often interpret their automatic actions and behaviors in value terms. These include innate approach and withdrawal tendencies such as the avoidance of looming objects, the experience of pain (and the avoidance of pain producing objects), and the taste of sweet substances. It is the secondary effect of these tendencies, such as our observations of our own approaches and withdrawals, that is one of the conditions that produces judgments of positive and negative values. The observations of our own actions may inform the value that is generated in a situation. This approach is similar to Bem's descriptions of self-perception (Bem, 1967). The experience of value arises out of our perception of our approaches and withdrawals. However, it is equally possible that approach and withdrawal themselves are the expressions of value as Schneirla (1959) suggested.[7] Actions are frequently innately determined but in the adult a large variety of approach/avoidance tendencies have been acquired and form the basis of this class of values.

A second source of affective values are cultural, social, and idiosyncratic predications—what I have called "social values" in the present context. The social context determines to a large extent how various objects and events are to be represented and how they are valued. Events and objects—whether actually encountered or not—are predicated to have certain values as a result of social or personal learning experiences and contexts. Food aversions (such as frogs' legs or spinach or liver) are frequently acquired without any contact with the actual substances, as are likes and dislikes of people and groups of people. Culturally acquired esthetic judgments of beauty, whether of people, landscapes, or paintings, may be similarly acquired.

The third source of value in the construction of emotion is structural. There are three different structural contributions to the emergence of values: patterning, consistency, and discrepancy. Patterning addresses the cognitive structure of objects and events. Patterning depends on the relations *among* features and attributes, rather than on the presence or absence of certain features. Scenery, paintings, people can be seen as beautiful or ugly as a function of a particular structural concatenation, a particular pattern of their constituent features. Value may arise out of differentiating patterns, in contrast to the mere identification of objects or events. The valence of a specific patterned object or event is determined to a large part by our experience with them and our analyses of their constituent features. Except for some esthetic patterns, it is the social context that defines which pattern will be judged as positive or negative. Thus, it is the patterning of sounds that describes acceptable music for a particular culture, and it is the pattern of the features of the human body that determines local standards of beauty. Feature patterning is a representation of value, whereas the two aspects of structure to be discussed next—consistency and discrepancy—are more important for the generation of values.

---

[7] Facial expressions (usually considered to *expressions* of emotion) fall into this category. I have suggested that these are evolutionary remnants of a primitive nonverbal communication system. As such, they express value and inform the quality of emotions (cf. G. Mandler, 1984).

Familiarity, Discrepancies, and Contradictions

One of the factors that influences judgments arising out of structural consideration is the frequency of occurrences and encounters. The more frequently an object or event has been encountered, the more consistent the representational schema. If an experience fits an existing schema it is—ceteris paribus—an acceptable/expected event. In most cases it is the preferred state of the world. We generally prefer the known to the unknown. If we see a building that conforms to our acquired views of what such a building should look like, we tend to like it.

The available evidence supports the hypothesis that sheer exposure and mere frequency of encounters generates familiarity, acceptance and schematic "fit." However, it is possible that the sense of familiarity and acceptability arises out of the fact that repeated exposures make an event comprehensible and understandable. Such comprehension arises in part out of consistency with expectations. Under such a view, it is the acquisition of knowledge about a domain of experience as well as its fit with a model of the world and one's environ that generates comprehension and acceptance.[8]

Frequent experiences with negatively valued events appear to present a paradox for this theoretical treatment. Do we eventually like what we initially disliked? The experimental evidence is contradictory: repeated exposure to initially negatively valued events may increase or decrease the negative evaluation [e.g., Brickman et al. (1972) and Mandler & Shebo (1983) for increasing negative value, and Gaver & Mandler (1987) for positive changes in the case of music appreciation]. Everyday experiences with novel and unfamiliar music, food, arts, and people suggest that extended experiences may change initially negative reactions to positive ones (see below). More important, the negative value of a particular event—its noxious aspects—is often maintained together with the familiarity/acceptance value generated by frequent exposures. The aversive nature of living in a fascist state or enduring a malicious neighbor coexists eventually with an acceptance of the status quo. Such a situation generates one of the more pervasive ambivalences of human life—the apparent acceptance of a basically unpleasant way of life. Stories of long-time prisoners who are reluctant to leave their jail after many years of "residence" illustrate one of the more extreme examples. Values are not unidimensional and many different sources of value generate a multifaceted way of perceiving the world.

Schema theory generates a psychological picture of humans that makes comprehensible their conservatism as well as their acceptance and

[8] I am grateful to Lynn Cooper for suggesting this alternative view.

generation of change. Order arises in part out of repeated experiences with our personal world, giving rise to a conservative organism who prefers the known to the novel, the old to the new. However, the world is not constant—it presents us with changed conditions, with reordered social relations, power positions, and dependencies. Change is often inherent in the structure of a society that generates inconsistent expectations and contrasting values and requirements. Such social inconsistencies are often referred to as social contradictions. Contradictions imply change and emotional involvement. Discrepancies and disorders are an inherent aspect of our world; we attempt to impose structure and order on the disorder, and the attempted resolutions of contradictions in our lives lead to new discrepancies.

Schemas change in the course of one's interactions with the world, and do so dramatically in early life. For the adult, schemas become powerful organizers of expectations, beliefs, opinions, and actions. Eventually, little change occurs in our perception of the social environment and even less for the physical environment. Normally the world changes relatively slowly and schemas easily assimilate changes in our world of communication, production, transportation etc. Television did not suddenly replace radio and automobiles only slowly displaced horses. The social world is somewhat more changeable, we encounter new people, make new friends, construct new conditions of work and play. Accommodation and assimilation describe the major agents of schematic change. Assimilation refers to one end of a continuum where new information and new events are assimilated into existing schemas without generating any important changes in the prototypical relevant schema. When the new information cannot be assimilated, we refer to the other end of the continuum—accommodation—which implies a change in a schema in order to integrate information that could not be assimilated to its current variables.

Our species operates on a principle of least effort when it comes to schematic change. Current schemas—our current view of the world and ourselves—are changed only with effort and whenever possible the organism stays with what it knows and with past actions and beliefs. The degree to which an existing schematic view of the world will change will depend on the degree of consistency and integration of the schema on the one hand, and the challenge that new information provides on the other. Accommodation requires cognitive effort, and in the absence of some motive for change, we stay with current conceptions and perceptions. The motives for change may be the availability of alternative views of the world that promise better conditions of existence or intolerable current conditions that require change. Habitual ways of knowing and perceiving are typically preferred to novel constructions that require mental—and often physical—effort. Assimilation is the preferred mode of dealing with the world and, I shall argue, is in fact one of the basic values that informs human thought and action. What is known and expected is—ceteris paribus—preferred to what is unknown and unexpected. The more experiences we have had with a particular event (be it a person, a home, a career, or a food) the more likely it is that we will find it acceptable. An extensive experimental literature has shown that repeated encounters (development of stable schemas) increase the acceptability of and preference for the repeated event (see, for example, Gaver & Mandler, 1987; Mandler & Shebo, 1983; Zajonc, 1968). As I have noted before, such encounters also affect the experience of initially disliked objects. A not surprising demonstration of the parallel between knowing and liking was demonstrated in one of our studies in which undergraduate students made judgments of whether they knew, i.e., had seen before, and whether they liked (or not) slides of paintings (Mandler & Shebo, 1983). The slides were selected from the renaissance, nineteenth and twentieth century (mostly impressionists), or modern abstract periods. Knowledge decreased precipitously from 66 to 24% as a function of the chronology and liking also decreased for the three periods.[9]

Another way of approaching the same issue is to consider the basic schema of an event or object, together with its default values, as the prototype of that kind of event (cf. J. M. Mandler, 1984; Rosch, 1978). To the extent that an event "fits" that prototype it will be considered typical of that class of events and should be preferred or liked. In a study by Purcell, subjects judged the typicality (goodness of example), interestingness, and liking (preference) for a wide variety of buildings.[10] Purcell found that typicality and preference were highly correlated ($r = .77$), particularly when interestingness was held constant ($r_{partial} = .94$). Typicality and interestingness, on the other hand, were negatively correlated ($r = -.29$, with preference controlled $r_{partial} = -.87$). Interestingness may be thought of as an index of deviation from typicality or of complexity. In this case, preference was directly related to typicality, independent of interestingness. In another study of 20 selected paintings, Purcell again found a high correlation (.80) between the mean ratings of typicality and preference.[11] Van Orden has explored the relation between typicality and liking ratings of unfamiliar examples of bird-

[9] The main finding of the study was to show that cognitive judgments (knowing a painting) are made faster than affective ones (liking a painting). The argument is that affective/value judgments require more processing of features and structures than do judgments of mere recognition.

[10] T. Purcell, unpublished study, University of Sydney.

[11] T. Purcell, *Relations between preference and typicality in the experience of paintings*. Unpublished paper, University of Sydney.

songs, seashells, and rocks.[12] He also found that judgments of typicality were highly correlated with preference judgments. Of course, correlation does not necessarily imply a causal relation between typicality and liking—it could be that things were judged as more typical *because* they were liked. In any case, these findings support the idea that we tend to like things we perceive as typical of their kind.

I have asserted that if an experience fits an existing schema it is positively valued. There are of course many situations where we do not seem to like or prefer the familiar. On analysis it is usually the case that other sources of value override the mere structural fit. But when nothing but structural comparisons predominate in a situation we will find the preference for the familiar. Boredom exemplifies the intrusion of other values on the preference for the familiar. It is usually the case that boredom is experienced when a particular event, often—but not always—somewhat repetitive, produces a negative reaction because the object or event fails to conform to some standard or expectation. Boring lecturers repetitively tell us what we already know or what they have already said before; boring movies fail to conform to the expectation of being entertaining; boring clothes fail to respond to a need to be trendy.

I have struggled with the problem of defining, i.e., of finding the just right expression for, the sense of preference or liking that arises out of the familiar. We really do not have the right words for it—but it seems to be related to a sense of comfort, nostalgia, a sense of belonging and similar "sentiments." It is a sense of avoiding cognitive effort, i.e., the cognitive structures do not need to be changed, and we passively accept their familiar contents. Consider another more unusual example of the familiar being the accepted and acceptable. Abusing parents have sometimes been found to have been the victims of parental abuse during their childhood. Abuse and the violence of the parent/child interaction is the regnant schema, they are the familiar aspects of the family situation. Parental love and security are intimately tied to the occurrence of abuse—being a victim is part of the implicit and accepted definition of being a child. And the masochistic experience also represents a sought out concatenation of pain with love and acceptance. It should be noted that the value aspect of "familiarity" is just one facet of the effect of prior experiences. Other aspects play an important role in human memory, where the symptom of "familiarity" is a central phenomenon in the automatic (implicit) effects of prior activation, to be contrasted with deliberate (explicit) access to mental contents (cf. Mandler, 1989c).

So much for the conservative, status quo maintaining aspect of human nature. But our social world in particular is often a world of discrepancies. What we have experienced and expect is contradicted by new social conditions, by changes in the social order. The contradictions introduced by the economic, social, and interpersonal world are the very discrepancies that generate arousal.[13]

If we accept that discrepancies and contradictions abound in our world, then we need to consider how these discrepancies are resolved. The dominant model in psychology has been one based on simple tension reduction and the achievement of orderliness and quietude, as in Freud. Another approach has been to borrow Walter Cannon's model of the homeostatic resolution of imbalance and to apply it to psychological states. In an important essay on disorder and order, Rudolf Arnheim tackled the problem from the point of view of Gestalt psychology. He rejected simple tension reduction and homeostatic models of disorder resolution and opted for the achievement of a new structure. He noted that in contrast to mere orderliness, the imposition of order in the face of disorder (and tension) requires active process; the individual must effortfully find and impose a new ordering on percepts and concepts. Disorder "is not the absence of all order but rather the clash of uncoordinated orders" (Arnheim, 1966: 125). In terms of the present discussion, disorder implies contradictions which suggests that discrepancy and contradictions require accommodation, i.e., the establishment of new schematic structures.

Within the context of emotional reactions, I have described the various possible resolutions that may follow different degrees of discrepancy or discontinuity. Figure 1 shows increasing discrepancy from left to right (congruity to severe incongruity). Starting at the right of the figure, it is assumed that for severe incongruity assimilation is not possible and accommodation (change of schema) is necessary. Such a change can be successful when the new schema "fits" the new experience. If successful, the very fact of successful accommodation may produce a positive value and, in addition, tension/arousal is presumably ameliorated and the value will be positive. On the other hand, the incongruity may produce a negative tone, and in some cases intensely so; for example if the accommodation requires the forceful removal of a disruptive event (aggression). Conversely, such events as unexpected praise or recovering a lost person or object would lead to a positive evaluation. In the case of unsuccessful accommodation, I assume that the sign of the subjective value will be negative. What the specific negative value will be depends on the context of the event and past experience with the event itself. If, however, a previously established alternate way of handling the situation

[13] For the sake of interdisciplinary communication, it would be gratifying if my descriptions of social contradictions are the psychological counterpart of the contradictions addressed by Harrison White (this volume).

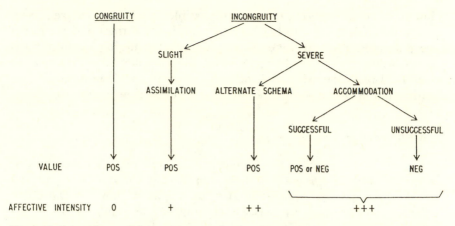

Figure 1. Several possible outcomes of schema congruity and incongruity in terms of both values and affective intensity. The resultant value is shown as either positive (POS) or negative (NEG). Degree of affective intensity is shown to vary from zero to $+++$. Reproduced from Mandler (1984).

is found (e.g., as in denial) arousal is attenuated and the value of the event is likely to be positive. In the case of assimilation, on the other hand, I assume that all outcomes involve no further mental effort and the values tend to be positive. The positive value arises at least in part out of the fact of successful assimilation—the very act of assimilating an experience may well be positively valued. I have also suggested (Mandler, 1984) that a parallel of such assimilation, i.e., successfully completing an intended action or thought sequence, has positive value—resulting in what might be called the "joy of completion."

The preceding discussion suggests that accommodation involves the generation of a new structure, a new ordering of experience. However, we should note that the imposition of structure (and order) on an event or experience does not necessarily produce a state of quiescence. The newly imposed or discovered order will bring with it its own discrepancies and contradictions. For example, Arnheim notes that "[o]rder and complexity are antagonistic, in that order tends to reduce complexity while complexity tends to reduce order" (Arnheim, 1966: 124). Complexity requires coping with a variety of different attributes and relations among them, and as a result structures may change and reduce the ability to cope with the event. New structures may also bring with them values of their own. The affective state following a state of discrepancy depends on the evaluation of the new, changed state. It is only rarely that the perceiver discovers the optimal order with a structure and complexity that can be accepted unchanged and unchallenged. Depending on the particular context and the person's preparation for the new situation, a variety of different reactions is possible. If past experience predisposes one to deal effectively with new complexities, then positive values are generated. If one feels helpless in the face of changing conditions, the values will be negative. In some cases the complex structure may be preferred just *because* it invites new explorations, new tension, and new contradictions to be resolved in ever new perceptions of the world.

The Challenge of Novelty

Novelty is not an all-or-none concept; an event may be novel because some well-known evidence is encountered that has not been encountered in a particular context before, or it may be novel because it is entirely "new," and a number of variations of these themes all deserve the label of novelty. Frequently the novel produces negative affect—it does not fit and there is no way in which we can accommodate to its demands. New styles of music and painting, new ways of structuring our social world, new modes of organization are usually greeted with negative evaluations. When is the novel positively valued—as it often is?

One possible explanation for the search for novelty lies in the positive evaluative state when a novel event or experience can be assimilated into existing schematic structures (cf. Figure 1). The positive affect generated by smooth assimilation would encourage the search for novel, but not extremely discrepant, situations.[14] Another candidate for coloring the novel positive is some other evaluative structure that interacts with the novel event. Such structures may be social, e.g., when a novel aspect of a difficult problem is seen as a possible solution, or it may be individual, i.e., for people who seek the novel and find positive value in problem solving, whether cognitive or aesthetic (e.g., the creative individual who seeks out complexity; see Dellas & Gaier, 1970). The creative artist and scientist both are part of a cultural tradition that values the novel construction and that seeks out novelty. On the other hand, there are social and cultural conditions in which the novel is avoided and considered inappropriate (e.g., in authoritarian societies).

There may also be phyletic differences since most animals react negatively to novelty, i.e., they are unable to accommodate to the new situation. Primates as well as the young human and other animals, on the other hand, apparently seek out novelty as a major mechanism in understanding and mastering their world. Whether or not we are an information-seeking species as such is still open to argument. The basic preference for the old emerges in human children after schemas about

---

[14] The attraction of play might have similar roots.

the world have been well established as, for example, in stranger anxiety. New information is sought whenever the physical and social world changes and requires new adjustments. In the modern industrial world we apparently have become novelty junkies, but in the light of very stable societies (as in some parts of Micronesia) it seems premature to generalize our own experience to an assertion about human nature.

The novel and particularly the creative event produces discrepancies and discontinuities. New ways of doing and seeing are by definition of this order, but the creative act often is seen as destructive and alien. This is usually the case in social action, but it is most easily demonstrated in the arts where the new way of seeing or hearing creates strong dissonances in the viewer and hearer. Beethoven's music provides one of many examples. A contemporary critic of the *Eroica* symphony noted that one left the concert hall "crushed by the mass of unconnected and overloaded ideas and a continuing tumult by all the instruments" (cited by Rosen, 1971: 393).[15]

There are reasons other than structural change why discrepancy and contradiction foster value-laden reactions. I have previously suggested one other possibility, i.e., that sympathetic nervous system arousal may have an additional (adaptive) function of alerting the organism to examine the environment, to discern what it is that has changed that has brought about the autonomic alerting reaction. Any such renewed analysis of the world would bring with it some evaluative reaction. A parallel argument can be developed out of considerations of the role of consciousness in human thought and action. One occasion that produces new states of consciousness—new conscious mental contents—is a change in currently active schemas and structures. Any change in current mental contents—independent of its effect on the sympathetic nervous system—would bring with it some evaluation of the new state of affairs.[16]

The import of the preceding is that discrepancies and contradictions are the occasion for the development or imposition of new values, that changes in values are most likely to occur when contradictions have to be faced. This is to be contrasted with the conservatism of holding to the familiarity and comfort of well-established, habitual schemas. Which of these two roads will dominate in a situation depends on the general system of schemas that characterize the individual's value system. The outcome of the dialectic between conservatism and change is in turn

---

[15] This brings up the question of the role of creative individuals and their peculiar function in creating discrepancies and new values. I have discussed their need to accept the necessary destructiveness of their actions in Mandler (1984).

[16] I cannot develop these themes here, and the reader is referred to Mandler (1975, 1985, Ch. 3, 1988) for extensive discussions of these issues.

determined by historical and social aspects of the society and the personal history of the individual within that society.

The Arts and Discrepancies

The most intense interest in the role of discrepancy and discontinuity and their effect on value has developed in the arts, both in visual arts and in music. I have already had occasion to refer to the work of the noted psychologist of art, Rudolf Arnheim. Still in the visual arts, the art critic John Berger (1988) suggested a pervasive disjunction or discrepancy in art:

> Before any impressive painting one discovers the same enigma. The continuity of space (the logic of the whereabouts) will somewhere on the canvas be broken and replaced by a haunting discontinuity. This is true of a Caravaggio or a Rubens as of a Juan Gris or a Beckmann. The painted images are always held within a broken space. Each historical period has its particular system of breaking. Tintoretto typically breaks between foreground and background. Cezanne miraculously exchanges the far for the near. Yet always one is forced to ask: What I'm being shown, what I'm being made to believe in, is exactly where? Perspective cannot provide the answer. The question is both material and symbolic, for every painted image of something is also about the absence of the real thing. All painting is about the presence of absence. This is why man paints. The broken pictorial space confesses the art's wishfulness.

In the analysis of musical aesthetics, Leonard Meyer (1956) is the most emphatic modern writer in tying affect *directly* to the interruption or inhibition of expectations. Meyer's discussion is concerned almost exclusively with affect as it is found in music—its composition and performance. Starting with principles of Gestalt psychology, he has described in depth how expectations, their products and their violations, produce meaning and emotion in music. Another eminent writer on the musical world, Charles Rosen, has also spoken about the role of discrepancies and discontinuities. Thus, "what is important is the periodic breaking of continuity" (1971: 58). "The emotional force of the classical style is clearly bound up with [the] contrast between dramatic tension and stability" (p. 74). "I do not want to turn Haydn, Mozart, and Beethoven into Hegelians, but the simplest way to summarize classical form is as the symmetrical resolution of opposing forces" (p. 83).

I cite these instances in order to draw attention to the fact that problems of value, in this case of aesthetic value, have not been unattended, and that when they are analyzed phenomena of contradiction and discrepancy appear just as they do in the analysis of the social order.

The Social Context

The schemas that give rise to feelings of quiescence/familiarity on the one hand and contradictions on the other develop out of experience in the social context—they depend by definition on the experiences that the individual can have and has had in his or her social world. In addition to the schema driven values that depend to a large extent on actual experiences in the world, social contexts frequently generate individual values independent of any experience with the valued object or event. A society and its members may reject as bad a variety of different people, objects, and events even though the majority of its members have not had any contact with the offending object, and we also often accept as benign or good similarly unexperienced objects. This applies to social and racial prejudices as well as to the mundane world of food and clothing preferences. Americans "know" that socialism, frog legs, and kilts are unacceptable to be espoused, eaten or worn, just as members of other societies "know" that capitalism, pumpkin pie, and faded jeans are unacceptable. These values and beliefs are not necessarily directly "taught;" they are part and parcel of the society in which one grows up and lives. Nor are they learned by a neutral organism, but the very conditions of living at a particular time and place—in a specific historical and social milieu—determine what can and will be known and valued. These values are often adopted without any specific, concrete experiences with the liked or disliked event or object. However, they may be just as powerful in influencing the social experience of the individual—they represent the schemas that determine the cognitive structure of a particular society. How uniformly they are held depends to a large extent on the means whereby they are promulgated. When the major means of communication and dissemination are primarily in the hands of a particular group or class or interests (as in the United States and in the Soviet Union), they become unassailable parts of the society's structure. Cognitive contents are not only not context free—they reflect, incorporate, and constitute the society in which they are formed.

Social (cultural) conditions also determine many value-laden actions and beliefs that are considered by some to be innately determined. I have previously presented an analysis of aggression and hostility that derives such a state from a biologically determined condition, i.e., reactions to thwarting, but makes its emergence as aggression dependent on social conditions (G. Mandler, 1984). In brief, the very young child reacts to the removal of a (still visible) object with increased persistence and force. In addition such a removal (thwarting) represents a discrepancy and generates sympathetic nervous system activity. When the object is removed by a human agent then the persistence and force will be exercised on that agent. If the object is recovered by such a series of actions, and if forceful actions on the agent of removal are repeated many times, the child learns that such "aggression" is a useful action. The combination of ANS activation together with the cognitive and perceptual schemas developed about agents and situations will then generate the "feeling" of aggression and hostility in conditions of thwarting. If, however, the child is discouraged from such solutions to the problem of removed objects, aggressive, violent feelings are less likely to develop.[17] It is this kind of analysis of the proximal causes of complex values, such as hostility and violence, which I favor in assessing the interaction of biological factors (persistence, force, ANS reactions) and social ones (solutions to problems of thwarting).

Social values form their own schemas, and often the most stable ones. What social factors favor such stable values? We can assume that stable societies lead to stable systems of values. But such stable values may be also most vulnerable when they encounter serious discrepancies because the discrepancy has not been previously encountered—it is indeed novel and disruptive. There is extensive evidence in the psychological literature that experiential schemas that incorporate possible deviations and failures are most impervious to disruption.[18]

Serious challenges to value systems and ensuing difficulties in maintaining social stability occur when stable systems encounter inevitable contradictions. Social values develop from the interactions of people and groups of people. Such values may be competitive or cooperative, they may emphasize submission or dominance, depending on the social and historical matrix in which they develop. Only exceptional social (and personal) circumstances that generate unusual discrepancies and contradictions produce rapid changes in values and value systems. Such a gradualist view of values and their change is based on the assumption that the consciousness of values arises with and out of the structure of the society, which in turn depends on the slow change of groups of people acting in accord and forming their accepted value schemas. Such change produces new values as well as their generational transmission. Only the most extreme utopians have believed that values can be changed quickly by either instruction or revolution in the absence of the appropriate social climate.[19]

[17] See, for example, the Semai people (Dentan, 1968).
[18] See, for example, the literature on partial reinforcement and extinction.
[19] It is sometimes overlooked that even Karl Marx was a gradualist in this sense; he saw changes in social consciousness developing slowly *after* the proletarian revolution (cf. for example, his discussion in the *Critique of the Gotha Programme*).

Rationality and Universality

I have previously indicated my reluctance to discuss the issue of rational moral theory. One problem for a psychologist is that there does not yet exist any reasonable agreement on what a rational argument or a rational theory is—from a psychological point of view. However, the simple values that I have primarily addressed are sometimes taken as the basis of the emotivist argument for moral theory. MacIntyre has characterized emotivism as "the doctrine that all evaluative judgments and more specifically all moral judgments are *nothing but* expressions of preference, expressions of attitude or feeling, insofar as they are moral or evaluative in character" (MacIntyre, 1981: 11). My interest has been to investigate the psychological basis of these preferences, feelings, and attitudes. It was not intended to go much beyond such an investigation, and in particular my goal was not to advance psychological states such as feelings or preferences as constituting moral judgments. MacIntyre (1981) went on to criticize the emotivist position and to demonstrate its poverty in providing a basis for a system of moral judgments. I agree that the kind of argument I have advanced for the origins of values is inadequate to justify a system of moral judgments. But what is meant when we speak of rational judgments and values?

No clarification of rationality has significantly improved on William James' definition of the core of rationality as the assertion that the world *is* intelligible "after the pattern of *some* ideal system" (James, 1890, Vol. 1: 677). As James adds, of course, the question then is "which system?" within the present framework, a system of moral values is a system of social and evaluative schemas.[20] These schemas are built as a function of the specific social and historical experiences of the individual *as a member of a particular social group or groups*. A moral value system also requires two other characteristics far beyond the intent of this chapter—cognitive consistency and conscious accessibility. To justify a moral value, we require that it be consistent with other values, and—by definition—such a moral system must be accessible for conscious constructions.

Finally, I need to address the question of universal ethical or moral values. It is the actions, thoughts, and ideas of people, usually at first in very small groups and latter growing to encompass more and more of the society and culture, that define what is valued, what is a contradiction, what becomes in an important sense familiar, and accepted because familiar. In another language, it is the infrastructure that creates the superstructure, and a stable superstructure harbors the reassurance of

---

[20] I read a very similar argument in Stephen Stich's presentation (this volume).

absolutes, of transcendent values. If and when it is stabilized, such a system escapes relativism because the social values are seen as un-challenged. I assume that the only other escape from a disordering relativism is a stable ideology that orders actions and values under some superordinate scheme that is socially accepted and acceptable.

A cognate position has been developed by MacIntyre who has mounted the most recent attack on attempts to find a universally accept-able set of moral principles. He argues for ethical principles that are developed and accepted by a narrower group of people—those formed by a common "tradition." By tradition MacIntyre refers to the historical, social, and cultural background that informs a particular social grouping and its moral principles. Such a view is, of course, consistent with the slow and accretional development of values. MacIntyre implies that rele-vant groups of people are likely to find and subscribe to a set of moral principles that do not depend on or make a claim for a priori univer-sality. He decries any attempt to find moral principles that are likely to be "found undeniable by all rational persons." The formulation of accep-tability by "rational persons" seems to describe most universalist at-tempts, though Nagel (1988) considers it a travesty and prefers the aim "to construct gradually a point of view which all reasonable persons can be asked to share." I find this formulation no more appetizing that the "travesty." There does not really seem to be much difference between a system that is undeniable by rational persons and one that is shared by reasonable ones. As a psychologist I have great difficulty understanding any acceptable definition of "rational" persons, nor am I sure that defini-tions of "reasonable persons" are ever untainted by the social values of the moment.[21] There is no Archimedian place "to stand" from whence we can move values or see them unshaded.

Conclusion: Interdependence, Biology, and a Contradiction

A psychology of value does not and cannot generate a theory that provides a scientific account of what values should be. I have attempted to show that it can attempt to describe the conditions that generate values—without a commitment as to the content of those values. To that extent I am in agreement with Barry Schwartz (this volume) who has shown how particular values "can be created and destroyed." I do believe that an analysis of the regularities/consistencies and the inconsisten-

---

[21] I remember an interchange between a philosopher and psychologist in which the for-mer condemned a particular psychological theoretical model of human thought as producing only "pseudorationality." The psychologist replied: "But that is all there is."

cies/contradictions of human life and social institutions can inform our understanding of the creation and destruction of values.

My discussion of the various sources of values has been somewhat isolated from the interdependent context in which all these sources operate. Values are constrained by social and biological conditions, and in addition by the limitations that each of the sources of value places on the others. The sources of "external" constraint are biological, structural, and environmental. Biology constrains the kinds of actions we can undertake (because of our physique and biological constitution) and it also determines to some extent what will be considered pleasant or unpleasant. These biological constraints include the innate approach/avoidance tendencies and their derived actions that are perceived as positive or negative. The ANS reaction to discrepancy and the preference for the schematically acceptable event are also biologically given aspects of the human organism. One might conjecture that these factors determine the basic dimension of pleasantness/unpleasantness, the inherent conditions that make situations good or bad.[22] Structural constraints are provided by the kinds of experiences that can or cannot cooccur, whether as a function of the limitations of the structural apparatus or as a function of the features and attributes available to the organism. Finally, the world we live in—with its ecology, meteorology, gravity, etc.—determines the kind of schemas that can be developed and the kinds of structures that can occur. The biology of the organism constrains the kind of structures that can be formed and the kind of social organization that is possible, but the social organization also constrains how the innate reactions can be experienced or exercised.

None of the sources of value presumably ever produces an experienced or exercised value in its "pure" or unattenuated form. Innate sources inform structural and social formations, and those in turn modify the derived innate expressions. Values are mostly schema dependent and schemas are developed primarily in the social context. My brief suggestion about the origins of aggressive and hostile values illustrates one such interactive, interdependent example where an important social value is derived from innate biological conditions, from structural factors, and from the social context in which it is developed.

I conclude with a final example—the analysis of and similarities between two emotional states: grief and guilt (from Mandler, 1984). The basic condition of grief (sadness) involves the loss of an object that cannot be recovered; guilt involves an act that cannot be undone. In both cases, the individual attempts to reconstitute a situation—life with the

---

[22] It would be most interesting if these diverse events all find a neurophysiological endpoint in the pleasure centers described by Keith Franklin (this volume).

lost object or life "prior to" the unacceptable act. Both of these are discrepancies and produce ANS arousal and often strong emotional reactions. Universal emotional states are universal because of the way the human world is constructed. For example, attachment and cathexes of people and objects are common human characteristics and some form of grief/sadness will be found in all human societies, but the specific nature and content of the grief, guilt, etc. will be determined by the social context, including the way society defines important (love) objects and unacceptable actions.

I started by reasserting my attempt to move psychologists to discuss seriously and in a principled way the sources and conditions of values. I certainly do not claim any kind of completeness for this account, nor any certainty for the propositions advanced here. I do hope that they will be the beginning of a study of value—even if it begins by questioning what I have tried to do here. There is at least one good reason why the study of value has been avoided—it is difficult and harbors the seeds of its own doubts. How can one have a theory of value when that theory may be just another instance of contemporary and evanescent social values? The study of values harbors its own contradictions when it becomes a social version of Zeno's paradox: with every advance we seem to be at best half way toward our goal—never quite to reach it. Societies always change, sometimes slowly, sometimes quite radically; the values that they generate are constantly in a state of flux. And these values, in turn, inform and constrain a psychology of value. Can a psychology of value arise out of a society that seems to inhibit the study of values; would such a psychology contradict the basis of its social existence? The social sciences are not, and probably cannot be, value free. In recognizing that constraint, we can try to face up to our particulate value systems and the values that our society and sciences have been bequeathed by social and historical conditions. In our understanding of our own value systems we can strive for a better academy and a better approach to a scientific understanding of values (cf. P. Mandler, 1989). Once social scientists are beginning to understand the origins and uses of values, maybe they can strive to do what so horrified our positivistic and "pure science" ancestors—to search for and to justify the good and the ethical.

Acknowledgments

Preparation of this chapter was supported in part by a grant from the Spencer Foundation. I am very grateful to Michael Mandler, who suggested important emendations, and to Roy D'Andrade, William Kessen, and Jean M. Mandler for helpful critical comments. The author retains the copyright for this chapter.

References

Arnheim, R. (1966). *Toward a psychology of art.* Berkeley, CA: University of California Press.

Bem, D. J. (1967). Self-perception: An alternative interpretation of cognitive dissonance phenomena. *Psychological Review, 74,* 183–200.

Berger, J. (1988). The art of the interior. *New Statesman & Society, 116,* 32–34.

Berscheid, E. (1983). Emotion. In H. H. Kelley, E. Berscheid, A. Christensen, J. H. Harvey, T. L. Huston, G. Levinger, E. McClintock, L. A. Peplau, & D. R. Peterson (Eds.), *Close relationships* (pp. 110–168). San Francisco: Freeman.

Brickman, P., Redfield, J., Harrison, A. A., & Crandall, R. (1972). Drive and predisposition as factors in the attitudinal effects of mere exposure. *Journal of Experimental Social Psychology, 8,* 31–44.

Cannon, W. B. (1929). *Bodily changes in pain, hunger, fear and rage* (2nd ed.). New York: Appleton-Century-Crofts.

Dellas, M. & Gaier, E. L. (1970). Identification of creativity. *Psychological Bulletin, 73,* 55–73.

Dentan, R. K. (1968). *The Semai, a nonviolent people of Malaya.* New York: Holt, Rinehart & Winston.

Gaver, W. & Mandler, G. (1987). Play it again, Sam: On liking music. *Cognition and Emotion, 1,* 259–282.

Geertz, C. (1973). *The interpretation of cultures: Selected essays.* New York: Basic Books.

James, W. (1890). *Principles of psychology.* New York: Holt.

Köhler, W. (1938). *The place of value in a world of facts.* New York: Liveright.

Köhler, W. (1944). Value and fact. *The Journal of Philosophy, 41,* 197–212.

MacDowell, K. A. & Mandler, G. (1989). Constructions of emotion: Discrepancy, arousal, and mood. *Motivation and Emotion, 13,* 105–124.

MacIntyre, A. (1981). *After virtue: a study in moral theory.* London: Duckworth.

MacIntyre, A. (1988). *Whose justice? Which rationality?* London: Duckworth.

Mandler, G. (1964). The interruption of behavior. In E. Levine (Ed.), *Nebraska symposium on motivation: 1964* (pp. 163–219). Lincoln, NE: University of Nebraska Press.

Mandler, G. (1975). *Mind and emotion.* New York: Wiley.

Mandler, G. (1982). The structure of value: Accounting for taste. In M. S. Clark & S. T. Fiske (Eds.), *Affect and cognition; The Seventeenth Annual Carnegie Symposium on Cognition.* Hillsdale, NJ: Lawrence Erlbaum.

Mandler, G. (1984). *Mind and body: Psychology of emotion and stress.* New York: Norton.

Mandler, G. (1985). *Cognitive psychology: An essay in cognitive science.* Hillsdale, NJ: Lawrence Erlbaum.

Mandler, G. (1988). Problems and directions in the study of consciousness. In M. Horowitz (Ed.), *Psychodynamics and cognitions* (pp. 21–45). Chicago: Chicago University Press.

Mandler, G. (1989a). Affect and learning: Causes and consequences of emotional interactions. In D. B. McLeod & V. M. Adams (Eds.), *Affect and mathematical problem solving: A new perspective* (pp. 3–19). New York: Springer-Verlag.

Mandler, G. (1989b). Affect and learning: Reflections and prospects. In D. B. McLeod & V. M. Adams (Eds.), *Affect and mathematical problem solving: A new perspective*. New York: Springer-Verlag.

Mandler, G. (1989c). Memory: Conscious and unconscious. In P. R. Solomon, G. R. Goethals, C. M. Kelley, & B. R. Stephens (Eds.), *Memory: Interdisciplinary approaches* (pp. 84–106). New York: Springer-Verlag.

Mandler, G. (1990). A constructivist theory of emotion. In N. S. Stein, B. L. Leventhal & T. Trabasso (Eds.), *Psychological and biological approaches to emotion* (pp. 21–43). Hillsdale, NJ: Lawrence Erlbaum.

Mandler, G. & Shebo, B. J. (1983). Knowing and liking. *Motivation and Emotion, 7*, 125–144.

Mandler, J. M. (1984). *Stories, scripts, and scenes: Aspects of schema theory*. Hillsdale, NJ: Lawrence Erlbaum.

Mandler, P. (1989, Winter). The "double life" in academia. *Dissent*, 94–99.

Marcel, A. J. (1983). Conscious and unconscious perception: An approach to the relations between phenomenal experience and perceptual processes. *Cognitive Psychology, 15*, 238–300.

Meyer, L. B. (1956). *Emotion and meaning in music*. Chicago: University of Chicago Press.

Nagel, T. (1988). Agreeing in principle. *The Times Literary Supplement, No. 4449*, 747–748.

Ortony, A., Clore, G. L., & Collins, A. (1988). *The cognitive structure of emotions*. New York: Cambridge University Press.

Perry, R. B. (1926). *General theory of value: Its meaning and basic principles construed in terms of interest*. Cambridge: Harvard University Press.

Rokeach, M. (1973). *The nature of human values*. New York: The Free Press.

Rosch, E. (1978). Principles of categorization. In E. Rosch & B. B. Lloyd (Eds.), *Cognition and categorization*. Hillsdale, NJ: Lawrence Erlbaum.

Rosen, C. (1971). *The classical style*. New York: Viking Press.

Schneirla, T. R. (1959). An evolutionary and developmental theory of biphasic processes underlying approach and withdrawal. In M. R. Jones (Ed.), *Nebraska symposium on motivation: 1959*. Lincoln, NE: University of Nebraska Press.

Schweder, R. A. (1982). Beyond self-constructed knowledge: The study of culture and morality. *Merrill-Palmer Quarterly, 28*, 41–69.

Strum, S. C. (1987). *Almost human*. New York: Random House.

Toda, M. (1982). *Man, robot, and society*. Boston: Martinus Nijhoff.

Zajonc, R. B. (1968). Attitudinal effects of mere exposure. *Journal of Personality and Social Psychology Monograph, 9*, 1–28.

Part III

Biological Perspectives

12

Biology and the Origin of Values

Richard E. Michod

Science involves both the search for generalities and their underlying principles. What principles might underlie a scientific analysis of human values? Like any biological species, human beings exist because of the evolutionary process. What, if anything, can the principles of evolutionary biology say about human values or values in general? There are several aspects to the problem of values. First, there is the problem of the origin of the *capacity* to modify behavior to attain desired goals. Second, there is the problem of organized systems of values, such as religious or political value systems. Finally, there is the issue of particular individuals' values.

Like all scientific explanations, evolutionary explanations have an *explanandum* and an *explanans*.[1] In evolutionary explanations based on natural selection, the *explanans* is usually the presence of a particular trait in a species or population. Concerning values, this refers to either (1) the capacity of using values to modify behavior, or (2) the particular values that are so used (either individual values or systems of values).

What does the *explanans* of natural selection explanations consist of? Darwin (1859) deduced the process of natural selection from the existence of variability and heritability in traits that affect an organism's ability to compete successfully in the struggle to survive and reproduce.[2] Heritable traits that are advantageous—those that increase the fitness of their carriers—are passed on to future generations in greater numbers than are disadvantageous traits. It is this increase in the frequency of

[1] For a discussion of evolutionary explanation and its relation to explanation in other sciences, see Michod (1981, 1986) and Byerly and Michod (1991).

[2] Evolutionary biologists now appreciate that competition among individuals, emphasized by Darwin in the struggle to survive and reproduce, is only one kind of interaction that can lead to selection. Cooperation, even altruism, at the level of individuals can lead to selection of genes and change in gene frequencies (e.g., kin selection, for review see Michod, 1982; reciprocal altruism, see Trivers, 1971; Axelrod & Hamilton, 1981; Brown, Sanderson, & Michod, 1982).

advantageous traits and the corresponding decrease in the frequency of disadvantageous traits that Darwin called natural selection. The *explanans* of natural selection explanations must include reference to the factors emphasized by Darwin, the two central factors being variation in fitness and heritability.

The ideas of fitness and heritability, although simple to define, are complex to put in practice (Byerly & Michod, 1990). In the simplest formulation, fitness either refers to an organism's *ability* to survive and reproduce successfully or to its *actual* survival and reproductive success.[3] No two organisms are identical, and, thus, they are not equally able to survive and reproduce. Because of the traits they possess, some organisms are more fit than others. For example, those ancestors of the modern giraffe with longer necks than their peers could better withstand an environment in which food was to be found high in trees. Differences between organisms can be selected only if they are heritable—that is passed from parent to offspring.

Heritability refers to the positive correlation between parent and offspring traits that must exist for selection to occur. The need for heritability is basic. If parents have increased fitness by virtue of possessing the trait in question (the first requirement), the trait will not persist and increase through time if it is not passed on to offspring. Darwin knew little about the mechanisms underlying heritability. However, he did appreciate that offspring tend to resemble their parents and further, that this resemblance was necessary for evolution by natural selection. Traits can have high heritability for a variety of reasons. Today we know that heritability of most biological traits results from the faithful and accurate replication of the information contained in DNA molecules. Offspring resemble their parents because they possess copies of their parents' DNA sequences, or genes. But there are other reasons that offspring resemble parents.

Offspring may have traits similar to those of their parents because of learning. This is especially true of behavioral traits and psychological traits such as values. Consider religious preference. Children tend to have the same religion as their parents not because religious preference has a genetic basis but because parents often impose religion on their children. Thus, there is high heritability for religious preference. This kind of

---

[3] When relatives are present in an organism's environment, as they almost always are in human societies, the concept of fitness must be expanded to that of "inclusive fitness," as discussed below. For the time being, however, I ignore this complication. I will not go into the philosophical and practical problems involved with estimating an organism's ability to survive and reproduce independently from its actual survival and reproductive success (Byerly & Michod, 1991).

heritability results from cultural transmission and is termed *vertical transmission*. It is difficult to distinguish vertical transmission from genetic transmission (Cavalli-Sforza, this volume). Religion, eating habits, values, and almost any behavioral trait could be subjected to this kind of learning and therefore could have high heritability without being genetically based. Thus, like genetic transmission, cultural transmission can produce heritability in human traits. It is reasonable that the capacity to modify behavior in an environmentally contingent manner is genetically heritable, as may be tendencies to behave in certain ways. Yet it is unlikely that specific values like religious preference are genetically heritable, although they could be culturally heritable (Cavalli-Sforza, this volume).

Selection can operate between any two traits with high heritability regardless of the cause of heritability, so long as the traits have different effects on fitness. Continuing with the example of religion, consider two religions: one that favored birth control and another that opposed it. As a result of these different values, family size would often be larger for families belonging to the religion opposed to birth control. That is, religious doctrine would cause differences in biological fitness. Because of these fitness differences and the high heritability of religion, selection could occur on the basis of religious preference. All other factors being equal, the frequency of the religion opposed to birth control would increase in the population.

Using these evolutionary principles we could inquire into the selective factors that led to the origin of the capacity for values by asking the following kind of question. "In what situations would an animal that had the capacity of changing its behavior by combining information from its environment with internal goals (values) increase in frequency over other animals that did not have this capacity?" The evolutionary analysis of this question would involve several steps. First, the goals, behaviors and environment must be specified. Second, a rule must be assumed by which a goal-in-an-environment is translated into a specific behavior.[4] Third, the fitness consequences of each behavior in each environment must be specified. Finally, the heritability of the rule and the pattern of change of the environmental states must be specified. If all of these steps are taken then the answer to such a question can be determined by traditional population genetics techniques. Similarly, one also might inquire into the selective factors leading to the establishment of certain value systems, such as one based on the rule "try to act in such a way as to benefit your kin."

---

[4] As pointed out by Franklin (this volume), "the development of the ability to evaluate was a major step in the evolution of complex organisms."

The Origin of Values

The Adaptive Significance of Values

To evolve by natural selection a trait must increase fitness. How might the capacity for values increase fitness? Values occur in a cultural context. Concerning culture, Cavalli-Sforza (this volume) states that "its transmissibility is the basis for its adaptedness, for it permits the accumulation of knowledge over generations." More precisely, Boyd and Richerson (1985) propose that the question of the adaptive significance of culture comes down to the following issue: when is it advantageous for an organism not to learn by experience in its environment (on its own, so to speak), but to learn by copying mom, dad, or another member of its species? To understand the adaptive significance of individual learning versus social learning is to understand the evolutionary origin of the capacity for culture. At the basis of Boyd and Richerson's (1985) approach is the assumption that individual learning is imperfect because the knowledge available to any particular individual is limited. As a result, individual learning produces errors. According to this view, culture acts as a repository for the collective knowledge of individuals, both living and dead. A stable environment is required for social learning to be favored over individual learning so that the rules taught by a culture are adaptive in the present environment. On the other hand, individual learning is adaptive when the environment changes rapidly and cultural knowledge is out of date.

There is no simple relation between culture and values. As discussed below, the question of the origin of the capacity for values is a different question than the origin of culture as posed above. Value systems may either respond[5] or resist[6] change as the culture accumulates new information. By definition cultural traits must be learned, whereas values are not necessarily transmitted only by learning. Thus the question of the adaptive significance of values is a different question than the question of the adaptive significance of culture.

What then is the adaptive significance of values? Values may be surrogate variables, but for what do they stand? This question needs careful evolutionary analysis, and I am not familiar with any rigorous treatment of it. However, for the purposes of discussion I suggest that the evolu-

---

[5] For example, medical ethics and the accompanying laws are currently adapting to new biological technologies such as gene cloning.

[6] One is reminded here of the existing pressure to change catholic doctrine by, for example, allowing women to be priests or to use birth control, so as to be more in step with cultural change.

tionary approach to values outlined in the previous section might lead to the following conclusion. The adaptive significance of values, at least originally, was that they produced fitness enhancing behavior in variable (novel?) environments, without the need of specifying a specific behavioral response for each environmental state. According to the views of values and culture mentioned above, values and culture appear to be adaptive, at least initially, in opposite situations. The capacity for values is most adaptive in variable environments, while culture (social learning) is most adaptive in stable environments. However, variable environments may be stable—thus the variation between the four seasons is predictable from one year to the next—and so there is no inherent contradiction to supposing that value systems and culture coevolved.

What is necessary for the evolution of the capacity to have values? For values to intervene, behavior must be decoupled from sensory input. Evidence for such decoupling can be found in Franklin's chapter (this volume). Franklin argues that "the neural mechanisms that underlie motivation are somewhat independent of the sensory analysis that normally leads to their activation." This decoupling of sensory input from motivation is critical for the evolution of values, since it allows evaluation of sensory input according to goals or values. However, this decoupling also may allow motivation to become divorced from biological fitness, especially in extreme environments. The critical word in Franklin's quotation, from the point of view of this discussion, is *normally*.

As Tiger (this volume) points out, much of our biological evolution occurred 2–4 million years ago, while most of our cultural evolution occurred within the last 10 generations. The normal environment for a hunter–gatherer primate is far removed from that of modern industrial man. Yet, many of our adaptations, including the capacity for values, evolved 2–4 million years ago in a completely different environment from the one we now inhabit.[7] For example, consider drug abuse. Although our primate ancestor's environment contained naturally occurring chemicals that could directly stimulate the nervous system, it also tended to provide prompt reprisal for their abuse. In our primate ancestor's environment, drug abuse would likely lead immediately to decreased biological fitness. But, in our modern society, where many are buffered from the sources of mortality that threatened our primate ancestor, there is more free time to experiment with direct stimulation of the nervous system and bypass the normal sensory context in which the neural substrates that underlie motivation evolved.

[7] This does not mean that humans have stopped evolving, for they have not. It means only that the recent cultural changes in our environment have been too rapid to expect genetic adaptation to them.

Do Values Really Exist?

Do values really exist, or are they simply heuristic devices needed by social science to explain regularities in behavior (Barth, this volume)? The idea of values presupposes the existence of systems capable of evaluation. Before the evolution of nervous systems, the only process that could evaluate alternative states was natural selection, which constantly and mechanically evaluates alternative heritable traits according to their effects on inclusive fitness. Heritable traits that have higher inclusive fitness effects increase in frequency over those that have lower inclusive fitness effects. Thus, the original value must have been inclusive fitness. Although it may be an anthropomorphism to think of a mechanical process like natural selection as having values, when nervous systems and brains first evolved they likely adopted inclusive fitness as their guiding value.

The basic function of nervous systems is to elicit conditional behavior. The capacity to bias behavior requires that positive value be placed on certain outcomes. Presumably this capacity first evolved under the guidance of natural selection in which biological values, such as hunger, pain, or pleasure, were tightly linked to effects on inclusive fitness. Therefore, the original values were likely surrogate variables for increased inclusive fitness. What is inclusive fitness?

Inclusive Fitness

The basic matter addressed by inclusive fitness concerns the operation of natural selection in populations in which relatives are present. This makes the concept especially relevant to human evolution that has occurred for the most part in small groups of extended family members. The concept of inclusive fitness, and the attendant cost/benefit rule for spread of an altruistic gene, were developed by W. D. Hamilton (1963, 1964a,b) and have revolutionized the way biologists and some social scientists view behavior. In addition, inclusive fitness and Hamilton's rule [Eq. (3) below] provide a formal framework for many empirical studies on the evolution of behavior.

Relatives share genes. Because they have at least one common ancestor (parents, grandparents, greatgrandparents, etc.), relatives possess copies of the same DNA sequence. These shared genes are termed "identical by descent," since they are identical by virtue of the fact that they are copies of a DNA sequence in a common ancestor and, therefore, are descended from that ancestor. In the simple but common case of a population structured into family units, different siblings carry genes that are identical by descent from their parents. In sexually reproducing populations, copies of ancestor's genes exist in different individuals to varying degrees. Inclusive fitness takes this complex issue into account in predicting how interactions between individuals should evolve. For discussion, the individuals involved in an interaction are often called the "donor" and "recipient" of the behavior of interest.

Inclusive fitness thinking is based on the realization that an individual's offspring, such as the donor's offspring, are simply one kind of relative. Other relatives, the siblings or first-cousins also carry genes that are identical with those in the donor. So these other kin can serve as vehicles for the perpetuation of the donor's genes, just as the donor's offspring. Because of sexual reproduction, the donor's offspring carry approximately one-half the donor's genes. Other relatives may carry an equally substantial portion of the donor's genes. For the same reason that the donor can pass on more of its genes by helping its offspring (for example, by providing parental care), so the donor may increase the frequency of its genes by helping these other relatives.

In population genetics inclusive fitness begins with a baseline individual fitness to which the different effects of the behavior are added. It is important to realize that the baseline fitness is the individual fitness that the donor would have without any social interactions. (This baseline fitness is usually assumed to be standardized to one.) The effects of the donor's behavior considered in inclusive fitness are the effects of the behavior on the donor's and recipient's baseline fitnesses, where the effects on the recipient's fitnesses are weighted by the degree of genetic relatedness of recipient and donor, R. (The relatedness of the donor to itself is, of course, one.) Assuming the donor of interest is of genotype i and letting c_i and b_i be the additive effects of the donor's behavior on itself and the recipient, the inclusive fitness effect of i's behavior is simply

$$c_i + Rb_i \tag{1}$$

Inclusive fitness has three important functions in the study of natural selection in populations in which relatives are present. First, genes affecting behavior can be shown to increase or decrease as a function of their positive or negative inclusive fitness effects respectively. In other words for i's behavior to spread,

$$c_i + Rb_i > 0 \tag{2}$$

An altruistic behavior is one in which the effect on the fitness of the donor is negative and the effect on the fitness of the recipient is positive ($c_i < 0$ *and* $b_i > 0$). Requiring the inclusive fitness effect to be positive [Eq. (2)] for an altruistic behavior ($c_i < 0$ *and* $b_i > 0$), gives Hamilton's rule

$$-c_i b_i < R \qquad\qquad (3)$$

for spread of the altruistic gene. Thus, the concept of inclusive fitness and Hamilton's cost–benefit rule are intimately related. Second, the average inclusive fitness effect in the population increases, and is eventually maximized, by natural selection.[8] Finally, the inclusive fitness effect is a simple and straightforward quantity, depending as it does on just three parameters, c, b, and R. The most attractive aspect of inclusive fitness is its apparent simplicity. Nevertheless, it summarizes the qualitative outcome of selection in a complicated frequency-dependent situation.

What is meant by an organism's inclusive fitness? The previous discussion dealt with the effects of behaviors on inclusive fitness and how these effects determine the evolution of genes affecting behavior. Based on this discussion, we can see that an organism's inclusive fitness is nothing more than the sum of the inclusive fitness effects of all its behaviors.

Values in Modern Society

As discussed above, we have a scientific theory for the origin of the capacity to have values and indeed a theory for the original value itself. What can this tell us about values in current human societies?

It is important to realize what is *not* an issue in asking this question. The issue is not whether human behavior is genetically determined. In fact, just the opposite is really the claim. The idea is that *evolution provided us with values instead of programming us genetically.* There can be no question that human behavior is highly conditional on circumstances. The unsolved problem is whether inclusive fitness is a kind of umbrella value in current value systems. Is human behavior, and the value systems that motivate it, generally guided by one overriding rule, or value—that of increased inclusive fitness—or do other values unrelated to inclusive fitness come into play? The answer may be one of relative proportion, how much of the diversity in human value systems can be explained by the umbrella value of inclusive fitness.

Whether increased inclusive fitness acts as an umbrella value in value systems is an empirical question that I cannot evaluate, for I am unfamiliar with the requisite data. In both Tiger's and de Waal's chapters values are implicitly viewed as biases in behavior that increase inclusive fitness.[9] Tiger (this volume), among many others, argues that the umbrella value

[8] The conditions under which these first two properties hold are discussed in Michod and Abugov (1980) and Michod (1982).

[9] Especially, in their assumed scenarios concerning the human species' evolutionary past.

of inclusive fitness does explain many interesting features of human behavior, for example, why murderers tend to kill unrelated individuals, the generality of the incest taboo, and the occurrence of mother's brother, among many others. On the other hand, according to George Mandler (this volume), "we now have enough sophisticated evidence both from anthropology and from primate studies to realize that human and simian diversity place somewhat weak constraints on the range of possible human values."

Although increased inclusive fitness was the first value, it does not necessarily follow that inclusive fitness retains its potency in our current environment. There are many examples of biological traits that evolve for one reason but are used for another. The human brain and nervous system did not evolve in environments in which there were violins, but this did not discourage Beethoven. The capacity to evaluate outcomes according to inclusive fitness effects could be used to evaluate outcomes according to other criteria. This leads to the question of whether the capacity to modify behavior on the basis of values allowed the construction of new value systems unrelated to inclusive fitness.

A casual glance at modern industrial society suggests that this may have happened. The lives of modern persons are filled with biologically insignificant and risky behavior. Why? Examples of risky behaviors are plentiful: smoking and drug use are just two. Why and how can the same motivational systems that generate biologically significant behaviors such as having sex and eating be used to generate biologically insignificant or even biologically risky and harmful behaviors?

Evolution may have produced the capacity to have values without providing much guidance concerning what values individuals adopt. This possibility strikes me as unlikely. The capacity to have values is based on sophisticated neural and hormonal systems that are costly. Costly traits cannot evolve by natural selection unless there are correspondingly large benefits. It is hard to reconcile the evolution of a costly, sophisticated trait—such as the capacity for values—with the idea that evolution would have not constrained its use to biologically significant matters *at least in the environment in which the capacity evolved first*. Therefore, we expect that the capacity for values initially had large beneficial effects on inclusive fitness. So why is a costly, sophisticated, and well-designed trait used for meaningless or even harmful ends? I am not sure of the answer to this question, although the following interrelated points seem relevant.

First, much apparently meaningless and harmful behavior may, in the final analysis, be important in shaping skills and abilities that are ultimately important to fitness. Much of this apparently meaningless or harmful behavior may be the functional equivalent of play. Behavioral ecologists and evolutionary biologists are just beginning to understand the biological function of animal play (e.g., Fagen, 1981). We need only note here that play can function in the development of many activities that are important in determining fitness. While activities like sky diving, gymnastics, or dancing may be categorized as play, it is hard to do so with an activity like drug abuse.

Second, there is the matter of free time. For any living organism, one can consider the time that must be expended on matters of biological survival and reproduction—time spent eating, reproducing, etc. By free time, I simply mean the time left over. Of course, the activities undertaken during free time may affect biological fitness (for example, drug abuse), but it is not necessary that they do so. Anyone familiar with watching animals knows that for much of the time animals appear to be doing nothing. The invention of culture creates even more free time. Free time in an organism with a nervous system in which motivation is only loosely coupled to biological circumstance provides opportunity for biologically insignificant behavior.

Finally, our modern environment may be so different from the environment in which we evolved, that the rules (involving values) that once translated the environment into useful behaviors no longer do so. Our biological situation in modern society is radically different from the environment in which we—and the capacity to have values—evolved. As already mentioned, Franklin (this volume) discusses the point that the sensory input that often leads to motivation is decoupled from the neural mechanisms that underlie motivation. If this is the case we should not be surprised that in radically new environments the neural mechanisms leading to motivation and action may be activated by new, and possibly biologically insignificant (or even harmful) events. On the other hand, this view is a bit unsatisfactory in light of the hypothesis that values evolved for the function of coping with changing and variable environments. The issue hinges on what distinguishes a novel or variable environment from a radically new environment.

The evolutionary advantage of value systems lies in their flexibility in coping with varying environments and changed circumstances. This flexibility demands a circuit in which action is decoupled from circumstance. However, it is precisely this decoupling of circumstance from action that allows arousal of biologically significant behavior in biologically meaningless contexts. The circuit works from the biological point of view, so long as the changed circumstances are not too different from that in which it evolved. Yet in radically different environments the rules and cues used in evaluation may no longer work. Like the sensory capacity that causes the moth to fly into the light, the capacity to modify behavior according to values may not always serve our biological fitness.

References

Axelrod, R., & Hamilton, W. D. (1981). The evolution of cooperation. *Science 211*, 1390–1396.

Boyd, R., & Richerson, P. J. (1985). *Culture and the evolutionary process*. Chicago: University of Chicago Press.

Brown, J. S., Sanderson, M., & Michod, R. E. (1982). Evolution of social behavior by reciprocation. *Journal of Theoretical Biology, 99,* 319–339.

Byerly, H. C., & Michod, R. E. (1991). Fitness and evolutionary explanation. *Biology and Philosophy, 6,* 1–22.

Darwin, C. (1859). *On the origin of species by means of natural selection*. London: John Murray.

Fagen, R. (1981). *Animal play behavior*. Oxford: Oxford University Press.

Hamilton, W. D. (1963). The evolution of altruistic behavior. *American Naturalist, 97,* 354–356.

Hamilton, W. D. (1964a). The genetical evolution of social behaviour, I. *Journal of Theoretical Biology, 7,* 1–16.

Hamilton, W. D. (1964b). The genetical evolution of social behaviour, II. *Journal of Theoretical Biology, 7,* 17–52.

Michod, R. E. (1981). Positive heuristics in evolutionary biology. *British Journal of Philosophical Science, 32,* 1–36.

Michod, R. E. (1982). The theory of kin selection. *Annual Review of Ecological Systems, 13,* 23–55.

Michod, R. E. (1986). On adaptedness and fitness and their role in evolutionary explanation. *Journal of History Biology, 19,* 289–302.

Michod, R. E., & Abugov, R. (1980). Adaptive topography in family-structured models of kin selection. *Science, 210,* 667–669.

Trivers, R. L. (1971). The evolution of reciprocal altruism. *Quarterly Review of Biology, 46,* 35–57.

13

The Neural Basis of Pleasure and Pain

Keith B. J. Franklin

To the psychologist, value is defined by effort and choice. An object or state of affairs has positive value if an individual selects it from a choice of options or will expend effort to obtain it. It has negative value if an individual rejects it from a selection of alternatives and will expend effort to avoid it. For the psychobiologist, the problem of value is to understand why some states of affairs are highly valued at a given time by a member of a particular species, and how the decisions about value are generated by the nervous system. These are fundamental questions in psychobiology and one could say that the development of the ability to evaluate was a major step in the evolution of complex organisms.

The basic mechanism organisms use to identify objects and events is called "stimulus filtering"[1]—a cell or group of cells in the nervous system is tuned to respond to a particular pattern or combination of features in the sensory input and is unresponsive to other possible features. The feature may be as specific as a particular chemical substance or as general as movement somewhere in the visual field. The response of these neurons constitutes a mental representation of the object that is associated with the feature. In simpler organisms, such as insects, objects are defined by a small number of features and the cells that respond to these features are closely connected to cells that control motor responses. If we may speak of perception and value in such organisms, perception, evaluation, and initiation of action are virtually simultaneous and indistinguishable. The stimulus filters possessed by an organism are closely tied to its life-style and have been selected through evolution to detect features that are strongly correlated with objects and events important for survival and reproduction. A classic example is the mated female tick that clings to a bush waiting for a mammal that will provide the blood meal she needs to produce her eggs. For the tick, a

[1] This concept and fascinating examples are discussed in Hinde (1979).

mammal is represented by the smell of butyric acid, which is produced by mammalian skin glands.

As animals adapted to ecological niches that require mobility and flexibility of behavior they developed more elaborate sensory systems that, compared to those of simpler organisms, greatly increase the range of circumstances under which the animal can distinguish and identify biologically significant objects and events. The increase in the discriminating power of sensory systems is achieved by hierarchies of filters in which those closest to the sensory organ detect relatively small or simple details of the sensory environment—in the visual system these appear to be oriented lines and edges, both static and moving (Hubel & Wiesel, 1959; Michael, 1969). Representations of complex features and objects are built up from combinations of lower order features.[2] However, the enormous amount of information that permits fine discriminations between objects and events creates a problem of classification. The precise combinations of features that define individual instances of biologically important events (e.g., predators) may be quite variable across time and space and thus evolutionary selection, which requires much time, does not favor the development of higher order feature detectors that can filter them and yet retain the detail that permits discrimination. Complex organisms have a built-in ability to recognize important events but these detectors respond to very general characteristics. For example, organisms with eyes that form images will draw back if presented with a visual image that increases rapidly in size. Such an image is produced by an object moving toward the organism at high speed and rapid avoidance is obviously advantageous. This response is shown by spiders and humans. In human infants it is easily produced by the rapid inflation of a balloon.

With the benefit of hindsight we know that the problem of building object detectors that can utilize the information about details can be solved by a nervous system that modifies itself in response to the outcomes of previous decisions, that is, by a system that learns. However, this flexibility has a cost. If sensory input is to be interpretable on the basis of experience, sensory channels (i.e., outputs from detectors tuned to certain patterns) cannot be hard-wired to the circuits that generate motor commands. There must, as well, be systems to promote advantageous linkages, and these systems must be connected to some sensory channels that have built-in capability to recognize biologically significant

---

[2] This statement glosses over a vast literature dealing with a very difficult problem that has been most extensively investigated in the visual system. While it is generally accepted that perception is accomplished by hierarchies of feature detector cells, how such hierarchies are arranged remains a matter of intensive research and debate. In particular it is now believed that different qualities of the visual image (i.e., motion, pattern, color, depth, etc.) may be processed simultaneously in different pathways (DeYoe & Van Essen, 1988).

events. This latter provision is important. If an organism is to modify its evaluation of sensory events in accordance with its experience of the consequences of approaching or escaping them, it must have some built-in capacity to recognize that an advantageous or disadvantageous state of affairs has occurred.

People have long recognized that some stimuli are more intimately linked to emotional or motivational states than others. Certain tastes, smells, and sensations can hardly be experienced without evoking a response of acceptance or rejection. Consider the taste of sugar or salt versus the taste of alkali, the smell of roses or sweet herbs versus the smell of rotting meat, the feel of warm fur on the skin versus the penetration of sharp thorns. It is often noted that tastes and smells figure prominently in any such list of motivationally charged sensory events. This is not surprising from a biological point of view. Both senses detect chemicals, which, unlike sights and sounds, are relatively unambiguous signals for biologically significant events (Steiner, 1974). Thus sweet tastes are, with few and rare exceptions, indicative of the presence of carbohydrates, while rotting meat odors usually indicate the presence of decaying flesh. Whether an organism accepts or rejects the substance depends on the species, but the tastes and odors are almost perfect indicators of the presence of potential foods. Neuroanatomists have recognized that the elaboration of neural systems of smell and taste is phylogenetically old. In mammals the taste system is very closely connected to oropharyngeal motor centers, and acceptance and rejection can be determined at a low level in the nervous system. We know that decerebrate rats (Grill & Norgren, 1978) and humans (Steiner, 1974) exhibit normal reactions to taste. Human anencephalic infants respond with smiling and swallowing to sweet substances, and grimacing and spitting out to bitter tastes. It seems that the value of tastes is assessed as soon as they are identified, and since they are almost inside the body the important responses are ingestion or rejection.

Pain caused by actual or impending injury to tissue is another unambiguous stimulus. Simple withdrawal reflexes are organized in the spinal cord and more elaborate reactions, including mobile escape and vocalization occur as long as the brain stem is intact (Carroll & Lim, 1960). Electrical stimulation of these systems in the brain elicits emotional reactions of aversion or escape (Olds & Olds, 1963).

In contrast, if we follow the auditory or visual information as it is processed through the thalamus and the various cortical representations we find no hint of emotional reaction. One of the striking findings from the early investigations of electrical stimulation of the cortex was the absence of emotional content of sensations and movements evoked from the cortex (Penfield & Jasper, 1954). Thus we may conclude that in the sensory systems of the distance receptors the greater part of sensory perception occurs without evaluation. This, of course, is in accord with our conclusions from subjective experience.

In the early 1950s investigators began to stimulate the inner core of the brain in both humans and animals and they found sites in the brain at which electrical stimulation appeared to be pleasurable (Olds & Milner, 1954). Animals would work at various tasks to acquire this brain stimulation, and brain stimulation appeared to produce more highly motivated behavior than any incentive previously known to experimental psychologists. There were also sites at which stimulation appeared to be highly aversive. Animals would work to escape or avoid stimulation of these sites (Olds & Olds, 1963). The conclusion that these findings were really indicative of a neural substrate of pleasure and pain was reinforced by investigations of brain stimulation in humans, who reported pleasurable and disagreeable sensations from stimulation of sites in some of the areas mapped by James Olds in the rat (Heath, 1963; Ervin & Martin, 1986). In many cases the feelings elicited by brain stimulation were ineffable and the origin of the feelings was obscure. This showed that the stimulation was not simply evoking affectively tinged memories or synthetic sensations—rather the stimulation seemed to be evoking feelings without relevant sensory content. This is what we would expect if the neural mechanisms of emotion and motivation are somewhat independent of the sensory perceptions that normally leads to their activation.

The most vigorous and sustained self-stimulation is observed at sites that run in a line from the anterior midbrain through to the deep anterior forebrain (see Figure 1). These sites lie along the course of a large fiber tract, the medial forebrain bundle, that connects the ventral forebrain with the midbrain. Most other positive sites are in structures that have connections with this tract. Along its course the tract gives off and receives fibers from many nuclei in the hypothalamus that are involved in basic biological activities such as feeding, drinking, sexual behavior, and hormone release. When the rewarding sites are stimulated behavioral activation is often observed (St. Laurent, 1988) and, if appropriate goal objects are present, active exploration of the environment may focus on the object and develop into consummatory behaviors (Valenstein, Cox, & Kakolewski, 1968).

If the stimulation is applied when the animal is approaching a particular place, the exploration becomes more and more restricted to the spot where the stimulation is turned on. Thus, environmental stimuli that are associated with arousal and exploration come to control spontaneous exploration.

These phenomena might have remained a laboratory curiosity had the

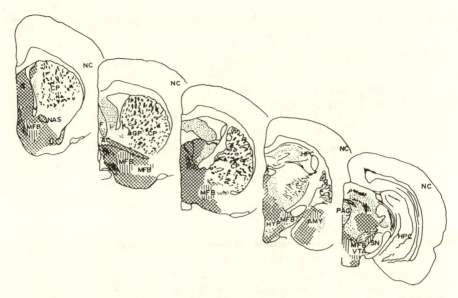

Figure 1. The figure shows a series of drawings of transverse sections of the left side of a rat's brain from the anterior forebrain (top left) to the midbrain (bottom right). Areas in which rats will work to obtain stimulation are shaded with vertical lines, areas in which stimulation is strongly aversive are shaded with dots, areas in which rats will both work to obtain stimulation and to escape stimulation are cross hatched. AC, anterior commissure; AMY, amygdala; CP, caudate-putamen; F, fornix; GP, globus pallidus; HPC, hippocampus; MFB, medial forebrain bundle; NC, neocortex; PAG, periaqueductal gray; S, septum; SN, substantia nigra; VTA, ventral tegmental area. Figure modified from Olds and Olds (1963).

developing pharmaceutical industry not begun to produce a variety of psychoactive drugs to reduce appetite and anxiety, to kill pain, and to reverse depression. Some of these drugs turned out to be addictive. The addictive drugs produce euphoria or improve mood (Henningfield, Johnson, & Jasinski, 1987) and people who take them have a strong tendency to rearrange their lives so that continued access to the drug becomes one of their highest ranked values. Moreover drug-directed behavior turned out to be easy to develop in animals. Animals will self-administer most of the drugs abused by humans and with similar preferences. Some of the common drugs they will self-administer are listed in Table 1.

The fact that animals readily learn to self-administer drugs shows that drug self-administration is not to be explained away as an aspect of human psychopathology. Rather, it must reflect some aspect of the natural organization of the brain that has come under the influence of an

Table 1. Some Drugs That Are Self-Administered by Animals and Humans

Stimulants	*Opioids*	*Tranquilizers*
Amphetamine	Morphine	Chlordiazepoxide
Methamphetamine	Heroin	Diazepam
Cocaine	Methadone	Pentobarbital
Phenmetrazine	Codeine	Amobarbital
Methlphenidate	Pentazocine	Alcohol
Pipradrol	Meperidine	
Diethylproprion		
Nicotine		

unnatural stimulus—a purified chemical. In studying the mechanisms of action of self-administered drugs it soon became clear that they acted on neural systems that had much in common with those that had been found in the brain stimulation studies. Experiments by Larry Stein in the early 1960s showed that self-stimulation behavior was extraordinarily sensitive to the stimulant effect of amphetamine (Stein, 1964)—a drug that is highly addictive and produces arousing effects very similar to those produced by brain stimulation. Moreover, both self-stimulation and the stimulant effects of amphetamine could be blocked by drugs that depleted the brain of some neurotransmitters that had recently been localized in the brain.

One of these neurotransmitters was dopamine, which derives from cells that are clustered at the midbrain–diencephalic junction (the VTA and SN in Figure 1) and send their axons along the MFB to almost all structures that support self-stimulation. Both self-stimulation and amphetamine release dopamine at the terminals of the dopamine system (Hernandez & Hoebel, 1988; Phillips, Jacubovic, & Fibiger, 1987). Moreover dopamine release in the terminal regions stimulates locomotor activity and exploration. There is now a great deal of evidence that the rewarding effect of brain stimulation and drugs involves the release of dopamine or other neurotransmitters in the structures innervated by the dopamine system. In humans, who can report directly on their subjective experience, dopamine-blocking drugs abolish the stimulant and euphoriant effects of amphetamine (Gunne, Anggard, & Jönsson, 1972). In animals dopamine-blocking drugs reduce the effectiveness of brain stimulation reward (Franklin, 1978) and self-administration of the dopamine-releasing drugs, amphetamine and cocaine, are blocked when the dopamine neurons are destroyed (Roberts & Zito, 1987). More recently it has been shown that animals will self-administer minute amounts of morphine or heroin directly into the brain (Wise, 1987; Koob, Vaccarino, Amalric, & Bloom, 1987) when they are injected into the region that contains the dopamine cells or their targets in the nucleus accumbens (NAS in Figure 1).

Because drugs and electrical stimulation produce their effects by acting directly on the neural mechanisms of motivation, and bypass the sensory systems that normally activate them, we are able to see clearly how activation of these systems transforms the value of sensory perceptions. I have already mentioned how rewarding brain stimulation seems to make a neutral place or object become the target of goal-directed behavior. A similar phenomenon is observed if animals are given an injection of amphetamine or an opiate in a particular place (van der Kooy, 1987). That place becomes a spot the animal will seek out if given a choice. Drugs and brain stimulation will also modify the evaluation of other sensory modalities such as taste. If a rat is allowed to taste a novel solution (e.g., coffee, to which the rat has a mild aversion) and is, immediately afterward, given a period of self-stimulation, on the next exposure to the solution the rat exhibits a preference for coffee solution and drinks more of it (Ettenberg & White, 1978). It is important to note that the rat has not been trained or rewarded for drinking the solution, but has merely experienced the taste in close temporal relationship with vigorous activation of the self-stimulation system.

The separability and interaction of the sensory and evaluative mechanisms can be further illustrated through the phenomena of pain and the effects of analgesic drugs. Pain is a psychological concept that has two aspects. On the one hand, pain is a sensation with qualities that can be described and quantified psychophysically. An individual can, for instance, describe it as pricking and burning with a magnitude of 4 on a 6-point scale. Pain also refers to a motive state that is highly aversive, and evokes reflex and voluntary behaviors directed to removing the source of pain. There are, however, circumstances in which responses to pain are suppressed or modified by other biologically significant stimuli. Analgesic drugs and brain stimulation can activate these inhibitory systems. One type of analgesia has been quite extensively studied. It is evoked by opioids or brain stimulation acting at sites in the brain stem core, which in turn stimulate pathways descending into the spinal cord where they inhibit the transmission of sensory input from peripheral pain receptors (Basbaum & Fields, 1984). A consequence of this is that the threshold for eliciting reflex and voluntary escape behaviors is raised. A natural stimulus for this mechanism appears to be fear or other highly stressful states. Many of these sites at which brain stimulation blocks pain sensitivity are in regions classified as aversive by Olds. Stressors such as restraint and shock can induce this type of analgesia (Akil, Watson, Young, Lewis,

Khachaturian, & Walker, 1984) and potentiate the analgesic effect of morphine. Its biological function may be to suppress responses to pain during emergency actions.

Analgesia is not only associated with stress. Indeed clinical analgesia produced by opiates is associated with warm comfortable feelings, and clinical lore suggests that analgesia may be reduced by anxiety or mild stress. An interesting observation is that there is a strong association between a drug being a good analgesic and it having abuse potential. A number of analgesic drugs are not used because of their abuse potential: amphetamine is a good example. In clinical trials amphetamine increases the potency of morphine and does not have some of the undesirable side effects (Forrest et al., 1977). Using an animal model of injury-produced pain Michael Morgan and I recently found evidence that amphetamine and morphine can produce analgesia through some of the neural pathways that are involved in drug self-administration (Franklin, 1989). The analgesic effect of morphine and amphetamine is blocked by destruction of the dopamine neurons and reduced by pharmacological antagonists of dopamine. Furthermore analgesia is induced by microinjections of morphine into the dopamine cell group in the VTA or the nucleus accumbens—the structures into which animals self-administer microinjections of opioids. We might interpret this analgesia as a transformation of the motivational significance of painful sensations and there is some evidence to support this idea. In one recent study we examined the effect of morphine in humans who had undergone abdominal surgery. In this experiment (which was done for other reasons) we had patients rate the intensity of their pain on several sensory dimensions (burning, pricking, and so forth) while they were allowed generous doses of morphine on demand. Initially patients reported quite severe pain and their behavior was consistent with their reports—they were pale, drawn, and preoccupied with their suffering, and they requested morphine. After several successive small doses of morphine had been administered their behavior suddenly changed—they became relaxed, began to speak spontaneously, and refused further morphine saying they were comfortable. At the same time they continued to rate the intensity of the pain much as before morphine. Some patients seemed to be aware of the discrepancy between their behavior in refusing medication and their description of their pain experience. One patient remarked "I don't have pain—it hurts."

Such transformations of the evaluations of even highly aversive stimuli is not merely an artifact of using powerful drugs. Many years ago Pavlov used an aversive stimulus, such as cutting or burning of the skin, as a signal for food presented to a hungry dog. At first the stimulus produced its unconditioned reaction of struggling and whining. After a number of trials in which the noxious stimulus signaled the presentation of food the dog began to salivate when the noxious stimulus was presented and ceased to show distress (Pavlov, 1927).

I have used these examples to argue that we have now identified some neural mechanisms that give sensory perceptions their motivational significance. I have concentrated on positive evaluation because more is known about that system though a parallel system of negative evaluation clearly exists. However, we know less about the neurochemistry of aversion, possibly because we have not found any neurotransmitter that holds such a central role as does dopamine in positive evaluation. Nevertheless, recent studies of the mode of action of antianxiety drugs do confirm the presence and location of brain structures involved in aversion. It is now believed that these drugs act by facilitating the effect of a ubiquitous inhibitory transmitter (γ-aminobutyric acid or GABA) in the brain regions mapped as aversive by Olds.

Microinjections of antianxiety drugs or GABA into the periaqueductal gray, medial hypothalamus, or amygdala (see Figure 1) inhibit defense reactions elicited by electrical stimulation of these sites or by peripheral electric shocks (Milani & Graeff, 1987; Audi & Graeff, 1984). In addition some drugs with a pharmacological action opposite to the antianxiety drugs have been developed. One of these, β-carboxylic acid ethyl ester, has been given to both monkeys and humans, and found to induce severe anxiety or fear (Dorow, Horowski, Paschelke, Amin, & Braestrup, 1983; Ninan, Insel, Cohen, Skolnick, & Paul, 1982). One of the human experimenters took the drug in the laboratory and became so overwhelmed by feelings of threat that he would not let his undrugged coinvestigator leave him alone in the lab (Dorow et al., 1983).

We do not know where in the brain the information about stimulus significance becomes attached to sensory perception, nor where it is remembered and recalled. However, there is reason to think that an important stage in this process may occur in the amygdala—a cluster of phylogenetically ancient subcortical nuclei underneath the temporal lobe (see Figure 1). In the amygdala the outputs from the highest levels of sensory processing merge with inputs from the structures of the motivational systems of the diencephalon and hindbrain (Aggleton & Mishkin, 1986). In animals and humans, stimulation of the amygdala evokes strong emotional reactions together with their physiological concomitants (Ervin & Martin, 1986). The amygdala does not seem to be part of the motivation organizing systems, however, because removing it does not prevent the expression of approach or avoidance behaviors. When the lesions are large, perhaps because they extend into the overlying temporal lobe, animals show a peculiar syndrome in which objects appear to have lost their significance (Kluver & Bucy, 1939). The most commonly observed effect in several species is attenuation of fear or defense reactions. Monkeys with these lesions are excessively tame, emotionally unresponsive, and have severe disruption of social relationships in the group. Free living monkeys with such lesions withdraw from social interaction (Kling & Steklis, 1976).

The importance of the high level sensory inputs to the amygdala for the evaluative aspect of perception is shown in a classic experiment (Downer, 1961). The experimenters removed the tip of the temporal lobe and amygdala on one side of the brain of a monkey and also cut the fibers connecting the two halves of the brain so that the visual input from each eye was restricted to its own hemisphere. Normally the information from half the visual field is transmitted from each eye to the opposite hemisphere. The animals behavioral reactions to visual stimuli appeared normal, showing that the monkey's capacity to respond emotionally was not impaired. The monkey can see through either eye, however, if the monkey was allowed to use only one eye, it reacted normally to stimuli presented to the eye on the side with the intact amygdala and temporal lobe but reacted weakly or not at all to stimuli presented through the side with the lesion. Thus the emotional response to visual signals was deficient when the results of visual analysis were disconnected from the pathways through the temporal lobe and amygdala to the motivational mechanisms of the diencephalon.

I have very briefly outlined some of the evidence that leads us to believe that we are beginning to map the neural substrates of motivation. the picture that emerges seems to me to support a very old idea—that the value that attaches to percepts derives from two sources. Some stimuli have intrinsic value because the sensory analyzers that detect them have come to be connected to circuits that organize biologically significant behaviors in the course of evolution. The clearest example of this mechanism lies in the taste system. An alternate route to value is through association of stimuli with the arousal or execution of biologically significant behaviors. I suggest that part of the scientific analysis of values lies in the study of the biological history of the species, and the brain mechanisms that evolved through that history. Other answers lie in the history of the individual and the environment in which the individual lives.

References

Aggleton, J. P., & Mishkin, M. (1986). The amygdala: Sensory gateway to the emotions. In R. Plutchik & H. Kellerman (Eds.), *Emotion theory, research, and experience* (pp. 281–299). Orlando: Academic Press.

Akil, H., Watson, S. J., Young, E., Lewis, M. E., Khachaturian, H., & Walker, J. M. (1984). Endogenous opioids: Biology and function. *Annual Review of Neuroscience, 7*, 223–255.

Audi, E. A., & Graeff, F. G. (1984). Benzodiazepine receptors in the peri-aqueductal grey mediate anti-aversive drug action. *European Journal of Pharmacology, 103,* 279–285.

Basbaum, A. I., & Fields, H. L. (1984). Endogenous pain control mechanisms: brainstem pathways and endorphin circuitry. *Annual Review of Neuroscience, 7,* 309–338.

Carroll, M. N., & Lim, R. K. S. (1960). Observations on the neuropharmacology of morphine and morphinelike analgesia. *Archives Internationales de Pharmacodynamie et Thérapie, 125,* 383–403.

DeYoe, E. A., & Van Essen, D. C. (1988). Concurrent processing streams in monkey visual cortex. *Trends in Neuroscience, 11,* 219–226.

Dorow, R., Horowski, R., Paschelke, G., Amin, M., & Braestrup, C. (1983). Severe anxiety induced by F.G. 7142 a β-carboline ligand for benzodiazepine receptors. *Lancet, 2,* 98–99.

Downer, J. L. de C. (1961). Changes in visual gnostic functions and emotional behaviour following unilateral temporal pole damage in the 'split-brain' monkey. *Nature (London), 191,* 50–51.

Ervin, F. R., & Martin, J. (1986). Neurophysiological bases of the primary emotions. In R. Plutchik & H. Kellerman (Eds.), *Emotion—Theory, research, and experience* (pp. 145–170). Orlando: Academic Press.

Ettenberg, A., & White, N. (1978). Conditioned taste preferences in the rat induced by self-stimulation. *Physiology and Behaviour, 21,* 363–368.

Forrest, W. H., Jr., Brown, B. W., Brown, C. R., Defalque, R., Gold, M., Gordon, H. E., James, K. E., Katz, J., Mahler, D. L., Schroff, P., & Teutsch, G. (1977). Dextroamphetamine with morphine for the treatment of postoperative pain. *New England Journal of Medicine, 296,* 712–715.

Franklin, K. B. J. (1978). Catecholamines and self-stimulation: reward and performance effects dissociated. *Pharmacology Biochemistry and Behavior, 9,* 813–820.

Franklin, K. B. J. (1989). Analgesia and the neural substrate of reward. *Neuroscience and Biobehavioral Reviews, 35,* 157–163.

Grill, H. J., & Norgren, R. (1978). Neurological tests and behavioral deficits in chronic thalamic and chronic decerebrate rats. *Brain Research, 143,* 299–312.

Gunne, L. M., Anggard, E., & Jönsson, L. E. (1972). Clinical trials with amphetamine-blocking drugs. *Journal Psychiatria Neurologia Neurochirugia (Amsterdam), 75,* 225–226.

Heath, R. G. (1963). Electrical self-stimulation of the brain in man. *American Journal of Psychiatry, 120,* 574–577.

Henningfield, J. E., Johnson, R. E., & Jasinski, D. R. (1987). Clinical procedures for the assessment of abuse potential. In M. A. Bozarth (Ed.), *Methods of assessing the reinforcing properties of abused drugs* (pp. 573–590). New York: Springer-Verlag.

Hernandez, L., & Hoebel, B. G. (1988). Food reward and cocaine increase extracellular dopamine in the nucleus accumbens as measured by microdialysis. *Life Sciences, 42,* 1705–1712.

Hinde, R. A. (1979). *Animal behaviour,* New York: McGraw-Hill.

Hubel, D. H., & Wiesel, T. N. (1959). Receptive fields of single neurons in the cat's striate cortex. *Journal of Physiology (London), 148,* 574–591.

Kling, A., & Steklis, H. D. (1976). A neural substrate for affiliative behavior in primates. *Brain Behavior and Evolution, 13,* 216–238.

Kluver, H., & Bucy, P. C. (1939). Preliminary analysis of functions of the temporal lobes in monkeys. *Archives of Neurology and Psychiatry, 42,* 979–1000.

Koob, G. F., Vaccarino, F. J., Amalric, M., & Bloom, F. E. (1987). Positive reinforcement properties of drugs: Search for neural substrates. In J. Engel & L. Oreland (Eds.), *Brain reward systems and abuse* (pp. 35–50). New York: Raven Press.

Michael, C. R. (1969). Retinal processing of visual images. *Scientific American, 220*(5), 104–114.

Milani, H., & Graeff, F. G. (1987). GABA-Benzodiazepine modulation of aversion in the medial hypothalamus of the rat. *Pharmacology Biochemistry and Behavior, 28,* 21–27.

Ninan, P. T., Insel, T. M., Cohen, R. M., Skolnick, P., & Paul, S. M. (1982). Benzodiazepine receptor-mediated experimental "anxiety" in primates. *Science, 218,* 1332–1334.

Olds, J., & Milner, P. M. (1954). Positive reinforcement produced by electrical stimulation of the septal area and other regions of rat brain. *Journal of Comparative Physiology and Psychology, 47,* 419–427.

Olds, M. E., & Olds, J. (1963). Approach-avoidance analysis of rat diencephalon. *Journal of Comparative Neurology, 120,* 259–295.

Pavlov, I. P. (1927). *Conditioned reflexes.* Oxford: Oxford University Press.

Penfield, W., & Jasper, H. (1954). *Epilepsy and the functional anatomy of the human brain.* Boston: Little Brown.

Phillips, A. G., Jacubovic, A., & Fibiger, H. C. (1987). Increased in vivo tyrosine hydroxylase activity in rat telencephalon produced by self-stimulation of the ventral tegmental area. *Brain Research, 402,* 109–116.

Roberts, D. C. S., & Zito, K. A. (1987). Interpretation of lesion effects on stimulant self-administration. In M. A. Bozarth (Ed.), *Methods of assessing the reinforcing properties of abused drugs* (pp. 87–103). New York: Springer-Verlag.

St. Laurent, J. (1988). Behavioral correlates of self-stimulation, flight and ambivalence. *Brain Research Bulletin, 21,* 61–77.

Stein, L. (1964). Self-stimulation of the brain and the central stimulant action of amphetamine. *Federation Proceedings, 23,* 836–850.

Steiner, J. E. (1974). Innate, discriminative human facial expressions to taste and smell stimulation. *Annals of the New York Academy of Science, 237,* 229–233.

Valenstein, E. S., Cox, V. C., & Kakolewski, J. W. (1968). Modification of motivated behavior elicited by electrical stimulation of the hypothalamus. *Science, 159,* 1119–1121.

van der Kooy, D. (1987). Place conditioning: a simple and effective method for assessing the motivational properties of drugs. In M. A. Bozarth (Ed.), *Methods of assessing the reinforcing properties of abused drugs* (pp. 229–240). New York: Springer-Verlag.

Wise, R. A. (1987). The role of reward pathways in the development of drug dependence. *Pharmacological Therapy, 35,* 227–263.

14

Sex Differences in Chimpanzee (and Human) Behavior: A Matter of Social Values?

Frans B. M. de Waal

This chapter emphasizes two gender differences in a large captive colony of chimpanzees (1) males form flexible aggressive coalitions, with changing partners, in the pursuit of high status; females form stable defense coalitions, with close friends and kin, to protect themselves against aggression. (2) Reconciliations (i.e., reunions between former opponents, often with kissing and embracing) are more common among males than females. Explanations of these gender characteristics in terms of a direct link between genes and behavior are rejected as it can be demonstrated that female chimpanzees are perfectly capable of and understand the more opportunistic male behavior patterns. Females, for example, actively influence male power struggles, and mediate when reconciliation attempts between male rivals remain unsuccessful. A relatively simple difference in social goals appears to account for and elegantly connect the observed gender differences. The value systems determining these goals are assumed to be innate. Their evolution is discussed in view of the community life of wild chimpanzees.

Introduction

Our closest primate relative, the chimpanzee (*Pan troglodytes;* Figure 1), shows striking sex differences in social behavior that appear remarkably human-like. These differences came to light in the late 1970s during studies of a large captive colony of chimpanzees, which lives on an island of nearly 1 hectare at the Arnhem Zoo (Netherlands). While the exploration of sex differences was not the primary objective of this research, it turned out that the actor's sex was one of the most important independent variables for the interpretation of behavior. This variable could be

Figure 1. A fully adult male chimpanzee. From de Waal (1982).

investigated in much greater detail in semicaptivity than possible in the
natural habitat, with its reduced visibility and complex logistics. I will
regularly refer to fieldwork, though, to show that most of the sex differences observed in Arnhem are representative of the species, and to place
them in an evolutionary perspective.

Sex differences are a highly controversial topic insofar as humans are
concerned. The debate revolves around innate versus environmental
origins. This dichotomy makes most biologists uncomfortable as we believe that virtually everything humans do is determined by a combination of influences. Men and women differ genetically, anatomically, hor-
monally, and behaviorally; it simply does not make sense to try to
separate the last difference from the former three. On the other hand,
behavioral differences do not need to follow directly from genetic programs that "dictate" the behavior of each sex. Such instinctivistic explanations cannot even begin to deal with the great individual variation
observed, nor with the obvious influence of the social environment. This
holds for chimpanzees as well as for humans.

In the course of time, I have changed my opinion about sex differences in chimpanzees from explaining them as inborn behavioral tendencies to viewing them as reflecting divergent social objectives in males
and females. If the sexes, so to speak, are trying to get something differ-

ent out of life we obviously expect this to affect their behavior: the road to goal X requires a different behavioral strategy than the road to goal Y. In intelligent species, these strategies need not be genetically specified; they often develop through experience and learning. Humans, in particular, are masters of acquired behavioral strategies. Take the millions of people who make a living in the urban jungle. Their basic goals are more or less the same as those of their hunter–gatherer ancestors (i.e., survival and reproduction), but their strategies involve quite a few new elements.

The rejection of gender-specific behavior in favor of gender-specific goals by no means eliminates the influence of genes. The crucial difference between the two views is in the *level* at which genes affect behavior: I believe that genes specify social goals rather than behavior patterns. This leaves the organism free, so to speak, to choose from alternative strategies to realize these goals. This more flexible framework to interpret the relation between genes and behavior is no luxury when faced with the psychological complexity of the chimpanzee. It is also of direct relevance to the theme of this meeting as it is the *value* attached to particular end-situations that determines the priority order among goals.

As regards sex differences, this approach makes no assumptions about sex-specific behavioral and mental capacities (although sex specificity is not excluded, and obviously does exist in the area of sexual behavior). Consequently, it allows us to address questions such as why each sex, under particular circumstances, seems perfectly capable of acting in ways typical of the opposite sex. It also raises the important question why the sexes use their rich behavioral potential to pursue different goals. Insofar as this difference is due to genetically "implanted" value systems, it must relate to the different ways in which the sexes reproduce. Natural selection obviously favors value systems that promote reproduction. This is not to say that all value systems are genetically determined; especially in our own species the situation is much more complex (see Cavalli-Sforza, this volume, for a discussion of culturally transmitted value systems).

Since the present contribution is intended for readers unfamiliar with primate behavior, I will first explain basic concepts such as coalition formation, social dominance, and reconciliation behavior. Subsequently, I will review the various sex differences in chimpanzees. In the last section I will try to relate these differences to life in the natural habitat, and compare them with gender roles in *Homo sapiens*.

It should be kept in mind that the picture sketched of the Arnhem chimpanzees is based on hundreds of hours of careful data collection by my students and myself, and on extensive computer analyses of this material. Here, I will ignore the statistical details. I will also not go into a discussion of methodology, which is standard ethology. The reader is referred to de Waal (1984, 1986) for technical presentations of the data discussed here, and to de Waal (1982, 1989) for popularized accounts of primate personalities, politics, and peacemaking.

Basic Social Concepts

My interest in primate behavior focuses on conflict as well as its resolution. This is an extensive field of investigation that touches on virtually every aspect of social life. Paradoxically, competition is often of a cooperative character, that is, individuals help one another in confrontations; this is called coalition formation. Further, to maintain an integrated community, and particularly to protect valuable partnerships, relationships need to be repaired after aggression; this is done by means of so-called reconciliation behavior. Because of these social mechanisms, aggressive competition cannot fruitfully be studied in isolation from cooperative and affiliative relationships. Let me give a brief introduction into the social sophistication of the chimpanzee.

Social Dominance

The hierarchy is expressed in greeting rituals in which the subordinate approaches the dominant, bows for him with bobbing movements, and utters a series of deep throaty grunts, known as pant-grunts. The dominant makes himself look big, puffing up his chest and raising his hair, while receiving these submissive gestures. The result is a postural contrast that leaves no doubt about which of the two parties is boss (Figure 2). This communication is absolutely unidirectional, that is, if individual A greets B in this manner during a given period, B will during the same period never greet A. Greetings have an appeasing quality in that they convey the message to the dominant that his position is safe and accepted. The dominant may perform an embrace, or groom the subordinate, as a way of accepting the greeting.

These ceremonies express *formal* dominance relationships, that is, dominance relationships agreed on by both parties. The interesting thing about chimpanzees is that their communicated positions do not always correspond with other measures of social dominance. Just as an elder statesman may have more influence behind the scenes than his official position would suggest, it is not unusual among chimpanzees to observe discrepancies between formal rank and the distribution of power and privileges. This discrepancy is mostly due to the ability of older,

Figure 2. A subordinate male bows and pant-grunts to the alpha male (right) who sits upright with his hair standing out. The adopted postures create the false impression that the two males differ in size. Such greeting ceremonies are common among males, but rare among females. From de Waal (1989).

more experienced individuals to form coalitions. Thus, I consider the oldest male and the oldest female the most influential individuals in the Arnhem colony, although neither occupies the highest formal rank (de Waal, 1982).

Serious tensions arise if an individual who used to greet the alpha male (i.e., the top-ranking male) ceases to do so. This is a sign of upcoming instability. Aggression levels increase, at first because the dominant tries to force the other back into a submissive attitude. This phase may be followed by overt challenges to the alpha position. The challenging individual, always another male, tries to provoke and intimidate the dominant male by so-called charging displays, in which he hurls objects at his rival, makes tremendous noise, and looks larger than life because of the remarkable pilo-erection chimpanzees are capable of. The confrontation will go back and forth, as the alpha male responds with similar behavior. These incidents occasionally escalate to a fight, although damaging aggression is rare. In Arnhem, rank reversals usually took several months to complete, involving hundreds of confrontations. The process ends when the previously dominant male bows and grunts for the other, thus formalizing the new order. The reason why rank reversals take such a long time is that they involve the entire community.

Coalition Formation

Aggressive confrontations among chimpanzees rarely remain limited to the two original combatants. Others join the fray, taking sides for the one or the other. A mother will defend her offspring against aggression, even if this means a fight with dominant individuals. But also unrelated adults help one another, and chimpanzees have a rich repertoire of sounds and gestures to recruit supporters. For example, one of the participants may run to and stretch out a hand to a third individual, begging him for support. In the meantime, the opponent may go to her best friend, put an arm around her shoulder, and return with this friend on her side. Figure 3 shows a coalition of four against one; such scenes may develop further, leading to confrontations between entire sections of the community.

Coalition formation is crucial during dominance processes; none of the males in Arnhem could dominate the colony entirely on his own.

Figure 3. An adult male (right) is chased off by a coalition of three screaming adults (background) and one juvenile (center) after the male had attacked one of them. From de Waal (1982).

High rank is therefore as much a matter of making the right friends as of fighting abilities. This lends a political quality to "campaigns" for the top position, with males competing over valuable coalition partners. Thus, a challenging male may groom the females and gently play with their offspring, much in the same way as candidates for the presidency hold babies in front of the cameras.

So-called separating interventions are part of this strategy, that is, an individual may break up contact between two others to prevent the formation of coalitions hostile to his own interests. For example, the alpha male will interrupt contact between his coalition partner and his main rival whenever he sees them together. This divide-and-rule tactic is fundamental for the stability of his position.

Reconciliation Behavior

Following an aggressive incident, there exists an increased probability of contact between opponents. In the chimpanzee, postconflict reunions are characterized by kissing and embracing, often followed by mutual grooming. This behavior, resulting in a distance reduction among antagonists, contrasts sharply with the traditional view of aggression as a socially negative, dispersive mechanism. Reconciliation is a relatively new area of investigation reviewed by de Waal (1989). The first studies indicate that reconciliation serves both arousal reduction (i.e., psychological stability) and the repair of damaged relationships (i.e., social stability).

Sex Differences in Chimpanzees

In terms of formal dominance, every fully adult male (i.e., 15 years or older) outranks every female. One hundred percent of the greeting ceremonies between adult members of the opposite sex are directed from female to male.

According to other measures, however, the difference in dominance is less pronounced, or even reversed. First, females win a minority of aggressive confrontations with males. These exceptional outcomes are largely due to coalition formation, that is, a female under attack may scream to mobilize the entire female population against her attacker. Second, competition over objects, small food items, places to sit, and social partners may be won by females; the three highest ranking females even win *most* of this competition with males. It is not at all unusual, for instance, for one of these females to shove an adult male out of a rubber tire that she wants to use as a seat herself (Noë, de Waal & van Hoof, 1980).

Such female priority may seem puzzling in view of the formal dominance by males, which dominance is backed by physical attributes. Male chimpanzees are faster, more muscular, and better armed than female chimpanzees (e.g., only the males possess large canines). We have tried to explain the discrepancy between formal rank and the outcome of competition on the basis of cooperation between the sexes. Females may support males during dominance struggles, reassure males after fights, cooperate when males try to arrange sexual encounters away from more dominant males, and so on. These benefits cannot be obtained by force, hence it is in the interest of males to develop good relationships with females. One way to do so is by granting privileges. In this view, then, priority rules between the sexes reflect a give-and-take between the male's physical dominance and the female's social and sexual "leverage" (Noë, de Waal & van Hoof, 1980; Smuts, 1987).

More interesting, perhaps, than the dominance relation between the sexes, is the difference in hierarchical relations among males as compared to those among females. As has also been noted in the wild (e.g., Bygott, 1974), the female hierarchy is rather vague compared to the male's. Elsewhere, I have provided systematic data and a literature review bearing on the unifying effect of formalized dominance (de Waal, 1986). Peaceful coexistence depends on unequivocal status communication. Without such communication relations are often seriously disturbed, and the probability of damaging fights increases dramatically. Reconciliations after fights are generally preceded by rituals in which the subordinate confirms the inequality in status by bowing for the dominant. In short, well-established dominance relationships appear to be a prerequisite for relaxed, tolerant relationships.

This unifying effect of hierarchies is not limited to male chimpanzees or males in general. Female macaques and baboons, for example, are united in remarkably stable rank orders, and these females are very dominance oriented. Female chimpanzees are exceptional in that they have no formalized hierarchy. Their rank order, insofar as it exists in terms of the outcome of aggressive encounters, is neither communicated on a regular basis nor, as it seems, linked to processes of conflict resolution. Greeting rituals, which serve to communicate status, are rare among females; between some females such a ritual has not been observed a single time during years of observation in Arnhem. Reconciliation following aggression by female chimpanzees is also considerably less frequent than that following male aggression, both in the wild and in captivity (de Waal, 1986; Goodall, 1986). This difference persists after correction for the lower frequency of aggression among females: in Arnhem, 47% of the fights among males are reconciled within half an hour, compared to only 18% of the fights among females.

Female chimpanzees in the wild avoid competition by spreading out over the forest, living largely solitary lives with their dependent offspring. They differ in this respect from male conspecifics (as well as from the female macaques and baboons mentioned above), which are considerably more sociable. Male chimpanzees are faced with the danger of gang attacks by males from neighboring communities, and therefore have good reasons to stick together when patrolling the borders of their territory (e.g., Goodall, 1986). Female chimpanzees, on the other hand, appear to gain little from each other's presence (Wrangham, 1979). This difference in the social dependency among male and female chimpanzees provides an evolutionary explanation of both the observed differences in conflict resolution and the absence of a formalized hierarchy among females.

These sex differences concern the impact of competition on relationships. Female chimpanzees respond with decreased contact to competition among themselves, whereas male chimpanzees employ powerful coping mechanisms to preserve unity. This is not to say that male chimpanzees are angels of peace. On the contrary, the aggression level is 20 times higher among the adult males in the Arnhem colony than among the adult females. Yet, in spite of this, one also sees a high level of affiliative contact among males. Male chimpanzees provide a prime example of fierce competitors unified in a hierarchy. The following sex differences in coalition formation must be interpreted in this light:

1. Female coalitions are committed to a limited number of female friends, and to the offspring of both the female herself and these friends. Stability of these coalitions has been documented in Arnhem for nearly two decades.

2. Male coalitions are flexible in that they change over time. One year, male A may support male B in his quest for dominance, only to ally the next year with male C against B if such cooperation offers better prospects for A's own status enhancement.

3. Females tend to fragment into subgroups with high internal solidarity (Figure 4). Their coalitions strongly overlap with other measures of positive behavior such as association and grooming. Sympathies and antipathies appear to be the main determinants of coalition formation among females.

Figure 4. Females maintain intimate relations with a small circle of friends and kin to whom they are very loyal. Here an adult female holds her adolescent daughter still while grooming her face. From de Waal (1989).

4. Rather than depending on social bonds and personal preferences, males take sides in fights dependent on strategic considerations. According to data from both the Arnhem colony and the natural habitat, the dissociation between political choices and affiliative behavior is most pronounced in males past their physical prime. These males build powerful positions by playing off ambitious younger and stronger males against one another. So, social manipulation by males appears to increase with age and experience (de Waal, 1982; Nishida, 1983).

   In short, the male community is characterized by ever-changing internal alliances but high solidarity in the face of external threats. The female community is characterized by stable subgroups with little coherence among them. Table 1 summarizes these differences. One point in need of clarification is that of female–female relations in Arnhem compared to in the natural habitat.

   Social bonding among unrelated adult females is quite strong in Arnhem as reflected in frequent grooming, and in social services such as the supervision and defense of one another's offspring. Although most posi-

Table 1. Summary of Sex Differences in Social Behavior Observed in the Arnhem Chimpanzee Colony[a]

	Females	Males
Hierarchy	Nonhierarchical	Hierarchical
	Little status competition	Fierce status competition
		Peaceful coexistence is linked to a formalized hierarchy
Reconciliation	Passive peace	Active peace
	Low aggression (avoid competition in the wild)	High aggression
	Reconciliation is rare	Reconciliation is common
Coalitions	Stable commitments	Opportunistic relations
	Coalitions correspond with affiliative preferences	Coalitions are changeable, and less dependent on affiliative preferences
Affiliation	Stay away from rivals	Association with both allies and rivals
	Competition excludes association	Group unity has priority over internal competition

[a] Based on behavioral frequencies presented by de Waal (1984, 1986).

tive interactions occur within the female subgroups, there also exists a wider female network. This is evident, for instance, when all females band together to chase off a male who attacked one of them. The virtual absence of food competition in captive settings no doubt contributes to the development of such female solidarity. Thus, the characterization of "passive peace" (Table 1) refers to the low frequency of aggression among females in an environment with an abundant food supply, such as a zoo, and the avoidance of aggression (through spacing) in an environment with scarce or irregular food resources, such as the natural habitat. In the latter type of environment competition "forces" females apart; close relationships are not characteristic of female chimpanzees in the wild (e.g., Wrangham, 1979; Nishida, 1979; Goodall, 1986).

The effect of the captive environment on male behavior, on the other hand, seems minimal except of course for the absence of territorial encounters with neighboring males. The relationships described for the Arnhem males are in many ways similar to what is known about males in the wild. Males compete primarily over sexually receptive females rather than over food (Figure 5). This competition is probably intensified in a captive setting, but this does not prevent the Arnhem males from combining high levels of competition with high levels of affiliation and cooperation, just as their wild counterparts.

Figure 5. The main goal of male strategies is to gain access to sexually receptive females. Access is partly decided through competition with other males, either directly over females or indirectly through competition over status (high rank correlates with mating success). Here the alpha male mates with an adolescent female, who squeals during the climax. From de Waal (1982).

Comparisons with Human Behavior

The popular notion of females as noncompetitive by nature does not hold up to critical evalution. It also does not make sense from the stand-point of evolution. Resources are limited, and every organism, male or female, needs to compete for its share. The share needed by a female with dependent offspring is often greater than that of a male. Hrdy's (1981) and Smuts' (1987) reviews of the primate literature show that competitiveness is by no means limited to males. Females of most species fight, and occasionally kill one another in the continual struggle for survival.

As for people, we are faced with the puzzle that "competition between females is documented for every well-studied species of primate save one: our own" (Hrdy, 1981: 129). Feminist authors may present women as pacifists (e.g., French, 1985), yet this view was recently challenged, not with data, but with a work of fiction. In *Cat's Eye,* Atwood (1989) addresses the issue of female competition, contrasting the tormentations to which girls subject one another with the straightforward competition among boys. At one point, the principal character complains: "I considered telling my [older] brother, asking him for help. But tell what exactly? I have no black eyes, no bloody noses to report: Cordelia does nothing physical. If it was boys, chasing or teasing, he would know what to do, but I don't suffer from boys in this way. Against girls and their indirectness, their whisperings, he would be helpless" (Atwood, 1989: 166).

A study by Lagerspetz, Bjorkqvist and Peltonen (1988) confirms that aggression among 11- to 12-year-old girls is less direct, hence less visible than aggression among boys. Interestingly, this study also supports the common observation that discords among girls outlast those among boys. The authors quote girls as stating that a person could be angry with another for "either one minute or for the rest of her life" (Lagerspetz, Bjorkqvist & Peltonen, 1988: 411). Persistence of bad feelings may be the flip side of the same coin that produces the enduring, intimate female friendships that have received quite a bit more attention (L. Rubin, 1985). If girls and women distance themselves from rivals, this would make their rivalries less obvious than those among men. A possible hypothesis, then, is that there exists great intensity and stability in both socially negative and socially positive relations among women, and that the second type is just more conspicuous than the first.

Similarly, in recent years, we have begun to interpret the frequent "grudges" among female primates as reflecting *selectivity* in peacemaking efforts; that is, females reconcile readily with a limited set of partners (e.g., offspring, other relatives, close female associates), but may maintain simmering conflict relations with others (de Waal, 1989). In the chimpanzee, in particular, this contrasts sharply with male behavior. Instead of an absolute distinction between friend and foe, the line is blurred for males. Males maintain group unity by all means even if this requires reconciliation with their greatest rival. This tendency, in turn, parallels that in the human male, who is widely recognized as a group animal. Already at an early age boys aggregate in groups, while girls seek dyadic associations (Hutt, 1972; Loots, 1981). In the words of Z. Rubin (1980: 106): "While boys tend to see the group as a collective entity, emphasizing loyalty and solidarity, girls are more likely to view the group as a network of intimate two-person friendships."

Studies by political scientists and social psychologists support the idea of greater stability in interpersonal attitudes among women, and greater flexibility (or, if one wishes, opportunism) among men. Masters (1989) measured responses to televised political leaders, finding that prior attitudes have a stronger influence on women, whereas men respond more to the specific competitive configuration of which the politician is part. Similarly, experimental studies of human coalition formation suggest that men select partners on the basis of the power distribution and the prospects of winning, whereas women do so predominantly on the basis of personal attraction (Bond & Vinacke, 1961; Nacci & Tedeschi, 1976). So, male attitudes may be more context dependent and female attitudes more person dependent.

Overall, there is quite an argument to be made that humans share important sex differences with chimpanzees in the manner in which they operate in a competitive arena. I would sum up as follows: the male strategy is to be competitive within a larger cohesive framework, which is often recognizable as a hierarchy with changing alliances and frequent compromise (e.g., the corporate ladder). The female strategy is to emphasize cohesion and commitment in some relationships, while letting competition run its course in others.

Discussion

Let me open this discussion with the observation that things are not as simple as presented. Because there has been surprisingly little research on the social impact of competition in humans, the sex differences discussed above must be considered largely hypothetical. Most social scientists isolate aggressive behavior as a problem area in human behavior rather than viewing conflict, and the aggressive form it sometimes takes, as an integrated part of social life. Their studies focus on destructive violence—such as murder, rape, and domestic abuse—and ignore the forms of aggression we are most of the time quite comfortable with, such as the daily quarrels that serve to negotiate relationships. Consequently, we know more about conflict resolution and reconciliation in animals than in our own species (de Waal, 1989).

In addition, the little knowledge that we do possess about these mechanisms in humans largely concerns Western cultures. Although cultural variation is not as great as some anthropologists have wanted us to believe (e.g., Freeman's, 1983, criticism of Margaret Mead), there is enough reason to be careful with generalizations. This holds equally for chimpanzees, which in the wild show marked intergroup variation in technical skills and social customs. This variation may reflect local traditions, in which the younger generation learns certain habits from the older generation (Goodall, 1986; Nishida, 1987).

One intergroup difference in social organization has already been discussed: females in the Arnhem colony are more strongly bonded, express greater solidarity, and hence exert more influence on community life than observed in the natural habitat. Calling this an "artifact" of captivity misses the point; every potential counts in the exploration of a species' social behavior. Also, because chimpanzees live in a great variety of ecological settings, "the" natural habitat does not exist. It should not be surprising that at least one free-living group of chimpanzees manifests the same potential as observed in Arnhem. Sugiyama (1988) observed a group of chimpanzees isolated in a relatively small forested area in which relationships among females were closer than usual, perhaps due to the limited opportunities for dispersal and migration.

Laboratory studies, too, have demonstrated that sex differences depend on the social and physical environment. For example, female rhesus monkeys housed in all-female groups act more like males than do females in mixed-sex groups. Goldfoot and Neff (1985) review the limitations of measuring behavioral sex differences. They conclude that "the separate behavioral components of male and female gender-role behavior can be separately and independently sensitive to changes in particular social conditions" (Goldfoot & Neff, 1985: 781). These investigators find it virtually impossible to separate biological factors from environmental ones; they emphasize the interplay between the two.

The point of discussing this variation in behavior is not to undermine the argument that males and females differ, but to make clear that there exists hardly any behavior in primates that can be said to be absolutely sex linked. What we observe are *average* differences between the sexes, evident under most but not necessarily all conditions. There exists a potential in both males and females to adopt the behavior typical of the opposite sex. For example, the entire repertoire of intimidation and bluff gestures typical of dominant male chimpanzees can be shown by females. Normally, females do not perform this rather spectacular behavior, and if they do their display usually is an incomplete, abbreviated version of the males'. Yet, during the first few years of the Arnhem colony the oldest female exhibited full-blown charging displays that were in no way less impressive than those of males (de Waal, 1982). Male chimpanzees, on the other hand, have been known to adopt juvenile orphans, both in captivity and in the wild, acting in a nurturant, protective manner normally associated with females (e.g., Nishida, 1979; personal observation).

Hence, the first explanation that I wish to reject here is the one linking specific behavior patterns directly to genetic sex differences. To stay with the above example, there is no gene for charging displays that males possess and females lack. This also applies to more complex social skills, such as reconciliation behavior: female chimpanzees are perfectly capable of reconciliation, but they just seem to use this capacity differently than male chimpanzees. Needless to say, I feel that the ideas of some sociobiologists, postulating direct effects of genes on behavior, are to be treated with great reservation. I agree with Crook (1989: 13) that their writings have given rise to "a curious metabiology lacking anchorage in known genetic facts."

The second explanation that we can safely reject is the one linking the observed sex differences to variation in cognitive capacities. One could argue that the male strategy, characterized by calculated shifts in allegiance and strategic relations with both rivals and allies, requires greater intelligence. The first counterargument here is that a large number, perhaps the majority of experimental demonstrations of striking intelligence in chimpanzees involved females, such as Washoe, the first ape to learn sign-language (Gardner & Gardner, 1969). Second, there is ample evidence that females have no trouble understanding the social strategies of males; they anticipate their moves and influence the process.

One example is the way female chimpanzees in Arnhem interfere in status struggles among males. This is the only situation in which female coalitions are less stable than depicted in previous sections; females tend to support the dominant male, changing allegiance once a new alpha male has gained power (de Waal, 1982). Another example is female mediation during reconciliations among males. De Waal and van Roosmalen (1979) describe how females may bring unreconciled males together. Females have also been observed to "confiscate" the weapons of males engaged in a confrontation by walking up to them and removing a heavy rock or stick from their hands. Operation in this charged social atmosphere, without becoming the victim of tensions oneself, requires extensive familiarity with male relationships. It is noteworthy that older females perform this role more often than young adult females.

In short, the males' social maneuvers are by no means a mystery to females. The females carefully watch the ongoing events and react appropriately, often intervening with great insight. This is quite different from the behavior of juveniles, which do make social mistakes (such as initiating play with a male whose rival is gearing up for a display), and may get into trouble as a result. Interestingly, the way in which females try to influence male rivalries appears to aim at stabilization. Opposition to challengers of the established alpha male, confiscation of weapons, and mediation in conflicts serve to conserve the peace. Thus, although showing little reconciliation among themselves, females contribute to the "active peace" among males. Since females are often the target of redirected male aggression, it is in their interest to keep things as stable as possible.

This brings us to the explanation of sex differences that I wish to propose, namely the *goal-directedness* of behavior. It appears that female chimpanzees value (1) supportive relations with a small circle of friends and relatives, and (2) social stability in the larger community. Male chimpanzees, on the other hand, value (1) unity among themselves, and (2) high rank within the male team. All behavioral sex difference discussed in this chapter can be regarded as flowing from this relatively simple sex difference in social values. The value approach provides an elegant explanation while at the same time accommodating the observed flexibility in behavior since there is no assumption of genetically specified ways to realize the apparent goals. On the contrary, we have discussed sophisticated social skills, such as coalition formation and reconciliation, that are probably profoundly influenced by learning.

As explained in the Introduction, the genetic make-up of a species does play a central role in all this by setting the desired end-situations. Since inherited characteristics are shaped by the evolutionary process, the reason for sex differences in social values must be sought in different reproductive consequences of particular end-situations for each sex. Inherited goals that, if realized, resulted in an increased number of offspring were promoted during evolution, whereas goals that interfered with reproduction were selected against.

In the chimpanzee, females do not appear to derive significant benefits from one another's company in the wild. These apes are big and strong enough that they do not need others for defense against predators, for example. Females have therefore evolved a tendency to avoid competition rather than stay together. They also have an interest in securing a safe environment to raise their offspring, which may explain their conciliatory role in a situation, such as the Arnhem Zoo, in which they are forced to live together with adult males. Males, on the other hand, do strongly depend on one another in the wild; cooperation is a matter of life and death during territorial encounters with neighboring groups. Males therefore evolved a tendency to establish a close-knit hierarchically organized group within which each male seeks to establish dominance over the others. The male's reproduction is served by maximizing the number of available females (which depends on the size of the territory) and the number of offspring sired (which may correlate with rank; Nishida, 1979; de Waal, 1982).

What the argument boils down to, then, is that the sexes differ in which social conditions best serve their reproduction, and that each sex has inherited a tendency to value and strive for these optimal conditions. It is up to the individuals to develop the most appropriate and successful behavioral strategies to reach a secure social environment (for females) and optimal access to fertile mates (for males). For this purpose each species has an array of behavioral potentials at its disposal. In some species, such as insects, the number of behavioral potentials is so limited that there is hardly any flexibility. In other species, such as the chimpanzee, the number of potentials is so great, and the role of experience so expanded through slow maturation, that each individual arrives at its own strategies, which we recognize as differences in personality. In this framework, differences between the sexes are interpreted as resulting not so much from a difference in behavioral potentials, but from a difference in genetically specified goals of life.

To what extent the same argument applies to human gender roles remains to be seen. Our species shares a long evolutionary history with the chimpanzee, but also has had a short independent history of its own during which, among other things, our ancestors began to live in small settlements with males and females spending much time together. This may have had an effect on the evolution of sex-typical value systems, perhaps increasing the overlap between these systems as both sexes faced the same environmental dangers and uncertainties. The parallels between human and chimpanzee sex differences are provocative, however, and a full understanding of human social organization can probably not be achieved without considering the primate evidence.

References

Atwood, M. E. (1989). *Cat's eye*. New York: Doubleday.

Bond, J., & Vinacke, W. (1961). Coalitions in mixed-sex triads. *Sociometry, 24,* 61–75.

Bygott, D. (1974). *Agonistic behaviour and dominance in wild chimpanzees*. Ph.D. thesis, University of Cambridge.

Crook, J. (1989). Socioecological paradigms, evolution and history: Perspectives for the 1990s. In V. Standen & R. Foley (Eds.), *Comparative socioecology: The behavioral ecology of humans and other mammals* (pp. 1–36). Oxford: Blackwell.

de Waal, F. B. M. (1982). *Chimpanzee politics*. Baltimore: Johns Hopkins University Press, 1989.

de Waal, F. B. M. (1984). Sex differences in the formation of coalitions among chimpanzees. *Ethology and Sociobiology, 5,* 239–255.

de Waal, F. B. M. (1986). Integration of dominance and social bonding in primates. *Quarterly Review of Biology, 61,* 459–479.

de Waal, F. B. M. (1989). *Peacemaking among primates*. Cambridge, MA: Harvard University Press.

de Waal, F. B. M., & van Roosmalen, A. (1979). Reconciliation and consolation among chimpanzees. *Behavioral Ecology and Sociobiology, 5,* 55–66.

Freeman, D. (1983). *Margaret Mead and Samoa*. Cambridge, MA: Harvard University Press.

French, M. (1985). *Beyond power*. New York: Ballantine.

Gardner, R., & Gardner, B. (1969). Teaching sign-language to a chimpanzee. *Science, 165,* 664–672.

Goldfoot, D. A., & Neff, D. A. (1985). On measuring sex differences in social contexts. In N. Adler, D. Pfaff, & R. Goy (Eds.), *Handbook of behavioral neurobiology* (Vol. 7, pp. 767–783). New York: Plenum.

Goodall, J. (1986). *The chimpanzees of Gombe*. Cambridge, MA: Belknap.

Hrdy, S. B. (1981). *The woman that never evolved*. Cambridge, MA: Harvard University Press.

Hutt, C. (1972). *Males and females*. Harmondsworth: Penguin.

Lagerspetz, K. M., Bjorkqvist, K., & Peltonen, T. (1988). Is indirect aggression typical of females? *Aggressive behavior, 14*, 403–414.

Loots, G. M. P. (1981). Een ethologisch onderzoek naar differentiatie in sociaal gedrag bij kinderen. In *ZWO Jaarboek 1980* (pp. 146–178). The Hague: Roepers.

Masters, R. D. (1989). Gender and political cognition: Integrating evolutionary biology and political science. *Politics and the Life Sciences, 8*, 3–39.

Nacci, P., & Tedeschi, J. (1976). Liking and power as factors affecting coalition choices in the triad. *Social Behavior and Personality, 4*, 27–32.

Nishida, T. (1979). The social structure of chimpanzees in the Mahale Mountains. In D. Hamburg & E. McCown (Eds.), *The great apes* (pp. 73–121). California: Benjamin/Cummings.

Nishida, T. (1983). Alpha status and agonistic alliance in wild chimpanzees. *Primates, 24*, 16–34.

Nishida, T. (1987). Local traditions and cultural transmission. In B. Smuts, D. Cheney, R. Seyfarth, R. Wrangham, & T. Struhsaker (Eds.), *Primate societies* (pp. 462–474). Chicago: The University of Chicago Press.

Noë, R., de Waal, F., & van Hoof, J. (1980). Types of dominance in a chimpanzee colony. *Folia Primatologica, 34*, 90–110.

Rubin, L. B. (1985). *Just friends*. New York: Harper & Row.

Rubin, Z. (1987). *Children's friendships*. Cambridge, MA: Harvard University Press.

Smuts, B. B. (1987). Gender, aggression and influence. In B. Smuts, D. Cheney, R. Seyfarth, R. Wrangham, & T. Struhsaker (Eds.), *Primate societies* (pp. 400–412). Chicago: The University of Chicago Press.

Sugiyama, Y. (1988). Grooming interactions among adult chimpanzees at Bossou, Guinea, with special reference to social structure. *International Journal of Primatology, 9*, 393–408.

Wrangham, R. (1979). Sex differences in chimpanzee dispersion. In D. Hamburg & E. McCown (Eds.), *The great apes* (pp. 481–490). California: Benjamin/Cummings.

15

How Are Values Transmitted?

L. Luca Cavalli-Sforza

The word "values" may be defined in several ways. I have been attracted by the idea that values are important in motivating human decisions and have therefore chosen an inclusive definition, putting in this concept all factors, be they beliefs, fantasies, drives, desires, and so on which affect such motivations and therefore determine our standards of behavior. This brings in a variety of biological factors such as hunger, fatigue, and sex drives as well as psychological ones, including dimensions of personality, attitudes, opinions, beliefs, customs, ethical, legal and religious rules, probably a much larger group than others may like to accept. Several of these factors are likely to have a strong biological component, but many others are determined by social culture, individual history, education, early conditioning, and a multitude of random events. In considering this I realize there is a danger of feeling overwhelmed, since there is so little hope of clearly expressing or measuring most if not all of them, but at least there is a smaller chance of leaving out important ones before beginning the analysis of the factors that determine our standards of behavior.

It is perfectly legitimate, of course, to classify these factors in categories but it is unlikely that the list will be complete and the categories sharp. Some will prefer to confine the word "values" to a particular class. But even if one is anxious to classify e.g., pulsions and drives, separately from values intended in a narrow sense, the fact remains that our decisions are likely to depend on a large number of factors coming from several of these categories.

How can one hope to list these factors and give them a relative rank or role in a particular decision or type of decision? The best hope is a pragmatic approach fixing one's attention on actual examples of decisions, which may be as basic as the particular reasons for certain events such as marriage or divorce, choice of a career, or involvement in misdemeanors and crimes. At the other extreme of a scale of seriousness of decisions, one may consider the choice of a particular brand of a common product; this more trivial set of decisions may have the advantage of finding substantive information from market research. After choosing a specific area of investigation and a sample of subjects one would then analyze the factors that have determined the particular choice that was made. There is real difficulty in obtaining good information. Introspective analysis might supply some results, but the role of subconscious factors is likely to be important, and in a variety of decisions certain determining elements may be sufficiently embarrassing that they are not willingly communicated to others. The use of questionnaires might be unadvisable, while an external interviewer who is an able and experienced counselor could perhaps obtain sounder information. Reliability tests might be devised to make conclusions more acceptable. This is a suggestion for a wide field of investigations; however, a good literature search would probably show that some simple knowledge is already in existence. I should add that I prefer to speak of *human* decisions and do not try to include animals, because our species offers the advantage of communication to a degree that is unavailable in other animals; and cultural values are more likely to be involved in all decisions, but I see no reason why some of the basic factors would not be found also in nonhuman animals.

From introspection I have formed a very simple model of how decisions take place especially when there is a conflict between different decisions. I believe there is a process of internal weighting of pros and cons, which is sometimes conscious. The weights given to the various factors are highly individualistic. In particular when referring to future events that cannot be predicted with certainty, there must also be some subconscious evaluation of prior probabilities that take part in the decision. In other words, one may consciously or not, practice a calculus of expected gains and losses associated with each possible decision, which are estimated on a positive/negative reward scale. The times at which rewards may be expected is also a variable in the calculus. These computations are likely to be extremely rough and often wrong in many ways: important possible solutions are ignored, guesses of gains and losses, and the relevant weights and probabilities may be seriously wrong. Nevertheless, the general approach even if largely subconscious may be a rational one, in agreement with a model by G. S. Becker (1976), which is in a way derived from Jeremy Bentham's ideas.

I have already erred in venturing too far into uncharted territory of unknown subjects. I believe it is possible and useful to research the transmission of values involved in the decisions that constitute behavior. Some may be of biological nature, others are clearly cultural. But many, perhaps most may be difficult to classify in one or the other way and may be the result of the interaction of biology and culture. This is a complication since we are interested in *mechanisms that affect the maintenance of values in populations,* and the rules of transmission across generations are quite different for biology and culture.

Some geneticists tend to see a strong genetic determination behind every difference among individuals or populations, and there might well be a little bit of it in most traits, but it is likely, a priori, that culturally determined differences have also a strong effect in almost every behavioral trait, especially when considering differences between populations or social layers.

At this stage one might feel the need for a definition of cultural determination. Following the one adopted by L. Cavalli-Sforza and Feldman (1981), it is the result of transmission by communication from other individuals, whether it takes the form of observation, imitation, conditioning or education.

Genetic and Cultural Differences between Groups and Individuals

A relevant a priori consideration stems from the observation of differences in behavior between ethnic groups. For a number of characters there is no substantial variation among individuals of a group, but there may be major differences among ethnic groups. The lack of direct observations shows the extent of differences or their mechanism of origin (cultural or not), one may cite the American experience, which shows at least qualitatively that many differences connected with ethnic origin tend to disappear after a few generations. The melting pot was not really effective in reducing genetic differences, at least sharper ones, but it usually helped reduce cultural ones, diluting them in various generations. The greater difference found for many cultural traits among groups than among individuals is characteristic of the cultural traits themselves. These considerations are presented without data, but two considerations may be sufficient. First, many cultural traits are of social nature and as such, there is automatically little difference among individuals. Second, if the above statement were not true national stereotypes, of which there is an abundant series of examples would not be possible. The rapid disappearance and replacement of the original stereotypes of immigrants that one notes in American societies is often a sufficient clue to consider them as cultural.

Traits studied by cultural anthropologists however show extreme dif-

ferences among ethnic groups, even biologically close ones, as can be
seen by a perusal of Murdock's atlas of cultural variation. The traits
studied by Murdock involve customs regarding family and kinship, economic demography, division of labor, how food is obtained, how houses
are built, and so on. It is not clear if and to what extent each of these
traits is related to values, but it is likely that many of them are, directly or
indirectly. Geographic plots of Murdock's data are instructive in showing
the extent of cultural variation and the mechanisms determining them
(Guglielmino et al., 1983). Many cultural traits tend to vary little among
individuals of a population because cultural norms are easily pervasive
in a society and often define the society itself; but there is more freedom
of variation among groups because many mechanisms that operate in
homogenizing culturally a social group do not easily operate among
groups, as will be discussed later.

By contrast, when one considers *bona fide* genetic traits that vary from
one group to the other it is almost the rule that they also vary among
individuals of a group. Those that are more easily amenable to study
have a simple genetic determination, and are controlled by differences
in a single gene. They are called genetic polymorphisms, and the variance in frequencies of polymorphic genes among populations is small
compared to the variance among individuals within populations; in fact,
the ratio of the former to the latter is between 10–20% (Lewontin, 1972;
Nei & Roychoudhury, 1972). An important exception are certain largely
inherited traits influenced by many genes such as skin color, stature, and
other bodily and facial traits that show greater variation among populations, but they are likely to be the result of strong climatic adaptations
or, in some cases, of sexual selection. Bodmer and Cavalli-Sforza (1976),
Matessi et al. (1979) have discussed these points further.

Statements of this kind may simply irritate extremists in both fields,
staunch supporters of complete genetic determination of almost every
trait, and at the other extreme, believers in total conditioning of our
behavior. Probably most people, however, will recognize them as basically sound. It may help to discuss in slightly more detail two basic
questions. First, how can one distinguish for a specific trait the roles of
genetic and cultural transmission, and, hence, determination? We have
considerable knowledge about the generalities of genetic transmission,
which I will not summarize here except for the simple statement that
genetic transmission is strictly from parent-to-child. This simple fact
establishes the major difference between genetic and cultural transmission, which is more complicated and less well-known. The second question is: What can one say about cultural transmission that is relevant to
the present subject? The two questions are obviously related and they
will be discussed in the rest of this chapter.

Distinguishing between Genetic and Cultural Transmission

There is one major tool for this distinction—the study of adoptions, that is, comparison of foster relatives with biological ones. The simple comparison of the similarity between identical twins and that between fraternal twins is simply the first step for testing the possible presence of biological inheritance, but does not supply strong evidence for it, unless it is supplemented by the study of identical twins reared apart, which is just one special case of the adoption method. Adoptions studies have serious drawbacks: in the human species they refer only to postnatal effects, they usually do not have the desired randomness; their statistical power is very limited because data that can be obtained in practice are basically rare and potentially biased. Even so, there have been many applications, of which the most extensive are to mental disease and IQ. Major mental diseases such as manic-depressive psychosis and schizophrenia have been shown to have a genetic component by means of a number of independent adoption studies that have given coherent results. It is also clear that genetics is not the only determinant, because monozygous twins, which are genetically identical, often show considerable differences.

The application to IQ is an excellent example of the difficulties of this type of research. In the 1960s and 1970s increasing "evidence" indicated that IQ was determined almost exclusively by genetic factors. This included results later proved to be largely invented (Kamin, 1974). The work done in this period never included a serious consideration of cultural transmission, or even of the possibility that it could affect results in spite of theoretical models showing the biases introduced by neglecting cultural factors (Cavalli-Sforza & Feldman, 1973, 1981). An attempt in the late 1970s to evaluate the relative roles of cultural and genetic transmission, using Wright's path coefficients, indicated that the role of cultural transmission was negligible (Rao et al., 1978). The same authors (Rao et al., 1982), however, retracted their conclusions after their path coefficient model was proved inadequate (Rice et at., 1981). At present, the accepted conclusion is that cultural and genetic transmission have about the same role, each determining about one-third of the variance of IQ in the Western world, with the last one-third determined by random or unaccountable factors. These estimates are based on a linear model of transmission and there may be other complexities that are presently unsolved.

In the 1980s, an alternative approach to testing genetic transmission was developed, using linkage to genetic markers. Linkage is the tendency of genes that are physically close on a chromosome, to be transmitted together, the more so, the closer they are. It has provided many new answers to old problems of genetic pathology, as for example, in diseases such as Huntington's chorea, cystic fibrosis, and neurofibromatosis, in which it has been possible to isolate, or come close to, the gene responsible for them. The linkage approach is, at least in humans, limited so far to uncomplicated "Mendelian" traits, caused by a single gene, where the trait studied is sharply bimodal or, in some cases multimodal and is transmitted according to strict Mendelian rules. This is not the case for IQ, in which the genetic contribution is certainly the result of many genes (and also nongenetic factors); such polygenic traits are much harder to approach by linkage analysis. Nevertheless, in many cases the linkage approach remains the most powerful test of genetic determination. For it to become useful in the study of human behavioral characters may require many more years of development.

Further considerations may be made after a brief survey of cultural transmission. This is a largely neglected field in which I became interested in when I started traveling to Africa for a study of the population genetics of Pygmies, perhaps the largest surviving group of relatively nonacculturated hunter–gatherers (L. Cavalli-Sforza, 1986). There is a deep gulf between the social and economic life of Pygmies and that of economically advanced societies, and yet no major potential difference seems to exist that would justify such a profound socioeconomic hiatus, other than opportunities and social attitudes. One is surprised at the ingenuity of achievements of the Pygmies within the constraints of a migratory economy of forest dwellers, in particular their remarkable social adaptations. African Pygmies are highly intelligent, have a sense of humor, and have developed artistic skills. Their ethical and social behavior is remarkable, and so is their lack of interest in a monetary economy, or in a technology that enormously attracts their neighbors, the African farmers. In spite of this they are willing to communicate and share with foreigners when they sense they are friendly.

African Pygmies are just one of many different cultures that exist in the world, but one cannot fail to be impressed by the differences in, and by the stability of their customs, which are found over and over again in Pygmy tribes living in very distant places. Some of these tribes have exchanged enough genes with their close neighbors to be quite different genetically one from the other, and sometimes quite similar to their farming neighbors, but they still conserve most of the peculiar social and cultural attributes of Pygmies, which are profoundly different from those of other neighboring ethnic groups. Several Pygmy customs are typical also of many other hunting–gathering groups of very different locations and ethnic origins, indicating high cultural conservation which keeps hunter–gatherers societies sharply distinct from societies which live in other economies (farming, pastoralism, industrial development).

Pygmies are brave hunters, but in principle abhor violence and aggression. There is some general tendency among laymen and a temptation among scientists to view aggression as genetically determined. There is no proof for this. A comparison of Scandinavians of thousand years ago—the ferocious Vikings—with modern Scandinavians, certainly the most peaceful people in Europe, makes me feel that aggression is largely determined by cultural factors. For all we know of population genetics it would be very difficult to explain such rapid and massive transformation on the basis of a genetic change. It has been suggested by some, that maybe all aggressive Scandinavians died, but this explanation would be acceptable only if one could accept not only that aggressiveness is highly heritable, but also that aggressive individuals are very few but their example is somehow extremely contagious; once they are dead, everybody else is peaceful. The importance of single individuals in determining social behavior of large masses may in some cases be extreme (Hitler's example may teach), but there is probably little or no genetic determination involved in these phenomena.

Can one transform these vague impressions and barely scientific considerations into more substantive knowledge? Some progress can be made, and I will briefly summarize a few results of theory and observation. It is clear that culture is transmitted, and in fact its transmissibility is the basis for its adaptive value, for it permits the accumulation of knowledge over generations. Being subject to change it continuously evolves, and in different circumstances it may change very slowly or very fast. Sometimes the rate of cultural change is such that substantial modifications may occur in the life of an individual. By contrast, some cultural factors are very stable: most major religions have been in existence for 2000 years or more. The average age of a language before it loses mutual intelligibility with a sister language developing in a nearby area is of the order of 1000 years. It is likely that many social customs, especially those concerning family and kinship structure, as discussed later are highly conserved, and therefore on average much older.

Some Properties of Cultural Transmission

First, I will briefly summarize some theoretical work on cultural transmission by Cavalli-Sforza and Feldman (1981).

To predict the evolution of cultural traits we have studied the kinetics of population change in a number of models, which can be grouped into four major types on the basis of the numbers of transmitters and receivers and their age relations. For simplicity, only two generations are considered here. All models have been studied for qualitative and quantitative traits: we prefer this word to define a character under study, as we find unwarranted at this stage the attempt of defining units of cultural transmission, an equivalent of "genes of culture." Empirical studies can be done on all sorts of traits, be they beliefs, customs and values as long as they are easy to score or measure reliably.

1. *Parent-child (vertical transmission).* Complete and indefinite maintenance over generations of a trait is ensured only if the probability of transmission is 1, in which case the frequency of the trait is stable over generations. With 2 transmitting parents, an equilibrium is reached slowly. This mechanism of transmission is the one most similar to genetic transmission, from which it may sometimes be distinguished only with difficulty.

2. *Transmission from a trait carrier ("teacher") to one other who initially does not carry the trait.* The process is repeated a number of times in a population. If transmitter and receiver belong to different generations we call it *oblique,* and if they are of the same generation we call it *horizontal,* but we refer to both as horizontal, a term that originates from epidemiology, when generational differences are not of the essence. The kinetics is of a logistic type, similar to that of epidemics of infectious diseases. An equilibrium with a qualitative trait frequency different from 0 or 1 can be reached, with rules that differ somewhat for the oblique and the horizontal case. This is a type of transmission that is considered as typically "cultural," but is by no means the only one.

3. *Transmission from one trait carrier (teacher, social or political leader) to many individuals.* This mechanism of transmission is practically absent among hunter–gatherers, and becomes more and more frequent as social hierarchies, schools, and indirect communication systems develop.

4. *Social group pressure,* in which many individuals, usually from the older generation, influence one individual (and often also all or many of the others) in a coherent direction, so that their teachings reinforce each other.

In general, individual variation tends to remain high in a population especially with mechanism 1, which can conserve mean and variance. Equally and even more highly conservative is mechanism 4, but, unlike vertical transmission, it tends to destroy individual variation and to create population homogeneity.

Mechanisms 2 and 3 can determine rapid cultural change, the third faster than the second. Homogeneity is more easily and rapidly attained under the third than under the second mechanism.

These formal rules can help understand the kinetics of cultural change. It is assumed that the information passed by the trait carrier— the teaching of the teacher, the orders of the political leader, the example of the social leaders—is followed, obeyed, and accepted. This may well depend on the ability, the persuasion, prestige or authority of the transmitter. It will also depend on the acceptability of the information, teaching, or suggestion. A funny story may spread around very quickly, but it is not likely that an order to commit mass suicide will be carried out (although it has happened). Other factors, moreover, modulate the process of acceptance and it will be important to consider them.

A study of cultural transmission may be easy for certain traits and conditions. In a survey of attitudes, beliefs, and customs carried out on Stanford students (Cavalli-Sforza et al., 1981) similarity between parents and students or students and friends existed only for certain traits; similarity between parents and children was generally higher than between students and friends, that between the two parents was highest indicating strong assortative mating and/or reciprocal influence over life among spouses (see also Price et al., 1981).

Religious attitudes showed the highest correlations, followed by political beliefs. In a survey based on similarities one can never easily exclude factors other than cultural transmission: in principle, it is not always possible to exclude genetic predisposition in the case of parent and child similarities, or assortment at mating for similarities between spouses, and others. Age effects and social stratification are easier to exclude. In some case, however, the distinctions are possible. For instance, spouses are very strongly assorted for religious denomination; but it is clear that in the marriages between individuals of different denomination, that of the mother prevails in influencing the religion followed by the offspring. The frequency of prayer shows an even stronger effect of only one parent, the mother. It would be strange if this strong sexual bias were due to genetic transmission; this could happen only in very special, highly unlikely situations.

A more direct study of cultural influences can be made by questions directed to ascertain who were the teachers of each individual for specific traits. A survey on African Pygmies (Hewlett & Cavalli-Sforza, 1986) showed that it was easy for individuals to identify the teacher for each of the traits used (skills and usual tasks). The most frequent teachers were parents (close to 90%), and usually only one of them for tasks for which there is sex specialization. A few traits were learned socially (especially dancing). Only 1 of 60 traits showed learning from individuals outside the Pygmy society: the building of a hunting weapon, the crossbow, which was recently adopted from African farmers. Once imported into Pygmy society, the transmission of this trait tended to become vertical.

African Pygmies live in small social groups, usually limited to an average of 30 individuals, the camp, for a shorter fraction of the time in aggregates of camps (the band), and rarely in larger aggregates (Cavalli-

Sforza, 1986). The influence of African farmers, with whom there exist multiple economic ties, is usually modest. There are no schools, no social hierarchies, and very few age peers. It is therefore not surprising that parental teaching is the major cultural process, and that sociocultural life is accordingly very highly conserved.

Cultural Adaptation

Culture is a powerful mechanism of adaptation, which is by no means unique to humans but is certainly most highly developed in our species. Our capacity of communication is clearly superior to that of other animals, and is an essential ingredient in cultural transmission.

It must clearly have developed by natural selection as an alternative to building specific genetic drives for each particular need. Being able to learn by a very general mechanism, and transmitting the necessary skills for survival to progeny and other members of the group, gives the possibility of occupying new environmental niches much faster than by developing specific genetic adaptations. But cultural adaptation does not always work to increase our Darwinian fitness. In fact, it sometimes fails miserably, as we are witnessing for instance in the epidemics of drug abuse. Thus, there are conflicts of biological and cultural adaptations. On average, however, for the mere fact that it exists culture is likely to increase Darwinian fitness. There must also be considerable positive interaction between genetic and cultural adaptation; very often, major skills develop from the combination of biological drives and cultural transmission. We would not have developed our language skills without a strong drive for learning language at a young age. The instincts of predation might not sustain a feline that loses its mother at an early age.

The variety of mechanisms of cultural adaptation in existence give to cultural traits the necessary flexibility or rigidity. Basic cultural learnings must be stable for life and highly conserved over generations. Many of them are acquired at a young age, when learning is usually easier, parental teaching is most common, and high conservation is thus assured. But there probably is further reinforcement by specific biological predispositions: for instance, sensitive periods for learning certain attitudes or activities can assure the acquisition of a cultural trait with high probability and make it essentially irreversible during life.

In humans there is perhaps no example of true imprinting as exists in some birds, in which the recognition of the mother and of conspecifics is determined in the first 24 or 48 hours. Sensitive periods are less well defined but examples are known. I would like to cite the following:

1. The incest taboo, prohibiting the development of later sexual attachment for individuals familiar before puberty (see review in Durham, 1991);
2. The acquisition of a new language, which at least from a phonetic point of view is almost never acquired perfectly after puberty (Lenneberg, 1967);
3. The preference for a specific type of physical environment: here there is no strong evidence for a specific sensitive period, but in a research on Stanford students there was a strong effect of the period spent in a specific environment, possibly tied with early exposure to it (Gurling and Cavalli-Sforza, unpublished).

Other beliefs and customs acquired during development are probably also fairly irreversible. Gypsies were originally from India, traditionally nomadic entertainers, therefore adapted to a migratory life. In recent times, especially in some European countries, they have often been forced to resort to begging, stealing, and prostitution—some of the very few ways of making a living that is today compatible with a nomadic way of life in the middle of modern society. If it were easy for individual Gypsies to adapt to non-nomadic ways of life their culture would not have survived, and spread to many European countries over the centuries. It has been attempted by several governments, usually without success, to make sedentary other migratory hunter-gatherers such as Pygmies, or pastoral nomads such as desert Bedouins. In part, this may depend on an imprinted preference for a certain physical environment and mode of life. This conditioning must be satisfactory enough so that it would take great temptation or considerable coercion to change it.

Another largely irreversible group of attitudes may be found in the political sphere. Le Bras and Todd (1981) have shown that there is a correlation, in France, between the traditional types of family (strictly nuclear, extended authoritarian, and extended egalitarian) and political preferences (economic liberalism, monarchy or equivalent authoritarian systems, and socialism, respectively). Todd (1983) has extended this correlation outside the boundaries of France. The explanation may be summarized by saying that the microcosm of the family is projected to the whole of society. One cannot fail to see that, if this conclusion is accepted, early conditioning is at play, and is especially powerful since parental teaching and pressure of the familial social group join forces in determining high conservation of these attitudes for the rest of individual life and over generations.

Finally, in the study by Guglielmino et al. (1983) an analysis of the geographic, ecological and linguistic correlates of systems of family and kinship in Africa has clearly shown that they are, on average, more highly conserved than all other cultural traits, probably because they are transmitted in the family and thus by the highly conservative vertical and social pressure mechanisms. In addition, they are further stabilized by early conditioning, as children they are raised by families, and exposed to the influence of parents, older siblings and other relatives from a very early age.

What little research has been carried out on cultural transmission was done on traits that are not, themselves, values as defined before, but are often closely related to them. A direct study of the transmission of values themselves is worth the effort, for it can explain their permanence through generations. I anticipate that strong, highly conservative cultural transmission (i.e., determination) will be found for many values, but in some cases more complex situations of interaction with genetic transmission may emerge.

References

Becker, G. S. (1976). *The economic approach to human behavior.* Chicago, IL: University of Chicago Press.

Bentham, J. (1963). *An introduction to the principles of morals and legislation.* New York: Hafner.

Bodmer, W. F., and Cavalli-Sforza, L. L. (1976). *Genetics, Evolution and Man.* San Francisco, CA: W. H. Freeman.

Cavalli-Sforza, L. L. (Ed.). (1986). *African Pygmies.* Orlando, FL: Academic Press.

Cavalli-Sforza, L. L., & Feldman, M. W. (1973). Cultural versus biological inheritance: Phenotypic transmission from parent to child. *American Journal of Human Genetics, 25:* 618–637.

Cavalli-Sforza, L. L., & Feldman, M. (1981). *Cultural Transmission and Evolution: A Quantitative Approach.* Princeton, NJ: Princeton University Press.

Cavalli-Sforza, L. L., & Feldman, M. W. (1983). Paradox of the evolution of communication and of social interactivity. *Proceedings of the National Academy of Sciences of the United States, 80,* 2017–2021.

Cavalli-Sforza, L. L., Feldman, M. W., Chen, K. H., & Dornbusch, S. M. (1982). Theory and observation in cultural transmission. *Science, 218,* 19–27.

Durham, W. H. (1991). *Coevolution.* Stanford, CA: Stanford University Press.

Hewlett, B. S., & Cavalli-Sforza, L. L. (1986). Cultural transmission among Aka Pygmies. *American Anthropologist, 88,* 922–934.

Kamin, L. (1974). *The science and politics of IQ.* Philadelphia, PA: Lawrence Erlbaum.

Le Bras, H., & Todd, E. (1981). *L'Invention de la France,* Paris: Librairie Générale Française.

Lenneberg, E. H. (1967). *Biological Foundations of Language.* New York: Wiley.

Lewontin, R. C. (1972). The apportionment of human diversity. *Evolutionary Biology, 6,* 301–398.

Matessi, R., Gluckman, P., & Cavalli-Sforza, L. L. (1979). Climate and the evolution of skull metrics in man. *American Journal of Physical Anthropology, 50,* 549–564.

Guglielmino, C., Viganotti, C., & Cavalli-Sforza, L. L. (1983). Spatial distributions and correlations of cultural traits in Africa. *Instituto di Analisi Numerica del Consiglio Nazionale della Ricerche,* Pavia.

Nei, M., & Roychoudhury, A. K. (1972). Gene differences between Caucasian, Negro and Japanese populations. *Science, 177,* 434–435.

Price, R. A., Chen, K.-H., Cavalli-Sforza, L. L., & Feldman, M. W. (1981). Models of spouse influence and their application to smoking behavior. *Social Biology, 28,* 14–29.

Rao, D. C., Morton, N. E., & Yee, S. (1976). Resolution of cultural and biological inheritance by path analysis. *American Journal of Human Genetics, 28,* 228–242.

Rao, D. C., Morton, N. E., Lalouel, J. M., & Lew, R. (1982). Path analysis under generalized assortative mating: II. American IQ. *Genetical Research Camb, 39,* 187–198.

Rice, J., Cloninger, C. R., & Reich, T. (1980). Analysis of behavioral traits in the presence of cultural transmission and assortative mating: Applications to IQ and SES. *Behavior Genetics, 10,* (1), 73–92.

Todd, E. (1983). *La Troisieme Planète: Structures Familiale et Systèmes Idéologiques.* Edition du Seuil, Paris.

16

Morality Recapitulates Phylogeny

Lionel Tiger

We can begin with Joseph Conrad's formulation in *Heart of Darkness* that "The mind of man is capable of anything—because everything is in it, all the past as well as all the future." Without indulging in Jungian arias about colorful and persistent archetypes, my effort in these remarks will be to extract from a reconstructed hominid past a plausible array of behavioral predispositions, which could when summarized in part support a biogenically based web of values. This is intrinsically (but not deliberately) controversial. First, it depends on a set of data about a period of history—human prehistory—about which we have only inferential knowledge. Its interpretation is subject to seemingly chronic and certainly colorful disagreement. Second, and more juicily, it questions the formal and practical adequacy of the nature–culture divide, which exists both in folk and religious analysis as well as in much of social science. Nevertheless our species exists, and so does an extensive and comprehensive set of scientific judgments about our chronological antiquity, our evolutionary relationship to other primate and mammalian species (Edey & Johanson, 1989), and the remarkably complex and physiologically rooted processes that sustain human biosocial life (Konner, 1983).

The essence of the argument here is that those values and ethics that effectively served our evolving ancestors, whose genes we carry and that are inevitably associated with our ontogeny, remain in some fashion encoded in our cognitive and behavioral apparatus. In a cross-time version of the Law of Parsimony, the earlier and more general the pattern was in the past the more likely it is to find some expression in the present. Physiological equivalents of this principle are suggested by the relatively common form of the spinal system among the vertebrates as well as the retention in *Homo sapiens* of structures of the brain common to other mammals and primates onto which has been added the characteristic human cortical tissue. Paul Maclean (1972) produced an early and still influential triune model of human brain that suggests that as with so much other physiology humans did not so much lose tissue through evolution but rather added more on to the common core. And there is logical if not also biological reason to conjecture that just as important elements of physiological structure have been maintained, so perhaps have elements of behavioral function.

How Cultural Variation Preserves Biological Unity

Let me deal immediately with the matter of human cultural variation. This is held by some students of the matter to provide evidence that humans are exempt from common genetically based influence over social behavior that could commonly influence different groups of the human genotype. In this view, our cultural options are as unlimited as the *tabula rasa* assumption about psychological development could imply. So the fact that there is plainly enormous variety of human social forms is treated as a convincing demonstration of the general irrelevance of the genetic codes for human social organization. Thus culture is a realm unto itself; the social sciences need have no formal and inevitable link with the ongoing process of biological science. It is interesting in itself that the social and natural sciences are so dichotomously defined, particularly by the university whose function is presumably to unify knowledge.

But let me turn this all the way around. The existence of extensive cultural variation among human groups can be seen as a particularly hominid expression of Romer's Law, as I adapt it. Romer's Law broadly is that animals evolve small adaptations in order to avoid larger ones involving its master systems such as locomotion, thermoregulation, and reproductive mode. Therefore an animal faced with a new predator that runs faster than it adapts by adjusting its fur color to its environment, to achieve secrecy rather than evolving wings to achieve speed. An animal whose soft food source disappears selects for large teeth and strong jaws to consume muskrats rather than become aquatic in order to dine on squid. For human beings, cultural variation is the way in which groups adapt to specific historical, social, geographic, demographic, and similar circumstances so that basic hominid patterns such as group formation, reproductive access, spatial management, and resource distribution can persist within species-specific norms. That is, *humans generate cultural variation to be able to maintain their basic behavioral social biology.* We can adapt to an array of diverse circumstances with an array of heterogeneous forms and yet maintain the capacity to readily interbreed, thus fulfilling the core requirement for a viable species. (Culture is clearly not a reliably independent marker; the enthusiasm for intercultural inter-breeding is sufficiently robust that earnest prohibitions against it are exceedingly common.)

This adaptation of Romer implicitly contains a large claim. But it is no larger than one which would dispute Conrad's assertion that contemporary life encapsulates past experience, or the phylogeneticist's one that miserly nature keeps everything such as the appendix and principally overcomes or supercedes earlier forms if it does not actually employ them. We are talking history here, even though some still distinguish between history and prehistory while others (I being one) see an unbroken continuity, the smoother since the road back to Eden is, if you will, paved with genes (Dawkins, 1982; Morin, 1982).

A note is in order on the anthropological overview that informs my comments and that I also think encapsulates the broad historical process of which contemporary society is the current outcome. We must take the industrial system to be a relatively exotic social form that has existed in the world for barely 10 generations and in many communities for barely three. Most Americans are very likely to be within two or three generations of agriculture. The agricultural and pastoral patterns are themselves relatively new, having emerged relatively suddenly between 8000 and 13,000 years ago, though there are some new indications that some social features of the agricultural mode existed in hunting–gathering communities. Notwithstanding this, the preeminent form of *Homo sapiens* has been as hunter–gatherer, a form that endured in an evidently stable manner for up to 4 million years. To the extent that there is a human nature, it was formed during this extensive period, and there has simply been insufficient time for any significant alteration in behavioral repertoires and possibly even cognitive predispositions to have occurred in response to the new circumstances of agriculture, let alone industry.

The Ethical Triangle

It is intriguing and pertinent that the legal and ethical systems that we currently employ emerged out of the transition to agriculture and pastoralism or thereafter, but before industrialism. The Buddhist, Greco-Roman, Judeo-Christian, Confucian, Islamic, and Hindu formulations are essentially products of small farmers and shepherds. Yet these are the preeminent ethical and value systems that underlie legal systems and that currently operate the planet. There is no commanding ethical system that has been produced by the industrial way, with the possible exception of Marxism, which was as much a cry of pain as an assertion of antipathy to an existing ethic, which was seen to be inadequate.

Hence we have a 2- to 4-million-old hunting–gathering primate governing a 10-generation-old industrial system with hortatory doctrines from 100 to 500 generations old. This is a structural strain of great dimension, the complexity and sweep of which pertain to and perhaps explain the concerns about the nature and origin of values that occupy us here. Certainly the emergence of a priesthood as a formal group—possibly the first leisured organisms in history—which accompanied the moral crises presumably associated with the movement to agriculture and pastoralism, suggests that the ongoing problems were sufficiently trying that a specialist corps of practitioners had to be created and supported to deal with them adequately. I have outlined this argument more fully elsewhere (Tiger, 1987).

Perhaps it is so as wrote James Madison in *The Federalist Papers* (1787) 10 generations ago that "If men were angels, no government would be necessary." Not only are people not angels but the world in which they must make their way is not the kind of world that made them. Not only are we not angels, but we are not even in an environment remotely like our heaven. We have had to make and adapt to a major chronomigration. If nothing else the scale of contemporary societies that puts a premium on impersonal managerial analytical skills may only very suboptimally involve those interpersonal psychoemotional capacities that members would necessarily employ in the groups of some 50 to 200 souls in which we are likely to have evolved. Because of this structured strain, it would appear highly likely if not inevitable that confidence about ethics would be at a premium in industrial societies—except among self-conscious fundamentalist groups that embrace various sectarian assertions usually predicated on well-articulated rumors of divine certification or at least favoritism. As with some recent Islamic fundamentalism, it seems rather likely that such strong sectarian assertions are in fact as much signals of rebellion against or disaffection with industrial ways of life as they reveal commitment to particular belief systems. Certainly the model of ideal behavior conjured up by fundamentalist assertions is closer to agripastoral styles of life than industrial ones.

Gender-Blinded

One of the most interesting relationships here is among values, law, and gender. It is clear that among most animals and among the highly social mammals in particular significant behavioral outcomes flow from being male or female. Biographical trajectory, use of time and energy, and even the brutal reality of longevity appear to have some chronic and predictable linkage to gender. Among humans, with our very long and demanding period of physical and social dependency during growth, the sex differences that are involved in sexual and natural selection are possibly enhanced by the requirements of child rearing.

In general, most communities make substantial distinctions between the treatment of males and females in various socioeconomic and emotional milieux; this has been amply and widely demonstrated on a cross-cultural basis both by ethnographers who have synthesized data from many cultures, and more recently by feminist scholars who have interpreted similar data as evidence of systematic antifemale exploitation. Notwithstanding the obvious political and moral implications of this, certainly until effective female-controlled contraception became available in the 1960s, with the pill, there was legitimate presumption that male–female relations were charged with potential reproductive consequences. Values and perhaps laws (e.g., even a law so quaint by contemporary standards as breach of promise) had to acknowledge such consequences and protect possible offspring if not also mothers from cavalier or indifferent treatment by sexual partners in particular and communities in general. As Tiger and Fox (1970) suggested, one of the irreducible functions of human kinship systems is to protect the mother–infant bond from the vagaries, frailties, and vicissitudes of the male–female bond. (The story is told with startling metaphorical clarity in the description of Mary and the baby Jesus as they seek room at the inn from a heartless community, which only later, once Jesus is defined as the Son of God, comes to understand its profound misbehavior. The giving of gifts symbolizes anew each year the basic obligation of generosity, and it is appropriate that this is linked to the central mammalian issue of supporting the mother–child dyad.)

Particularly in the United States there has been a deep-rooted effort to abolish both procedural and legal distinctions between males and females. Sex-blind standards have been urged for legal, familial, economic, educational, political, and cognate activities. This has also been accompanied by efforts to demonstrate that any apparent differences between male and female behavior flow from discriminatory structures, usually exploitative of females, and do not represent expression of any inherent differences between males and females rooted in our biological nature. It is significant that the legal instruments to accomplish the gender-abolitionists' goals were in the United States linked to efforts to eliminate discrimination on the basis of race. In fact, the addition of the category "sex" to the enabling legislation was proposed as a joke by a southern Congressman who concluded that the race-linked legislation was so risible and unlikely to pass that he added gender to the list to exaggerate what he considered the proposal's farcical character. Of course the legislation became law for utterly clear and justifiable moral and legal reasons.

A practical problem remains. There may be a significant category conflation here. On biological and anthropological grounds it is clear there are no substantial and interesting differences among the races whereas there are many between males and females. While there may be behavioral and economic differences between, say, blacks and whites in communities in which they arrived under different circumstances—e.g., ownership or slavery—nevertheless black communities say in West Africa and white ones say in Scandinavia display very similar patterns of division of labor, age-grading, political process, and the like.

However, in all communities of whatever race, males and females comport themselves along different statistical tracks. It becomes perhaps a majestic experiment or an empirical folly to adhere to legal and value systems that presuppose that they should and will behave the same (Tiger & Shepher, 1975). It is interesting that in her widely cited *In a Different Voice*, Carol Gilligan (1982) claims male and female children display significantly different approaches to and processes of moral decision making. (Gilligan does not consider the possibility that the most parsimonious explanation of her finding lies in a biosocial interpretation of how males and females prepare in childhood for different adult reproductive strategies. Nevertheless, her empirical account is wholly consistent with contemporary biological understandings of the relationship between social decision making and gender.)

This becomes most consequential where reproduction is concerned. The most peculiar and striking indication of the effect of the abolitionists' initiative is that under American legislation a woman applying for maternity benefits must request payment for disability—rather than for an ability that is what she has—because otherwise the law would discriminate unfairly against males who cannot and women who do not bear children. Of course one can understand and sympathize with the thinking behind this, and there is some reason—for example, from recent Brazilian evidence[1] (Simons, 1988), to expect that legislation offering women special maternity benefits will result in employers being less willing to hire them. Nevertheless on semantic, moral, and common sense grounds, to require a woman who has had a child to define herself as disabled constitutes an historical and practical novelty (Sommers, 1988).

---

[1] New legislation extends maternity leave from three to four months and there are indications that pregnant women or those deemed likely to become pregnant are passed over in favor of men or women beyond childbearing age. Public discussion of the so-called "mommy track" is of course a version of a similar concern (see Simon, 1988).

So in terms of the fact–value distinction, here is a colorful case of opposition between ethnographic fact and legal–attitudinal initiative. I cannot pretend to offer a practical amelioration. However, it seems reasonably clear that much of the difficulty faced with such issues as daycare and the support of unmarried mothers flows from what may be the necessarily problematic outcomes of intellectual positions at significant variance from the gender-linked behavioral propensities of human beings (Jagger, 1983).

There is also the possibility that the historically low birth rates of the industrial countries (for example, even Roman Catholic Italy shows a birth rate of 1.3, while replacement is 2.2 children per woman), which have in general become committed to the gender-abolitionist practice if not theory, reflects more than the opportunity for conscious choice by women and men able to control fertility. The industrial countries are very productive but not very reproductive, which may suggest the incompatibility between an industrial economic system that assumes men and women live their lives in much the same ways and to similar schedules, and the behavioral propensities of reproduction. If we adopt the terminology about the reproductive system that economists use for the productive one, many industrial countries have been in reproductive depression—negative growth for two quarters—for years. And in the wider context of how species govern reproduction, the industrial societies are something of a novelty in nature because they do not convert resources into offspring.

Of course major questions remain about the relationship between "human nature" theories and legal process, such as have been raised by Donald Elliott (1988) of the Yale Law School, Dr. Margaret Gruter (1982) in her exploration of recent data in biology and their meaning for lawyers, and political scientist Roger Masters (1992) in his remarkable new synthesis. Notwithstanding the good questions that endure, there exists sufficient reason to begin questioning the empirical validity of the gender-abolitionist analysis and hence the likelihood that it will produce legal and normative outcomes that will interact with human beings in the desired way. As the Fabians in England understood when the welfare state was being projected there, the first step was to find out what was actually happening in the communities that were to be administered, and to base policy on existing realities as a starting point. (This program led in part to the founding of London School of Economics and Political Science where there was a Chair of Social Biology whose last holder was the polymath Lancelot Hogben. It has not been filled for decades— presumably a relatively rare case of academics abandoning an asset.) A biological Fabianism seems equally plausible today (Tiger, 1970).

A brief comment is in order about the "is"–"ought" distinction or problem, because my assertions here may seem to suggest that patterns of behavior that may on scientific grounds of varying sturdiness seem to be "natural" must then also be desirable on moral grounds. That is, if sex differences exist in nature and are encoded in the genotype therefore sex differences in social behavior and organizational conduct are ethically preferable to patterns not found in nature.

But this does not follow at all. It is the same as saying that because cancer is found in nature, therefore cancer is desirable. Or that if homicide may serve "natural" genetic purposes therefore there ought to be no laws against homicide. However, what does follow is that if cancer exists and prospers at the biogenetic level, then it is at this level that remedies to it should at least in part be sought. With social situations, it is helpful to understand the potentially biosocial bases of them if planned, desirable change is to occur. This is not to deny the importance of environment and social stimuli but rather to emphasize them. I use here the seminal formulation of David Hamburg who as early as 1963 asserted that the interesting question about the nature of learning in animal studies was not, strictly, what was genetic and what cultural, but rather what is easy for a species to learn. That is, if human sex differences are fairly substantially rooted in hormonal, maturational, cognitive, and other subcultural processes, and hence if males and females are likely to respond with some degree of difference to similar stimuli, then it is merely sensible to appreciate this and to try to plan, for example, school systems in order to take these responsive propensities into account, not to deny their existence.

Is There a Genetics of Homicide?

Values and legal principles are obviously most clearly exemplified in action. I want to discuss briefly some recent findings on the relationship between kinship and killing both because of the intrinsic interest of the dramatic data and their interpretation and also because they may reveal in extreme form the operation of biosocial principles that are close to behavioral bedrock. I am making the assumption that killing people reflects crucial and ramified articulation of social structure. Killing is also relatively convenient to study insofar as it is a clear and finite event less subject than most behavior to gradations and mitigations of motivation and intensity. Either it happens or it does not.

About the two main sources I cite I must first declare a form of scientific interest insofar as both authors received very early in the projects on which they report grants from the Harry Frank Guggenheim Foundation at the time I was Research Director there. I acknowledge there is something self-serving about helping fund research and then approvingly citing it in support of a particular favorite position. Two rejoinders: the material in question is linked to very substantial theory and bodies of work by others; and the particular articles cited were both lead articles in *Science* and thus hardly in print without the most responsible refereeing and multifacetted scrutiny. I know for a fact that at least one of the two articles was the subject of much internal discussion if not controversy among *Science* and its consultants and its subsequent publication reflected no small amount of colloquy.

There is a general article (Daly & Wilson, 1988a) and a more specific ethnographic one with broad resonance (Chagnon, 1988). Daly and Wilson (1988a) essentially argue that homicide occurs with clear consistency with genetic relatedness, even though the individuals involved may have not a clue about the influences on their behavior or on the pattern it takes. That is, people are far less likely to kill genetic kin than relatives by marriage: "19% of Detroit homicide victims in 1972 were related to their killers by marriage compared to 6% by blood . . . 10% of Miami victims in 1980 were marital relatives of their killers compared to 1.8% blood relatives." Nonrelated (by blood) coresidents were 11 times more likely to be murder victims than blood kin. "A child living with one or more substitute parents in the United States in 1976 was approximately 100 times more likely to be fatally abused than a same-age child living with genetic parents." That all this is related to reproductive outcomes is strongly suggested by the fact that spouses who share offspring also share more marital harmony while those with children of former unions experience more disharmony.

The principal focus of marital violence is male sexual possessiveness—jealousy is the leading motive attributed to spousal homicide. In particular danger are younger wives who are estranged or threaten estrangement from husbands. There are various other patterns of homicide that are predictable by biosocial theory, which enjoy added interest because by and large these data are all about individuals of the same social and ethnic class who by definition share the most intimate of circumstances, living together. A fuller treatment of the issue by the same authors is their *Homicide* (Daly & Wilson, 1988b).

Chagnon's report is based on 23 years of study of the Yanomamo Indians of Amazonas, a relatively bellicose group whose demography is well known by Chagnon. The author asserts that blood revenge, homicide, kinship obligations, and warfare are tightly linked by underlying processes susceptible to parsimonious explanation by biosocial theory. For example, 44% of males over 25 have participated in killing another person and "men who have killed have more wives and offspring than men who have not killed." Groups that retaliate swiftly when fights begin between their members and those of other groups, usually over sexual issues, appear to deter the violence of neighbors while also deterring such predation as the abduction of nubile females by other groups. In his contribution to this volume, Frederick Barth cites data from the community he has studied that appear to suggest a similar process.

There is a strong association of support from kinsmen during aggressive interaction with subsequent political success or failure of members of particular family lineages. Headmen of these are usually polygynous; a successful headman may over a lifetime have a dozen or more wives, and father a commensurate number of children; one individual fathered 43 offspring. Along other dimensions as well, there is positive association between cooperative kin-based aggression and reproductive success, which is what one would expect from a theory that attended to biosocial subtext as well as of others such as economic distribution and political ambition. The point is that even the extreme issues of violence and death, which incorporate values and norms surrounding less extreme episodes, are parsimoniously explicable in a biosocial context. Of course in the Yanomamo case, we are dealing with a small-scale tribal society far different from our own industrial ones. Nevertheless, similarity exists in the sexual basis of much homicide, suggesting possibly common motivations. Certainly the association between kinship and energetic social action suggests the strength of the link between social behavior and reproductive outcome.

Culture Reduces Biological Variation

Having made some comment about the general role of cultural variation in permitting human radiation so successfully throughout the planet, let me comment finally about the role of culture, which is inextricably linked with values, in the operations of individual cultural groups. Within every culture, there is more or less variation between the individual members along an array of lines—height, bone width, rate of speaking, acceptance of authority, etc. I always tell students, and not altogether whimsically, that when they are studying an animal or human group, *the shortest analytical distance between two points is a normal curve.* My proposition is that a principal function of cultural pattern is to reduce or at least monitor the amount of variation permitted to members of a community. While one view of culture is that it is the mechanism for self-expression, for offering the opportunity for achieving differentiation from others, my sense is the opposite—that the role of cultural patterns is to ensure some predictable and reliable amount of interindividual coherence and similarity.

The principal function of culture is to reduce the amount of variation that biology makes possible. Indeed, the responsiveness of people to social cues, as expressed in fashion, moral convention, and so on, reveals that cultural patterning is easy to learn, especially during childhood and even later as Colin Irwin (1987) has shown in the strenuous dialect commitments of teenagers—their way of defining appropriate courting groups. That is one central reason why school systems are so concerned with the issue of inculcating values, and why when people challenge the culture, this is so perilous that specialized rules such as about academic freedom or civil liberties or free expression must be invoked to protect individuals who in other situations are routinely imprisoned, somehow sanctioned, ostracized, or even physically punished.

A noncontroversial prediction from this would be that the more threatened a culture, such as during a dangerous war, the more intensely will the cultural values be upheld and violators stifled, for example, as traitors during war time. The general implication here is that the ideal of the Renaissance and thereafter that a particularly sweet fruit of cultivation is interesting individual differentiation is in fact a relatively exotic concept. While it remains an effective and intensely satisfying value, with vast socioeconomic implications, nevertheless we know that it is nonetheless relatively fragile and is consistently under real, potential, or near attack by censors, fundamentalists, ideologues, and so on. As my sociological mentor at the University of British Columbia Kaspar Naegele told me: "The clearing is very small." And perhaps the underlying reason for this is that firm protection of variation far from the central tendency of the normal curve of social response is phylogenetically rare and hence psychologically difficult for those who vary—think of their courage—and those who evaluate the variation— think of their outrage. The conflict may be as passionate in the arts, which are about expression and pleasure, as in politics, which may often be about survival or at least the sense of social security.

This is another way of describing the inevitably strong bias in favor of a central tendency among communities of highly gregarious species.

Then what has happened in contemporary communities to suggest there is some form of crisis or bewilderment about values, when values should if you will be natural? The impact of science and the inevitable secularization it produces are of course major factors in this. However, I want to highlight what may be pertinent changes that result from the particular nature of the industrial system as we understand it. There is obviously a major set of impacts on personal values set in motion by the invention and broad dominance of the corporate structure, in which the "corporate veil" protects individuals (or has in the past—there are changes underway) from prosecution as individuals for actions taken as agents of the corporation. But I am especially interested here in the general pattern of economic individualism that prevails, and that in essence requires that members of industrial communities as early as kindergarten begin to treat themselves and be treated as independent contractors who are in effective competition with all other members of their age grade.

This is a form of impersonal contest both reflected and abetted by the proliferation of highly consequential tests of what is purported to be technical competence and personal character. This point I need not elaborate, except to note that within the past 25 years the independent contractor category has come to include nearly all females, many of whom could in the past expect with some reasonable confidence that they would marry and focus for large periods of their adult lives on reproductive not productive activity. That is no longer so. Even the long-term sexual interdependence for reproduction that has been associated customarily with family life is now optional, with results expressed very obviously in the record of divorce, and more consequentially in declined and declining reproductive rates such that by and large some industrial communities as I have noted are barely replacing themselves while many are technically below replacement. The enormous difficulty faced by increasing numbers of single mothers in the industrial countries, even in highly supportive and programmatic societies such as Sweden, which has one of the world's lowest birth rates and smallest average family sizes, suggests the scope and consequence of the change (Popenoe, 1988; Hewlett, 1986). It takes little hyperimagination to wonder if the reluctance or inability for people to undertake the central biological process of reproduction with confidence and effect has something to do with the unavailability of a broad sense of shared values, even values that pertain to the most intimate spheres of human conduct. Discerning the direction and intensity of the causal link here, if there is one, is another matter.

References

Chagnon, N. (1988). Life histories, blood revenge, and warfare in a tribal population. *Science, 239*, 989–992.
Daly, M., & Wilson, M. (1988a). Evolutionary social psychology and family homicide. *Science, 242*, 519–524.
Daly, M., & Wilson, M. (1988b). *Homicide*. Hawthorne, NY: Aldine de Gruyter.
Dawkins, R. (1982). *The extended phenotype*. New York: Freeman.
Edey, M., & Johanson, D. (1989). *Blueprints: Solving the mystery of evolution*. New York: Little Brown.

Elliott, D. (1988). Toward an ethological theory of legal obligation: Developments in American legal scholarship. von Siemans Stiftung, Munich, February.

Gilligan, C. (1982). *In a different voice: Psychological theory and women's development.* Cambridge: Harvard University Press.

Gruter, M. (1982). Biologically based behavioral research and the facts of law. *Journal of Social and Biological Structures, 5,* 315–323.

Hewlett, S. A. (1986). *A lesser life: The myth of women's liberation in America.* New York: William Morrow.

Irwin, C. (1987). Inuit and the evolution of limited group conflict. European Sociobiological Society, Van Leer Foundation, Jerusalem, Israel.

Jagger, A. (1983). *Feminist politics and human nature.* Totowa, NJ: Rowman & Allanheld.

Konner, M. (1983). *The tangled wing: Biological constraints on the human spirit.* New York: Harper Colophon.

Maclean, P. (1972). Cerebral evolution and emotional processes: New findings on the striated complex. *Annals of the New York Academy of Sciences, 193,* 137–149.

Madison, J. (1787). *The Federalist,* No. 51, at 160 (r. Fairfield ed. 1961).

Masters, R. (1992). *The nature of politics.* New Haven: Yale University Press, in press.

Morin, E. (1982). *Science avec conscience.* Paris: Fayard.

Popenoe, D. (1988). *Disturbing the nest: Family change and decline in modern societies.* Hawthorne, NY: Aldine de Gruyter.

Simons, M. (1988). Brazilian women find fertility may cost jobs. *New York Times,* December 8.

Sommers, C. H. (1988). Philosophers against the family. In H. Lafollette & G. Graham (Eds.), *Person to person.* Philadelphia: Temple University Press.

Tiger, L. (1970). Biological Fabianism. *The Canadian Forum, 50,* 1.

Tiger, L. (1987). *The manufacture of evil: Ethics, evolution, and the industrial system.* New York: Bessie Books/Harper & Row.

Tiger, L., & Fox, R. (1970). *The imperial animal.* New York: Holt; see also second edition, New York: Holt, 1989.

Tiger, L., & Shepher, J. (1975). *Women in the kibbutz.* New York: Harcourt, Brace Jovanovich.

Biographical Sketches of the Contributors

George A. Akerlof is the son of Gosta Akerlof, a chemist who emigrated from Sweden in 1920, and Rosalie Hirschfeld Akerlof. He was born in New Haven, Connecticut in 1940 and grew up, after the age of ten, in Princeton, New Jersey. He got his undergraduate degree from Yale in 1962 and in 1966 he received his Ph.D. from M.I.T. where his thesis supervisor was Robert Solow. Since 1966 he has been at the University of California, Berkeley with a brief hiatus from 1978 to 1980 when he was Cassel Professor of Money and Banking at the London School of Economics. He has also worked at the planning unit of the Indian Statistical Institute in New Delhi, the Federal Reserve Board and the President's Council of Economic Advisers. He is married to Janet L. Yellen.

Fredrik Barth was born in 1928 and lives in Norway. He received his M.A. in anthropology at the University of Chicago in 1949 and his Ph.D. from Cambridge University in 1957. He is presently Research Associate under the Ministry of Culture in Norway, and Professor of Anthropology at Emory University. Barth has taught as professor of anthropology at the universities of Bergen and Oslo in Norway, and has been visiting professor at several American universities. He has done anthropological fieldwork in various parts of the Middle East, and in the Sudan, New Guinea, Bali, and Bhutan. He has published widely on these materials and on theoretical topics.

L. Luca Cavalli-Sforza is a Professor of Genetics at Stanford University since 1970 and prior to this date he taught the same discipline at the Universities of Parma and of Pavia in Italy. His main interest is human evolution, from both the genetic and the cultural points of view.

Baruch Fischhoff is Professor of Social and Decision Sciences and of Engineering and Public Policy at Carnegie Mellon University. He holds a B.S. in mathematics from Wayne State University and an M.A. and Ph.D. in psychology from the Hebrew University of Jerusalem. He is a recipient of the American Psychological Association's Early Career Awards for Distinguished Scientific Contribution to Psychology and for Contributions to Psychology in the Public Interest. His current research includes risk communication, adolescent decision making, evaluation of environmental damages and insurance-related behavior.

Keith B. J. Franklin was born in England in 1943 and grew up in Malaya and New Zealand. He received his B.A. and M.A. (Hons) in Psychology from the

University of Auckland, New Zealand. He moved to England to study for his Ph.D. with L. J. Herberg at the Institute of Neurology, Queen Square, London and received his Ph.D. from the University of London in 1976. After a post-doctoral fellowship in Canada with Peter M. Milner at McGill University, he joined the McGill Department of Psychology, where he is now Associate Professor. His wife, Frances V. Abbott, is also a neuroscientist. They have three children to occupy their spare time.

Michael Hechter is Professor of Sociology and Fellow at the Udall Center for Studies in Public Policy at The University of Arizona. His books include *Internal Colonialism: The Celtic Fringe in British National Development 1536–1966* (1975), *The Microfoundations of Macrosociology* (edited in 1983), *Principles of Group Solidarity* (1987) and the forthcoming *Explaining Nationalism*. His most recent research has focused on the scope and limits of rational choice theory.

Richard J. Herrnstein is Edgar Pierce Professor of Psychology at Harvard University, where he has been a faculty member since 1958. His research on the behavioral effects of reward and punishment started in the early 1950s and has continued to the present.

George Mandler, Ph.D. Yale 1953, taught at Harvard University and the University of Toronto before moving in 1965 to the University of California, San Diego as founding chair of their Psychology Department. He is a Fellow of the American Academy of Arts and Sciences, has been a Fellow at the Center for Advanced Study in the Behavioral Sciences and a J. S. Guggenheim Fellow, and received the William James Award, American Psychological Association. His books include *The Language of Psychology* (with W. Kessen), *Thinking: From Association to Gestalt* (with J. M. Mandler), *Mind and Emotion, Mind and Body: Psychology of Emotion and Stress,* and *Cognitive Psychology: An Essay in Cognitive Science.* He currently divides his year between the University of California, San Diego and University College London.

Richard E. Michod is Professor of Ecology and Evolutionary Biology at The University of Arizona. He is editor of the book *Evolution of Sex* and has published over sixty articles in the area of genetics and evolution. His research interests involve the evolution of sex and social behavior and the philosophy of biology.

Barry Schwartz is Professor of Psychology and former department head at Swarthmore College. He has been at Swarthmore since 1971, when he received his Ph.D. in experimental psychology from the University of Pennsylvania. He has published widely in the area of learning and motivation, focusing on biological constraints on learning and on the undermining of intrinsic motivation by extrinsic incentives. His books include *The Psychology of Learning and Behavior* (3rd Edition, 1989), *Behaviorism, Science, and Human Nature* (with Hugh Lacey, 1982), *Learning and Memory* (with Dan Reisberg, 1991), and *The Battle for Human Nature* (1986). His latest book, *Why the Best Things in Life Should Be Free* (1993), is directly related to the themes developed in his contribution to this volume.

Tibor Scitovsky is Eberle Professor of Economics, emeritus, at Stanford University. He was born in 1910 in Budapest, and educated at the London School of Economics and the University of Budapest. In addition to Stanford, he has taught at Yale, the University of California at Berkeley, the London School of Economics, and the University of California at Santa Cruz. A Distinguished Fellow of the American Economic Association and member of the American Academy of Arts and Sciences and the British Academy, his books include *The Joyless Economy* (1976) and *Human Desire and Economic Satisfaction* (1986).

Stephen P. Stich is the author of *From Folk Psychology to Cognitive Science* (MIT Press, 1983) and *The Fragmentation of Reason* (MIT Press, 1990). He has taught at the University of Michigan, the University of Maryland and the University of California at San Diego, and has held visiting appointments at Bristol University and the University of Sydney. He is currently Professor of Philosophy and Cognitive Science at Rutgers University.

Lionel Tiger is Charles Darwin Professor of Anthropology at Rutgers University. He was educated at McGill University and the London School of Economics of the University of London. He has also taught at McGill and the Universities of Ghana and British Columbia. From 1972 until 1984 he was Research Director of the Harry Frank Guggenheim Foundation in New York and he has been Chairman of the Board of Social Scientists at *US News and World Report*. Among his books are *Men in Groups, The Imperial Animal* (with Robin Fox), *Women in the Kibbutz* (with Joseph Shepher), *Optimism: The Biology of Hope*, and *The Manufacture of Evil: Ethics, Evolution, and the Industrial System*. His most recent book is *The Pursuit of Pleasure*.

Frans B. M. de Waal is Research Professor in the Division of Behavioral Biology at the Yerkes Regional Primate Research Center and Associate Professor in the Department of Psychology at Emory University. He has worked for twenty years on the social behavior of non-human primates first in the Netherlands and, since 1981, in the United States. He is the author of *Chimpanzee Politics* (1982) and *Peacemaking Among Primates* (1989).

Harrison C. White is Chair of the Department of Sociology and Director of the Center for the Social Sciences at Columbia University. He is the author of the recent book *Identity and Control: A Structural Theory of Social Action* (Princeton University Press 1992), *Social Forces in the Arts* (Westview Press 1993) and various articles on mathematical models of market and organization.

Aaron Wildavsky is Class of 1940 Professor of Political Science and Public Policy and a member of the Survey Research Center at the University of California at Berkeley. He is a Fellow of the Association of Public Policy Analysis and Management, American Academy of Arts and Sciences, and the National Academy of Public Administration. He is the author of *Speaking Truth to Power, Searching for Safety,* and *Cultural Theory* (with Michael Thompson and Richard Ellis).

Janet L. Yellen is the daughter of Julius Yellen, a doctor in Brooklyn, New York, where she grew up, and Anna Blumenthal Yellen. She was born in 1940. She got her undergraduate degree from Brown in 1967 and in 1971 she received her Ph.D. from Yale, where her thesis supervisor was James Tobin. Since 1980 she has taught at the University of California, Berkeley, where she is currently the Bernard T. Rocca Professor of International Business and Trade. Previous jobs were at Harvard, The Board of Governors of the Federal Reserve, and the London School of Economics. She is married to George A. Akerlof.

Index

Addictive drugs, 277
Altruism, 47, 58–59
American academic science (*See* Science)
Amphetamine, 278, 279
Amygdala, 281–282
Analgesic drugs, 279–280
Animal behavior
  chimpanzees, 291–296
  marmots, 14
ANS reaction, 238, 252, 255
Anthropology
  absence of theory of values in, 17, 31–33
  Baktaman, 37–39
  Balinese, 39–42
  Barth's value studies, 34–35
  complexity of values, 44–45
  Firth's value studies, 35–36
  Haviland's value studies, 45
  historical situation of values, 45–46
  Kluckhohn's value studies, 33, 35
  Parsons's value studies, 33–34
Antianxiety drugs, 281
Articulated values, philosophy of, 188, 198–200
Arts, 250
Attitudes, 313, 315
Attributes, 188–189
Aversive stimuli, 280–281

Baktaman, 37–39
Balinese, 39–42
Basic values paradigm
  discrepancies interest and, 207
  experimental ability and, 208–209
  interest criterion and, 210
  order interest and, 207–208
  philosophy of, 188, 189, 200–204
  precision of search and, 209
Behavior (*See* Animal behavior; Human behavior)

Beliefs, 313, 315
Biological determinants, 15–16
Biological unity, 320–321
Biological variation, 328–330
Biology (*See also* Science)
  existence of values and, 266
  heritability and, 261–263
  inclusive fitness and, 266–268
  modern society's values and, 268–270
  origin of values and, 264–265
  psychology and, 254–256

Caste system
  change in values in, 77–79
  science and, 70–72
Categorization, 222–225
Catholic Christianity, 79–82
Change in values
  in caste system, 77–79
  derivative of, 67
  as dimensions, 85–86
  illustration of, 67
  mating and, 77
  questions concerning, 75–76
  in science, 77–79
Chimpanzees, 291–296
Coalition formation, 290–291
Coercion, 47, 51–53
Cognitive evaluation, 237
Collective goods, 96–97
Competitive consumer markets and, 94–96
Concepts, 222–225
Confirmation bias, 166
Consent, 47, 51–53
Contradictions, 242, 246, 254–256
Cultural accounting, 59–60
Cultural adaptation, 314–316
Cultural differences
  biological unity and, 320–321
  biological variation and, 328–330

Cultural differences (*cont.*)
  morality and, 320–321
  transmission of values and, 307–308
Cultural transmission of values
  cultural adaptation and, 314–316
  genetic transmission of values and, 309–311
  properties of, 311–314
Customs, 313, 315

Destruction of values
  economic imperialism and, 178–183
  means-ends relations and, creation of new, 157–160
Discrepancies
  arts and, 250
  basic values paradigm and, 207
  emotion and values and, 238, 245–248
Disease, 195–196
Diseconomies, 98–100
Distinctions
  consensus of, 47
  consent versus coercion, 47, 51–53
  cultural accounting of, 59–60
  overview of, 47, 60
  public versus private goods, 47, 53–58
  self-interest versus altruism, 47, 58–59
  voluntary versus involuntary risks, 48–51
Dopamine, 278–279

Ebionite Church, 80
Ecological determinants, 15
Economic imperialism, 147, 178–183
Economics (*See also* Fair wage-effort hypothesis)
  collective goods and, 96–97
  competitive consumer markets and, 94–96
  diseconomies and, 98–100
  equity and, 97–98
  external economies and, 98–99
  internal economies and, 99–100
  merit goods and, 98
  national income estimates and, 103–105

national product and, 103–105
  scarcity values and, 100–105
  utility and, 5–6
  values research in, 93–96
  wealth maximization and, 9–10
Elicitation of values (*See also* Basic values paradigm)
  lability and, 210–211
  overview of, 187–188
  paradigms
    articulated values, philosophy of, 188, 189, 198–200
    basic values, philosophy of, 188, 189, 200–204
    concept of, 196
    partial perspectives, philosophy of, 204–206
    samples, 197
    problematic preferences
      paradigms, choice of, 189–192
      philosophies, continuum of, 188–189
    sample problems, 192–196
Emotion and value
  arts and, 250
  contradictions and, 242, 246
  discrepancies and, 238, 245–248
  familiarity and, 242
  novelty and, challenge of, 248–250
  schemas and, 239–240, 242–245
  source of values and, 240–241
  theories of, 235–239
Equity, 97–98
Equity theory, 109–110
Ethical triangle, 321–322 (*See also* Morality)
Ethics (*See* Morality)
Euphoria, 277
External economies, 98–99
Externalities, 54

Fair wage-effort hypothesis (*See also* Relative deprivation model)
  equation of, 107
  equity theory and, 109–110
  jealousy and, 114
  overview of, 107–108
  personnel management and, 115
  relative deprivation theory and, 110–111
  retribution and, 114

social exchange theory and, 111–112

unemployment and, 21, 117–118

wage patterns and, 116–117

wage-salary secrecy and, 115–116

work restriction in workplace and, 112–114

Familiarity, 242

Free-rider problem, 56

GABA (*y*-aminobutyric acid), 281

Gamble, 195

Gender-blinded morality, 322–326

Gender differences (*See* Sex differences)

Generosity, 39–42

Genetic differences

homicide and, 326–328

morality and, 326–328

transmission of values and, 307–308

Genetic transmission of values, 309–311

Goods

collective, 96–97

merit, 98

private versus public, 47, 53–58

Greed, 39–42

Happiness, 192–194

Hard-wired values, 13–14

Headache, 194–195

Heritability, 261–263

Homicide, 326–328

Human behavior (*See also* specific acts and ethnic groups)

matching law and, 140

sex differences in, 296–298

utility and, 137–140

Human prehistory, 319–320

Immanent values, 4–5

Imperialism, economic, 147, 178–183

Imprinting, 314

Inclusive fitness, 266–268

Individual experience, 15, 16

Industrialization, 159–160

Institutional determinants, 16

Instrumental values, 4, 11

Interdependence, 254–256

Interest criterion, 210

Intergroup differences in values, 15, 298–299

Internal economies, 99–100

Internalities, 54

Involuntary risks, 48–51

IQ tests, 309–310

Jealousy, 114

Lability, 210–211

Labor supply, 127–128, 129

Law of diminishing marginal returns, 5–6, 144

Law of Parsimony, 319

Marmots, 14

Matching, 21, 141

Matching law, 140

Mathematics, 86–87

Means-ends relations

destruction of values and, creation of new, 157–160

laboratory evidence of creation of new, 161–176

Melioration

concept of, 140–141

reinforcement returns on two commodities, 142–146

utility maximization and, 141, 146

Mental representation

alternative models for, 225–228

categorization and, 222–225

concepts and, 222–225

morally relevant differences arguments and, 218–222

overview of, 215–216

Plato's moral philosophy and, 216–218

Merit goods, 98

Missionary religion, 79–82

Model building on unconventional postulated values, 19–21

Models (*See* specific types of)

Moral concepts (*See* Morality)

Morality (*See also* Mental representation)

cultural differences and, 320–321

ethical triangle and, 321–322

genetic differences and, 326–328

human prehistory and, 319–320

morally relevant difference arguments and, 218–222

Morality (*cont.*)
  Plato's, 216–218
  sex differences and, 322–326

National income estimates, 103–105
National product, 103–105
Naturalism (*See* Anthropology)
Natural selection, 261–263
Need reduction theory, 7
Nested values, 15–16
Networks of values, 63, 68, 84
Novelty, 248–250

Object detectors, 273–275
Operating strategy, 38
Opiate, 279
Order, interest in, 207–208

Pain, 275, 279–282
Paradigms (*See also* Basic values paradigm)
  articulated values, philosophy of, 188, 189, 198–200
  basic values, philosophy of, 188, 189, 200–204
  choice of, 189–192
  concept of, 196
  partial perspectives, philosophy of, 204–206
  samples of, 197
Partial perspectives, philosophy of, 204–206
Personnel management, 115
Pleasure, 276–279
Political attitudes, 315
Postulating values, 9–10, 19–21
Practices, 176–178
Precision of search, 209
Principle of Utility, 137–138, 147
Private goods, 47, 53–58
Problematic preferences (*See also* Paradigms)
  paradigms, choice of, 189–192
  philosophies, continuum of, 188–189
  sample problems, 192–196
Productivity shocks, 128–129
Protest response, 201–202
Psychology (*See also* Emotion and value)
  biology and, 254–256

definitions of values and, 233–235
interdependent context of, 255–256
overview of values in, 229–233
rationality and, 253–254
reinforcement theories in, 7–8
social context of values and, 251–252
sources of values and, 229
universality and, 253–254
Public goods, 47, 53–58
Pygmies, 310–311, 313–314

Rape, 51–53
Rationality, 253–254
Reconciliation behavior, 291
Reinforcement, 7–8, 162, 166 (*See also* Melioration)
Relative deprivation model (*See also* Fair wage-effort hypothesis)
  assumptions in, 121–123
  comparative statics in, 127–129
  fully segregated equilibria in, 130–131
  integrated equilibria in, 123–127
  overview of, 120–121
  partially segregated equilibria in, 129–130
Relative deprivation theory, 110–111
Religion, missionary, 79–82
Religious attitudes, 313
Religious values, 9
Representative sampling, 208–209
Research (*See* specific topics of; Values research in social and behavioral sciences)
Retribution, 114
Revealed preference, 12–13
Risks, 48–61
Rock 'n roll music, 70, 82–84
Romer's Law, 320–321

Sample problems
  disease, 195–196
  gamble, 195
  happiness, 192–194
  headache, 194–195
Samples of subjects, 208–209
Scandinavians, 311
Scarcity values, 100–105
Schemas, 239–240, 242–245

Science (*See also* Biology)
  caste system and, 70–72
  change in values in, 77–79
  generalities and, 261
  practice of, 153–156
  values and, 155–157
Science of values, 153–158
Self-interest, 47, 58–59
Selfishness, 47, 58–59
Self-stimulation, 276, 278
Sensory systems
  amygdala and, 281–282
  evaluation and, lack of, 275–276, 279
  interpretations by, 274–275
  pain and, 275, 279–282
  pleasure and, 276–279
  stimuli and, 275, 280–281
  stimulus filtering and, 273–274
Sets of values, 66
Sex differences
  in chimpanzees, 291–296
  in human behavior, 296–298
  morality and, 322–326
  overview of, 285–288
  social concepts and, basic, 288–291
  variation in, discussion of, 298–302
Simple values, 231
Social behavior theory, 8–9
Social concepts, basic, 288–291
Social dominance, 288–290
Social exchange theory, 111–112
Sociohistorical analysis, 17–19
Sociology, 8–9
Spousal rape, 52
Stimuli, 275, 280–281
Stimulus filtering, 273–274
Stress, 238, 280
Styles of values
  case studies of, 69–70
  networks and, 67–69
  values as symbolic packages and, 63–64, 68–69
  values from structural equivalence and, 84–85
Subjective values, 93

Transactions, model of, 34
Transmission of values (*See also* Cultural transmission of values; Genetic transmission of values)

cultural differences and, 307–308
genetic differences and, 307–308
overview of, 305–307

Unemployment
  fair wage-effort hypothesis and, 21, 117–118
  model of, 118–120
Universality, 253–254
Utility
  Bentham's studies of, 137–138
  of commodity, 142
  economics and, 5–6
  human behavior and, 137–140
  importance of, 147–148
  law of diminishing marginal returns and, 5–6
  maximization, 21, 141, 146
  Principle of, 137–138, 147

Value networks, 63, 68, 84
Values (*See also* specific types of; Values research in social and behavioral sciences)
  adaptive significance of, 264–265
  content of, 23
  Cozzens' studies on, 65–66, 76
  definitions of, 3–5, 233–235, 305
  dynamics of, 23
  embodiments of, 155
  existence of, 266
  Goffman's studies on, 64–65
  historical situation of, 45–46
  level of analysis of, 5
  in modern society, 268–270
  origin of, 264–265
  Parsons's studies on, 64–65
  science and, 155–156
  scope of application of, 3
  scope of control of, 3
  sets of, 66
  sharing of, social, 3–5
  sources of, 229, 240–241, 255
  study of, 2–3
  as symbolic package, 63–64, 68–69
  theories of, 2, 5–9
Value sets, 66
Values research in social and behavioral sciences (*See also* Anthropology; Economics; Psychology)

Values research (*cont.*)
  defining values and, 3–5
  direction of, 16–24
  focus on values and, 1–3
  genesis of values and, 13–16
  interdisciplinary, 22–23
  measurement problems and, 10–13
  model building based on uncon-
    ventional postulated values
    and, 19–21
  in 1950s and 1960s, 31
  novel measurement and, 21–22
  postulating values and, 9–10

  sociohistorical analysis and, 17–19
  theoretical synthesis of, 23–24
  theoretical traditions and, 5–9
Value styles (*See* Styles of values)
Voluntary risks, 48–51

Wage patterns, 116–117
Wage-salary secrecy, 115–116
Wealth maximization, 9–10
Wealth, pursuit of, 43–44
Welfare, 103–105
Work restriction in workplace, 112–
  114